CW00924262

# Bell Aircraft

FRONTIER

# Bell Aircraft since 1935

Alain J Pelletier

*FRONTISPIECE: Bell Model 212 C-FNSA (c/n 30524) of Frontier Helicopters dropping water during a demonstration. (Conair)*



First published in Great Britain 1992 by
Putnam Aeronautical Books, an imprint of
Conway Maritime Press Ltd
101 Fleet Street
London EC4Y 1DE

*British Library Cataloguing in Publication Data*
Pelletier, A.J.
Bell aircraft since 1935
1. United States. Aircraft, history
I. Title
629.133

ISBN 0–85177–851–8



Typesetting and page make-up by
The Word Shop, Bury, Lancashire
Printed and bound in Great Britain by
Butler & Tanner Ltd, Frome

# Contents

'Although human subtlety makes a variety of inventions, it will never devise an invention more beautiful, more simple or more direct than does nature, because in her inventions, nothing is lacking and nothing is superfluous.'

Lawrence D Bell

# Preface and Acknowledgements

Bell is a unique manufacturer in United States aviation history. Born as a tiny company with a handful of employees and virtually no design contracts, it became a significant aircraft manufacturer within a few years through a full series of innovative fixed-wing aircraft. Now when we look at these designs, from the twin-engined XFM-1 Airacuda to the ducted-fan X-22 VTOL research aircraft, we must admit that none of them was conventional. And all this was done thanks to the tireless work of two outstanding personalities, both animated by the strongest will to succeed, Lawrence D. Bell and Robert J. Woods.

This innovative path was reinforced a few years later when a third man joined the team. His name was Arthur Young and with him Bell began to explore a nearly unknown territory, that of vertical flight. Even this exploration was hard and full of traps but it proved successful to such an extent that today Bell has become one of the world's major helicopter manufacturers. One helicopter out of two flying in the western world is a Bell. This fact is so true that in the minds of most people the name of Bell has simply become synonymous with the helicopter.

For both the personalities involved and the products designed, the history of Bell had to be written. This account will give the reader a complete panorama of Bell activities since 1935 up to the present, through its aeroplanes and helicopters as well as some of its projects and other flying machines.

Of course such a book could not have been written by a single isolated person. In fact, this is the work of a full team comprising individuals throughout the world who shared their knowledge. That is why I remain indebted to all those mentioned here (plus those I may have overlooked):

Bob Leder, Ted Hayes and Terry A Arnold of Bell Helicopter Textron Inc; Eleanor L Ponto of Bell Aerospace Textron; Hélène Carrier of Textron Canada Ltée; my fellow historians Peter M Bowers, Robert L Burns, Michel Cristescu, Richard Currie, Robert F Dorr, Jean-Pierre Dubois, Jeffrey L Ethell, Edward F Furler Jr, J M G Gradidge, Joseph G Handelmann, Peter J Marson, David W Menard, David W Ostrowski, Arthur Pearcy Jr, Jean-Jacques Petit, Louis Sampité, Jerry Scutts, Jean-Pierre Tedesco, Carl Waldenmaier and John Wegg.

Thanks also to Agusta SpA, Boeing Helicopters (Madelyn Bush), Conair (Robert M Stitt), GIAT (Martine Chayrigues), ITPN Nusantara Aircraft Industries Ltd (Suripto Sugondo), the Museum of Army Flying (J R Cross), the NASA Lyndon B Johnson Space Center (Mike Gentry), the National Air and Space Museum/Smithsonian Institution (Paul Silbermann), the US Army, the US Army Aviation Museum (Thomas J Sabiston), the US Army Center of Military History, the US Coast Guards (R L Scheina); the embassies of Austria (Maj Winkler), Israel (Attias Saguit), New Zealand (D Dunn), Norway (Sigurd Hellström) and Spain (Gravalos Guzman).

A very special thanks to my good friend René J Francillon for his prolonged assistance and encouragement. My gratitude also goes to the Putnam editorial team for their confidence in my project. And finally, I wish to express my deepest thanks to Maryse, my wife, who has endured more than she should have for the sake of this book.

As illustrations have been gathered from a variety of collections, every attempt has been made to credit the original photographer but with the passing of time some names have been lost; my sincere apologies to those slighted by an incorrect credit line.

Alain J Pelletier
Bures, January, 1992

# Author's Notes

This book conforms with most other Putnam titles. Only the histories of aircraft have been covered and these are presented in chronological order. Where applicable the aeroplanes are identified by both Bell Model number and customer designation. At the end of the book, numerous appendices are devoted to selected projects and miscellaneous types as well as to non-technical data such as production details (construction numbers, serial numbers, etc), lists and milestones.

From the beginning Bell used to assign a Model number during the preliminary phase of each project. For a long period, these Model numbers were allocated in sequential order and remained in use as designation numbers for the commercial types. Variants were given a suffix letter (in alphabetical order) and sub-variants a suffix number. At a later date, this designation system was used in a different way. Chosen Model numbers were not necessarily given in sequential order, thereby creating gaps, the first digit sometimes indicating the number of rotor blades. In addition the suffix letters were not necessarily allocated in alphabetical order and sometimes had a meaning (U standing for Utility, L for Long or SP for Special Performance, etc). The US military designations, where applicable, were given in the traditional way with the usual sequence of type symbol letter, model number, series letter, block number, and manufacturer identification letters. For Bell, the last were as follows:

BA Bell Atlanta, Georgia
BC Bell Aerosystems, Buffalo, New York
BE Bell, Buffalo, New York
BF Bell, Fort Worth, Texas

Manufacturer's serial numbers, generally called constructor's numbers or c/ns, have been allocated by sequence for each model.

# Origin and Corporate History

*A strong personality, Lawrence Dale Bell, the founder of Bell Aircraft Corporation. (Bell)*

Lawrence (Larry) Dale Bell(*) was born on 5 April, 1894, in the little town of Mentone, Indiana. He was the youngest of the ten children of Isaac Evans Bell and Harriet Sarber Bell. The young Lawrence was only 13 when his parents decided to retire to Santa Monica, California. 1910 was an important year for Larry, he got his first paid job, and he and two of his brothers (Vaughn and Grover) saw an aeroplane for the first time at the Dominguez Field aviation meeting (10–20 January, 1910). This event was an eye-opener for the three boys who in due course began to build model aeroplanes and kites. In 1912, Larry completed his studies at the Santa Monica Polytechnic and decided to join his brother Grover who was at this time working with Glenn L Martin as an exhibition flyer. Unfortunately, a year later, on 4 July, 1913, Grover died in a crash while flying a Curtiss Pusher Model D. This was a shock for Larry who then decided to give up aviation.

Thanks to the obstinacy of his friend Dave Hunt, he returned and both built wing-floats for floatplanes. Soon after, Larry entered the Martin Company and one of his first tasks was to prepare a biplane which had been sold to Pancho Villa, the Mexican revolutionary. In August 1915, the 23-year old Donald W Douglas joined Glenn L Martin as chief engineer; he would soon design the Martin MB-2. Two years later, Martin decided to merge with the Wright company to form

*Robert J Woods, father of many Bell designs. (Bell)*

* Not to be confused with the famous inventor and aviation pioneer Alexander Graham Bell (see *Canadian Aircraft since 1909*, pages 101–104), nor with the English pioneer pilot C Gordon Bell who tested the Humphreys monoplane in 1911.

*Lawrence Bell at the controls of his brother's biplane in 1912. (Bell)*

Wright-Martin Aircraft Company. A new figure arrived, a draftsman named J H 'Dutch' Kindelberger but Donald Douglas left because of a dispute with Larry Bell. The latter became vice-president and general manager of Martin, but the relationship between Bell and Martin was getting worse everyday. Late in 1924, Bell gave an ultimatum: either he was going to have a share in the ownership or he would leave. Martin refused and Bell quit on 18 January, 1925.

For more than three years Larry Bell kept away from aviation; he sold machine-tools and did various jobs. By July 1928, he was selling second-hand goods in Los Angeles when Reuben H Fleet asked him to join the Consolidated company, in Buffalo, as manager–salesman. A year later, he was promoted to general manager and Ray Whitman was appointed assistant general manager. The Consolidated Fleetster transport monoplane appeared in March 1929; it was the first American production aeroplane to have an all-metal monocoque fuselage. In 1931, the Detroit Aircraft Corporation was faced with severe financial difficulties and was unable to fulfill a contract with the US Army Air Corps for five YP-25 two-seat monoplanes. Larry Bell jumped on this opportunity: he enlisted Robert J Woods, the designer of the aircraft, and convinced USAAC representatives to give Consolidated the YP-25 work. Nevertheless, the main activity of Consolidated remained the building of floatplanes (NY-2) and flying-boats (P2Y Ranger) for the Navy. The P3Y, precursor of the famous PBY Catalina, was not yet on the drawing boards.

In the early thirties, Fleet began to consider moving his activities to the west coast while Bell yearned to have a company of his own. In June 1935, Fleet decided to move to San Diego and Larry Bell told him of his intention to stay in Buffalo to 'capitalize on what [Fleet was] forced to leave behind'(**). Fleet promised Bell two million dollars worth of sub-contract work to help the new born company. Immediately, Larry Bell got in touch with friends and businessmen and convinced Robert Woods to join the venture. With Ray Whitman, Bell drew plans to form a new company in Buffalo.

*Edwin J Ducayet, president of Bell Helicopter Corporation from 2 July, 1960, until 1 January, 1972. (Bell)*

Things went quickly. On 20 June, 1935, Larry Bell, Robert Woods and Irene Bernhardt resigned from Consolidated and twenty days later, on Wednesday 10 July, 1935, the Bell Aircraft Corporation was legally founded.

## The Bell Aircraft Corporation

The newly formed company was capitalized at $500,000. Larry Bell was president, Ray Whitman was vice-president, treasurer and purchasing agent, and Bob Woods was chief design engineer. Buildings of the former Consolidated factory were rented for a year from the American Radiator Co. At first, the Bell Aircraft Corporation produced exhaust pipes and radio masts. On 28 January, 1936, as he had promised, Reuben H Fleet signed a $878,330.38 contract with Bell for the building of 146 wing panels to be mounted on the PBY-2/3 flying-boats. This contract was followed by a $24,995 contract from the USAAC for the installation and testing of the Allison V-1710 engine in a Consolidated A-11A airframe. These contracts helped launch Bell Aircraft and on 25 March, 1936, the company announced a net loss of only $5,843.02.

At the end of 1936, Bell had 642 employees, 145,000 sq ft of floor space and more than $2,100,000 backlog. Soon, Bell was committed with Lockheed in a USAAC programme for a heavy fighter and the innovative Bell XFM-1 Airacuda was selected. The construction of the first aeroplane began in May 1936 and a follow-on order for 13 service trials machines was signed in May 1938. Nevertheless the mighty Airacuda did not enter service with USAAC combat units, mainly because of its high price, more than $219,000 each!

On 19 March, 1937, the Air Corps published its specification No. X-609 for a new high-performance single-seat fighter. Bell answered it with two rather radical proposals, the Models 3 and 4 in which the engine had been moved back near the centre of gravity to

*Leonard M 'Jack' Horner, president of Bell Helicopter Textron Inc, joined the company in 1974. (Bell)*

** Quoted by Donald J Norton in *Larry, a biography of Lawrence D Bell.*

*P-39N Airacobras in full mass production in Buffalo. Unit cost of a P-39N was then $62,794. (Bell)*

provide better manoeuvrability, nosewheel undercarriage, improved pilot view and heavier armament. Model 4 was eventually selected and ordered as the XP-39. However, the aircraft which flew for the first time on 6 April, 1938, differed appreciably from the original Model 4 but its performance was impressive. Unfortunately, numerous and successive modifications introduced throughout its career made the P-39 steadily heavier, and reduced its performance so that it was gradually relegated to ground-support missions.

## The Second World War

Larry Bell was still busy on the YFM-1s and the XP-39 when President Roosevelt asked him to go to Europe to collect information on the aviation industry there. During his trip, Bell visited Messerschmitt, Heinkel and Focke-Wulf factories in Germany and was very impressed by the way the Germans had organized mass production. After his return to the States, he wrote an in-depth report for the US government stressing Germany's strength as well as Great Britain and France's great weaknesses.

In early 1940, the company ran into serious financial difficulties. The Airacuda was a very costly programme and there were still too few production orders for the P-39.

*Bell's first achievement, the sleek and innovative Airacuda, resulted from the ill-fated Fighter, Multiseat category. Illustrated is the YFM-1B powered by two Allison V1710-41 engines. (Bell)*

*The sole Bell mass produced fighter, the P-39 Airacobra, a rugged aircraft but with limited performance. Illustrated is a P-39N flying over McChord AFB. (P M Bowers)*

Due to the war in Europe, some fresh finance arrived at the right moment. The Anglo-French Purchasing Commission signed a $9 million contract for the delivery of two hundred P-400s (export variant of the P-39), with a $2 million advance in cash. On 13 April, 1940, Great Britain signed for 675 P-39Ds and after the collapse of France, in June 1940, the French contract was taken over by the British. During the autumn of 1940, in order to meet these orders, Bell obtained authorization to build new facilities near Niagara Falls Airport, north of Buffalo, bringing floor space from 474,262sq ft to more than 1,000,000 sq ft. In 1940, Bell had manufactured thirteen aircraft; 926 were to leave the production lines in 1941, 1,973 in 1942, 4,947 in 1943 and 1,729 in 1944, the last and 9,588th P-39 being rolled out on 24 July, 1944. The average unit cost of a P-39, which was $77,159 in 1939–41, had fallen to $69,534 in 1942 and $50,666 in 1944. In the same period the number of employees had grown from 1,170 in January 1940 to 50,674 in February 1944, working in three shifts.

In early 1943, Bell opened new facilities for the Ordnance Division in Burlington, Vermont. At first, 589 employees were sent to Burlington; there would be 2,538 in June 1944. The task of this division was to produce gun mounts for the Army and the Navy and it eventually won the 'Army–Navy E' for production excellence. Later in the war, the Ordnance Division was to manufacture B-29 parts as well as equipment and shells for the Chemical Warfare Service. Other facilities included Camp Cataract for the training of Army mechanics, the Bell Modification Center for the modification of aircraft due to be delivered to the USSR (P-39s and P-63s but also P-51s, PBYs, etc), the Atlanta plant which produced several hundred Boeing B-29 Superfortresses, and a former Ford Motor Company shop, in Main Street, Buffalo, inside which the first American jet aeroplane was to be built.

On 5 September, 1941, Larry Bell and chief engineer Harlan M Poyer had been asked by Generals Echols and Arnold to design an aeroplane

*Bell's Fort Worth facility, Texas. (Bell)*

*An advertisement for the Airacobra in the March 1941 issue of Fortune.*

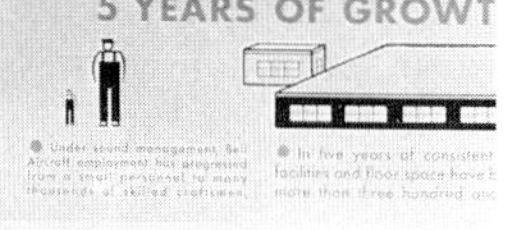

around the General Electric built British turbojet. The aircraft, known as the XP-59 was built in great secrecy and accomplished its maiden flight on 30 September, 1942. After much experimentation, one hundred aircraft were ordered by the Army on 11 March, 1944, but only 50 were eventually produced.

During the war, the Air Force accepted 13,575 Bell aircraft of all types, representing 53,037 tons of airframe weight ie 2.7 per cent of the American aircraft industry output during this period. Bell's product line also included rear gun enclosures, elevators and tailplanes for the Boeing B-17. During that period, Bell was also committed to a light fighter programme which would eventually lead to the XP-77.

*The famous Huey was used worldwide and produced by several licencees. Here is seen a flight of Austrian Air Force Agusta-built Model 204Bs. The aircraft in the foreground is c/n 3204 coded 4D-BY. (Austrian Embassy)*

*UH-1s in production at Bell's Fort Worth facility. (Bell)*

*Model 206B-IIIs and Model 412s on the production line at Bell Helicopter Textron Canada. (Bell)*

At the end of the war, the Georgia Division was rapidly closed down: of the 26,514 employees working there in August 1944, there were only 92 left on 30 September, 1944. The plant was eventually shut down and the unfinished aircraft were scrapped. Activities in the Niagara Frontier Division were also considerably slowed: 28,325 people were employed in early 1944; there were 19,264 in early 1945 and only 5,326 by the end of June 1945. However, Bell stayed in business in Buffalo and Burlington. The latter won a large contract from Graham-Paige Motors Corp for the production of 80,000 5hp two-cycle engines but the contract was cancelled after only half had been built and Bell had to shut down this plant.

## Enter the Helicopter

In order to maintain some activity, Bell soon produced a motorized wheelbarrow known as the 'Bell Prime Mover'. But development of the first Bell helicopter had begun in 1941 under the direction of Arthur M Young and with the backing of Larry Bell. Young had tested helicopter scale-models for 13 years before he joined Bell and his collaboration with Bell resulted in the Model 30 which flew for the first

*Arthur Young. (Bell)*

time in December 1942.

In 1945, the Air Force asked Robert Woods to go to Germany at the head of a team of engineers in order to examine captured technical materials. This team, called Combined Advanced Field Team (CAFT), was assigned as its primary mission the investigation of everything about Messerschmitt activities and advanced research. On 7 May, 1945, the team arrived in Messerschmitt's headquarters in Oberammergau and among tons of documents discovered some interesting items concerning swept-wing theory, transonic flight, and anti-aircraft missiles. The Americans also discovered a nearly-completed variable-geometry swept-wing prototype known as the Messerschmitt P.1011 and this eventually served as a basis for the Bell X-5. At the end of the war, the Americans also 'captured' some German brains and several of them came to work at Bell. The most famous of these personalities was certainly Prof Walter R Dornberger who, with Werner von Braun, had been responsible for the V 2 ballistic missile programme.

*Floyd W Carlson, logged numerous achievements as a helicopter test pilot for Bell. (Bell)*

On 8 March, 1946, the famous Model 47 helicopter was certificated by the CAA opening the door to commercial sales. In due course Bell began production for commercial, industrial and government uses. That year, sales totalled $11.5 million but losses increased to $657,900.

*Bart Kelley (left) and Arthur Young (right) reminisce about the early days. (Bell)*

The 25th of January, 1946, marked a very important milestone for the company; the experimental supersonic prototype Bell X-1 accomplished its first gliding flight with Jack Woolams at the controls, the first powered flight occurring on 9 December. On Tuesday, 14 October, 1947, Capt Charles 'Chuck' Yeager would become the first supersonic man in aviation history.

## 1947–48, the Troubled Years

In February 1947, Bell ran into difficulties when a group of dissident shareholders led by Jackson Martindell gathered Bell common stock in a campaign against Larry Bell's control of his company. At the time, the company had $31.6 million in assets and only $12.8 million in liabilities. This group proposed a new board of directors in place of Bell, Beard, Whitman and Woods. But at last, in April 1947, after a proxy fight, the Bell management was maintained.

In 1948, Bell had 1,861 employees and ran again into serious difficulties. For the third consecutive year there were losses ($657,000 in 1946, $1,200,000 in 1947 and $350,000 in 1948). The unions were strengthened, especially UAW Local 501. On 10 March, 1949, a new leadership of the Local 501 was elected and laid down a set of demands. After much discussion, the concessions of the management were rejected and Local 501 voted for a strike on 13 June. The strike was very tough and lasted until 17 October when an agreement was reached. This strike delayed the inspection of Model 60/X-5's mock-up until December (it was originally scheduled for 28 June, 1949).

The helicopter division was moved to Fort Worth, Texas, in

1951. A 55-acre site had been selected on 30 January, 1951, the ground breaking ceremonies were held on 21 May and the personnel began occupying the facility on 3 December. This decision had been prompted by the company's winning a competition which called for manufacturing a number of ASM helicopters (Model 61/HSL-1). While this plant was under construction, production was kept at the old Globe Aircraft plant, in Saginaw, which had been leased in early 1951. In 1951 too, Bell initiated the study of a hypersonic glider, first as a private venture then with Air Force backing. This aircraft would have been boosted to high altitude by rockct propulsion and thcn completed its mission in a glide. For that year, sales totalled $82 million.

*The Model 47 earned its reputation by performing rescue missions. Seen here is the Bell 47G-2 c/n 1465, F-BHKZ, of the French Protection Civile in June 1957. It has two outside stretchers. (Protection Civile via J P Tedesco)*

*Bell Model 222s under construction. In the foreground is the eighth production aircraft, to be delivered to Wells Fargo Leasing Corp as N5007L. (Bell)*

*Production of the AH-1 Cobra at Fort Worth. (Bell)*

At the end of 1952, the Texas plant had manufactured a total of 416 helicopters; in December alone 67 aircraft had been delivered. Employment had grown from 259 to 2,600 workers.

On 10 April, 1953, the 1,000th Model 47 was rolled off the assembly line. Meanwhile, the 'Goldfish bowl' as it was known, had been deployed in Korea where it performed outstandingly well. During the summer of 1953, Larry Bell took a ride near the frontline. This was a very tiring experience for him and he complained of a pain across his chest (examination would later reveal an hypertensive cardiovascular disease). The following year, the company reported $185.6 million in sales and employment was 18,850. In 1955, the US Navy automatic All-weather Carrier Landing System (ACLS), which had been under development for four years, entered production. The first fully automatic landing of an F3D Skyray naval shipboard fighter had taken place at Niagara Falls Airport on 5 May, 1954, and the ACLS was eventually installed aboard all the Navy's aircraft carriers.

In February 1955, Bell won an industry-wide competition to develop and produce a turbine-

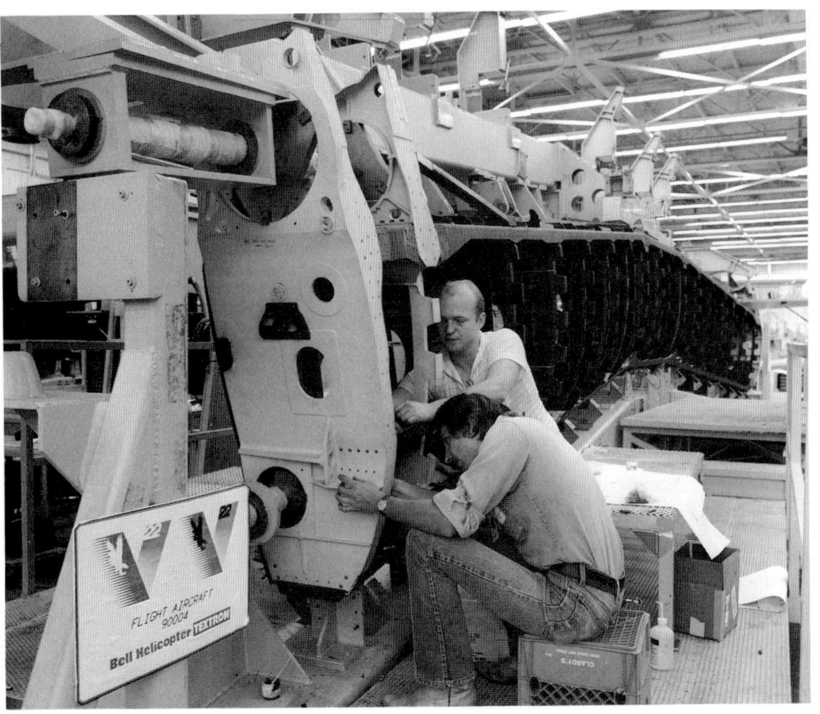


*The wing of the fourth V-22 Osprey prototype being assembled. (Bell)*

powered utility helicopter for the US Army. This would eventually become the famed 'Huey'. Deliveries of the UH-1 began in September 1958 and the line was closed in December 1980, 22 years later, after more than 10,000 military and 1,200 commercial variants had been produced. But the line was eventually reopened in 1983 to fill a co-assembly contract with the government of Turkey.

During all this time, test programmes had been pursued with Bell's experimental supersonic aircraft. On 27 September, 1956, Capt Milburn G Apt in the Bell X-2 became the first man to reach Mach 3 but he was killed a few seconds after he lost control of the aircraft. As a matter of fact, the same year, with the cancellation of the X-16 high-altitude reconnaissance aircraft programme, the days of Bell fixed-wing aircraft production programmes came to an end. Larry Bell's health deteriorated rapidly and on 24 May, 1956, he had suffered a severe stroke. On 10 October he had a heart attack and succumbed ten days later, the day of the Model 204/XH-40's maiden flight. He was still chairman at the time of his death on Saturday, 20 October, 1956. Edwin J Ducayet became in turn president of Bell Helicopter (he had joined Bell Aircraft Corp as assistant to the vice-president in charge of the helicopter division in 1950 and would remain at the head of Bell until 1 January, 1972, when he became chairman, a position he held until his retirement from Bell at the end of that year).

*Larry Bell and Charles 'Chuck' Yeager with the Bell X-1A.*

## The Bell Helicopter Corporation

By 1956, the company's helicopter activities had become so extensive that, on 1 January, 1957, the Helicopter Division at Fort Worth was given full corporate status, becoming the Bell Helicopter Corporation. A further reorganisation took place in February 1958 when it was decided that all defence product activities in the Buffalo and the Niagara Frontier plants would be operated by a newly established autonomous unit called Niagara Frontier Division. At the same time, vice-president R J Sandstrom was assigned to direct the activities in the high-altitude and space field. At the end of 1957, employment totalled 13,404 of which 10,095 were in the aircraft, avionics, rocket and special weapons divisions and 3,309 in the Bell Helicopter Corp.

In 1958, the XV-3 convertiplane made aviation history with the first 100 per cent conversion of a tilting propeller-rotor aircraft. Feasibility of the concept was established by 125 flying hours and 110 full conversions. The following year, Bell began development of the Model 8096 Agena engine as a weapon pod to be carried by the Convair B-58 Hustler and later used on the Lockheed-built Agena vehicle.

The year 1960 marked an important new step in Bell history. In July, Textron Inc of Providence, Rhode Island, bought various Bell Aircraft Corporation properties, including the helicopter operation. Textron organized a wholly-owned subsidiary, Bell Aerospace Corp, which came into existence that year, and the helicopter operation was renamed Bell Helicopter Company. Bell Aerospace Corp was responsible for the design of the secondary propulsion system for the Agena target vehicle (Model 8247) and other space contracts included the manufacture of reaction controls for the North American X-15A, Minuteman and Centaur rockets. Its research and development programmes in the VTOL/STOL field included ground effect vehicles such as the X-22A, rocket belts and the Lunar landing training vehicles (LLTV).

The early sixties were marked by an impressive set of world records established both by the Model 47 and the Model 204. In September 1965, Bell announced development of the JetRanger and of the HueyCobra, a company-funded product improvement to meet a battlefield requirement in Vietnam. The Army took delivery of the initial AH-1G in June 1967, only 14 months after contract award! By October of the same year, the HueyCobra was deployed in Vietnam. Production grew steadily and by the end of March 1969, Bell had built and delivered 12,000 production helicopters of all types and more than 10,500 people were employed. By the end of 1969, Bell had built and delivered 13,000 production helicopters, including more commercial helicopters than all other US manufacturers combined. On 24 November, 1971, Bell announced that it was co-operating with the Bendix Corporation on a new traffic terminal approach and landing system (the Microwave Landing System). In December 1971, E J Ducayet became chairman and James F Atkins took over as president of Bell Helicopter. In 1972, the US Army/NASA Tilt Rotor Research Aircraft Progamme was initiated to demonstrate the concept. Bell was selected to design, build and accomplish initial contractor flight testing of two XV-15 aircraft. At the end of 1973, the Model 47 was discontinued after 27 years of continuous production covering more than twenty different basic configurations and, on 23 April, 1974, Bell Helicopter announced the delivery of the 20,000th helicopter, an important milestone in the company's history. Out of this total, 80 per cent had been delivered since the beginning of 1964.

In January 1976, the name of the company was changed to Bell Helicopter Textron and, in January 1982, it was incorporated as Bell Helicopter Textron Inc, a wholly-owned subsidiary of Textron Inc. In the middle of the year, Bell and Boeing Vertol Co teamed to participate in the Joint Services Vertical Lift Aircraft (JVX) programme. Preliminary design contracts were awarded to Bell-Boeing in April 1983 and again in May 1984. The V-22 programme is today's most significant programme underway at Bell Helicopter with first deliveries scheduled to start in 1992.

On the commercial side, in December 1982, the Canadian Government requested proposals for the establishment of a helicopter manufacturing industry in Canada. The proposal submitted by Bell Helicopter was the one selected and, in December 1985, Bell Helicopter Textron, a division of Textron Canada Ltd, moved into its new Canadian facility, situated 20 miles north of Montreal. The original mandate was to build a family of new light twin-engined helicopters, the first being the Model 400. Unfortunately because of market conditions, development of the Model 400 was suspended. This resulted in the decision to move the manufacturing of the Model 206B JetRanger III and 206L LongRanger III into the

*The Landing Craft Air Cushion (LCAC), a product of Textron Marine Systems, can cruise at speeds of more than 40kt. (Bell)*

*Lawrence Dale Bell was born in Mentone, Indiana, on 5 April, 1894. (Smithsonian Institution)*

Canadian facility. Textron Canada is also due to produce the future Model 230.

In another important programme for the mid-to-late 1990s, Bell Helicopter has joined with McDonnell Douglas in the US Army's LHX preliminary design competition. Demonstration and validation contracts were awarded in 1988 to McDonnell Douglas-Bell and Boeing-Sikorsky. A full-scale development contract was expected to be awarded to the winning team in late 1990. Current plans call for the production of approximately 2,100 LHX helicopters. Unfortunately for Bell the final decision was in favour of Boeing-Sikorsky.

## Today's Bell

Today, Textron Inc is a multi-industry company with operations in three business sectors: aerospace technology, commercial products, and financial services. Aerospace and defence divisions include Bell Helicopter Textron in Fort Worth, Texas; Textron Lycoming in Stratford, Connecticut (producing engines among which are the AGT1500 gas turbine for the US Army's M1 Abrams main battle tank and the ALF502 turbofan for the British Aerospace BAe 146 commuter airliner); Textron Defense Systems in Wilmington, Massachusetts; Cadillac Gage Textron in Warren, Michigan, Textron Aerostructures in Nashville, Tennessee (involved in major wing programmes for the Rockwell B-1B and the Lockheed C-5A/B and will produce components for the Airbus A330/340 and McDonnell Douglas C-17); Textron Marine Systems in New Orleans, Louisiana (which is producing the LCAC amphibious craft for the Navy/Marines); Bell Aerospace Textron in Buffalo, New York; Aircraft Engine Components Textron in Newington, Connecticut; Airfoil Textron in Lima, Ohio; Fuel Systems Textron in Zeeland, Michigan; HR Textron in Valencia, California; Cherry Textron in Santa Ana, California; and Textron Speciality Materials in Lowell, Massachusetts. Bell Helicopter Textron includes ten factories covering 3,000,000 sq ft (280,000sq m) and located in Fort Worth and Amarillo, Texas, and in Montreal. The total of employees worldwide is 9,300.

In 1989, Textron was the 61st largest American industrial corporation (it was ranked 72nd in 1987) with $7,440.1mn revenue and $259.2mn profits. The number of employees had dropped from 60,000 in 1988 to 58,000. Current chairman and chief executive officer of Textron is B F Dolan, president and chief operating officer is James F Hardymon and president of Bell Helicopter Textron is Leonard M 'Jack' Horner (who joined the company in 1974 and was previously vice-president of the Sikorsky Division of United Technologies). Textron's major current defence programmes include the AH-1W Super Cobra, the AHIP programme and the V-22 Osprey.

# The Aircraft

## XFM-1/YFM-1 Airacuda

In 1936, as the Boeing B-17 Flying Fortress was still under development, an operational requirement was issued for a long-range escort fighter to protect bombers on long-range bombing flights and the new designation FM (for Fighter Multiplace) was then introduced in USAAC terminology. Two manufacturers, Lockheed and Bell, answered this requirement under a $25,000 contract for preliminary engineering. The deadline was 15 March, 1936. Lockheed proposed the twin-engined XPB-3/XFM-2 which remained on the drawing board and was later cancelled in favour of the famous XP-38. Bell's answer was the XFM-1 Airacuda which was eventually retained by the Air Corps. Bell won the competition by 72 points to 71.6 out of 100 (the XFM-1 was found to have better military characteristics than its Lockheed counterpart).

In May 1936, a $400,000 contract was signed for the construction of a prototype. For the first Bell aircraft Robert J Woods and Art Fornoff, the project engineer, conceived a rather innovative layout which retained many of the design details from Woods' designs for Lockheed and Consolidated. This aircraft was a large twin-engined machine whose span of 69ft 10in was nearly equal to that of a medium bomber. Two supercharged 1,150hp Allison V-1710-13 liquid-cooled engines drove three-blade pusher propellers and were arranged in such a manner that the forward portion of each engine nacelle could be fashioned into a gunner's compartment. The XFM-1 had an all-metal structure with fabric-covered control surfaces. The fuselage comprised nose and tail sections joined at the wing front spar. The tail section was of semi-monocoque construction. A Plexiglas enclosed cabin extended from the nose to aft of the navigator's station. The wing was of stressed skin, box spar, cantilever construction consisting of a centre and two outer panels. The undercarriage was fully retractable.

Armament was to include a redesigned Madsen 37mm cannon (mounted in a hydraulic flexible cone) and a 0.30in machine-gun in each nacelle. The cannon could be fired by the gunner in the nacelle or

*The Bell XFM-1 is recognizable by the large airscoops on top of the engine nacelles and by the side mounted turbo-superchargers. (USAF)*

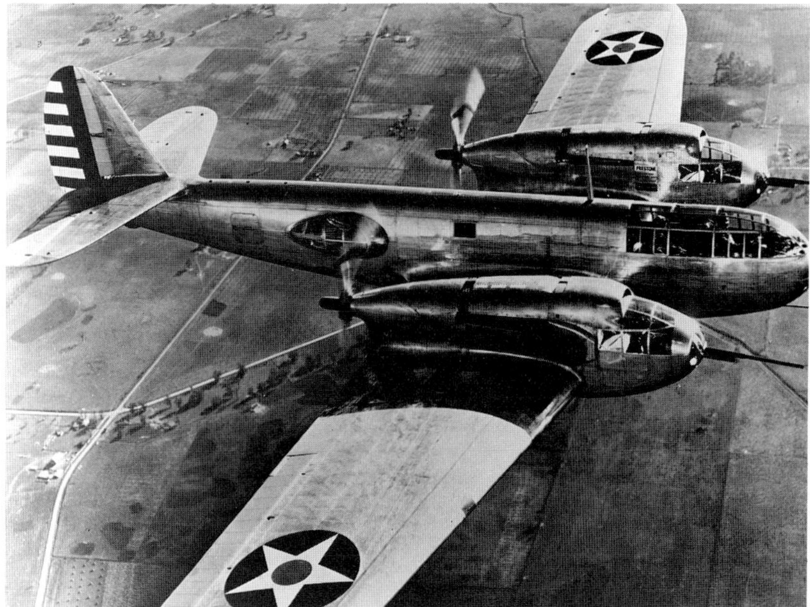

*The XFM-1. The observation blisters on the rear fuselage sides are clearly visible. The spinners have not been fitted. (USAF)*

*The Airacuda was quite innovative for its time. The ball-mounted cannon at the front of the engine nacelles are noteworthy. (USAF via J Ethell)*

*The XFM-1 suffered a hard landing on 24 September, 1937, when the starboard undercarriage unit collapsed. (Courtesy J Ethell)*

by the navigator through a central fire control system. A 0.50in machine-gun was to be operated through streamlined side blisters by a gunner stationed in the rear fuselage. The aircraft could also carry twenty 30lb T-5/M-5 bombs in the fuselage between the front and rear wing spars. The XFM-1 had a crew of five: pilot, co-pilot/navigator, radio operator-gunner and two gunners stationed in the front of the engine nacelles. Crew members communicated with each other by means of a telephone and could move from one position to another while in flight.

After a wooden mock-up had been built, construction of the prototype was initiated in May 1936 and the wings were mated to the fuselage at the end of July 1937. First Lieut Benjamin S Kelsey took the unarmed XFM-1 (s/n 36-351) on its first flight at Buffalo on 1 September, 1937. Unfortunately, during take-off, the port engine backfired and blew in the air ducts as well as the intercooler. Another incident occurred during the second flight, on 24 September, 1937: on landing, the starboard undercarriage remained unlocked and collapsed. The XFM-1 crash-landed damaging the starboard wing and propeller. After repairs and ten other test flights, the aeroplane was accepted at Wright Field on 21 October, 1937. The Airacuda was extensively tested at Langley Field during 1938 and 1939 where it became unpopular with maintenance crews responsible for keeping the 'plumber's nightmare', as they called it, in flying status. Maintenance apparently was a major problem. Nevertheless the XFM-1 was put on display with several other Air Corps prototypes at the famous Bolling Field Exhibition (19 to 24 January, 1940). President Roosevelt, accompanied by the Secretary of War, the Assistant Secretary of War and the Chief of the Materiel division, visited this display on 20 January. The XFM-1, camouflaged in olive-drab, was in hangar No. 1 together with the Bell XP-39.

*The second Bell YFM-1A, s/n 38-497, was powered by two Allison V-1710-23s. (USAF)*

*The YFM-1 without side blisters and turbo-superchargers. Propeller spinners have been added. Noteworthy is the high level of finish of this aeroplane (s/n 38-486).*

*An unarmed YFM-1. (USAF)*

Meanwhile, on 20 May, 1938, the War Department had contracted for thirteen XFM-1s for Service testing (s/n 38-486/498), but only nine (s/n 38-486/491, 493/495) were eventually completed as such. The YFM-1s were powered by two 1,150hp Allison V-1710-23 engines in modified cowlings (radiator air intakes were moved into the wing leading edge, superchargers were now built into the nacelles and propeller spinners were added). The fuselage was lengthened and the front fuselage redesigned. A periscope was fixed under the nose in order to detect attack from the underside. The armament was revised. The fixed 0.30in machine-guns were repositioned from the engine nacelle compartments to the nose section of the fuselage. The side blisters were replaced by hatches, and the two 0.30in machine-guns repositioned in ventral and dorsal hatches in the area of the wing trailing edges. The aircraft had now provision for underwing bomb-racks.

The first YFM-1 made its maiden flight on 28 September, 1939. This aircraft was delivered on 23 February, 1940, and the last one on 30 July of the same year. Three aircraft (s/n

*This view of the YFM-1 clearly shows its unusual layout. (USAF)*

*This view of a YFM-1A shows the large ailerons and cooling vents. The lack of rear visibility is also apparent. (USAF via J Ethell)*

38-496/498) were completed as YFM-1As and had nosewheel undercarriages. The main legs retracted inwards into the wing (they retracted rearwards previously) and the front leg retracted rearwards under the cockpit. This nosewheel undercarriage was the source of a serious problem, nosewheel shimmy. This was solved after numerous tests and the use of a car fitted with an Airacuda's nosewheel. Other incidents occurred; on 21 June, 1940, an Airacuda encountered serious difficulties during a routine flight. The pilot, Bryan Sparks, baled out and was injured while the co-pilot, Jack Strickler, decided to bring back the aircraft, but it crashed in a field and was damaged beyond repair. The wrecked airframe was eventually donated to Buffalo's Burgard High School.

Two of the YFM-1s (s/n 38-489/490) were converted to YFM-1Bs by the installation of 1,090hp Allison V-1710-41 engines and some internal equipment, but the performance remained virtually unchanged. The thirteenth aircraft (s/n 38-492) was not completed and most probably used for structural tests. For a number of reasons, but primarily due to the poor performance, complexity of the design and price ($219,000 each), further development on the Airacuda was discontinued. The twin-engined Bell aircraft was in fact

*The XFM-1 in November 1937. (USAF)*

nearly 30mph slower than the Boeing B-17B it was intended to escort! In addition, the Airacuda suffered severe flight limitations for a fighter: it was not allowed to make an Immelmann turn, fly inverted, spin or even loop and roll! It could not taxi because its cooling system only operated in the airflow created by flight. On the ground, the aeroplane had to be towed. In fact, the Airacuda was a mix of innovations and oddities.

In January 1942, the nine airworthy Airacudas were flown to Chanute Field, Illinois, and relegated to Air Corps Technical School's 10th Air Base Squadron where mechanics used them as instructional airframes. They were eventually scrapped and none of them has survived.

## XFM-1

Span 69ft 10in (21.28m); length 44ft 10in (13.66m); height 13ft 7in (4.14m); wing area 683.9sq ft (63.5sq m).

Empty weight 13,400lb (6,073kg); loaded weight 17,333lb (7,852kg).

Maximum speed 270mph (434km/h) at 12,600ft (3,840m); cruising speed 244mph (393km/h); service ceiling 30,500ft (9,300m); normal range 800 miles (1,285km); maximum range 2,600 miles (4,180km).

## YFM-1

Span 70ft (21.34m); length 45ft 11⅜in

*The unarmed Airacuda prototype in its original configuration. This aircraft flew for the first time on 1 September, 1937. (US Air Force)*

(14.00m); height 12ft 5in (3.78m); wing area 685.7sq ft (63.70sq m).

Loaded weight 19,000lb (8,607kg).

Maximum speed 268mph (431km/h) at 12,600ft (3,840m); cruising speed 200mph (322km/h) at 12,000ft (3,660m).

## YFM-1A

Dimensions as YFM-1 except height 19ft 6in (5.94m).

Empty weight 13,674lb (6,194kg); loaded weight 19,000lb (8,607kg); maximum weight 21,625lb (9,796kg).

Maximum speed 268mph (431km/h) at 12,600ft (3,840m); cruising speed 200mph (322km/h) at 12,000ft (3,660m).

*This view shows the neat lines of the Airacuda. Noteworthy is the under fuselage fire position. This aircraft (s/n 38-486) was the first of the service trials batch. (USAF)*

*This Bell YFM-1 Airacuda bears the designator and insignia of the 10th Air Base Squadron. (P M Bowers)*

## YFM-1B

Dimensions as YFM-1A.

Empty weight 13,674lb (6,194kg); loaded weight 18,373lb (8,323kg); maximum weight 21,625lb (9,796kg).

Maximum speed 268mph (431km/h) at 12,600ft (3,840m); cruising speed 200mph (322km/h) at 12,000ft (3,660m); normal range 1,670 miles (2,687km); maximum range 2,180 miles (3,508km); initial rate of climb 1,500ft/min (457m/min); service ceiling 29,900ft (9,113m); absolute ceiling 31,300ft (9,540m).

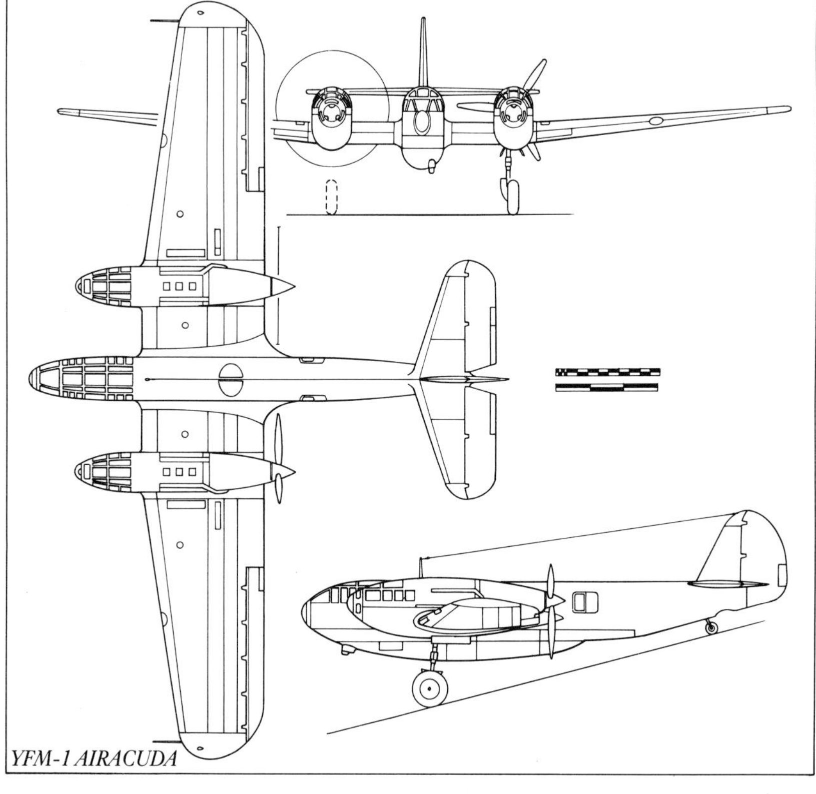

*YFM-1 AIRACUDA*

# Models 11/15, 26 and 33 P-39 Airacobra

In the mid-thirties, the main types of aircraft in the US Army Air Corps inventory were the Boeing P-26, Martin B-10B, Curtiss A-12 and the Douglas O-36; the first Seversky P-35s and Northrop A-17s had just been ordered. But all these were considered by the USAAC as interim types. A new generation of combat aircraft had to be designed. This situation was critical as far as fighters were concerned. At the time, some commercial aeroplanes were faster than the fighters on squadron inventory. That is why, in 1936, the Air Corps asked several manufacturers to submit single-seat fighter projects for evaluation, among them was the newly born Bell Corporation and its chief engineer Robert J Woods.

Bob Woods and Harland M Poyer began working in June 1936. On 19 March, 1937, the USAAC issued specification No. X-609 for a new fighter. As this specification was not very precise, the Bell team could design without many constraints what it thought to be the ultimate fighter. It wanted to design an aircraft possessing great fire-power, excellent visibility for the pilot, good take-off and landing characteristics, improved ground handling and, above all, superlative manoeuvrability.

Armament was a critical consideration. At the time, most American combat aeroplanes were lightly armed. Virtually no fighter had wing-mounted guns; all armament was in the nose above the engine. Thus, due to lack of available space, the only way to increase fire-power was to increase calibre. Woods had been very impressed by tests of the new 37mm T9 light gun designed by American Armament Corp, a subsidiary of Oldsmobile, and he decided to design the new aircraft

*A highly retouched photograph showing the prototype Airacobra in front of the Bell factory in Buffalo on 15 December, 1938. The oil cooler air intake was on the right-hand side while the supercharger air intake was on the left. (Bell)*

*The XP-39 in NACA's large wind tunnel at Langley Field, Virginia. (Courtesy P M Bowers)*

*One of the first models of an Airacobra seen during preliminary tests in the University of Michigan wind tunnel. (Courtesy P M Bowers)*

*One of the earliest standard P-39Cs. This model had rudimentary armour plating and its fuel tanks were not self-sealing. (US Air Force)*

around its armament. Two designs were then considered, one with a 25mm cannon and the other with the 37mm cannon. The barrels of both of these guns were too long; in consequence, the engine (a twelve-cylinder Allison V-1710 liquid-cooled engine) had to be moved rearward and equipped with an extension shaft. On the first design, called Model 3, the cockpit was also moved rearward, aft the engine. This position might not have been accepted for downward visibility. On the second design (Model 4), the positions were reversed: the engine was moved further aft and the cockpit installed in front of it, between

*The XP-39 (s/n 38-326) in its original form. The large air intake for the supercharger was later discarded. (Bell)*

*After tests at NACA, the XP-39 was redesignated XP-39B. The supercharger was abandoned and the air intake for the carburettor was resited on top of the fuselage. (Bell)*

*A YP-39. The main differences between the YP-39 and the prototype Airacobra were the larger fin and the armament. (Bell)*

the engine and the propeller. This configuration required an oversized extension shaft but, on the other hand, visibility was excellent and, above all, the engine was now placed very near to the centre of gravity, a theoretically ideal position for good manoeuvrability. Another innovation was that both Model 3 and 4 had tricycle undercarriages.

In May 1937, both designs were presented to the USAAC technical services and, after careful study, Model 4 was retained for further development. A contract was awarded on 7 October, 1937, requiring the construction of a single prototype under the USAAC designation XP-39. This was to be delivered by August 1938. Model 3 was put aside for a time but later served as a basis for the Bell Model 32.

Construction of the prototype then began in Buffalo. The aircraft was of all-metal construction with fabric-covered contral surfaces. The centre wing section was integral with the fuselage and the outer wing panels, incorporating the main undercarriage legs, were bolted to it. This later proved troublesome because it was impossible to remove the wing panels with the aircraft standing on its undercarriage and required a crane and jigs.

*A YP-39 on the Buffalo flight line on 16 October, 1940. Armament had not yet been installed. (Bell)*

The engine was a 1,150hp Allison V-1710–17 equipped with a Type B-5 supercharger, the airscoop of which was installed on the port side of the fuselage. This engine drove a three-bladed propeller via a lubricated reduction gear and an articulated extension shaft in order to compensate for fuselage deformations under high-manoeuvres.

At the beginning of spring 1938, construction was complete. The aircraft (s/n 38-326) was then disassembled and taken to Wright Field for preliminary flight testing. The maiden flight was on 6 April, 1938, with dive-bomber pilot Lieut James Taylor (USN Ret) at the controls. Bell's John L 'Mickey' McCarthy was the crew chief. The XP-39 had not then received its armament and weighed only 6,204lb and, during early flights, the speed of 390mph was reached and only 5 minutes needed to climb to 20,000ft. These figures were a little under those calculated (400mph). On 6 June, 1939, after some sixty flying hours had been logged, the XP-39 was sent to Langley Field NACA wind-tunnel. These tests led to the removal of the supercharger and its intake, and the aircraft was sent back to Buffalo for modifications. These included an engine replacement (a 1,090hp Allison V-1710-39), the moving of the carburettor air intake to the back of the fuselage aft of the cockpit, wing span reduced to 34ft, fuselage length increased to 29ft 9in and a lowered canopy. All this led to a weight increase, the aircraft now weighed 6,450lb, and a designation change to XP-39B.

The prototype was back in the air on 25 November, 1939. Low-altitude manoeuvrability was found to be better but high-altitude performance had deteriorated: maximum speed was now 375mph at 15,000ft and time to 20,000ft was 7½ minutes. Unfortunately, the aircraft was destroyed in an accident after only 28 hours flying.

Meanwhile, the USAAC had been impressed by the performance of the XP-39 and, on 13 April, 1939, had signed a contract with Bell for the construction of thirteen Service trials aircraft designated YP-39 (Model 12 under Bell terminology). These aircraft were to be identical to the XP-39B but with a V-1710-37 engine. The first YP-39 (s/n 40-027) made its maiden flight on 13 September, 1940. This aircraft had its full armament, ie a 37mm cannon, with 15 rounds, firing through the propeller hub, two 0.50in machine-guns with 200 rounds and one 0.30in machine-gun with 500 rounds. The vertical tail surfaces were enlarged and some armour had been installed in the cockpit area. All-up weight has been increased to 7,235lb.

*A P-39D. There is a landing light under the port wing. (Bell)*

*Among the P-39D's new features was the small fillet at the base of the fin. (Bell)*

The thirteen YP-39s (40-027/40-039) were delivered between 7 September and 16 December, 1940, and were used for evaluation. Some of them were sent back to Bell to be used in the development of improved versions. Most of them were destroyed in accidents: 40-027 during its 8th flight; 40-029 on 21 January, 1942; 40-030 on 10 May, 1943; 40-031 on 22 December, 1940; 40-036 on 26 March, 1942; and 40-039 on 10 June, 1942. The remaining examples were withdrawn from use.

## Production History

The first production contract was awarded on 10 August, 1939. This one, which received USAAC approval on 12 October, covered eighty examples of Bell Model 13 and, at first, were designated P-45 Airacobra, but this designation soon changed to P-39C and P-39D.

**P-39C (Model 13) and P-39D (Model 15).** These variants were almost identical to the YP-39 with the exception of the engine which was a 1,150hp Allison V-1710-35. Twenty aircraft were built as P-39Cs and the first of them flew in January 1941. These were followed by sixty P-39D-BEs. In comparison to the P-39C, the P-39D (Model 15) incorporated several improvements, the two 0.30in nose machine-guns were deleted and four guns of similar calibre were installed in the wings, an under-fuselage strong-point enabled the carrying of a jettisonable fuel tank, a 300lb M-31 bomb or a 600lb M-32 bomb. The fuel tanks were now self-sealing but their capacity was reduced to 120 US gal; some armour was added and a small fillet was added at the root of the vertical fin.

Further orders covered one hundred and twenty P-39D-1-BEs ordered on 9 September, 1940; 249 P-39D-1-BEs ordered on 13 September, 1940; 150 P-39D-1-BEs ordered on 11 June, 1941, and 344 P-39D-2-BEs ordered on 17 September, 1941. In all, a grand total of 923 P-39Ds was produced. The P-39D-1 was the variant which was due to be delivered to Great Britain under Lend-Lease. These aircraft were armed with a 20mm M1 cannon and incorporated a small dorsal fillet. P-39D-2-BEs were also Lend-Lease aircraft equipped with a 1,325hp V-1710-63 engine. Most of the D-1s and D-2s were delivered to the USSR and some dozens were taken in charge by USAAC squadrons. Most of these were later modified for the ground attack role with additional armour under the fuselage and K-24 and K-25 cameras in the fuselage thus becoming P-39D-3-BEs (26 ex-P-39D-BEs) and P-39D-4-BEs (11 ex-P-39D-1-BEs).

**Caribou and Airacobra I (Model 14):** At the time of the first USAAC contracts, the situation was getting worse in Europe. France and Great Britain were desperately seeking for military materiel in order to compensate their inferiority against the German threat. From 1939, a special commission began to negotiate for thousands of aircraft and engines. The Bell P-39 was concerned in this action and, after receiving War Department approval on 30 March, 1940, Bell signed a $9,000,000 contract with the French Government for the delivery of two hundred P-39s from October 1940. Needless to say these aircraft were never delivered. Great Britain ordered 675 Model 14s on 13 April, 1940, under the name Caribou. The Caribou differed from its American counterpart only by its armament which consisted of a 20mm Hispano M-1 cannon with 60 rounds, two 0.50in machine-guns in the nose with 270 rounds and four 0.30in machine-guns in the wings with 1,000 rounds.

Surprisingly, in the course of the eight months that followed this agreement, not a single British pilot flew the P-39; the very first was Christopher Clarkson who began aircraft evaluation only on 30 December, 1940. Meanwhile, production had begun and the first Caribou had left the assembly lines in April

1941. The aircraft were delivered by ship and the first crates were unloaded in Great Britain in July. In fact, the very first aircraft were three P-39Cs delivered under Lend-Lease (s/n 40-2981, 40-2983, 40-2984, respectively DS173, DS174 and DS175). They were assembled by a team from BOAC at RAF Colerne and the first of them flew on 6 July, 1941, with a USAAC pilot, Lieut M F McNickle, at the controls. DS173 was sent to A & AEE Boscombe Down and DS174 joined the Air Fighter Development Unit (AFDU). But the British were soon disappointed with their new fighter. Maximum speed did not exceed 359mph. This poor performance was mainly due to the lack of a turbo-supercharger which limited speed at high altitude.

*A P-39C in Royal Air Force colours. The RAF received three aircraft of this type before delivery of the Airacobra I. (Courtesy P M Bowers)*

*The Caribou AH573 at the A & AEE at Boscombe Down where the tests were disappointing. (Courtesy RAE)*

*A row of P-39Cs belonging to the 31st Pursuit Group, at Selfridge Field, Michigan. All aircraft are unarmed. (US Air Force)*

At the end of July, the first genuine Airacobra Is, as they were now known, arrived at Colerne. After assembly, some of them were sent to A & AEE for tests (AH573, AH574, AH589, AH701). AH573 was devoted to evaluation of climb and level performance and tested various exhaust pipes to comply with RAF regulations. AH574 tested the cooling system and was equipped with an automatic throttle. AH589 was used to study pollution with carbon dioxyde and AH701 served to evaluate general performance and gun heating. During these tests the following performance figures were registered: maximum level speed: 355mph at 13,000ft; climb to 10,000ft: 5min 6sec; climb to 20,000ft: 11min 42sec; service ceiling: 29,000ft. By comparison, at the same time, the Supermarine Spitfire Mk.VB was flying at 364mph; climbed to 20,000ft in 8min and had a service ceiling of 40,000ft. Even the Hawker Hurricane Mk.IIC climbed faster than the Airacobra I.

It was decided to re-equip No.601 City of London Squadron, flying the Hurricane Mk.IIB, with Airacobra Is. The first P-39Ds were taken in charge by No.601 Squadron on 7 August, 1941. But these were not fully operational. Not less than twenty-five modifications had been requested by the A & AEE and the

AFDU. Assembly of the new aircraft also caused problems, Airacobras arrived dismantled in crates without having undergone any earlier testing and spares were lacking. However, pilots of No.601 Squadron discovered that it was an aircraft pleasing to fly but with irritating shortcomings such as an unreliable compass, carbon dioxyde vapours invading the cockpit when firing the guns, and limited gun accessibility during ground maintenance. In September, four Aircobras were declared operational and sent to Manston. There, between 9 and 11 September, they accomplished two missions over the French coast. Unfortunately, the compass was still causing trouble and the four aircraft were sent back to Duxford. The British Government then decided to send most of its Airacobras to the USSR. The remaining machines were kept by the USAAC as P-400s. In January, 1942, No.601 Squadron moved to Acaster Malbis where, in March, it began to receive its first Supermarine Spitfire Mk.VB's.

Other tests were conducted in Great Britain with Airacobras. AH571 was equipped with a reduced area rudder and AH574 received an arrester hook and was tested aboard HMS *Indefatigable* during the summer of 1944. This aircraft was withdrawn from use on 18 March, 1948.

**P-39F and P-39J (Model 15B):** In 1942, Curtiss Electric propellers could no longer be delivered in sufficient quantities and some aircraft were even delivered without a propeller! The decision was taken to adapt an Aeroproducts propeller and this change gave birth to a new variant called P-39F. Initial orders (13 September, 1940) covered 254 aircraft but only 229 were eventually delivered. Among them, twenty-seven were converted for ground attack and tactical reconnaissance roles by the Field Modification Centers and became P-39F-2-BEs. Some aircraft were transformed into two-seat trainers (TP-39F). The 25 remaining aircraft of the initial order were equipped with an Allison V-1710-59 engine under the designation P-39J-BE.

**P-39G (Model 26):** This variant was not produced and the 1,800 ordered under this designation became P-39K, L, M and N.

**P-39K (Model 26A):** This variant was equipped with a 1,325hp V-1710-63 engine driving an 10ft 4in diameter Aeroproducts propeller. Two hundred and ten P-39K-1-BEs were ordered on 25 August, 1941, and eventually built. Half a dozen were later converted to ground attack P-39K-2-BEs and one became the prototype of the P-39N variant.

**P-39L (Model 26B):** This variant was identical to the P-39K but with a Curtiss Electric propeller and an increased gross weight of 9,100lb. Two hundred and fifty P-39L-1-BEs were produced of which eleven were subsequently modified for the ground attack role as P-39L-2-BEs.

**P-39M (Model 26D):** This variant was powered by a 1,200hp V-1710-83 engine driving an 11ft 1in diameter Aeroproducts propeller. Although less powerful than the V-1710-63, this engine enabled better high altitude performance. This variant could fly at 370mph at 15,000ft compared to 360mph for the P-39L. A total of 240 P-39M-1-BEs was produced (ordered on 25 August, 1941) of which eight were

*At first, the British P-39s were named Caribou but the name Airacobra was soon adopted.*

modified for the ground attack role as P-39M-2-BEs.

**P-39N (Models 26C and 26F):** This was one of the two main production variants of the Airacobra; 2,095 P-39Ns were produced. The engine was a 1,200hp V-1710-85. The first 166 production aeroplanes had 10ft 4in Aeroproducts propellers and twelve wing fuel tanks with a total capacity of 120US gal. The following aircraft were equipped with an augmented diameter Aeroproducts propeller of 11ft 7in and had four of the wing fuel tanks removed in order to reduce gross weight. Internal fuel capacity was reduced to 87US gal. Aircraft of the last block (P-39N-5-BE) benefitted from several improvements including an SCR-695 radio, modified armour, bullet-proof glass behind the pilot, a new oxygen system. There were numerous conversions to ground support variant: this concerned thirty-five P-39N-0-BEs (becoming P-39N-3-BE), 128 P-39N-1-BEs (becoming P-39N-2-BE) and 84 P-39N-5-BEs (becoming P-39N-6-BE). An order for 205 additional P-39Ns was cancelled.

**P-39Q (Model 26E):** This was the main production variant with 4,905 aircraft built. The engine remained the same as for the P-39N but the armament was altered. The 0.30in machine-guns were replaced by 0.50in machine-guns in a gondola under each wing and fed with 300 rounds each. These gondolas were not mounted on the P-39Q-21-BE, Q-25-BE and Q-30-BE.

There were slight variations from one block to an other. The P-39Q-1-BE had a 1,150hp V-1710-35 engine; the P-39Q-5-BE had ten wing tanks instead of eight and a capacity of 110US gal; the P-39Q-10-BE had full wing fuel capacity restored, a new microphone, AN-M-14 grenades and modified armour protection; the P-39Q-15-BE had new electric circuits, new oxygen system and flame dampers

*The P-400 BW146 belonging to the 67th Fighter Squadron in Plaines des Gaiacs, New Hebrides, in 1942. Its pilot (seen standing) was Flg Off Zed Fountain and the aircraft was named* Whistlin' britches. *(Courtesy Ed Furler)*

*W McDonough of the 40th Fighter Squadron won two aerial victories above Wauon, New Guinea, while flying this P-39L. (USAF via W Greenhalgh)*

*A P-39Q-1-BE of the 347th FG taking off from Makin in the Gilbert Islands, on 13 December, 1943. The aircraft was named Little Rebel. (US Air Force)*

*This P-400, named* Our friend, *is curiously painted in olive drab instead of retaining its original British camouflage. (P M Bowers)*

*In 1941, this P-39D was equipped with an external supercharger but tests proved inconclusive. (Bell)*

on wing guns. The P-39Q-20-BE was identical but with improved armour. The P-39Q-21-BE and Q-25-BE were recognizable by their four-blade 11ft 7in Aeroproduct propellers. The P-39Q-30-BEs were identical to the P-39Q-25-BEs but had three-blade propellers.

A large number of aircraft were modified for ground attack and tactical reconnaissance missions: five P-39Q-1-BEs were transformed as P-39Q-2-BEs; 148 P-39Q-5-BEs were transformed as P-39Q-6-BEs and eight P-39Q-10-BEs were transformed as P-39Q-11-BEs. A few P-39Q-20-BEs were also converted to two-seat unarmed trainers (P-39Q-22-BE). Two aircraft (s/ns 42-19976 and 42-20807) were transferred to the US Navy to be used as drones under the designation XTDL-1, later XF2L-1K.

*An Airacobra arriving at Casablanca in April 1944. The main undercarriage and wings were in one piece and a hoist was required to assemble the aircraft. (ECPA)*

**XP-39E (Model 33):** As it appears from this list of variants, there was no significant improvement of the P-39 between 1941 and 1944. However, the Bell design team was very concerned by this problem and worked in three directions: performance, fire power and maintenance. On 13 and 14 February, 1941, Bell representatives went to Wright Field to present projects for two improved variants of the P-39: the XP-39E and the XP-63. On 1 March, the specification of the XP-39E was published by Bell: the aircraft would receive a supercharged V-1710-E9 engine, a 37mm cannon and six 0.50in machine-guns. A month later, on 11 April, the USAAF ordered two prototypes under a $513,750 contract (contract No.AC18373).

The prototype (s/n 41-19501) made its maiden flight on 21 February, 1942, at Niagara Falls Airport. It had received a V-1710-E4 as the E9 variant was not ready at that time. The new aircraft differed from the standard P-39 in many respects: its wings had a laminar flow aerofoil, squared tips and 22in increased span; the fuselage was 20in longer and the tail unit had been completely redesigned. The air intake of the carburettor had been moved aft on the back of the fuselage and the size of the airscoops at the wing roots had been increased. Last but not the least, the undercarriage had been considerably strengthened due to

*The P-39L-1-BE named* Wild Flower *in North Africa during the summer of 1943. The camouflage colours are sand and brown. There are yellow bands around the wings. (Courtesy P M Bowers)*

the increased weight of the aircraft. The empty weight was now 6,951lb against 5,474lb for the P-39D.

The XP-39E had a fairly short life as on 26 March, 1942, after 35 flights and 14hr 55min, it was totally destroyed during spinning tests. But these flights had proved that the weight increase had not been compensated for by the more powerful engine. On 4 April, the second prototype (s/n 41-19502) flew at Niagara Falls powered by a V-1710-E9 but, unfortunately, on 15 May, it crash-landed near Spencerport (New York) during its 27th flight. The nose undercarriage and propeller were seriously damaged and the aircraft was grounded for repairs. Tests had to be stopped as there was no other prototype.

On 27 May, a third machine was ordered under a $271,735 contract. This aircraft (s/n 42-71464) flew for the first time on 19 September, 1942; it logged 5hr 40min flying before being transferred to Allison for engine tests. Meanwhile, the second aircraft had been repaired but it was the victim of another accident on 8 February, 1943. The third prototype was then brought back to Niagara Falls in order to continue the flight-test programme. This programme was terminated by summer 1943 and both aircraft were taken on charge by the USAAF. The second aircraft arrived at Wright Field on 12 June, 1943, and the third aircraft arrived on 9 June. Test flights had not shown any significant improvement in performance. When compared to the P-39D, the XP-39E had a slower climb, had a lower service ceiling, a higher landing speed, a longer take-off distance and if its maximum speed was higher it accelerated slower. Thus the XP-39E programme came to an end. The contract orders for 4,000 production aircraft (to be designated P-76-BE) were cancelled and both aircraft were later used in the development of the XP-63.

*A P-39G-BE (42-8926) which was later redisignated P-39N-O-BE. It has a three-blade Aeroproducts propeller. (Bell)*

There were relatively few modifications to the P-39 during its career. Bell tested various equipment on the P-39 such as an external under-fuselage turbo-supercharger, trials of which proved unsatisfactory, and several types of high-capacity under-fuselage fuel tanks. A number of P-39s were converted to two-seat trainers by adding a second cockpit

*A P-39L-1-BE (42-4626) equipped for trials with a high capacity under fuselage fuel tank. (Bell)*

*The task of P-39Ds belonging to the 1st Composite Squadron, at Wideawake Field, on Ascension Island, was to protect Allied aircraft over the South Atlantic. (US Air Force)*

in front of the original one. On these odd-looking machines, the tail fillet was enlarged and an additional fin was added under the rear fuselage. This conversion concerned one P-39F-1-BE (TP-39F-BE) and twelve P-39Q-20-BEs (being designated successively P-39Q-22-BE, TP-39Q-BE and RP-39Q-BE), a few of which were delivered to the USSR. It is possible that some P-39s were converted as powered targets under the designation A-7.

## Service History

The first production P-39s were taken on charge by USAAC units at the beginning of 1941. The first unit to be equipped was the 31st Pursuit Group stationed at Selfridge Field, Michigan. In December, this unit was deployed at Baer Field during the Carolina manoeuvres. When the Japanese attacked Pearl Harbor, 179 British Airacobras were still in the United States awaiting delivery. They were immediately taken over by the USAAC (designated P-400, they retained their British serial numbers and two-tone camouflage) and sent to the South Pacific. Early in 1942, the three Pursuit Squadrons of 31st PG were transferred to 35th PG stationed at Hamilton Field and, on 18 January, the 39th, 40th and 41st PS embarked in San Francisco for Australia and three new squadrons were created within the 31st PG: 307th, 308th and 309th PS. On 25 January, the Group was back in Baer Field and soon moved to New Orleans where plans were made to send the Group to Europe. After intensive training to fly the Airacobras across the Atlantic, the pilots were eventually sent by sea and the Group re-equipped in Great Britain with Spitfires.

Meanwhile, the 8th PG had moved to Brisbane and the 35th PG to New Delhi. The 8th PG sent detachments to New Guinea and was thus the first P-39 unit to see combat. Coming from Baton Rouge, the 67th PS/58th PG arrived in New Caledonia on 15 March with forty-five P-400s and two P-39Ds but everything had to be improvised. Due to lack of spares, one aircraft out of five had to be cannibalized. In June 1942, the Pursuit Groups were re-designated Fighter Groups. On 4 May, the 35th FG was back in Sydney, Australia, but, on 22 July, it was sent to Port Moresby in New Guinea. There, the Airacobras had a hard job intercepting the incoming Japanese bombers. The lack of turbo-supercharger was a dreadful handicap but if the Airacobra was in a good position to fight, the 37mm cannon was a pretty lethal weapon. The lightly constructed Japanese aircraft disintegrated when hit by a 37mm projectile. The American pilots also discovered the great efficiency of the Airacobra in close support missions. Light bombs and improvised fire bombs were used with fairly good results. The 8th FG's first combat tour ended on 1 June, 1942. Its pilots were sent to Townsville while the aircraft were taken over by 35th FG. On 18 September, the 8th FG arrived in Milne Bay, at the eastern end of New Guinea. In February 1943, this group was back in Australia while 18th FG left Esperito Santo for the Pacific theatre. It arrived at Guadalcanal on 17 April. In May, the 8th FG began its third tour of operations. The Allied Forces were progressing steadily. On 15 August, the 35th FG was in Tsili-Tsili (40 miles east of Lae) and moved to Nadzab, closer to Lae, on 5 October. On 23 December, the 8th FG was in Finschhafen and 35th FG arrived in Gusap on 7 February, 1944. From that date, the Airacobras were progressively withdrawn from use in the Pacific area and replaced by Lockheed P-38s (8th and 18th FG) and Republic P-47s (35th FG).

In the Mediterranean, following operation 'Torch', two Fighter Groups flying Airacobras were allocated to MTO (81st and 350th FGs). From January 1943, these units were based in Morocco, in Medouina and Oujda respectively, along with P-39s of the 154th Observation Squadron. They flew close support missions under the protection of 12th Air Force Spitfires and P-40s. Until July 1942, the Airacobras main role was to protect convoys in the Mediterranean. Then, they were involved in the invasion of Sicily and Italy. On 28 November, the 92nd FS (81st FG) arrived in Grottaglie and the day after the 91st FS arrived in Monte-Corvino from where they flew missions along the Dalmatian coast. Some of these missions were among the longest undertaken in the Mediterranean theatre (up to 1,100 miles). During this period enemy encounters were rare and only a few combats occurred. In January 1944, the Airacobras were involved in the attack against Anzio and, in February, the 350th FG arrived in Corsica while the 81st FG departed for Karachi, then in India, and Kwanghan in China where it was re-equipped with Curtiss P-40s. The 350th FG was sent to Tarquinia where, in September, its P-39s were replaced by P-47s.

During the war period numerous P-39s remained in the United States flying with training and reserve units. A handful was used by the NACA Ames Research Center for various tests (these were s/n 41-8849, -18476, -28268, -28328, -20790).

USAAF units equipped with P-39s
8th FG (35th, 36th, 80th FS);
15th FG (45th, 46th, 47th FS);
16th FG (24th, 29th, 43rd FS);
18th FG (6th, 19th, 78th FS);
20th FG (55th, 77th, 79th FS);
21st FG (46th, 72nd, 531st FS);
31st FG (39th, 40th, 41st FS);
32nd FG (51st, 52nd, 53rd FS);
33rd FG (58th, 59th, 60th FS);
35th FG (20th, 21st, 34th FS then 39th, 40th, 41st FS)
36th FG (22nd, 23rd, 32nd FS);
48th FG (492nd, 493rd, 494th, 495th FS);
52nd FG (2nd, 4th, 5th FS);
53rd FC (13th, 14th, 15th, 438th FS);
54th FG (42nd, 56th, 57th FS);
56th FG (61st, 62nd, 63rd FS);
58th FG (67th, 68th, 69th FS);
59th FG (447th, 488th, 489th, 490th FS);
81st FG (91st, 92nd, 93rd FS);
318th FG (44th, 72nd, 73rd FS);
328th FG (326th, 327th, 329th, 444th FS);
332nd FG (100th, 301st, 302nd FS);
338th FG (305th, 306th, 312th, 441st FS);
339th FG (485th, 503rd, 504th, 505th FS);
342nd CG (33rd, 50th, 337th FS);
347th FG (67th, 68th, 70th, 339th FS);
350th FG (345th, 346th, 347th FS);
354th FG (353rd, 355th, 356th FS);
357th FG (362nd, 363rd, 364th FS);
367th FG (392nd, 393rd, 394th FS);
369th FG (398th, 399th, 400th FS);
404th FG (506th, 507th, 508th FS);
405th FG (509th, 510th, 511th FS);
478th FG (544th, 545th, 546th FS);
10th, 26th, 66th, 68th, 69th, 70th, 71st, 72nd, 74th, 75th, 76th, 77th, 363rd and 432nd PRG.

## Foreign operators:

**Australia:** due to the Japanese threat a batch of twenty-two P-39D/Fs (serial numbers A53-1/22) was delivered to the Royal Australian Air Force on 27 July, 1942. A second batch of five aircraft was taken on charge in May 1943 and a third of three machines arrived in June 1943. They were used by 23rd, 24th, 82nd and 83rd Squadrons for a short time. All the aircraft were returned to the USAAF by autumn 1943.

**France:** in January 1943, following the Anfa conference, the Allied headquarters decided to re-equip all the Armée de l'Air squadrons stationed in North Africa (under Plan VII). On 13 May, 1943, the first Airacobras were delivered to GC III/6 Roussillon in Ain Sefra where they replaced the ageing Dewoitine D.520s. In June 1943, this group moved to Berkane, then Tafaraoui where GC I/5 Champagne was stationed with its new Airacobras. Both groups were then used on Coastal Command missions. Meanwhile, in La Réghaïa, the GC I/4 Navarre re-equipped with P-39s and began operations on 7 September. Most of the P-39Ns were second-hand aircraft and during the lengthy Coastal Command missions several accidents occurred due to engine failure. At one time all flights had to be stopped but soon brand new P-39Qs were delivered. In May 1944, P-39s were delivered to the fighter school in Meknès. In August, the GC II/6 Travail was commissioned, GC I/4 re-equipped with P-47s and the newly created GC I/9 Limousin took on charge its first P-39Qs. In September, a new unit was commissioned on P-39s, the GC II/9 Auvergne. In December, the GC II/9 received its first P-39Qs and GC

*Ladd Field, Alaska, on 8 March, 1944. Dozens of Soviet Airacobras are awaiting delivery.*

III/6 gave up its Airacobras for Thunderbolts.

The French P-39s operated mainly in the Alps area and northern Italy. At the end of the war, one of the groups received P-63s (GC II/6), others were decommissioned for budgetary reasons (GC I/9 and II/9).

The very last French Airacobras were used by the fighter school (CIC) in Meknès and the flight test centre (CEV) at Brétigny at the beginning of the fifties.

In all, the Armée de l'Air took on charge 165 P-39s, most of them being P-39Ns and P-39Qs.

**Great Britain:** *see* under Caribou and Airacobra I.

**Italy:** on 24 May, 1944, after the Italian capitulation, the Allied Supreme Headquarters decided to re-equip the co-belligerant air force with new aircraft. These deliveries included, among others, 149 Airacobras (75 P-39Qs and 74 P-39Ns) coming from 15th Air Force depots. The aircraft equipped 2nd, 9th, 10th, 12th Groups (Gruppi) and the fighter school (Scuola Addestramento Bombardamento e Caccia). They saw limited action in the Mediterranean and the Balkans and began to be replaced by P-38s in 1946. The last examples were withdrawn from use in 1951.

**Poland:** two aircraft were used in Poland. One P-39Q was taken on charge in November 1944 by the 2nd Squadron of the 2nd Air Regiment of the Polish Air Force. Its pilot was the Polish Air Force Commander-in-Chief Fiodor Polenine. This aircraft was withdrawn from use in 1948 and given to a technical school. The other aircraft, of Russian origin, was also used for ground instruction in Warsaw.

**Portugal:** in December 1942, a group of eighteen American P-39Ds flying to North Africa landed by mistake at Portela de Sacavem, in Portugal. These aircraft were interned and kept by the Portuguese after negotiations with United States authorities. From June 1943, they were used by Esquadrilha O.K. stationed in Ota and received serial numbers 301 to 318. Due to a shortage of spares the P-39s were grounded and scrapped in 1946.

**USSR:** among all Airacobra operators, the Soviet Air Force (V-VS) was by far the largest. More than a half of the entire P-39 output was sent to the USSR. Figures vary with sources from 4,700 up to 5,700 aircraft delivered but the most common figure is 4,924 Airacobras as follows: 108 P-39Ds, 40 P-39Ks, 137 P-39Ls, 157 P-39Ms, 1,113 P-39Ns, 3,291 P-39Qs and an unknown number of Airacobra Is (P-400) and some two-seaters. Of this total, 4,719 aircraft eventually reached the USSR, the others were lost during delivery. The first batches of aircraft were delivered in 1942 via the Arctic route. The following batches were delivered by sea and through Iran but most of the aircraft (2,618 aircraft) were ferried over the famous Alaska–Siberia route (ALSIB) by the pilots of the 7th Ferrying Group. Numerous Soviet fighter regiments flew the P-39 (32nd, 38th, 55th, 145th, 191st, 196th, 255th, 298th, 508th IAPs) as well as several Guards' Aviation regiments. The Soviets were particularly pleased with the American fighter and some of the country's highest aces were Airacobra pilots (A I Pokryshkin, G A Rechkalov, N D Gulayev).

**Racers** after the war was over, several Airacobras entered races. Skyline Unlimited used two P-39Qs with the unofficial support of Bell: one, painted red with black trim (registered NX92847 and nick-

*The P-39F-1-BE had twelve exhaust stacks and an Aeroproducts three-blade propeller. Here, an aircraft from the AAF Training Command central instructors school at Matagorda Penninsula, a sub-post of Foster Field. (US Air Force)*

*One of the two P-39Qs used by the US Navy and designated XTDL-1. This one is the P-39Q-5-BE s/n 42-19976, seen at the Bell factory on 6 February, 1946. (Courtesy E Furler)*

*The P-39N-1-BE s/n 42-9410, belonging to Groupe de Chasse II/6 of the French Air Force. Just visible above the stork insignia is the name* Lt de Villars. *(ECPA)*

*Bell converted a number of Airacobras into two-seat transition trainers. A second cockpit was added in front of the original one and the fin was modified. (Bell)*

named *Cobra I*), was piloted by Jack Woolams, and the other, painted yellow and black (registered NX92848 and nicknamed *Cobra II*), had Alvin 'Tex' Johnston as pilot. In August 1946, during the Cleveland Air Races, Woolams was killed in an accident during qualification but Johnston was the winner of the Thompson Trophy Race. The same summer, Clyde Adams was killed in Saratoga (Wyoming) while piloting P-39 NX61446. The following year, Jay Deming aboard *Cobra II* took third place in the Thompson Trophy Race and, in 1949, a P-39 registered N13381 took ninth place in the Sohio Trophy Race. Another aircraft worth mentioning is the heavily modified P-39Q of Mike Caroll which was destroyed during its first flight, on 10 August, 1968.

Today, some thirty P-39s are still in existence in various condition: four P-39Ds, one P-39F, one P-39K, ten P-39Ns, thirteen P-39Qs and two P-400s. A large number of them were recovered in the 1980s in Papua New Guinea. Very few of them are airworthy but there are several restoration projects underway. Recently, more airframes were recovered such as P-39G s/n 42-4962 in Yakutia, USSR, and P-39Q s/n 44-2485 from a Lake, 240 miles from Watson Lake, in Canada.

*The Bell XP-39E was an attempt to improve the performance of the Airacobra. (Bell)*

*The second production P-39Q-5-BE leaving the factory shows the gun gondolas under the wings. It has a high-capacity under fuselage fuel tank. (Bell)*

*The* Cobra II, *flown by Alvin 'Tex' Johnston, like the* Cobra I, *was used in races with the unofficial backing of Bell. (P M Bowers)*

## XP-39

Span 35ft 10in (10.92m); length 28ft 8in (8.73m); height 11ft (3.35m); wing area 200sq ft (18.58sq m).

Empty weight 3,995lb (1,810kg); loaded weight 5,550lb (2,514kg).

Maximum speed 390mph (627km/h); rate of climb 3,800ft/min (1,058m/min); service ceiling 32,000ft (9,753m).

## XP-39B

Span 34ft (10.36m); length 29ft 9in (9.07m); height 11ft 10in (3.60m); wing area 213sq ft (19.79sq m).

Empty weight 4,530lb (2,052kg); loaded weight 6,450lb (2,922kg).

Maximum speed 375mph (603km/h); cruising speed 310mph (498km/h); rate of climb 2,800ft/min (853m/min); service ceiling 36,000ft (10,970m); range 600miles (965km).

## P-39D

Span 34ft (10.36m); length 30ft 2in (9.21m); height 11ft 10in (3.60m), wing area 213sq ft (19.8sq m).

Empty weight 6,300lb (2,853kg); loaded weight 7,650lb (3,465kg); maximum weight 8,850lb (4,010kg).

Maximum speed 335mph (539km/h) at 5,000ft (1,525m), 360mph (579km/h) at 15,000ft (4,575m), 324mph (521km/h) at 25,000ft (7,625m); rate of climb 2,550ft/min (12.9m/sec) at 5,000ft (1,525m); time to 10,000ft (3,050m) 3.9min, to 20,000ft (6,100m) 9.1min, to 25,000ft (7,625m) 14min; service ceiling 31,900ft (9,726m); range at maximum cruising power 350miles (563km); maximum range with drop tank 1,100miles (1,770km).

## P-39N

Span, length and wing area as P-39D; height 12ft 5in (3.75m).

Empty weight 6,400lb (2,900kg); loaded weight 7,600lb (3,443kg); maximum take-off weight 8,800lb (3,986kg).

Maximum speed 330mph (531km/h) at 5,000ft (1,525m), 376mph (605km/h) at 15,000ft (4,575m), 368mph (592km/h) at 25,000ft (7,625m); rate of climb 2,600ft/min (13.2m/sec) at 5,000ft (1,525m); time to 5,000ft (1,525m) 2min, to 15,000ft (4,575m) 6.1min, to 25,000ft (7,625m) 11.9min; service ceiling 38,270ft (11,665m); range at maximum cruising power 300miles (483km); maximum range with drop tank 975miles (1,570km).

## P-39Q

Dimensions as P-39N.

Empty weight 5,680lb (2,573kg); loaded weight 7,651lb (3,466kg).

Maximum speed 382mph (616km/h) at 11,000ft (3,600m), time to 14,765ft (4,500m) 4.5min; service ceiling 34,790ft (10,605m); normal range 650miles (1,045km).

## XP-39E

Span 35ft 10in (10.92m); length 31ft 11.3in (9.73m); height 9ft 9.5in (2.98m); wing area 235.6sq ft (21.89sq m).

Empty weight 7,631lb (3,457kg); loaded weight 8,918lb (4,040kg).

Maximum speed 386mph (621km/h); cruising speed 205mph (330km/h); rate of climb 2,800ft/min (853m/min); service ceiling 35,200ft (10,730m); range 500 miles 805km).

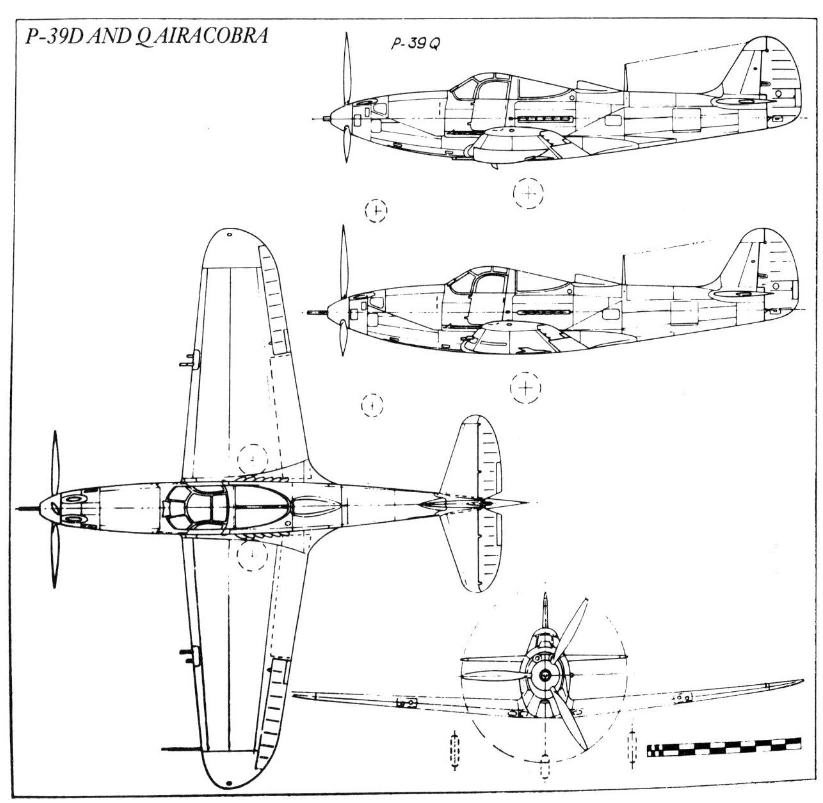


*P-39D AND Q AIRACOBRA*

# Model 5 XFL-1 Airabonita

On 1 January, 1938, the US Navy issued a specification for a light high-performance shipborne fighter to replace its obsolete fleet of biplane fighters. Several manufacturers submitted projects among which were Vought-Sikorsky with the Model V-166B, Grumman with the twin-engined Model G-34 and Bell with the Model 5. A contract (No.63629) for one prototype of the Bell design was placed on 8 November, 1938, under the designation XFL-1 Airabonita. This aircraft was in fact a navalized variant of the Air Corps' P-39 then under development but it differed from the latter in many respects. The engine retained was an 1,150hp Allison XV-1710-6 liquid-cooled engine driving a 10ft 4½in diameter Curtiss three-blade propeller. It was installed aft of the pilot and coolant radiators were located under the wing. This was the first time a naval fighter was powered by such an engine. The complete structure of the aircraft was reinforced for carrier-operation. Wingspan, chord and dihedral were greater than those of the P-39 but the fuselage was shorter. To reduce the stalling speed, the flaps were larger and made in three sections (one centre section under the fuselage and two underwing sections). The vertical tail surfaces were different too in order to maintain longitudinal stability at high angles of incidence. Contrary to its Army counterpart, the XFL-1 had a conventional undercarriage with a tailwheel, and an arrester hook was added. The main undercarriage legs were moved forward and attached to the front wing spar. The cockpit was raised to increase visibility but the car-like doors were retained. A small window was placed under the fuselage just ahead of the wing root to make landings onboard carriers easier.

*The XFL-1 differed from the XP-39 primarily in having a tailwheel undercarriage. (Bell)*

Provision was made for two 0.3in Browning synchronized machine-guns in the fuselage nose and a Browning 0.5in machine-gun or a 37mm cannon firing through the propeller hub, but this armament was never installed.

The prototype (BuNo 1588) made its first flight on 13 May, 1940, but

*The XFL-1 Airabonita (BuNo 1588) photographed on 16 July, 1940, during initial trials. (Bell)*

subsequent tests were somewhat prolonged because the Allison engine caused trouble, and problems were encountered with the balance of the aircraft (Bell engineers proposed introducing ballast in the nose but the Navy refused to agree). This delayed the delivery of the XFL-1 to the US Navy. Official evaluation began in July 1940 but the aeroplane failed to be certificated for carrier operations because of undercarriage trouble.

*XFL-1 with underwing radiators and arrester hook. (Bell)*

*The XFL-1 on low-speed approach, with the three-segment flaps lowered. (Bell)*

*The XFL-1 prototype on 16 July, 1940. It has a modified dorsal airscoop. (Bell)*

In December 1940, the prototype was returned to Bell for modifications and, in February 1941, the US Navy decided not to have the Airabonita put into production. The project was abandoned and the Navy chose the Vought contender which evolved eventually as the F4U Corsair. In February 1942, the unsuccessful XFL-1 was transferred to the Aircraft Armament Unit for anti-aircraft tests and subsequently destroyed. The remnants of this aircraft were still in the dump of Patuxent River Naval Air Test Center in the mid-1960s.

Span 35ft (10.67m); length 29ft 9⅛in (9.07m); height 12ft 9⅔in (3.90m); wing area 232sq ft (21,55sq m).

Empty weight 5,161lb (2,338kg); loaded weight 6,651lb (3,013kg); maximum weight 7,212lb (3,267kg).

Maximum speed 307mph (494km/h) at sea level; 336mph (540km/h) at 10,000ft (3,050m); 322mph (518km/h) at 20,000ft (6,100m); economic cruising speed 160mph (277km/h); landing speed 72mph (116km/h); initial rate of climb 2,630ft/min (800m/min); climb to 10,000ft (3,050m) in 3.75min; climb to 20,000ft (6,100m) in 9.2min; normal range 965miles (1,550km); maximum range 1,072miles (1,725km); endurance (60 per cent power) 4.9hr, (90 per cent power) 2hr, (full power) 1.2hr; service ceiling 30,900ft (9,420m).

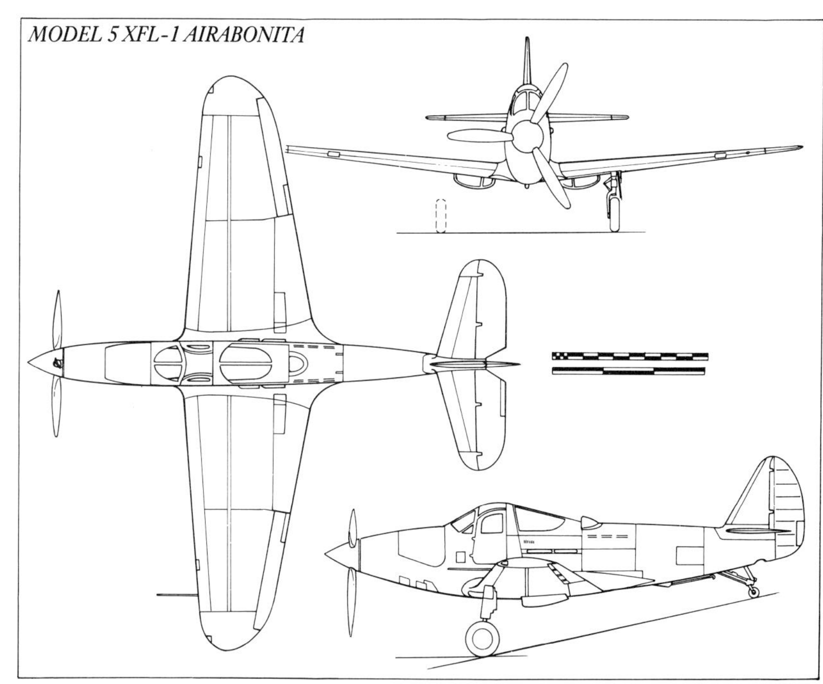

# Models 33 and 41 P-63 Kingcobra

Bell QF-63C (ex- RP-63C-BE) with buzz-number PL-074. This aircraft was probably painted bright red overall. No anti-glare panel was required due to the absence of a pilot.

The second variant of Model 33 which was presented at the Wright Field meeting (see Bell P-39E) was somewhat different although retaining the same configuration. This was a bigger and heavier aeroplane, weighing 8,800lb at full load. Like the XP-39E it had a low-drag laminar flow wing but was powered by a 1,325hp Allison V-1710-47 engine equipped with a new Allison-designed auxiliary hydraulically-driven supercharger in order to increase ceiling and high altitude performance.

Two prototypes were ordered by the US Army Air Force on 27 June, 1941 (contract No.AC-18966); these were designated XP-63. At Bell's design office, it was Dan J Fabricy who was put in charge of the project, assisted by Jack Strickler. Two sections of the wing of the new aeroplane were tested in the large NACA wind tunnel at Langley Field under the direction of Dr Eastman Jacobs and spinning tests were conducted with scale models in a vertical wind tunnel. The latter led to a modification of the tail unit. The effects of the propeller on the airflow characteristics were checked in the wind tunnel at Caltech. Even the cooling system had to be redesigned because of the more powerful engine of the XP-63.

The first prototype (s/n 42-45511) was built by a team led by Don Rowe and Bob Lapp. The maiden flight, with Bob Stanley (Bell's chief test pilot) at the controls, took place at Buffalo on Monday 7 December, 1942, the day after the surprise Japanese attack on Pearl Harbor. Stanley appreciated the aircraft's behaviour during this maiden flight and did not hesitate to compare the XP-63 with the Supermarine Spitfire! During the following test flights the XP-63 was flown by USAAF officers before being ferried to Muroc, California, in order to benefit from better weather conditions. Unfortunately the prototype was damaged beyond repair in an accident on 28 January, 1943. A joint broke in the main undercarriage which only went one-third of the way down. The aircraft was badly damaged during an attempted

*The second prototype, XP-63, first flown on 5 February, 1943, had a short career, it crashed in May. (Bell)*

*The sole P-63D-BE (s/n 43-11718) had a tear drop canopy for better visibility, and an enlarged wing. (Bell)*

crash landing at dawn. Jack Woolams who was at the controls was luckily unhurt. The prototype had then flown only 25hr 20min.

The second prototype (s/n 41-9512) flew at Niagara Falls Airport on 5 February, 1943, piloted by an Army test pilot, but on 25 May, 1943, the Allison engine lost a valve in flight and the aircraft was eventually lost. The following month, the US Air Force ordered a third machine, powered by a 1,325hp V-1710-93 engine (XP-63A, s/n 42-78015), which flew on 26 April, 1943. It was in fact the static test airframe which had been brought to flying status. This prototype incorporated several improvements such as a redesigned dorsal airscoop, new exhaust pipes and underwing hard points. Armament consisted of a single 37mm cannon firing through the propeller hub and two 0.50in machine-guns in the forward fuselage. A 500lb bomb or a 75US gal fuel tank could be carried under the fuselage. Some 88lb of armour protected the most critical parts of the aircraft. Thus, this aeroplane achieved most of the flight test programme which was concluded on 26 April, 1943.

*This view of the first production P-63E-1-BE (s/n 43-11720) shows the ventral fin to good advantage. (Bell, courtesy P M Bowers)*

## Production History

The first production contract was signed on 29 September, 1942, and the first production P-63A was delivered to the USAAF in October 1943. By summer 1944, the Bell P-63 was officially named Kingcobra by the War Department.

The P-63A was produced in seven blocks and aircraft incorporated slight changes in armament, armour and fuel capacity from one block to another as follows:

– The P-63A-1-BE was identical to XP-63E. It had 87.7lb of armour and an internal fuel capacity of 100US gal.

– The P-63A-5-BE had 178.8lb of armour and a fuselage strong point able to carry a 75US gal or 175US gal flush-fitting ferry fuel tank or one 500lb bomb.

*The third XP-63A flew on 26 April, 1943. Essentially a production prototype, it was powered by an Allison V-1710-93. There is a metal fairing over the rear portion of the cockpit.*

*The P-63F-1-BE is immediately recognisable by its redesigned fin. Here the first aircraft (s/n 43-11719) is seen in September 1946. (Courtesy P M Bowers)*

*The RP-63G Pinball target aeroplanes were painted bright orange overall with black circles around the lights that illuminated to register hits. Seen here is RP-63G-1-BE s/n 43-11724. (Bell)*

– The P-63A-6-BE had underwing racks for 75US gal fuel tanks or 500lb bombs, these improvements being first tested on aircraft s/n 42-68931.
– The P-63A-7-BE could carry 64US gal fuel tanks underwing.
– The P-63A-8-BE had 188.8lb of armour and a new type of propeller (Aeroproducts A6425–D3). This new propeller was first tested on aircraft s/n 42-69425.
– The P-63A-9-BE had 198.9lb of armour. The 37mm M-4 cannon was replaced by an M-10 of the same calibre with 58 rounds.
– The P-63A-10-BE had 236.3lb of armour and three rocket launchers under each wing.

Bell delivered 1,725 P-63As between October 1943 and December 1944, and then switched the production to the P-63C variant, 1,227 of which were eventually delivered.

The P-63C differed from the P-63A by its 1,325hp Allison V-1710–117 engine with increased war emergency power rating. Externally, the P-63C could be readily distinguished from the previous variant by its long anti-roll fin under the rear fuselage. On this variant, the internal fuel capacity was increased to 107US gal and the weight of the armour reached 201lb. Armament remained unchanged. The P-63C was to be produced in two blocks, P-63C-1-BE and P-63C-5-BE, aircraft from the later batch differing by their underwing racks.

The XP-63B was never built. It was to have been an XP-63A re-engined with a 1,400hp Packard-Merlin V-1650-5.

The next variant was the P-63D of which only one example was to be built. At the beginning of 1945, a P-63C was modified with a 1,425hp V-1710-109 engine, a bubble canopy and an enlarged wing (wingspan increased by 10in). In spite of the weight increase the performance of the P-63D were better than that of the P-63A. The P-63D flew at a maximum speed of 437mph at 30,000ft compared with the 408mph of the P-63A at the same altitude. Nevertheless, this good performance was roughly identical to that of the North American P-51D then in full mass production. This sole P-63D was destroyed during diving tests with Bob Borchert at the controls. The D variant was followed by the P-63E (Bell Model 41) which was identical to the P-63D in most aspects except for the canopy which remained classical with car-like doors. A total of thirteen aircraft was built and contracts for 2,930 more were cancelled after VJ-Day. However, two airframes from these contracts were completed under the P-63F designation. The P-63F had a 1,425hp V-1710–135 engine and an enlarged fin and rudder to increase longitudinal stability. One P-63F (s/n 43-11719) survived the war and was later sold on the civil market with registration N447AG.

*Bell tested several butterfly tail configurations on the P-63. (P M Bowers collection)*

*About two dozen P-63Es were modified with a rear cockpit for training. This one, registered N41964 (previously NX41964) is seen in April 1952. Note nose probe. (Sommerich, courtesy of P M Bowers)*

*This P-63C-5-BE (s/n 44-4126) was modified with a small bubble canopy and clipped wings for an attempt on the world's speed record at the 1972 Reno Nationals. Unfortunately, it crashed on a test flight and its pilot, Larry Havens, baled out safely. (H Allen Herr, courtesy of J A Cerdà)*

During 1943, the P-63 was involved in a new programme the purpose of which was the training of the medium and heavy bombers' gunners. The idea was to use aircraft with specially reinforced surface skin as gunnery targets against which frangible bullets (made of lead and plastic) could be fired. In August 1944, under contract No.AC29318, Bell converted five P-63As. All armament and internal armour was removed. All skinning was replaced by thicker metal sheet, the upper fuselage airscoop was replaced by a clam-shell intake and the canopy was armoured (38mm windshield and 25mm sidewindows). Not less than 110 microphones were buried under the skin. A light hidden in the propeller hub flashed each time a bullet hit the aircraft and each hit was recorded on an automatic counter located on the instrument panel.

These aircraft, designated RP-63A-11-BE, were powered by the V-1710–93 engine with water injection and had their internal fuel capacity increased to 126US gal. The first of them flew for the first time on 1 September, 1944, with Robert M Stanley at the controls and they became quickly known as the Pinballs.

The first flight tests were not completely successful because the modifications had altered the position of the centre of gravity by a considerable extent. This fault was overcome by repositioning some equipment inside the airframe. The hub light was hardly visible and additional lights were installed around the rear fuselage. A first batch of ninety-five aircraft was ordered in due course. These were designated RP-63A-12-BE. A second production batch concerned two hundred RP-63C-2-BEs which were powered by the V-1710–117 and had 1,487.7lb of armour. A third and last batch totalled thirty-two RP-63G-1-BEs with the V-1710–135 and 2,164.9lb of armour. Additional contracts for 420 more RP-63Gs were cancelled. In 1948,

*A French Kingcobra of Groupe de Chasse I/5 'Vendée', which fought in Indochina. It has the Joan of Arc insignia on the door.*

these target-aircraft had their designation changed to QF-63A, QF-63C and QF-63G respectively. They were used by the Yuma Flexible Gunnery School and by the 79th Fighter Training Wing.

In addition to these standard variants, several P-63s were also converted for experimental purposes:

– A single P-63E-1-BE was re-engined with a 1,425hp V-1710–127 for comparative trials. This aircraft was known as the XP-63H-BE.

– At least two Kingcobras received a V-tail unit. One of these was an RP-63G-1-BE (s/n 45-57300) but the identity of the other one remains unknown. Both aircraft were designated XP-63N.

– A P-63A-6-BE (s/n 42-68931) was mounted with a ski-undercarriage system designed by Luscombe Engineering Company. The tests began in July 1943 at Lake Ouimet, Montreal. They proved that skis were impractical on that kind of fighter and trials were discontinued in February 1945.

– About two dozen P-63s were modified with a second cockpit in the rear fuselage for use as instrument and equipment test beds. These were known as TP-63As and TP-63Cs.

*Another V-tail configuration was tested on XP-63N (s/n 45-57300) which was an ex-RP-63G as the rear cockpit metal fairing shows. Note wing probe and buzz-number PL-300.*

## Service History

The Kingcobra saw limited service with the USAAF. Only a handful of Advanced Training Units flew it. The aircraft were rapidly withdrawn from use and put into storage in Kingman, Arizona, and Ontario, California, before being scrapped. A few found their way to NACA research centres: P-63A s/n 42-68864 was modified with an under fuselage glycol cooler scoop and a large carburettor intake and tested at NACA Lewis Research Center; P-63A s/n 42-68868 was used for exhaust flame supression research; P-63As s/n 42-68892 and 42-68941 were used by Ames Research Center and three other P-63As (42-68861, -68881 and -68889) were flown at Langley Research Center.

Most of the production was in fact delivered abroad, mainly to the Soviet Union and France. Of the 3,303 P-63s built, 2,397 were delivered to the Soviet Union under Lend-Lease, via the ALSIB route (Alaska–Siberia), by the 3rd and 7th Ferrying Groups. All these were delivered between 1942 and 1945

*Bell QF-63C-2-BE s/n 43-10959 with code FM36 in May 1946. (Courtesy P M Bowers)*

*The French P-63C-5-BE s/n 43-11691 was used by the CEV (Flight Test Centre) at Brétigny. It is seen here equipped to test a jettisonable fuel tank converted as a photographic-reconnaissance pod. (CEV)*

and twenty-one were lost during ferrying operations. Unfortunately, almost nothing is known of the operational career of the Kingcobra with the V-VS (Russian Air Force).

A total of 300 P-63Cs was allocated to France under the MAP. In fact, it appears that far less than 300 aircraft were in fact taken on charge by the Armée de l'Air. The grand total of aircraft delivered seems not to have exceeded 150–200 machines.

At the end of the Second World War, the Armée de l'Air began to receive P-63Cs, the first five being taken on charge on 26 July, 1945. In due course, the GC 1/5 Vendée fighter group was the first French

*P-63A-9-BE s/n 42-69432. Deliveries of the P-63A began in October 1943. (Bell)*

*The prototype of the P-63 photographed on 7 December, 1942. The new tail unit and the four-blade propeller were easy recognition features. (Bell)*

*The RP-63C-2-BE (s/n 43-10972) wearing a highly colourful paint scheme. (Courtesy P M Bowers)*

unit to fly the type (this unit had been created in North Africa on 1 August, 1944). It was followed by GC 2/9 Auvergne based in Salon-de-Provence, in southern France. Both units were disbanded on 23 March, 1946, for budgetary reasons. When the war started in Indochina, most of the French fighter units stationed in France and North Africa were flying Republic P-47Ds but combat use of this type in Southeast Asia was then forbidden by the United States. Thus, several of the fighter units sent to the Indochina threatre of operations had to be re-equipped with P-63Cs. Additional batches of Kingcobras were then directly delivered in Saïgon by the French navy carrier *Dixmude* (ex-BAVG-3 *Biter*).

The 5th Escadre de Chasse (fighter wing) flew P-63Cs from July 1949 until the summer of 1950. This wing was composed of GC 1/5 Vendée (which had been re-commissioned) stationed in Lang-Son and GC 2/5 Ile de France in Hanoï. The two groups of the 6th Escadre de Chasse arrived in Asia at a later date. The GC 2/6 Normandie-Niémen, based in Saïgon-Tan Son Nhut, flew P-63Cs from October 1949 until November 1950 when it began to re-equip with Grumman F6F-5 Hellcats, and GC 3/6 Roussillon in Hanoï-Gia Lam (later in Bach Maï) flew Kingcobras from August 1950 until March 1951 when it began to convert to Grumman F8F Bearcats. The aircraft of GC 2/6 were transferred to GC1/9 Limousin (stationed in Haïphong-

*P-63A-9-BE FZ440 conducted various tests at the Royal Aircraft Establishment. It is seen at Farnborough, on 18 April, 1945. (Courtesy RAE)*

*The P-63A-1-BE s/n 42-68889 was owned by NACA Langley Research Center from 4 February, 1944, until 27 August, 1945. It is seen here while testing an enlarged fin and rudder. (Courtesy of P M Bowers)*

Cat Bi) which flew them until February 1951 when the fighter group received its first Bearcats.

It has to be mentioned that the French flight-test centre in Brétigny (CEV) also flew some P-63Cs as liaison aircraft and for various tests.

Two Kingcobras were used by the British during the Second World War and immediately thereafter. Great Britain received two P-63s through Lend-Lease (FR408, ex-42-68937, and FZ440, ex-42-69423) which were diverted to the Royal Aircraft Establishment at Farnborough to conduct research on low-drag laminar flow wings. FR408 flew for the first time on 18 May, 1944. It was later involved in a landing accident and had to be replaced by FZ440 (which had received a one-piece bubble canopy). These experiments demonstrated that low-drag laminar flow wings lost their efficiency if their contour was destroyed by crews walking on them, by refuelling hoses and even insects. FZ440 was withdrawn from use at the end of 1948.

Following the Rio Pact, in 1947, the Honduras Air Force (Aviacion Militar Hondureña) took delivery of five Bell P-63E-1-BEs (43-11727/11731; coded 400/404) together with seven Lockheed P-38L-5-LOs. These were delivered by air from Miami between October 1948 and July 1949. They were stationed at Tegucigalpa until 1957 when they were replaced by Chance-Vought F4U-4/5s. Four of them flew back to the States, the fifth remained in Honduras where it is still preserved as a gate guardian at Tegucigalpa FAH base.

Today, fourteen Kingcobras have survived (five P-63As, one P-63C, four P-63Es, one P-63F, one RP-63A, one RP-63C and one RP-63G) five of which are maintained in flying condition. A sixth flying example (P-63C s/n 44-4393/N62822) which had been acquired by the Fighter Collection at Duxford, England, was destroyed on 4 June, 1990, in France, killing John Larcombe.

*P-63F-1-BE s/n 43-11719 (registered N447AG) was owned by A T George of Atlanta, Georgia, circa 1969. It is now owned by the Confederate Air Force and registered N6763. (R J Francillon)*

*The ill-fated Fighter Collection owned P-63 the day before it crashed. The P-63C-5-BE s/n 44-4393, registered N62822 is seen here taking off from La Ferté Alais on 3 June, 1990, piloted by the late John Larcombe. (A Pelletier)*

## P-63A

Span 38ft 4in (11.69m); length 32ft 8⅜in (9.96m); height 12ft 6⅞in (3.83m); wing area 248sq ft (23.04sq m).

Empty weight 6,375lb (2,894kg); normal loaded weight 8,800lb (3,995kg); maximum gross weight 10,500lb (4,767kg).

Maximum speed 361mph (581km/h) at 5,000ft (1,525m), 392mph (631km/h) at 15,000ft (4,575m), 410mph (660km/h) at 25,000ft (7,625m); maximum cruising speed 378mph (608km/h); climb to 25,000ft (7,625m) 7.3min; service ceiling 43,000ft (13,115m); normal range 390–450 miles (628–724km); ferry range 2,575 miles (4,143km).

## P-63C

Span 38ft 4in (11.69m); length 32ft 8⅜in (9.96m); height 12ft 6⅞in (3.83m); wing area 248sq ft (23.04sq m).

Empty weight 6,795lb (3,085kg); normal loaded weight 8,800lb (3,995kg); maximum gross weight 10,715lb (4,854kg).

Maximum speed 410mph (660km/h) at 25,000ft (7,625m); maximum cruising speed 355mph (572km/h); climb to 25,000ft (7,625m) 8.5min; service ceiling 38,600ft (11,770m); normal range 320miles (514km); ferry range 2,100miles (3,380km).

## P-63D

Span 39ft 2in (11.93m); length 32ft 8⅜in (9.96m); height 11ft 1⅞in (3.40m); wing area 255sq ft (23.69sq m).

Empty weight 7,084lb (3,209kg); normal loaded weight 8,750lb (3,964kg); maximum gross weight 11,200lb (5,080kg).

Maximum speed 437mph (703km/h) at 30,000ft (9,140m); cruising speed 188mph (302km/h); climb to 28,000ft (8,534m) 11.2min; service ceiling 39,000ft (11,890m); range 700–950miles (1,126–1,530km); ferry range 2,000miles (3,220km).

## P-63E

Span 39ft 2in (11.93m); length 32ft 8⅜in (9.96m); height 12ft 8¾in (3.88m); wing area 255sq ft (23.69sq m).

Empty weight 7,310lb (3,311kg); normal loaded weight 9,413lb (4,264kg); maximum gross weight 11,200lb (5,080kg).

Maximum speed 410mph (660km/h) at 28,000ft (8,534m); cruising speed 188mph (302km/h); climb to 28,000ft (8,534m) 7.5min; range 727miles (1,170km); ferry range 2,150miles (3,460km).

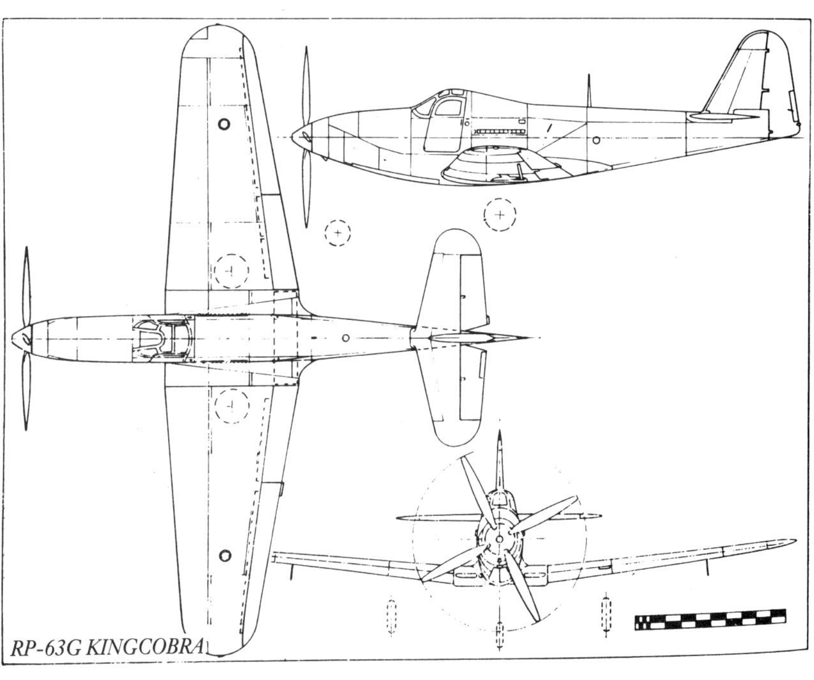

*RP-63G KINGCOBRA*

# Model 27
# P-59 Airacomet

It was thanks to British gas-turbine research that jet powered aircraft could be developed in the United States. Development of a jet fighter was initiated by the US Army Air Force during 1941 very soon after Maj-Gen H Arnold had seen Wing Cdr Frank Whittle's engine under test and the Gloster E.28/39 experimental aircraft. Rights for General Electric to develop further and produce the British engine were acquired in due course and, on 4 September, 1941, the USAAF took the decision to build a first batch of fifteen engines and to design an airframe to flight-test them. Because it was less overloaded by aircraft production, close to General Electric's facilities and, last but not the least, because of its imaginative engineering staff, Bell Aircraft was chosen for this exciting challenge. Indeed it was a challenge because the contract, signed on 30 September, 1941, required delivery of the first prototype not more than eight months after go-ahead!

Naturally the American jet fighter programme required a very high degree of secrecy. Numerous severe measures were taken concerning the people involved in the project, the building and, of course, the aircraft itself. Even its designation was carefully chosen. In fact, the new aircraft was designated XP-59A after a totally different design (XP-59) which was then on Bell's drawing boards (*see* Appendix I) and no serial numbers were allocated until after the prototypes had flown.

The Bell team worked fairly quickly and soon the outline of the Bell Model 27, as it was known inside the company, took shape. The general configuration of the XP-59 was quite conventional. It retained a straight cantilever mid-wing of relatively low aspect ratio and the two 1,300lb st General Electric I-A turbojets were buried in nacelles mounted in parallel under the wing roots. The tail unit was conventional and a wide-track electrically-operated nosewheel undercarriage was used. The airframe was of all-metal monocoque construction with flush-riveted light-alloy skin. All control surfaces were fabric-covered and manually operated (only the flaps were electrically actuated). The cockpit was pressurized, heated and de-iced by air ducted from the engines. At the time, the specified armament comprised two 37mm M4 cannon in the nose with 44 rounds per gun and internal fuel capacity was only 290US gal.

Construction of the first prototype (c/n 27-1, s/n 42-108784) began three months after the contract had been signed, in a toolshop leased for the work from the Ford Motor Co. Nevertheless, the contract schedule was not met due to delays in the delivery of the engines. It was on 12 September, 1942, that the aircraft was finally packed in crates and sent by train to Muroc. After re-assembly and necessary checks, Bell's chief test pilot Robert Stanley took the XP-59A into the air for the first time on 1 October, 1942. This first flight was made with the undercarriage locked down and at very low altitude (25ft). Three more flights were accomplished the same day, and four more the day after. During these flights, the XP-59A reached an altitute of 10,000ft. The ninth flight did not occur until 30 October because some modifications had to be made to the undercarriage. The reliability of the engines also left much to be desired. Detached turbine blades, overheated bearings and fuel pump failures were among the problems.

*The first prototype XP-59 entered flight test in October 1942 and was unarmed. A serial number was not allocated to this aircraft until after flight testing had begun. (Bell)*

*One of the US Navy's few P-59Bs, finished in classic two-shades of blue camouflage. (Courtesy Tailhook)*

*This view of an XP-59A shows its layout to advantage.*

The second prototype (c/n 27-2, s/n 42-108785) soon joined the first in the flight-test programme but encountered the same teething troubles as its stable mate. The flights were made at a rather slow rate and by April 1943 the first prototype had only totalled 15¼hr in 30 flights and the second prototype 13¾hr in 24 flights. At the beginning of April, due to heavy rain, the second prototype was towed (fitted with a dummy propeller and canvas covers) first to Hawes Field, then to Harpers Lake where it remained until 7 April and was brought back to Muroc. At the end of the same month, the third prototype (c/n 27-3, s/n 42-108786) joined the programme.

Meanwhile, on 26 March, 1943, the USAAF had ordered a Service trials batch of thirteen YP-59A-BEs (42-108771/108783). These aircraft differed from the three XP-59A-BEs in some respects. They featured a rearward-sliding canopy instead of the sideways-hinged one. The engines were intended to be 1,650lb st General Electric I-16s (later designated J31), but in fact I-A engines were fitted because the I-16s were not ready in time. The intended armament for the XP-59A was retained on the first nine YP-59As but the final four aircraft received a single 37mm cannon and three 0.50in machine-guns in the nose.

The first two YP-59As were delivered to Muroc in June 1943 and the first flight was made by 42-108772 on 18 August, 1943. With its temporary I-A engines, the YP-59A reached 389mph at 35,160ft and could reach 30,000ft in 18.82min. When the I-16 engines were installed the top speed was increased to 409mph at 35,000ft. The second YP-59A flew on 15 September, 1943, followed soon after by aircraft Nos.4 to 7. No.3 (42-108773) was sent to Britain for comparison with the Gloster Meteor. By this time the Bell fighter had been named Airacomet and, 42-108773, after receiving the official grey-green RAF camouflage with bright yellow undersides as well as the serial RJ362/G, made its first flight on 28 September, 1943, with Frank H Kelley Jr at the controls. Between 5 November, 1943, and April 1944, the Bell jet fighter flew only eleven times at Farnborough and it was returned to the United States early in 1945.

The six remaining aircraft of the Service trials batch were assigned to different tasks. Aircraft Nos.8 and 9 were delivered to the US Navy in

*An unidentified P-59A in bare metal finish. A bomb rack is installed under the wing. (Courtesy P M Bowers)*

*The Airacomet displayed at the Planes of Fame Museum in Chino, California, is a service trials batch aircraft (YP-59A-BE s/n 42-108777) converted to a two-seater. (A Pelletier)*

November 1942 (42-108778/108779 becoming BuNo 63960/63961) which kept them flying until 1947/49 (one crashed in December 1947, another was scrapped the same month and the third one last flew in 1949). Aircraft No.10 (42-108780) was modified as a drone for the development of radio control equipment (it was lost on 23 March, 1945). Aircraft Nos.11 and 12 (42-108781/108782) were sent to NACA for wind-tunnel experiments and aircraft No.13 (42-108783), after gunnery tests conducted in April 1944 which showed that the aircraft was a rather poor gun platform, was converted to a drone controller aircraft with a second cockpit installed in the nose, painted black overall and nicknamed *Mystic Mistress*. This modification was also applied to the third prototype and to the seventh YP-59A (42-108777).

*The P-59B-1-BE (s/n 44-22650) preserved by the US Air Force Museum has buzz-number PJ-650. (P M Bowers)*

*The third prototype XP-59A (s/n 42-108786) joined the test programme in April 1943. (US Air Force)*

*A US Navy P-59B-1-BE in overall dark sea-blue livery. (Courtesy P M Bowers)*

Spinning trials were initiated at the end of December 1943 and, as a result, a small ventral fin was introduced on the aircraft to enhance spin recovery characteristics. The Service tests began at Muroc on 5 December, 1944, with three YP-59As. Mock combat sorties were flown against the Lockheed P-38J Lightning and Republic P-47D Thunderbolt which revealed that the Airacomet was outclassed by the conventional piston-engined fighters, and the Airacomet was declared unsuitable for combat.

On 27 February, 1944, flight testing came to an end with a grand total of 242½hr flown by the three XP-59As and six YP-59As. During diving tests which followed two major incidents occurred. In June 1944, YP-59A 42-108781 made a belly landing and later that year a P-59A was lost after its entire tail unit had broken away.

On 11 March, 1944, a production contract for one hundred P-59A-BEs (44-22609/22708) was confirmed by the USAAF, fewer than Bell had hoped. A further 250 aircraft were also planned. The production models differed from the Service trials aircraft in many respects: they had squared-off wingtips which reduced the span from 49ft to 45ft 6in and the wing area from 400sq ft to 386sq ft. All control surfaces were now metal-covered. The fuselage had been strengthened, the fin and rudder had been redesigned and a ventral fin incorporated. The pitot tube was repositioned and there were other minor changes. The engines remained unchanged, as General Electric I-16s. The first P-59A-BEs were delivered at the end of 1944, but by that time the USAAF had decided to reduce its order to only thirty-nine aircraft, but in fact fifty were built due to economical considerations (it would have been more expensive to scrap nearly complete airframes than to deliver them). These fifty aircraft were built in two batches: twenty P-59A-BEs (44-22609/22628) and thirty P-59B-1-BEs (44-22629/22658) which differed by having a 66US gal tank in each outer wing panel and some P-59Bs were eventually fitted with 2,000lb st J31-GE-5 engines. By 27

August, 1945, all fifty had been delivered.

One P-59A was assigned to Wright Field while two others went to the AAF Proving Ground Command, at Eglin Field, Florida; a fourth was sent to the Extreme Temperature Operations Unit at Ladd Field, Alaska, where it performed quite well. Sixteen aircraft were taken on charge by the 412th Fighter Group of the 4th Air Force, this Group including 29th, 31st and 445th Fighter Squadrons. Of the P-59Bs, three were transferred to the US Navy as BuNos 64100, 64108/64109 (44-22651, 22656/22657) and, in September 1945, one (44-22650) went to NACA Lewis Research Center, Cleveland, where it was used for jet thrust performance and augmentation research until January 1949. A batch of nineteen P-59Bs was assigned to the 412th Fighter Group.

The 412th FG had been constituted at Muroc on 30 November, 1943, to be the USAAF's first jet unit and was stationed at Bakersfield, California. It had mission 'to train as the first operational fighter group utilising jet-propelled equipment, and, concurrently, to assist other personnel or units, as designated, in transition from conventional to jet-propelled type aircraft'.

*The YP-59A-BE s/n 42-108777 before a test flight. (US Air Force)*

*P-59B-1-BE s/n 44-22635. The P-59B had an additional 66US gallon bag tank in each outer wing.*

*The service trials batch YP-59A-BE s/n 42-108775. The YPs were substantially the same as the prototypes in external appearance but had rearward-sliding canopies. (Courtesy P M Bowers)*

*The XP-59A-BE on the Rogers Dry Lake where it accomplished its maiden flight on 1 October, 1942, with Bell's chief test pilot Robert Stanley at the controls. (US Air Force)*

*P-59A-1-BE s/n 44-22610 taxi-ing. The P-59A was the production version of the Airacomet but was built only in small numbers. (US Air Force)*

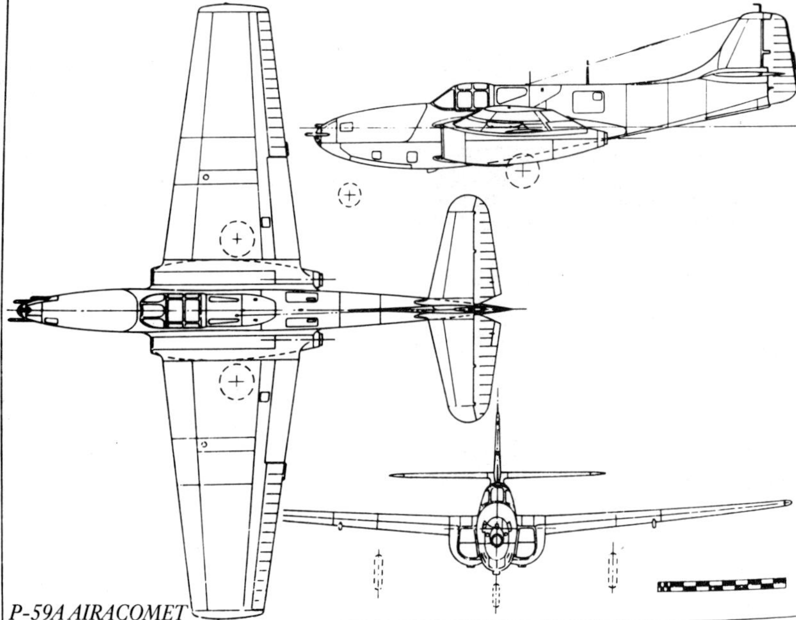

P-59A AIRACOMET

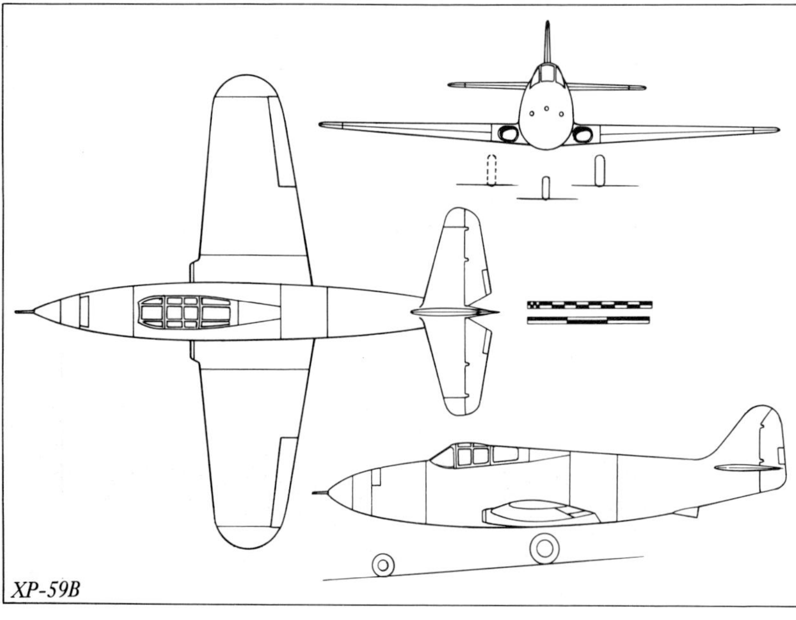

XP-59B

During March 1945, a captured Mitsubishi A6M5 Model 52 Zero was taken on charge by the 445th Fighter Squadron in order to conduct comparative tests with the P-59A and, on 10 July, 1945, the Group moved to Santa Maria Army Air Field, California, and then to March Field on 29 November, 1945. Soon after, the Group began to re-equip with the Lockheed P-80 Shooting Star and was inactivated on 3 July, 1946. The P-59 had thus been in active service for no more than a year.

A single-engined variant of the P-59, designated XP-59B, was studied for a while but abandoned when the P-80 was ordered from Lockheed. The XP-59B would have resembled a jet-powered Airacobra with air intakes in the wing roots and jetpipe emerging under the fuselage.

Six Airacomets are still in existence: one XP-59A (42-108784 at the National Air and Space Museum, in Washington, DC); one YP-59A (42-108777 at the Planes of Fame Museum, Chino, California, in two-seat configuration); one P-59A (44-22614 at March Field Museum, California) and three P-59Bs (44-22633 at the Flight Test Historical Museum, Edwards AFB, California; 44-22650 at the USAF Museum, Dayton, Ohio, and 44-22656 at the Harold Warp Pioneer Village, Minden, Nebraska).

## P-59A

Span 45ft 6in (13.87m); length 38ft 1½in (11.62m); height 12ft (3.65m); wing area 386sq ft (35.86sq m).

Empty weight 7,950lb (3,606kg); normal loaded weight 10,882lb (4,909kg); maximum weight 13,000lb (5,902kg).

Maximum speed 409mph (658km/h) at 35,000ft (10,670m), 376mph (605km/h) at 5,000ft (1,525m); cruising speed (60 per cent power) 298mph (480km/h) at 20,000ft (6,095m); cruising range 240 miles (386km) at 20,000ft (6,095m); rate of climb 3,200ft/min (16.3m/s) at 5,000ft (1,525m); time to 10,000ft (3,050m) 3.2min; time to 20,000ft (6,095m) 7.4min; time to 30,000ft (9,150m) 15.5m; service ceiling 46,200ft (14,090m); range with drop tanks 520miles (837km).

# Model 30

By the autumn of 1941, Arthur M Young had been testing helicopter scale-models on his farm in Pennsylvania for some thirteen years. After this period of research, many failures and his big breakthrough with the invention of the stabiliser bar, Young had perfected a design that would appeal to a manufacturer. Young's first attempts at interesting aircraft companies in his machine met with little enthusiasm until one of his friends visited Bell's factory. This led to an appointment for a demonstration on 3 September, 1941. Larry Bell and Arthur Young reached an agreement in due course and, on 24 November, 1941, Young and his assistant, Bart Kelley, arrived at Bell to supervise the initial building of two prototypes as specified in the contract. On 23 June, 1942, Young and his team (some fifteen people) were installed in an old Chrysler agency and garage in Gardenville, a suburb of Buffalo. Dave Forman was assigned to supervise the project.

The Model 30, as it was known inside the company, was a rather crude structure made of welded tubes with a wide four-legged undercarriage made of 3in aluminium tubing. The engine, a 160hp Franklin six-cylinder horizontally-opposed air-cooled unit was

*Model 30 No.1 (NX41867) in its late configuration with Arthur Young at the controls. The windshield remains to be added. (Bell)*

*The preserved Model 30 in its overall bright yellow livery. (Bell)*

*Arthur Young poses in the preserved Bell Model 30. (Bell)*

*Bart Kelley (left) assists Arthur Young in installing the transmission mast assembly in Model 30 No.1. (Bell)*

mounted vertically behind the cockpit within a steel-tube framework. The main two-blade rotor hub was mounted on a transmission mast by universal joint and was provided with a stabilising bar below and at right angles to the blades which were rigidly connected to the hub. This bar acted as a flywheel on a hinge. It kept the rotor blades level and independent from the movements of the fuselage, solving the problem of stability. The main rotor drive was done through a centrifugal clutch and a two-stage planetary transmission with a 9:1 reduction ratio. The blades, of symmetrical aerofoil section, were made of solid wood with a steel insert in the leading edge. The two-blade tail rotor (also made of solid wood) was mounted on a thin tube at the end of the fuselage.

The roll-out of the first Model 30 (c/n 1, later to be registered NX41867) took place on 24 December, 1942; a secretary broke a bottle of champagne on the fuselage and the aircraft was named *Genevieve.*

*Model 30 No.1 (NX41867) and No.2 (NX41868). Differences between the two aircraft are clearly visible in this view. (Bell)*

On this day, the engine was run up at 150rpm. The maiden flight occurred on 29 December when Young flew the tethered Model 30 at an altitude of 5ft; the same day Floyd Carlson also flew the aircraft. Early in January 1943, the prototype was victim of an accident and its pilot, Bob Stanley, was badly hurt. The aircraft was repaired and on 26 June, 1943, the cable was removed and Carlson took *Genevieve* on its first free flight. The aircraft performed well and by July 1943 was flying at speeds of over 70mph. At this time, a three-wheeled undercarriage was installed, the fuselage was covered and the aircraft was painted blue overall, so that it could be used for demonstration flights.

*Arthur Young checking Model 30 No.1 before a test flight in 1943. (Bell)*

*The Model 30 during a tethered flight at Gardenville; Floyd Carlson is at the controls. (Bell)*

*Floyd Carlson flying Model 30 No.1 (NX41867) hands off. There is a probe on the right hand undercarriage leg. (Bell)*

While flights of the Model 30 No.1 were underway, aircraft No.2 was being built. Several modifications were introduced in this machine: new undercarriage, semi-monocoque fuselage and new tail rotor mounting, but the most noticeable change was the enclosed cockpit, with car-like doors, for the pilot and one passenger. Unfortunately a setback occurred in September 1943 when the No.1 crashed with Carlson at the controls. Carlson was unhurt but the badly damaged aircraft had to be rebuilt. It was flying again within six months. Thus, in late September 1943, aircraft No.2 (registered NX41868) replaced No.1 as the test vehicle. One of the first passengers to fly in this aircraft was Larry Bell.

In 1944, Bell began a demonstration programme with aircraft No.2 which made its public debut in

*Floyd Carlson at the controls of* Genevieve, *Bell Model 30 No.1. (Bell)*

*The second Model 30, NX41868, inside Civil Air Patrol Armory in Buffalo. (Bell)*

*The Model 30 No.2 had accommodation for two people seated side-by-side. The undercarriage was rather crude and access to the cabin was via car-like doors. (Bell courtesy P M Bowers)*

March 1944. On 10 May, Floyd Carlson flew the aircraft indoors in a Buffalo armoury before Civil Air Patrol pilots and cadets. By the spring of 1944, aircraft No.1 had been rebuilt and was designated No.1A. Making a spectacular comeback, this helicopter was the star attraction at a soldier's benefit show, staged at Buffalo's Civil Stadium on 4 July.

On 5 January, 1945 the first rescue mission ever made by a Bell helicopter took place when Jack Woolams baled out of a P-59 Airacomet in trouble near Lockport. Floyd Carlson and Dr Thomas C Marriott took off in one of the Model 30s and, guided by Joe Masham flying a P-59, rescued the unfortunate pilot. But the first publicized rescue mission took place two months later, on 14 March, when two ice fishermen were rescued on Lake Erie. Carlson received the Treasury Department Silver Medal for this daring feat.

Meanwhile, the construction of a third aircraft had begun. Among the several improvements introduced on this machine were a four-wheel undercarriage, an advanced instrument panel and a tubular tailboom, but it retained the open cockpit of No.1. This helicopter (c/n 3, registered NX41869) flew for the first time on 25 April, 1945, and performed well, so well that it proved to be the best of the trio to demonstrate, but the open cockpit was a real handicap. To overcome this Young had the idea of covering the cockpit with a Plexiglass bubble thus providing both comfort and outstanding visibility for pilot and passenger. The shape of this aircraft was now very near to that of the Model 47.

Two of the Model 30s are still in existence: c/n 1A (NX41867) is on display at the National Air and Space Museum and c/n 3 (NX41869) is owned by Buffalo and Erie County Historical Society Museum, Amhurst, New York.

Rotor diameter: 32ft (9.75m); tail rotor diameter: 5ft (1.52m); disc area: 855sq ft (79.46sq m).

# Model 32 XP-77

During the course of the war, with the ever growing production of military equipment, shortages of raw material began to appear. Metals and alloys were the first to cause a problem. In 1941, a search began for replacement materials and for aeronautical designs using non-strategic materials. This trend led, for example, to the twin-engined Beechcraft AT-10 trainer in which most of the airframe was of wooden construction. Combat aircraft were also concerned and, from October 1941, discussions took place at Wright Field between USAAF engineers and aircraft manufacturers' representatives including those of Bell Aircraft Corp. These led, in April 1942, to a contract calling for the design and development of a lightweight fighter designated P-77 under USAAF terminology.

In fact for the Bell design team this was not an entirely new concept. When the P-39 design was initiated in 1936, Bob Woods considered two different layouts: one (Model 4) led to the P-39, the other (Model 3) was withdrawn. It was this latter design which served as a basis for the XP-77.

Successively known as the Tri.4, Design D-6 and finally Model 32, the XP-77 was a small low-wing monoplane using resin-bonded laminated Sitka spruce construction with stressed skin. The powerplant was a 520hp Ranger XV-770-7 twelve-cylinder air-cooled inline engine driving an Aeroproducts 9ft 6in diameter two-blade propeller. The cantilever single-spar wing had an aspect ratio of 7.56 and a NACA 65 low-drag laminar flow profile; dihedral was 5 degrees. The fuselage, of all-wood construction too, housed a 52US gal fuel tank and provision was made for a 38US gal auxiliary belly fuel tank. The Bell electrically-operated nosewheel undercarriage was retained and planned armament consisted of one 20mm cannon firing through the propeller hub and two 0.50in machine-guns in the forward fuselage. The cannon was later removed when the USAAF requested provision for a 300lb bomb or a 325lb depth charge to be carried. As far as performance was concerned, Bob Woods wanted to build 'a plane that meets that magic 4–4–4 combination', that is to say that with a 4,000lb gross weight and a 400hp engine, it could fly at 400mph. Calculated maximum speed with the supercharged version of the engine (XV-770-9) was 410mph at 27,000ft. Initial rate of climb was to be 3,200ft/min.

Under contract No.AC-30864 of 10 October, 1942, the USAAF ordered six prototypes of the XP-77-BE (43-34915/34920), plus two airframes for static tests, one full-scale mock-up and one full-scale model plus one ⅑th scale model for wind-tunnel tests, at the total cost of $698,761.88. The first aeroplane was to be delivered within six months following agreement.

The full-scale mock-up was inspected on 21/22 September, 1942, and no less than 54 changes were requested by USAAF representatives.

At the time, Bell was committed to the full-scale production of P-39s, development of the new P-63 and the P-59 jet fighter was also on the drawing boards. As the months passed, Bell requested more delays for deliveries. At the same time, the total cost of the programme jumped dramatically to $2,548,540.46! The availability of light alloys had improved by that time and the interest of the USAAF in a lightweight fighter made of non-strategic materials decreased. In August 1943, it was decided to cut down drastically the lightweight fighter programme and, on 20 December, 1943, Bell was advised that only two prototypes were to be built and these had to be delivered on 31 January, 1944, and 1 March, 1944.

New delays then occurred. The

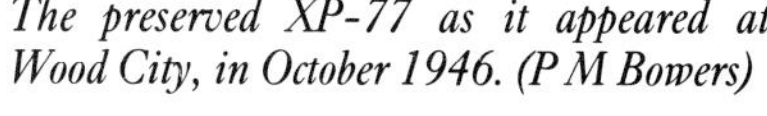
*The preserved XP-77 as it appeared at Wood City, in October 1946. (P M Bowers)*

*The second prototype XP-77-BE was lost on 2 October, 1944, when it entered an inverted spin. The pilot was able to bale out. (Bell)*

*The first prototype XP-77 at Wood City. The markings are certainly not authentic. (P M Bowers)*

*The XP-77 was an attempt to design a lightweight fighter made of non-strategic materials. The prototype, (XP-77-BE s/n 43-34915), first flew on 1 April, 1944.*

subcontractor (Vidal Research Corp) in charge of building the wings was unable to deliver these important components on schedule, the first wing panel arriving on 3 February, 1944. Delivery of the first aircraft was then postponed to 5 March. Subsequent difficulties with the undercarriage retraction system led to another month's delay and the first flight was only accomplished on 1 April, 1944, eight months beyond the initial schedule. This flight lasted 25 minutes and was found to be satisfactory. The aeroplane was then ferried to Wright Field on 2 May, 1944, to undergo flutter and vibration tests. At an unknown date, this first aircraft suffered a nose-wheel failure. On 22 July, after repairs had been made, it was sent, together with the second prototype, to Eglin Field for operational tests which were made in late July and early August. General handling characteristics were found satisfactory but overall performance was far below that specified. The XP-77 had a maximum speed of 328mph at 12,600ft and the rate of climb was found to be too slow for an interceptor. In short, the Bell fighter was slower than the heavier fighters of conventional construction then in the USAAF inventory. Unfortunately, the second prototype suffered a major accident on 2 October, 1944, when it entered an inverted spin obliging the pilot to bale out.

In most respects, the XP-77 was a misfit and it was recommended that no more consideration was to be given to its production. This led to the complete withdrawal of the programme in December 1944.

The first prototype survived the war and was put on display for a while in Wood City but its final fate remains unknown.

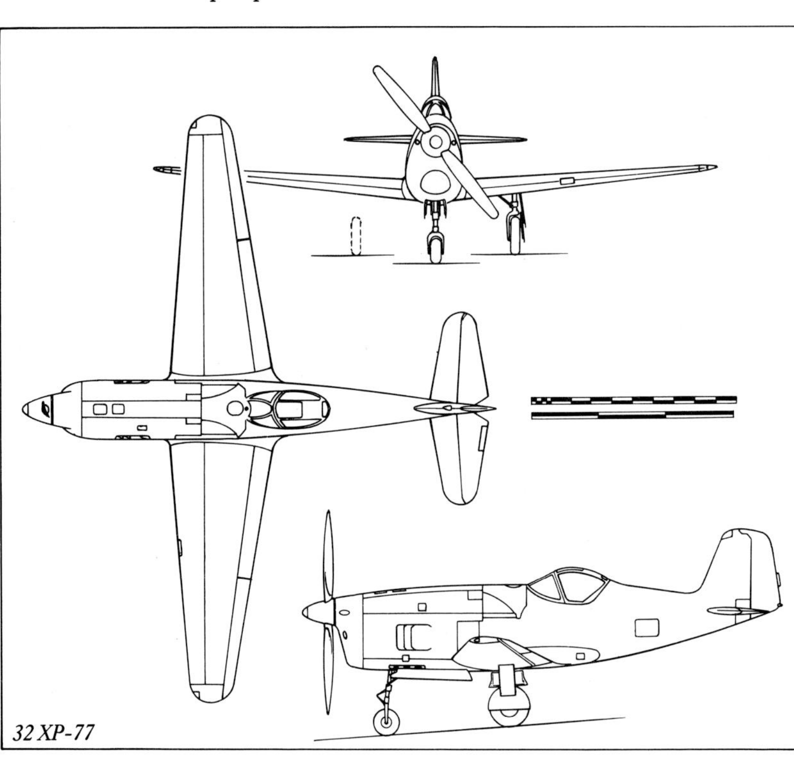

*32 XP-77*

Span 27ft 6in (8.39m); length 22ft 10½in (6.98m); height 8ft 2¼in (2.49m); wing area 100sq ft (9.29sq m).

Empty weight 2,855lb (1,296kg); loaded weight 3,672lb (1,667kg); maximum loaded weight 4,028lb (1,829kg).

Maximum speed 330mph (531km/h) at 4,000ft (1,220m), 328mph (528km/h) at 12,600ft (3,843m); initial rate of climb 3,600ft/min (18.3m/s); time to 9,000ft (2,745m) 3.7min; service ceiling 30,000ft (9,180m); normal range 305miles (491km); maximum range 550miles (885km).

# XP-83

Following the deadly attacks on unescorted bombers over Germany, the US Air Force was especially concerned with long-range escort fighters and early in 1944 Bell began the development of a long-range heavily armed derivative of its P-59 Airacomet jet fighter. This project attracted the attention of the Army Air Force which, on 31 July, 1944, ordered two prototypes under the designation XP-83-BE (s/n 44-84990/84991).

For the XP-83, Robert J Woods retained the basic layout of the Airacomet but the machine was somewhat bigger. The powerplants were two General Electric XJ33-GE-5 centrifugal-flow turbojets each rated at 4,000lb st for take-off at 11,500rpm and located alongside the fuselage in order to minimize asymmetric thrust in case of an engine failure but this layout was not aerodynamically ideal. The structure was of the all-metal semi-monocoque type with flush-riveted stressed skin. The straight wing was a two-spar structure (with auxiliary spar) with a low-drag laminar flow profile. Incidence varied from +1deg at the roots to −1deg 15min at the wingtips. Dihedral was 2deg and sweepback 8deg 2min. Movable surfaces comprised two power-assisted ailerons (with a trim-tab on the port aileron) and two large hydraulically-operated Fowler flaps located between the ailerons and wing roots. Hydraulic aileron boost was employed to reduce stick forces at high speeds. A hydraulically-operated dive-recovery flap was located under each wing near the wing root. The empennage, of cantilever monoplane type, had an adjustable tailplane by means of an electrically-controlled actuator and the elevators had trim tabs. The wide-track characteristic Bell nosewheel undercarriage was actuated by means of three electrical motors and retracted inwards.

To accomplish the long-range missions for which it had been designed the XP-83 had three self-sealing interconnected fuel cells (908US gal in the fuselage and three self-sealing cells (123US gal) in each wing. Additional jettisonable fuel tanks could be carried on hard points under the wings. The cockpit was pressurized and the canopy was jettisonable in case of emergency. Various armament configurations were considered and proposed by Bell. One of these comprised four 20mm cannon, another four 37mm cannon and a third a tremendous pack of twenty 0.50in machine-guns. In fact, a more conventional arrangement of six Browning 0.50in machine-guns in the nose with 300

*The XP-83 was powered by a pair of General Electric J33-GE-5 turbojets rated at 4,000lb st.*

*This view of the XP-83 shows the nose armament consisting of six 0.50in machine-guns with 300rpg. The aircraft also had provision for one 1,000lb bomb under each wing. (US Air Force)*

*The first prototype of the XP-83-BE long-range jet fighter. The general layout was quite similar to that of the Airacomet. (Bell)*

rounds was eventually decided on. The aircraft also had provision to carry two 1,000lb bombs or two 300US gal drop tanks under each wing.

The first prototype was rolled out in January 1945 and was flown on 25 February by Bell's chief test pilot, Jack Woolams. Performance was found somewhat disappointing. The flight tests revealed that the XF-83, as it had been redesignated, was underpowered and its manoeuvrability left much to be desired. The flight-test programme was quickly resumed but the USAAF did not order the XF-83 into production.

In 1946, the first prototype was transformed into a flying test-bed for ram-jet engines one of which was mounted at each wingtip. Unfortunately, in September 1946, during one of the test flights, the aircraft crashed and was completely lost. The second prototype also served as a test-bed for various experiments until 1947 and was eventually scrapped.

Span 53ft 0in (16.17m); length 44ft 10in (13.68m); height 15ft 3in (4.65m); wing area 431sq ft (40.04sq m).

Empty weight 14,105lb (6,404kg); normal gross weight 24,090lb (10,937kg); maximum weight 27,500lb (12,485kg).

Maximum speed at 15,660ft (4,776m) 522mph (840km/h); initial rate of climb 5,650ft/min (28.7 m/s); time to 30,000ft (9,150m) 11½min; service ceiling 45,000ft (13,715m); normal range 1,730miles (2,784km); maximum range 2,050miles (3,298km).

*Tested early in 1945 the XP-83 was soon abandoned and used only as a flying test-bed. (Bell)*

*The rather bulky appearance of the XP-83 is apparent in this view taken on 8 February, 1945, at Wright Field. (US Air Force)*

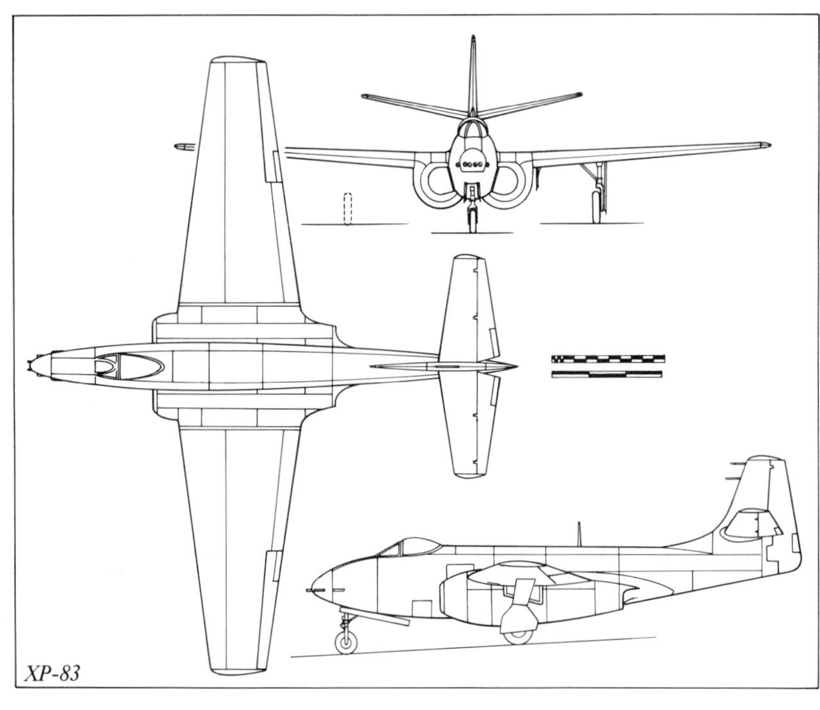

# Model 47 R-13/H-13/ HTL/HUL Sioux

On 24 June, 1945, the Gardenville group led by Arthur M Young was moved into Bell's new main factory in Niagara Falls which had larger installations including a hangar and model and machine shops. It was there that the Model 47 helicopter was born. The new prototype (c/n 1, registered NC1H) was evolved from Model 30 No.3. It was a two-seater and the engine retained was a vertically-mounted 175hp Franklin with clutch, drive shaft and rotor assembly integrated in a steel-tube framework with the engine supported on rubber mounts at top and bottom. Dual controls were fitted. The stabilising bar was retained; this bar, which was about 5ft long and weighted at the ends, was linked to the rotor in such a way that it tended to maintain the plane of the rotor horizontal irrespective of the angle of the mast. The Model 47 was rolled out six months later on 8 December, 1945, and made its first flight on the same day. Ten additional aircraft (c/ns 2 to 11) were built for tests, training and demonstration.

Larry D Bell was a constant passenger in the helicopter. One day, when Floyd Carlson was flying him to a Buffalo country club for a meeting, the aircraft's tail rotor drive-shaft broke on one of the Model 47 prototypes. Happily, Carlson safely autorotated into a field. There were no major problems during the certification by CAA (the Civil Aeronautics Administration had never certificated a commercial helicopter before). On 8 March, 1946, the Model 47 was awarded the world's first commercial helicopter licence ahead of Igor Sikorsky's efforts to do the same. Exactly two months later, Bell received Helicopter Type Certificate No.1 from the CAA.

*Several members of the Gardenville team take a ride aboard Model 47 NX41860. The pilot is Joe Mashman. (Bell)*

The Model 47 was priced at more than $20,000, more expensive than a fixed-wing aeroplane and there was a lack of demand from the military services. However, the Army was the first military branch to acquire a Bell helicopter (in December 1946).

In 1947, twenty-eight Model 47As (designated YR-13-BE, later YH-13-BE) were delivered to the US Air Force. These were powered by the 175hp Franklin O-335-1 engine and used for evaluation purposes. Three machines of this batch (s/n 46-228/230) were modified for cold-weather operations as YR-13A-BEs for trials in Alaska, the first two being taken there aboard a Fairchild C-82 on 6 January, 1947. Some of these aircraft later underwent hot weather trials in southern USA in temperatures up to 120deg F. Ten other machines (s/n 46-236/237, 242/244, 249/251 and 253/254) were transferred to the US Navy as HTL-1s, two being later transferred to the US Coast Guard.

The first commercial delivery was made on 31 December, 1946. The commercial production variant was the Model 47B which featured car-like windscreen and doors as well as a glazed nose made of Plexiglass. The majority of helicopters sold in 1947 were purchased one at a time by newly formed charter operators, a few corporations, crop dusters, and others. In fact, the first successful

*HTL-5 (BuNo 129971) of the US Navy at NAS Corpus Christie. There is an antenna loop inside the cockpit. (J Wegg)*

*Chief pilot Floyd Carlson demonstrates the stability of the Model 47 flying the prototype hands off on 8 March, 1946. (Bell)*

single Bell 47B, c/n 49 G-AKCX, to be used as a demonstrator. This last aircraft was damaged beyond repair at Heathfield on 7 February, 1946. In France, Fenwick Aviation became exclusive distributor for the Model 47 and approached the French Armée de l'Air as well as the Aéronavale (French naval air arm). In November 1950 tests were conducted aboard the cruiser *Emile Bertin* with the French Model 47 demonstrator (c/n 177, registered F-BDRU).

Early in 1948, the Model 47B was superseded by the Model 47D which incorporated a number of improvements, the most apparent being the plastic bubble-like cabin, the top of which could be removed to provide an open cockpit. In 1949, a new sub-variant appeared, the Model 47D-1 utility helicopter capable of carrying three people or 500lb of payload. The same year, Bell helicopters began to be used on air mail services in Chicago and a

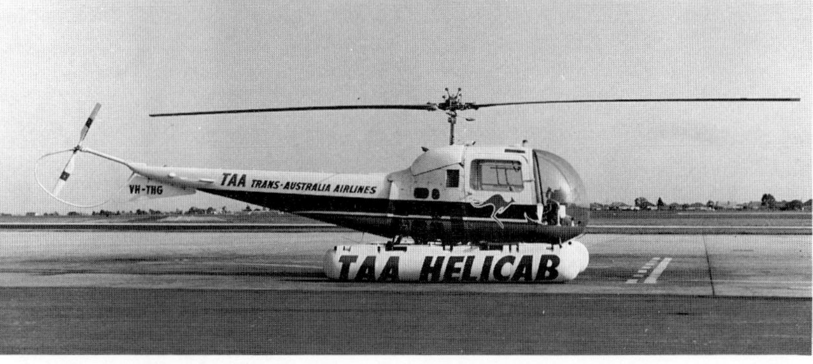


*Pontoon-equipped Model 47J-2 VH-THG of Trans-Australia Airlines. (Courtesy P M Bowers)*

commercial application of the Model 47 was on agricultural work and geophysical surveys. During the last seven months of 1947, more than thirty Bell helicopters treated tens of thousands of acres of flat crops and orchards. In September 1947, ten of these Model 47s were purchased by Trabajos Aereos Y Representaciones in Argentina and began a fairly efficient war against the annual locust invasion. In Europe, British European Airways formed its Experimental Helicopter Unit in Yeovil in July 1947: the fleet included two Bell 47B-3s (c/n 69 G-AKFA *Sir Balin* and c/n 73 G-AFKB *Sir Balan*) for training. These aircraft had been imported by Irvin-Bell Helicopter Sales Ltd together with a

*Westland Sioux XT211 of the British Army was later registered G-BFOH and 5B-CGO before being written off on 5 September, 1988. (Museum of Army Flying)*

Bell 47 set a new altitude record with 18,550ft (5,654m) as well as a new speed record with 133.9mph (215.45km/h). In 1950, a Bell 47D-1 became the first helicopter to fly over the Alps, and in Belgium the first European postal service by helicopter was set up by Sabena on 21 August, 1950. At the end of the same year, Bell 47s were used to take precise measurements over the Niagara Falls. But these were not the last achievements of the Goldfish bowl, as the Bell aircraft began to be known. On 17 September, 1952, Bell pilot, Elton J Smith set the world's straight line distance record for helicopters without payload (Class-E) at the controls of a Model 47D-1 registered N167B, flying nonstop from Hurst (Texas) to Buffalo (New-York): 1,217.137 miles (1,958.37km) in 12hr 57min. On 2 September, 1956, at the National Aircraft Show in Oklahoma City, an H-13H flown by an Army pilot stayed in the air for 57hr and 50min, an unofficial world's record.

Above all, the helicopter showed its great value in rescue operations. For example, during the tremendous storm in the North Sea and along the Dutch coasts, in February 1953, two Bell 47D-1s of Sabena (piloted by G Trémerie and Vervoort) rescued dozens of people and brought in food. On 10 September, 1954, a Model 47G was used by A H Voisin to rescue the victims of the Orléansville (Algeria) earthquake. In 1957, President Eisenhower flew in an H-13J from the White House lawn to a command post as part of a civil defence exercise and became the first president to fly in a helicopter.

*In 1956, the first H-13H (s/n 55-3355) remained airborne for 57hr 50min. It had modified fuel tanks mounted each side. (P M Bowers)*

On 31 October, 1959, the Model 47G-3 variant accomplished its maiden flight and the little Bell helicopter continued to accumulate records. At the beginning of 1961, the Model 47 with L W Hartwig at the controls set up a new series of records: on 31 January, with a Model 47J-2 weighing 2,059lb, he established a speed record over a 100km closed circuit (E.1b and E.1c classes) with 104.635mph (168.358km/

*An H-13G-BH. This variant was powered by a 250hp Lycoming VO-435-23. (Bell)*

*A Model 47B (NC102B) performing during an airshow in 1949. Car-type windscreen and doors were characteristic of this variant. (P M Bowers)*

h). A few days later, on 2 February, he set several other records in the E.1b class with a Model 47G-3: distance in a closed circuit, 641.436miles (1,032.070km); speed over 310miles (500km), 73.985mph (119.041km/h); speed over 621miles (1,000km), 73.351mph (118.022km/h) and on the same day broke three new records at the take-off weight of 2,204lb (998.4kg): distance in a closed circuit with 631.57 miles (1,016.2km); speed record over 500km (310miles) closed circuit, 74.000mph (119.067km/h) and speed over a 1,000km (621miles) closed circuit, 73.864mph (118.848km/h). The same month, D J Dougherty on a Model 47G-3 established the women's altitude record with 19,386ft (5,908.86m) and the women's distance record in a straight line with 405.92miles (653.12km). The nonstop distance record in a straight line was raised to 731.38miles (1,176.79km) by A P Averill piloting a Model 47G-3 on 8 February.

In 1961, Bell announced a whole new range of high-altitude capabilities for helicopter operations during flights by the new turbo-supercharged Model 47G-3B in a Pike's Peak test. A Model 47G-3 hovered atop Pikes Peak (14,110ft, 6deg C temperature) with a pilot and five passengers aboard. Useful load on this manoeuvre was 1,500lb.

Production of the Model 47 grew steadily and by the end of 1952, 416 helicopters had left the assembly line. In December alone, sixty-seven aircraft had been delivered. The 1,000th Model 47 was rolled out on 10 April, 1953, and the 2,000th Model 47, a 47J, was completed on 11 December, 1957. Bell ceased production of the Model 47 at the end of 1973. Nevertheless, the Model 47 still continued to be of invaluable assistance in a wide range of tasks. As an example, by 1977, Petroleum Helicopters Inc had logged 1,100,000 flying hours with its Model 47 fleet.

## Production History

As detailed here, the Model 47 was built by Bell and its licensees in a wide range of production models.

**Model 47:** prototype and service test batch; eleven aircraft built.

**Model 47A:** *see* under YR-13.

**Model 47B:** first production variant powered by a vertically mounted 175hp Franklin 6ALV-335 six-cylinder engine. The enclosed cabin, seating two side-by-side, featured two car-like doors. A total of 78 Model 47Bs (including 47B-3) were produced. Very few Model 47Bs survive today (c/n 11 registered N11HU, 57/N1575, 58/N138B and 70/N150B). In 1989, one example (c/n 36, N116B), was restored to flying condition by Douglas D Daigle of Santa Ana, California.

**Model 47B-3:** available in 1948, this model was the crop-dusting variant featuring a fully open cockpit. Bins were affixed aft of the cabin and could carry 400lb of dust.

*In 1961, a Model 47G-3, with a pilot and five passengers, hovered atop Pikes Peak. (P M Bowers collection)*

*The Agusta-Bell 47G-2 c/n 184 was first used by the French Air Force with F.SFWI call-sign, then by French Army Aviation before being transferred to the civil register as F-BTSY. (Author's collection)*

**Model 47D:** improved variant of the Model 47B powered by a 178hp Franklin 6V4-178-B32 engine. It featured a fully-enclosed cabin made of a full-blown Plexiglass canopy for greater visibility. The upper section of this canopy and the doors were quickly removable and could be replaced by a small windshield. Flexible nylon floats could be fitted for amphibious use. A few 47Ds survive today on the US register (c/n 5 registered N147B, 10/N156B, 20/N12888, 39/N39KH, 41/N855E).

**Model 47D-1:** this sub-variant had some earlier refinements deleted to provide for a 25 to 37 per cent greater payload. Empty weight was reduced from 1,482lb (673kg) to 1,380lb (626kg).

**Model 47G:** standard production model powered with 200hp Franklin 6V4-200-C32AB (O-335-5) engine. This version featured a small elevator which was geared to work in conjunction with rotor tilt. This permitted an increase in permissible centre of gravity travel and greatly improved stability. From 1954, this model was built under licence by Agusta with the Franklin 6V4-200-C22 engine.

**Model 47G-2 and G-2A:** introduced in 1955, this variant was basically similar to the Model 47G but featured a 200hp derated Lycoming VO-435-A1B engine in order to maintain maximum power up to 5,000ft and to increase engine life. The Model 47G-2 was built under licence by Agusta (304 aircraft) and 180 aircraft were produced under licence in Japan by Kawasaki (c/ns 101/280) of which 75 went to JGSDF with serials 30101/30175. In addition thirty-three Model 47G-2As were built by Kawasaki (c/n 501/533) of which eight went to JMSDF with serials 8751/8758.

**Model 47G-3:** this variant, first flown on 2 July, 1959, had a 225hp Franklin 6VS-335 engine. It also had greater rotor diameter and lengthened tail-boom. Production deliveries were begun in March 1960, and it was possible to convert the previous Model 47G-2 to G-3 configuration by means of a modifications kit

**Model 47G-3B:** presented in 1961, this sub-variant differed from the Model 47G-3 in having a 260hp Lycoming TVO-435 engine. In Japan, 210 Model 47G-3Bs were built by Kawasaki and designated Kawasaki 47G3B-KH4, nineteen of them went to JGSDF with serials 30201/30219.

**Model 47G-3B-1:** this model was basically similar to the Model 47G-3 but was powered by a 270hp turbo-supercharged Lycoming TVO-435-B1A engine, it also had increased fuel capacity and an 8in wider cabin. A 10lb weight was added to each blade-tip to improve autorotation characteristics and manoeuvrability. With these improvements, gross weight was increased by some 100lb. This model received FAA type approval on 25 January, 1963.

In Great Britain, in 1964, the Model 47G-3B-1 was chosen in preference to the Hiller UH-12E and to the Hughes Model 300 to replace the ageing Saro Skeeters flown by the British Army. A total of 253 machines of this type were produced in Great Britain by Westland (c/n WA.310/459, WA.505/527, WA.564/611, WA.699/731) most of which were procured by the British Army as Sioux AT Mk.1s (XT151/250, XT498/516, XT540/

*The Model 47G-1 c/n 6 was first registered N4929V. It went on the British register as G-ARIA on 8 March, 1961. It is seen here at the 1970 Hannover Air Show. (M Cristescu)*

*Bell HU-13P (BuNo 143143) used by the US Navy in NCSL Panama City. HU-13P was the new designation for the HUL-1 introduced from 1962. This helicopter is seen preserved at NAS Pensacola in August 1974. (M Cristescu)*

570, XT798/849, XW179/195) and dual-control Sioux HT Mk.2 (XV310/XV324). The first Westland Sioux flew at Yeovil (Somerset) on 9 March, 1965, and the last machine was delivered in December 1969. Six Westland Sioux (c/n WA.580/585) were supplied to the South Yemen Air Force with serials 401/406, and Bristow Helicopters Ltd used sixteen aircraft as trainers (c/n WA.716/731, G-AXKK–G-AXKP, G-AXKR–G-AXKZ and G-AXLA). Detail of Westland production is in Appendix X.

**Model 47G-3B-2:** introduced in 1968, this variant was basically similar to the Model 47G-3 but had a 280hp Lycoming TVO-435-G1A supercharged engine for better high-altitude performance over a wide range of temperatures. Fuel capacity was increased to 57US gal, the cabin widened by 8in to 5ft and all-up weight increased by 100lb. The FAA type certificate for this variant was issued on 17 January, 1968.

In all, a total of 389 Model 47G-3B-1s and -3B-2s was built by Bell. A similar variant was produced by Agusta in Italy.

**Model 47G-4A:** this variant, introduced in 1966, was a basic three-seat utility helicopter with 305hp (derated to 280hp) Lycoming VO-540-B1B3 engine. Cyclic and collective controls were hydraulically boosted. Dynamic components, cabin and centre-frame were interchangeable with those of the Model 47G-3B-1 or B-2. Between 6 and 11 May, 1969, a Bell 47G-4A owned by Pacific Southwest Airlines established an unofficial endurance record for helicopters of 121 hours, piloted by C E Keough and L Dolan. Deliveries began in December 1965 and production totalled 269 aircraft. A similar version was manufactured by Agusta in Italy, with 59 produced.

**Model 47G-5 and G-5A:** this model was introduced in 1966 and designed as a low-cost variant in which non-essential structures and components had been eliminated to

*The red and white Model 47B c/n 36 (N116B). This aircraft was still flying in 1990 and belonged to Douglas D Daigle of Santa Ana, California. (Bell)*

*One of the two H-13J-BFs (s/n 57-2729) specially built for President Dwight W Eisenhower. (P M Bowers)*

reduce the price and increase useful load to 1,191lb. Powered by a 265hp Lycoming VO-435-B1A, the Model 47G-5 retained the standard Model 47 rotor system, with stabilising bar, and hydraulically-boosted controls. New equipment included an automotive 12V electrical system and a compact low-profile instrument pedestal. This variant was also available as a two-seat agricultural model (Ag-5, which see), with Bell AgMaster chemical application system or as a three-seat utility model. Deliveries began in January 1966 and production totalled 336. This model was also produced by Agusta.

**Ag-5:** two-seat agricultural model of the 47G-5 equipped with the Bell AgMaster chemical application system (manufactured by Transland Aircraft) comprising various sprayboom lengths. This system weighed about 150lb and included two 60US gal glass-fibre hoppers. Fitted with this equipment, a Model 47 could spray up to 14.4 acres a minute while flying at 60mph.

**Model 47H and 47H-1 Bellairus:** introduced in 1955, this was a deluxe version of the Model 47G. It had an enclosed sound-proofed cabin which could accommodate one pilot and two passengers. The cabin had leather upholstery throughout as well as a leather covered dashboard grouping all electrical switches and carburettor controls. The metal monocoque tail boom contained a luggage compartment.

**Model 47J Ranger:** proposed in 1956, the Model 47J was a four-seat utility version of the Model 47G. The 47J was powered by a 220hp derated Lycoming VO-435. The enclosed cabin had accommodation for the pilot seated centrally in front and three passengers on a cross bench aft. This bench could be removed to allow the installation of two stretchers. The port door could also be removed to permit the use of an internal electrically-powered hoist for rescue missions. Alternative skid or pontoon landing gear could be fitted and metal rotor blades were optional permitting a loaded weight of 2,850lb. Larger capacity fuel tanks (48US gal) could also be installed providing an extended range of 250 miles. This model was also built under licence by Agusta with 152 aircraft built.

**Model 47J-1:** this sub-variant was basically similar to the Model 47J but was powererd by a Lycoming VO-435A.

**Model 47J-2 and J-2A Ranger:** introduced in 1960, this sub-variant was similar to Model 47J but had a 305hp (de-rated to 240hp) Lycoming VO-540-B1B, metal rotor blades, hydraulic power controls and a gross weight of 2,850lb. The Model 47J-2A of 1964 was produced in Italy by Agusta.

**Model 47J-3 SuperRanger:** this variant, produced by Agusta, was powered by a Lycoming VO-540 derated to 260hp. It differed from the standard J-2A in having a modified main transmission able to absorb greater power input. A special ASW version was designed for the Italian Navy with new instrumentation, high efficiency rotor brake and armed with a single Mk.44 torpedo.

**Model 47J-3B-1:** this sub-variant produced by Agusta was a high-altitude version powered by a 270hp Lycoming TVO-435-B1A and equipped with an exhaust-driven supercharger which maintained sea level conditions up to 14,000ft. This model also had a high-inertia rotor and servo-control on the pitch control systems. In all, Agusta produced 123 Model 47J-2/J-3s.

*Texas Helicopter M-79T Hornet is a tandem two-seater derivative of the Model 47 proposed as an armed trainer. (A Pelletier)*

*Model 47G-3 c/n 6859 registered N7965J and owned by James W Kruger, at West Glacier, Montana, in August 1989. (A Pelletier)*

**Model 47K:** *see* HTL-7.

**Model 47L:** *see* HUL-1M.

Some aircraft received special modifications such as a multi-bladed rigid rotor (1960) or a fixed wing with ailerons and flaps. This last aircraft (a Model 47G-2 registered N6723D and nicknamed *Wing Ding*) was converted under the leadership of Jan Drees and flown by Floyd Carlson and Lou Hartwig in 1963. The purpose of the *Wing Ding* programme was to develop an aircraft which would lift very large payloads in excess of its hover capability, taking advantage of running take-offs and landings. In addition to the wing the rotor's mast angle could be varied in flight.

## Military Variants

**YR-13:** in 1947, twenty-eight model 47As powered by the 175hp Franklin O-335-1 were delivered for test and evaluation purposes. They were re-designated YH-13-BE in 1962. Ten were diverted to the US Navy as HTL-1s and three modified as YR-13A-BEs.

**YR-13A:** Three YR-13s were modified for cold weather operations. They were re-designated YH-13A-BE in 1962.

**H-13B:** in 1948 the US Army placed a contract for sixty-five H-13Bs similar to the Model 47D (s/n 48-796/860). These were powered by the 200hp Franklin O-335-3, had the bubble canopy with removable top and retained the four-wheeled undercarriage.

**H-13C:** in 1950, one H-13B, designated YH-13C-BE, was modified by removal of the rear fuselage covering and installation of skids in place of wheels for test purposes. These proved successful and in 1952, fifteen H-13B-BEs were converted to H-13C-BE configuration and fitted with external stretcher carriers.

**H-13D:** similar to the H-13C-BE but powered by a 200hp Franklin O-335-5, with single control and skid undercarriage. A total of eighty-seven aircraft were delivered (s/n 51-2446/2531, 51-16642). In 1962, the remaining examples were re-designated OH-13D-BF.

**H-13E:** similar to the H-13D but with dual controls and a third seat. This variant also incorporated a new main transmission, new tail and a rotor gear box. The engine was a 200hp Franklin O-335-5B. A total of 490 machines was procured (s/n 51-13742/14231). In 1962, the surviving machines were re-designated OH-13E-BF.

**XH-13F (Model 201):** in early 1955, an H-13D-BF was experimentally re-engined with a 280hp Continental-Turboméca XT51-T-3 Artouste shaft-turbine.

**H-13G:** military version of the standard Model 47G fitted with the 200hp Lycoming VO-435. Generally similar to the H-13E-BF, it had a smaller controllable elevator with endplate fins, relocation of the fuel tank, added fuel capacity, new battery and other changes to provide increased stability. This model was geared to operate in conjunction

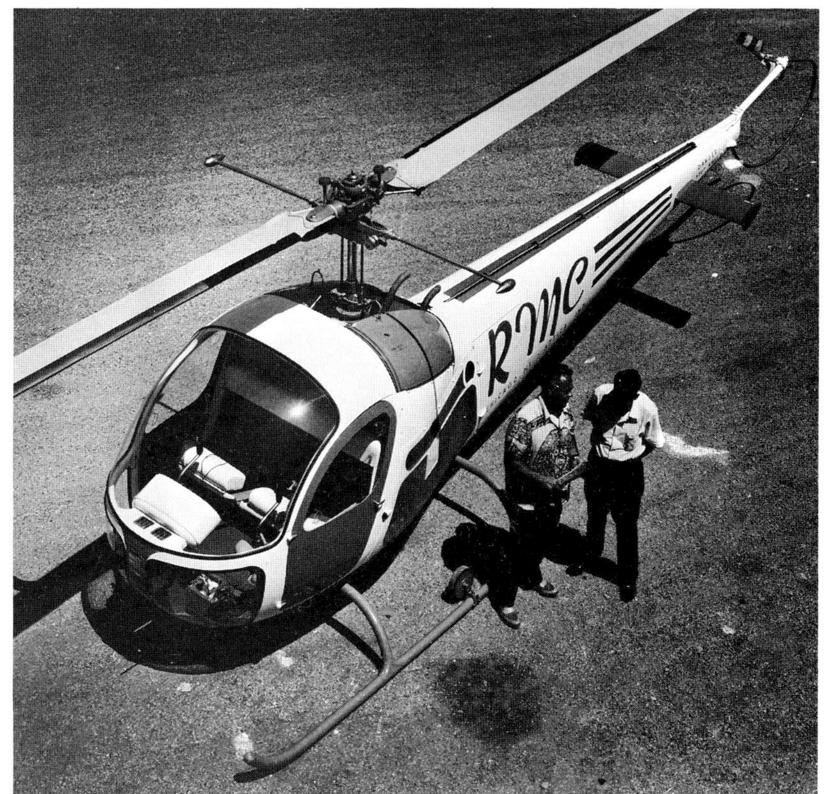

*The Model 47H was the de-luxe version of the Model 47G, here operated by R.M.C.*

with the rotor tilt to improve the centre of gravity range and stability. The H-13G could carry two external litters. A total of 265 examples was delivered to the US Army (s/n 51-14232/14241, 52-7790/7993, 53-3654/3674 and 53-3785/3814). A single machine (s/n 52-7873) was transferred to the US Navy and in 1962 the remaining examples became known as OH-13G-BFs. The naval training version was designated HTL-6 (which see).

**H-13H:** military version of the Model 47G-2 powered by a 250hp Lycoming VO-435-23. This variant was equipped with stretcher evacuation kits, two radios, dual controls, new-type skid undercarriage and bonded all-metal rotor blades. The first H-13H (s/n 55-3355) set up an international helicopter endurance record of 57hr 50min in 1956. Inflight refuelling was accomplished by pouring petrol at regular intervals from 5gal cans into modified tanks whilst hovering just clear of the ground.

Ordered in 1955, the first H-13Hs were delivered in December 1956, production eventually totalling 470 machines (s/n 55-3355/3356, 4613/4633; 56-2161/2244; 57-1792/1875, 6203/6244; 58-1497/1552, 5304/5395, 6984/6998; 59-4911/4972 and 60-6035/6046). Several batches of aircraft were delivered to foreign countries under MAP agreement and a few aircraft were transferred to the US Air Force and became UH-13H-BFs in 1962. At the same time, Army machines became OH-13H-BFs.

**H-13J:** military version of the luxury Model 47J powered by a 240hp Lycoming VO-435-21. Two were procured for use by President D W Eisenhower (s/n 57-2728/2729). They were equipped to carry three people and specially furnished. These aircraft were re-designated UH-13J-BE in 1962.

**H-13K:** late in 1960, two H-13H-BFs were converted to Model 47G-3 configuration by installation of a

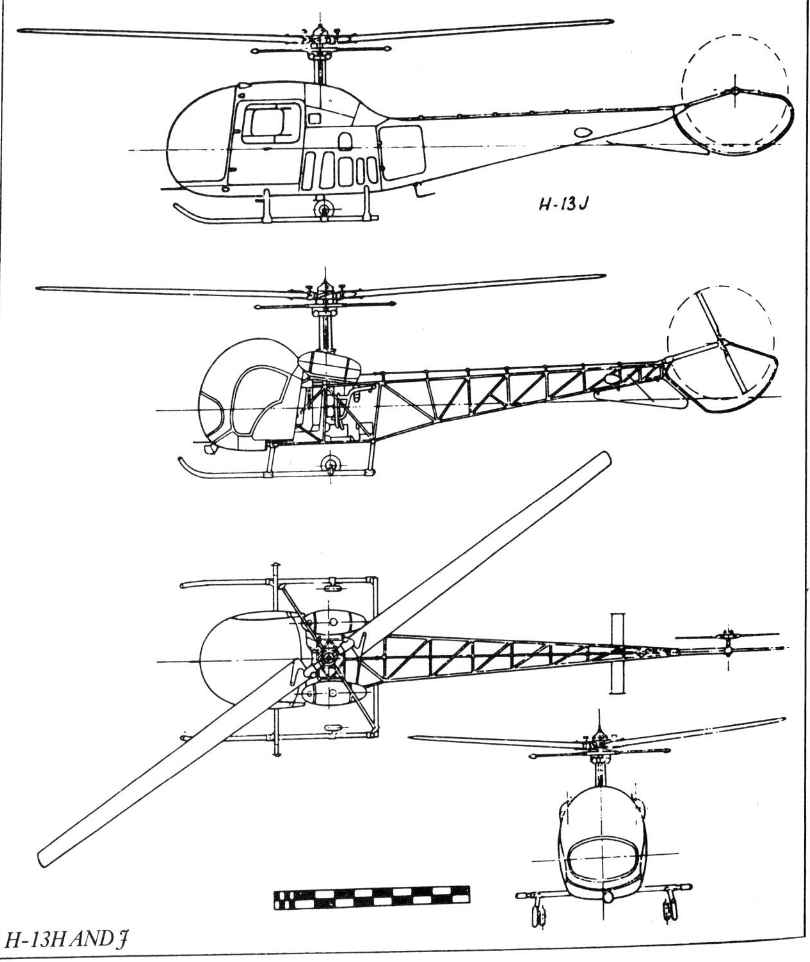

*H-13H AND J*

225hp Franklin 6VS-O-335 and a larger diameter rotor for high-altitude performance evaluation at Fort Rucker. These aircraft were re-designated OH-13K-BF in 1962.

**TH-13L:** new 1962 designation for HTL-4.

**TH-13M:** new 1962 designation for HTL-6.

**TH-13N:** new 1962 designation for HTL-7.

**UH-13P:** new 1962 designation for HUL-1.

**HH-13Q:** new 1962 designation for US Coast Guard's HUL-1G.

**UH-13R:** new 1962 designation for HUL-1M.

**OH-13S:** US Army three-seat observation version of Model 47G-3B procured to succeed the OH-13H. It was powered by 260hp turbo-supercharged Lycoming TVO-435-25(-D1B). The tail boom was extended by 14in, the rotor blades were 1ft longer, the tail rotor drive was extended and gross weight increased to 2,850lb. A total of 265 aircraft of this variant were delivered (s/n 63-9072/9221 and 64-15318/15432).

**TH-13T:** two-seat instrument training version of Model 47G-3B-1 powered by a 270hp Lycoming TVO-435-25(-D1B). The TH-13T was basically similar to OH-13S except that the cabin was 8in wider, with a tinted plastic bubble, the weight of the rotor blade tips was increased for additional inertia and hydraulic boost was installed on the collective control system. This variant also featured additional avionics including VOR, ADF, marker beacon receiver, ILS, gyro-magnetic compass, attitude gyro-system and blind flying hood. An order for 103 aircraft for the US Army was announced in June 1964, followed by further orders for 26 on 17 August, 1965, 91 on 15 October, 1965, 54 on 16 June, 1966, and 141 on 22 June, 1967. Production eventually totalled 411 machines (s/n 64-17845/17903; 65-8038/8080; 66-4273/4298, -8040/8130; 67-15912/15965, -17003/17144 and -17882/17885). First delivery was made in December 1964.

**HTL-1:** designation for a batch of ten YR-13-BEs transferred from the USAF for evaluation purposes (BuNo 122452/122461).

**HTL-2:** designation for twelve Model 47Ds (BuNo 122952/122963) delivered in 1949.

**HTL-3:** nine Model 47Es (BuNo 124561/124569) delivered in 1950/51; another three were procured some years later for the Brazilian Navy (BuNo 144693/144695).

**HTL-4:** Navy version of the Model 47D-1 of which 46 were delivered in 1950/51 (BuNo 128621/128636 and 128887/128916). They were re-designated TH-13L in 1962.

**HTL-5:** in 1951/52, thirty-six machines (BuNo 129942/129977) similar to the HTL-4 but powered by the 200hp Franklin O-335-5 engine, were delivered to the US Navy.

**HTL-6:** Naval training version of the H-13G-BF of which 48 were delivered in 1955/56 (BuNo 142373/142396 and 143148/143171). This variant was similar to the TH-13L with metal tail rotor blades, new rotor brakes, improved cyclic controls, synchronized elevators and other changes. These were all supplied with skid undercarriages but

*The Model 47G-2 c/n 2209 (N6723D) was fitted with a fixed wing to lift large payloads in excess of its hover capability. This aircraft, nicknamed 'Wing Ding' was later put back to its original configuration and owned by Terry L Ewing of North Canton, Ohio. (Bell)*

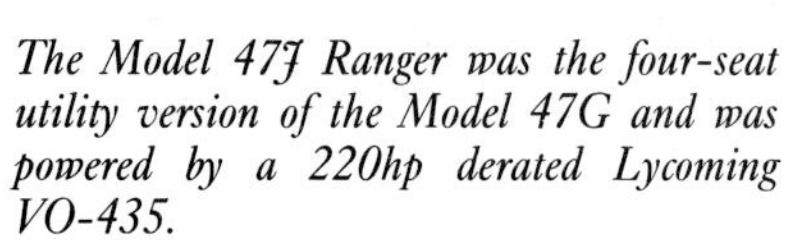

*The Model 47J Ranger was the four-seat utility version of the Model 47G and was powered by a 220hp derated Lycoming VO-435.*

*One of the two HUL-1Gs (No.1338) used by the US Coast Guard in the Behring Sea. (Courtesy of US Coast Guard)*

float kits could be installed. Aircraft BuNo 142386 was later transferred to the Royal Canadian Navy with RCN serial number 1387. In 1962, surviving examples became the TH-13M.

**HTL-7 (Model 47K):** ordered into production in 1957, this was the training version of the Model 47J for the US Navy. The HTL-7 retained the HUL-1 airframe from the firewall back with completely re-styled cabin with all-weather flight instruments, modified training engine (Lycoming O-435-6/-6A), dual controls and side-by-side pilots' seats. Deliveries totalled eighteen machines (BuNo 145837/145854) in 1958, the first of which was delivered in December 1957. Two were used by Bell for the Army–Navy Instrument Programme to develop ideal helicopter instrumentation. Two other examples were used by the US Coast Guards on ice-breakers as general purpose aircraft. In 1962, the remaining machines were re-designated TH-13N.

**HUL-1:** standard Model 47J for general utility and ice-breaker patrol duties with the US Navy, powered by the 260hp Lycoming VO-435-B1B. A total of twenty-eight aircraft was procured in 1955/56 (BuNo 142364/142372, 143134/143147, 147578/147581 and 148277) and one was cancelled (BuNo 142363). They were operated by squadrons HU-1 and VU-2. Two HUL-1s were fitted with HTL-7 flight instruments for operational tests in the Antarctic in the course of the US Navy's IGY Operation Deepfreeze III expedition in 1957–1958. In 1962, surviving examples became UH-13Ps.

**HUL-1G:** two HUL-1s were diverted to the US Coast Guards and modified for search and rescue in

*Bell Model 47G c/n 60 (N140B) owned by L A Heinemann of Boynton Beach, Florida, was converted as a sprayer with twin booms and open cockpit. (J M G Gradidge)*

the Behring Sea. They became HH-13Qs in 1962.

**HUL-1M (Model 47L):** basically similar to the HUL-1 but experimentally powered by the 250hp Allison YT-63-A-3 shaft-turbine. Gross weight was increased to 2,850lb. Two examples were built (BuNo 149838/149839) and they became UH-13Rs in 1962.

**HUL-2:** projected turboshaft-powered version of the HUL-1 with 250shp Allison YT-63-A-3 shaft-turbine; superseded by the HUL-1M.

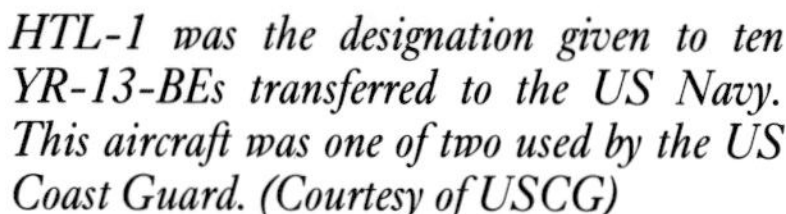

*HTL-1 was the designation given to ten YR-13-BEs transferred to the US Navy. This aircraft was one of two used by the US Coast Guard. (Courtesy of USCG)*

## Service History

The Model 47 was used by a wide range of Army, Navy and Marines units. It participated in war operations twice in the hands of American pilots. The first conflict to see widespread use of helicopters was the Korean war. US ground forces used its brand new Bell H-13Ds for the evacuation of wounded soldiers to the Mobile Army Surgical Hospital units (the famous MASHs). The H-13Ds, deployed in small units of four aircraft (the first of which was the 2nd Helicopter Detachment which arrived at the end of 1950), succeeded in evacuating some 17,700 casualties thanks to outside platforms able to carry stretchers. The Marines used their HTL-4s too, two of which were lost due to enemy action.

At the beginning of the Vietnam war the Army used a number of OH-13 Sioux for observation duties in which they performed well (1st Cavalry Division, 101st Airborne Division). They were replaced later in the conflict by the Hughes OH-6 Cayuse.

The US Coast Guards used two HUL-1Gs and two HTL-1s bought for the USAF for $49,290 in May/June 1947. One crashed in December 1962 (BuNo 122460 ex-s/n 46-253) and the other (BuNo 122461) was put up for disposal in January 1955.

## Foreign Military Customers

The Model 47 was operated by air forces or naval air arms of more than forty foreign countries:

**Argentina:** about six Model 47G-2As and Js were delivered to the Air Force while the Army received three Model 47G-2s and OH-13Hs. The Navy took delivery of six Model 47Ds and three Model 47G-4s which served with the II Escuadra Aeronaval. The Gendarmerie had two Model 47G-3B-1s.

**Australia:** the Royal Australian Air Force used 64 Model 47G-2/G-3/G-3B-1/G-4s (serialled A1- followed by the last three digits of the construction number). The last examples were operated by No.16 Squadron at Oakey along with Cessna 180s and Pilatus PC-6s.

**Austria:** in the mid-1950s, the Austrian Air Force took delivery of several batches of Model 47G-2s and Agusta 47G-2s, which were operated by the light helicopter flying school at Langenlebarn and the helicopter squadron at Hörsching. In 1960, several ex-US Army OH-13Hs were taken on charge by the 2nd Helicopter Squadron at Aigen.

**Brazil:** from 1959, the Força Aérea Brasileira received numerous Model 47s (three Model 47D-1s, twelve Model 47G-2s, three Model 47Js, thirty-six OH-13Hs) which were serialled in the 8500 and 8600 ranges. The Navy had six Model 47D-1s (serialled N-5001/5006) and four Model 47G/Js (serialled N-7003/7006).

*The Continental Tomcat is a specialised single-seat agricultural aircraft based on the Model 47G-2. Here, N9002T is seen at Salinas in October 1976. (J Wegg)*

*The HTL-6 was the naval training version of the H-13G-BF; forty-eight were delivered to the US Navy in 1955/56.*

667, No.2, 7, 11 and 16 Flights, Ind Flight, UNFICYP Flight, 3 CBAS, ARWF, D&T Squadron, 1 RTR, CFS and 28ANZUK Squadron. In addition, two aerobatic teams were established: the Tomahawks and the Blue Eagles. The last Sioux AH Mk.1 was retired on 22 February, 1978, when the last six of 666 Squadron made a flypast over RAF Topcliffe and were flown to RNAY Wroughton for disposal.

**Chile:** the Fuerza Aérea de Chile had three Model 47D-1s (serialled H-01/03) and the Servicio de Aviación Naval de Chile (Navy) had nine Model 47G/G-2As and three Model 47J-2s.

**Colombia:** the Fuerza Aérea Colombiana received 27 Model 47G-3Bs, OH-13D/G/H/J/Ss which were delivered between 1954 and 1961.

**Cuba:** in 1959, the Fuerza Aérea del Ejército de Cuba (FAEC) received four Model 47G-2s and four Model 47Js which were serialled in the H-6/-15 range.

**Dominican Republic:** two Model 47Gs were delivered.

**Ecuador:** the Fuerza Aérea Ecuatoriana used three Model 47Gs.

**France:** the French Air Force, Army, Navy and Gendarmerie operated about forty Model 47Gs and 110 Agusta 47Gs. The Armée de l'Air took delivery in 1956–57 of an estimated eighteen Model 47Gs and fifty AB 47Gs. These were withdrawn from use in 1964–65 and several of them were transferred to ALAT (Army Aviation) and Israel. A single machine found its way to Sénégal. The Aéronavale (French Naval Air Arm) received three Model 47D-1s, five Model 47Gs and eight AB 47Gs between October 1951 and July 1960 which were used by Escadrille 58S.

**Great Britain:** fifty Agusta-Bell 47G-3B-1s went to the British Army (XT101/XT150) as Sioux AH Mk.1s. The first (XT127) was delivered to the British Army on 4 June, 1964, and the last one (XT150) on 25 October, 1964. Aircraft of the XT101/126 batch were delivered to the Middle and Far East. Most of the 253 Model 47G-3B-1s produced by Westland were procured by the British Army as Sioux AT Mk.1s (XT151/250, XT498/516, XT540/570, XT798/849, XW179/195) and dual-control Sioux HT Mk.2s (XV310/XV324). The first Westland Sioux flew at Yeovil on 9 March, 1965, and the last machine was delivered in December 1969. Several Army units flew the Sioux: Squadrons 652 to

**Greece:** the Hellenic Air Force took delivery of six Model 47G-3B-2s and thirteen Model 47G-5s some of which are still operated by 357 Mira at Dekélia. The Army Aviation operates Model 47G-5s.

**Guatemala:** the Fuerza Aérea Guatemalteca operated a single Model 47B which was delivered in February 1949.

**Indonesia:** the Indonesian Air Force (TNI-AU) received a dozen Model 47G/Js some of which were ex-Australian examples.

**Israel:** the IDF/AF operated an unknown number of Model 47Gs and Agusta 47G-2s, some of which had been transferred from France.

**Italy:** the Aeronautica Militare Italiana received large numbers of Agusta 47G-2/Js the last of which

*The M-74 Wasp is a single-seat agricultural conversion of the Model 47G proposed by Texas Helicopter Co. (A Pelletier)*

were operated by Comando Generale delle Scuole at Foggia. The Army Aviation had twelve Agusta 47G-3B-1s, seventeen Agusta 47Js and a number of ex-US Army OH-13Hs. The Navy operated Agusta 47G/Js and Corpo Carabinieri had eleven Agusta 47G-3B-1s and three Agusta 47Js.

**Jamaica:** the Jamaican Air Force received two Model 47G-3B-1s which were delivered in 1963/64 and serialled JDFH-1/2.

**Japan:** the Japanese Ground Self-Defence Force (JGSDF) received seventy-five Kawasaki 47G-2s (serialled 30101/30175) and nineteen 47G-3B-KH4s (serialled 30201/30219) which were operated by 4th Hikotai at Metabaru and 7th Hikotai at Okadama. The Maritime Self-Defence Force (JMSDF) took delivery of eight Kawasaki 47G-2As (serialled 8751/8758).

**Libya:** the Libyan Arab Jamahiriyah Army Aviation operated ten Model 47G-4As and some Agusta 47Gs.

**Madagascar:** the Malagasy Air Force operated one Model 47G loaned from the French Army in 1961.

**Malaysia:** the Tentera Udara Diraja Malaysia took delivery of an unknown number of Model 47G-5As which were operated by 2nd Flying Training School at Keluang (the surviving examples were re-serialled FM2001/2006 and later M24-01 and up).

**Mexico:** the Fuerza Aérea Mexicana (FAM) operated eighteen OH-13s within Escuadrón Aéreo 209 based at Santa Lucia. In 1958 the Mexican Navy received at least six Model 47G/Js (including HMR-27, 29, 30, 128 and 131).

**New Zealand:** RNZAF operated thirteen Model 47G-3B-1/2s (serialled NZ3701/3713). The last five examples are serving with the Central Flying School at Wigram.

**Pakistan:** the Pakistan Army Aviation Wing operates an unknown quantity of Model 47Gs and ex-US Army OH-13s.

**Paraguay:** the Fuerza Aérea del Paraguay took delivery of an estimated twenty Model 47Gs and OH-13s of which two were later transferred to the Navy.

**Peru:** the Fuerza Aérea del Peru received thirty Model 47G/G-3B-1/G-3B-2A/G-5As (serialled in the 611/666 range) of which eight were later transferred to the Army. These were operated by Grupo de Helicópteros 3 at Callao. The Navy operated five Model 47Gs.

**Sénégal:** the Air Force received two Agusta 47Gs from France.

**South Yemen:** the Yemen People's Democratic Republic Air Force took delivery of six Westland 47G-3B-1s (serialled 401/406).

**Spain:** the Ejercito del Aire (Spanish Air Force) received twenty-one OH-13Hs, five Agusta 47G-2s, seven Agusta 47G-3Bs and three Agusta 47J-3B-1s which were operated by ALA75 which later became ALA78. The FAMET (Army aviation) received five OH-13Hs, six OH-13Ss and two Agusta 47G-3B-1s which served during 1967–84 within UHEL XI and CEFAMET. The Armada (Navy) took delivery of six Model 47Gs, one Model 47G-2A, one Model 47G-5, two HTL-4s, two Agusta 47G-2s, one Agusta 47G-2A and one Agusta 47G-2A-1 which equipped the Primera Escuadrilla from 1954 to 1987.

**Sri Lanka:** the Sri Lanka Air Force received six ex-US Army OH-13Hs.

*A Model 47B (possibly NX41967). The car-like cabin was discarded on later variants and replaced by the famous 'fish-bowl' cockpit bubble. (Bell)*

*The Model 47D-1 N78900.*

*The Model 47B-3 crop-dusting helicopter (NC142B) with open cockpit and 178hp Franklin engine was first tested with a covered rear fuselage. (J Wegg)*

**Sweden:** the Swedish Army Air Corps (Arméflygkår) operated a number of Model 47Gs (known as Hkp 1) which were later replaced by Agusta-Bell 206As (Hkp 6A).

**Taïwan:** the Chinese Nationalist Air Force took delivery of an unknown quantity of Model 47Gs and ex-US Army OH-13s.

**Thailand:** the Royal Thaï Army Aviation (RTAA) operated Model 47Gs and ex-US Army OH-13Ss.

**Turkey:** the Turkish Army Aviation received some fifty OH-13H/TH-13Ts.

**Uruguay:** the Air Force received three OH-13Gs (serialled BR-001/003) in April 1955 which were operated by Grupo de Aviación No.5 in Carrasco, and the Navy took delivery of four Model 47G-2s (serialled A-051/054).

**Venezuela:** the Fuerza Aérea Venezolana operated ten Model 47G/Js within Grupo Mixto de Enlace y Reconocimiento (Mixed Liaison and Reconnaissance Group) in Barquisimeto and the Navy had two Model 47Gs.

**West Germany:** the Luftwaffe operated fourteen Model 47G-2s (in 1968 surviving examples were serialled 74-27/74-38) and thirty-one Agusta 47G-2s (in 1968 existing examples were serialled 74-01/74-26). These were operated by HFS-S (Flying school) and were withdrawn from use in 1972–73.

**Zaïre:** the Force Aérienne Zaïroise operates half a dozen Model 47Gs.

**Zambia:** the Zambian Air Force took delivery of sixteen Agusta 47G-4As (serialled AF719/733).

## Model 47B

Rotor diameter 33ft 7½in (10.26m), tail rotor diameter 5ft 5in (1.65m).

Gross weight 2,100lb (956kg).

Cruising speed (75 per cent power) 80mph (128km/h); rate of climb 950ft/min (290m/min); service ceiling 9,700ft (2,960m); range 200miles (320km).

## Model 47D-1

Rotor diameter 35ft 1½in (10.72m); disc area 965sq ft (89.65sq m); overall length 41ft 2½in (12.56m); fuselage length 27ft 4in (8.33m); height 9ft 2in (2.79m).

Empty weight 1,380lb (626kg); loaded weight 2,078lb (943kg).

Maximum cruising speed at sea level 92mph (147km/h); maximum rate of climb at sea level 1,025ft/min (313m/min); climb to 5,000ft (1,525m) 6min; service ceiling 13,000ft (3,965m); hover ceiling in ground effect 6,300ft (1,920m); range (75 per cent power) 214miles (342km).

*The Model 47B NX41967, in front of Bell Aircraft's main building. The glazed nose provided better visibility during landing and take-off. (Bell)*

*The XH-13F-BF. The new engine arrangement is quite apparent. (Bell)*

## Model 47G

Rotor diameter 35ft 1½in (10.72m); disc area 965sq ft (89.65sq m); overall length 41ft 5in (12.62m); fuselage length 27ft 4in (8.33m); height 9ft 5in (2.87m).

Empty weight 1,435lb (651kg); maximum weight 2,350lb (1,067kg).

Maximum speed 86mph (138km/h); cruising speed 70mph (113km/h); initial rate of climb 780ft/min (238m/min); time to 5,000ft (1,525m) 8.2min; service ceiling 10,900ft (2,718m); hover ceiling in ground effect 3,600ft (1,098m); range 212miles (341km).

## Model 47G-2

Dimensions as for Model 47G.

Empty weight 1,564lb (709kg); loaded weight 2,450lb (1,111kg).

Maximum speed 100mph (161km/h); hover ceiling in ground effect 10,850ft (3,310m); range 238miles (383km).

## Model 47G-3B-2

Rotor diameter 37ft 1½in (11.32m); length overall 43ft 2½in (13.17m); fuselage length 32ft 6in (9.90m); height 9ft 3in (2.82m); disc area 1,083sq ft (100.61sq m).

Empty weight 1,860lb (843kg); maximum weight 2,950lb (1,338kg).

Maximum speed 105mph at sea level (169km/h); cruising speed 83mph (133km/h) at 5,000ft (1,525m); initial rate of climb 1,065ft/min (325m/min); service ceiling 17,600ft (5,365m); hover ceiling in ground effect 16,600ft (5,060m); hover ceiling out of ground effect 14,700ft (4,480m); maximum range 250miles (402km).

## Model 47G-4A

Dimensions as for Model 47G-3B-2.

Empty weight 1,823lb (827kg); maximum weight 2,950lb (1,338kg).

Maximum speed 105mph at sea level (169km/h); cruising speed 89mph (143km/h); initial rate of climb 800ft/min (244m/min); service ceiling 11,200ft (3,415m); hover ceiling in ground effect 7,700ft (2,347m); hover ceiling out of ground effect 3,900ft (1,190m); maximum range 259miles (416km).

## Model 47G-5

Dimensions as for Model 47G-3B-2.

Empty weight 1,650lb (748kg); maximum weight 2,850lb (1,293kg).

Maximum speed at sea level 105mph (169km/h); cruising speed at 5,000ft (1,525m) 85mph (137km/h); initial rate of climb 860ft/min (262m/min); service ceiling 10,500ft (3,200m); hover ceiling in ground effect 5,900ft (1,800m); hover ceiling out of ground effect 1,350ft (412m); maximum range 256miles (411km).

## Model 47H-1

Dimensions as for Model 47G except height 9ft 3in (2.82m).

Empty weight 1,502lb (681kg); loaded weight 2,350lb (1,067kg).

Maximum speed 100mph (161km/h); cruising speed 88mph (142km/h); initial rate of climb 820ft/min (250m/min); service ceiling 12,000ft (3,660m); hover ceiling in ground effect 4,300ft (1,310m); normal range 211 miles (339km).

## Model 47J-3B-1

Rotor diameter 37ft 1½in (11.32m); fuselage length 32ft 4¾in (9.87m); overall height 9ft 3½in (2.83m).

Empty weight 1,863lb (845kg); maximum take-off weight 2,950lb (1,340kg).

Maximum speed at sea level 105mph (169km/h); cruising speed at 5,000ft (1,525m) 86mph (138km/h); initial rate of climb 905ft/min (276m/min); service ceiling 17,500ft (5,340m); hover ceiling in ground effect 16,500ft (5,030m); hover ceiling out of ground effect 12,200ft (3,720m); maximum range 210miles (338km).

## Model OH-13S

Dimensions as Model 47G-3B.

Empty weight 1,936lb (878kg); maximum weight 2,850lb (1,293kg).

Maximum speed at sea level 105mph (169km/h); cruising speed at 5,000ft (1,525m) 83mph (133km/h); initial rate of climb 850ft/min (259m/min); service ceiling 18,500ft (5,640m); hover ceiling in ground effect 18,000ft (5,500m); hover ceiling out of ground effect 18,000ft (5,500m); maximum range 250miles (402km).

## HTL-7

Main rotor diameter 37ft 2in (11.33m); overall length 43ft 4in (13.2m); height 9ft 4in (2.84m).

Empty weight 1,618lb (734kg); maximum loaded weight 2,800lb (1,270kg).

Maximum speed 105mph (169km/h); cruising speed 100mph (160km/h); service ceiling 17,000ft (5,180m).

## Model 47 derivatives

The Model 47 design has been such a success that some manufacturers develop their own design re-using more or less Model 47 components or sub-assemblies:

**Carson Super C-4:** this company based in Pennsylvania introduced a number of conversion kits to improve performance of the Model 47. By mid-1963, it had re-engined some forty-five Model 47G/G-2s with the 240hp Franklin 6VS-335A turbo-supercharged engine. It had also designed a new cabin to convert the Model 47 to a four-seater. The latter was known as the Super C-4 and was made originally by splitting the cabin structure transversally and inserting a 24in plug of constant dimensions. At a later date, an entirely new cabin was introduced which was sold as a kit. Changes in weights and performance were as follows:

Maximum take-off weight 2,450lb (1,110kg); maximum speed at sea level 90mph (145km/h); normal cruising speed 80mph (129km/h).

**Continental Copters El Tomcat:** in 1959, Continental Copters Inc of Fort Worth, Texas, developed and produced a specialised single-seat agricultural aircraft based on the Bell Model 47G-2. Known as the El Tomcat Mk.II, this aircraft flew for the first time in April 1959 and received an FAA supplementary type certificate soon afterwards. An improved variant, the El Tomcat Mk.III, made its maiden flight in April 1965 and subsequent variants were progressively introduced: El Tomcat Mk.IIIA in January 1966, El Tomcat Mk.IIIB and El Tomcat Mk.IIIC first flown in May 1968. The Tomcat Mk.III is powered either by a 200hp Franklin 6V4-200-C32, a 210hp 6V-335-A or a 235hp 6V-350-A engine. It weighs empty 1,200lb and 2,450lb loaded. The El Tomcat Mk.V was first flown in June 1968. It is powered by a 220hp Lycoming VO-435-B1A (empty weight 1,375lb and maximum weight 2,450lb).

**Texas Helicopters:** Texas Helicopter Co, which was acquired in 1985 by Aerodyne Systems Engineering Ltd, has developed a single-seat agricultural conversion of the Model 47, known as the M-74 Wasp and a tandem two-seater known as the M-79T Hornet. The prototype of the latter (registered N1001X) received FAA certification on 25 April, 1985. This variant has also been proposed as an armed trainer for AH-64 Apache crews. In both Wasp and Hornet, the fuselage had been redesigned and the Allison 250-C20B engine repositioned. Maximum take-off weight of the Hornet is 3,200lb. In 1989, some thirty-five Wasps and Hornets were on the US civil register.

**Agusta A 115:** this aircraft which began trials during the summer of 1961 incorporated the cabin of the Model 47J, the rotor, tail boom, transmission and undercarriage of the Model 47G and a Turboméca Astazou II turbine derated to 320shp.

Empty weight 1,610lb (731kg); loaded weight 2,977lb (1,351kg).

Maximum speed 105mph (169km/h); hover ceiling in ground effect 13,800ft (4,200m) and range 161miles (260km).

**Elicotteri Meridionali EMA 124:** this three-seat light utility helicopter was designed by Costruzioni Aeronautiche Giovanni Agusta to be manufactured by EMA under licence agreement. The EMA 124 was a derivative of AB-47 with a two-blade semi-rigid main rotor and provision for blade folding. The engine was a 305hp Lycoming VO-540-B1B3 derated to 250hp. With a maximum take-off weight of 2,353lb, the EMA had a maximum speed at sea level of 106mph and a hover ceiling in ground effect of 8,200ft (2,500m). First flight was made in 1970.

**Kawasaki KH-4 and KHR-1:** the Kawasaki KH-4 was a four-seat general-purpose helicopter developed from the Model 47G-3B. Main changes incorporated an all-new cabin, a new instrument layout, a modified control system and larger fuel capacity. The engine retained was a 270hp Lycoming TVO-435-B1A or -D1A. An experimental variant of the KH-4 was the KHR-1 which was modified to test a three-blade rigid rotor system. This aircraft flew for the first time on 26 April, 1968.

**KH-4**

Rotor diameter 37ft 1½in (11.32m); length overall 43ft 7½in (13.30m); length of fuselage 32ft 7¼in (9.93m); height overall 9ft 3½in (2.84m).

Empty weight 1,800lb (816kg); maximum take-off weight 2,850kg (1,293kg).

Maximum level speed 105mph (169km/h); cruising speed 87mph (140km/h); service ceiling 18,500ft (5,640m); hover ceiling in ground effect 18,000ft (5,485m); maximum range 248miles (400km).

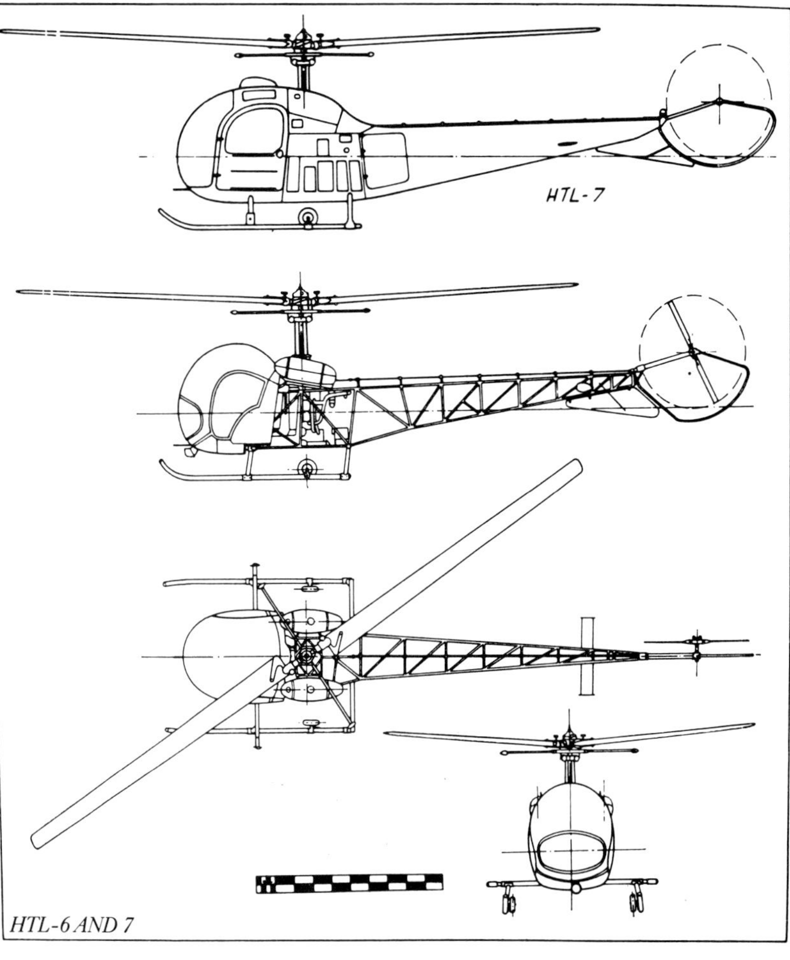

HTL-6 AND 7

# Model 42

*The Model 42 in front of the Niagara Falls plant. (Bell)*

In 1946, accepting the conclusions of a marketing survey, Larry Bell asked the main engineering department of his company to develop for the civil market a much larger helicopter than the Model 47. This was the Model 42 which was in fact a very ambitious aircraft for its time and was presented by Bell Aircraft Corp as 'the helicopter of the future'. It had been calculated to cruise at 130mph over a range of some 450 miles. The rather modern looking Model 42 was a streamlined all-metal helicopter which could carry five people: the pilot's and co-pilot's seat were situated in the fore part of the cabin, and a cross bench for three passengers was located aft. Access to the cabin was via two car-like doors. As powerplant Bell's engineers selected the 450hp Pratt & Whitney Wasp Junior R-985 nine-cylinder air-cooled radial. It was horizontally mounted in the rear fuselage and its adequate cooling was assured by a large airscoop located at the root of the main rotor mast. This rotor, made of wood, was of the symmetrical aerofoil section

*The prototype Model 42 hovering at the Bell factory. (Bell)*

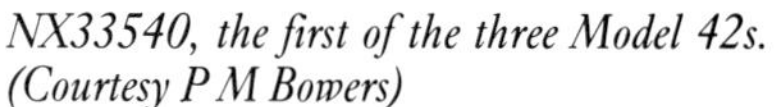

*NX33540, the first of the three Model 42s. (Courtesy P M Bowers)*

two-blade type with the now classic stabilising bar; it had a reduction gear with a ratio of 8.987:1. In addition to the free-wheeling coupling, the transmission included a rotor brake. A three-bladed anti-torque tail rotor, also made of laminated wood, was located on the starboard side of the semi-monocoque tail boom. The undercarriage was of the fixed tricycle type and fuel capacity was 65US gal.

Unfortunately for Bell, the Model 42 had been designed more as an aeroplane than a helicopter and developed teething troubles. As Richard S Tipton recalled, 'the Model 42 was a combination of beauty and the beast. Strip away the 42's comely cover and you'd find a monstrous tangle of cables winding around drums and a chamber of mechanical horrors'. Faced with unexpected difficulties, Larry Bell eventually decided to transfer the responsibility of the Model 42 development to the Gardenville team. After much work and re-design, Arthur Young and Bartram Kelley got most of the bugs out of the prototype (c/n 1, NX33540) and made it fly properly.

In December 1946, the Model 42 was displayed at the Cleveland Air Show. Unfortunately, in those days there was no potential market for such an aircraft. Two more examples were assembled and tested (c/n 2, NX42063; and c/n 3) but no firm orders were placed and the development of the Model 42 came to a halt. Nevertheless, the characteristic silhouette of the Model 42 would re-appear months later with the military Model 48.

None of the Model 42 seem to have survived.

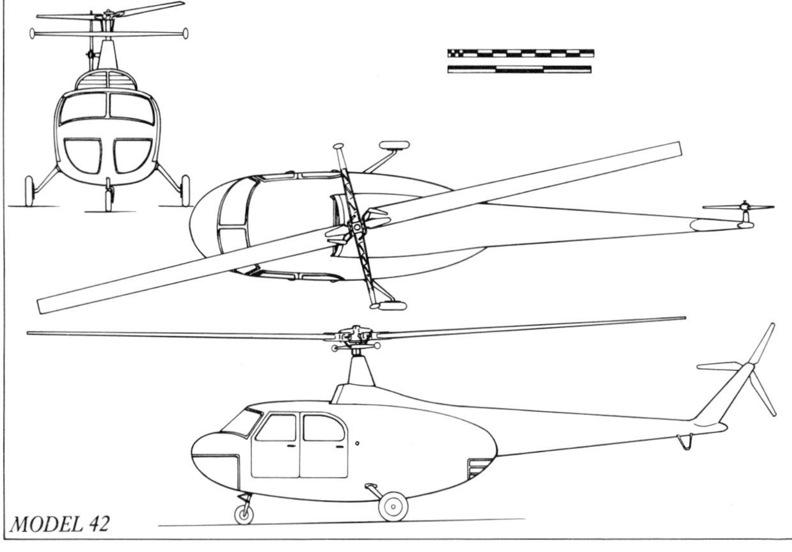

*MODEL 42*

Rotor diameter 47ft 6in (14.48m); tail rotor diameter 7ft 5in (2.25m).

Maximum weight 5,100lb (2,315kg); useful load 1,445lb (656kg).

Maximum speed at sea level 125mph (200km/h); cruising speed (75 per cent power) 100mph (160km/h); service ceiling 13,000ft (3,965m); range 300miles (480km).

# L-39

On 17 May, 1946, Bell Aircraft announced that 'experimentation with the use of sweptback wings in an effort to reach the ultimate goal of man-carrying flight beyond the speeds of sound has passed from the high-speed wind-tunnel stage to the use of full-scale aircraft'.

This announcement marked the first stage development of the US Navy research swept-back wing experimental programme. To do so, two P-63 airframes were diverted for modification: one was an XP-63N with 379 hours of flight time and received the model designation L-39-1 (BuNo 90060); the other was a P-63A-9-BE and received the model designation L-39-2 (BuNo 90061). The main modification consisted of mounting P-63E-like outer wing panels with 35 degrees sweepback. The main undercarriage was not retractable but the nosewheel was still retractable. To modify the centre of gravity position, ballast was installed in the rear fuselage. But it was later discovered that this ballast was insufficient and it was decided to change the four-blade propeller for a lighter three-blade one (from a P-39Q). After further tests, the fuselage was lengthened by four feet, a large ventral fin was added and wing slots installed in the wing leading-edges.

The maiden flight of the L-39-1 was made on 23 April, 1946, at Niagara Falls Airport with A M 'Tex' Johnston, Bell test pilot, at the controls. After several other test flights, the aircraft was ferried to NACA Langley Research Center on 22 August, 1946, by L W Grey. Meanwhile the L-39-2 had been flown by Johnston. This aeroplane was equipped with an automatic fuel equalizer designed to maintain a constant position of centre of gravity during flight. Both aircraft were used to correlate previous wind-tunnel experiments and were also used for various other experiments. For example, in August 1946, L-39-2 was fitted with a circular arc aerofoil developed for the future Grumman XS-2F Tracker.

All tests were halted on 26 August, 1946, and the entire programme was withdrawn. L-39-2 was sent to Langley on 11 December, 1946, and both aircraft were transferred to NACA Lewis Research Center in Cleveland, Ohio, on 12 December, 1949. The two airframes were eventually sold as scrap in 1955.

Span 33ft 6in (10.21m); length 36ft 8⅜in (11.18m); height 12ft 6⅞in (3.83m); wing area 250sq ft (23.22sq m).

Performance unknown.

*The L-39 was mainly developed to study swept wing characteristics. The first L-39 made its maiden flight on 24 April, 1946. (US Navy)*

*The L-39 had a P-63 stock fuselage but the wings incorporated 35degrees of sweep. (US Navy)*

*The second L-39 was modified to have a wing similar to that of the forthcoming X-2. It had a very sharp leading edge. (Bell)*

# Model 44 X-1 and X-1E Model 58 X-1A, B and D

When, during the Second World War, new generation fighters such as the Lockheed P-38 Lightning and the Republic P-47 Thunderbolt entered service, they were the first aircraft capable of reaching high-subsonic velocities in a dive, and thus the first aircraft to encounter the compressibility phenomenon. After numerous accidents had occurred, manufacturers introduced limitations in aircraft diving speeds and airframe strengthening which prevented some accidents (not all) but certainly did not overcome the problem. In fact, this phenomenon was not new to aerodynamicists and engineers. Back to 1935, men such as Theodore von Kármán and Ezra Kotcher had mentioned it and recommended that full-scale tests be conducted with specially built experimental aircraft. In 1943, at Bell, an engineer named Robert Wolf proposed such an aircraft be designed taking advantage of the turbojet engine under development at that time in both the United States and Great Britain. Kotcher also suggested obtaining the assistance of the Army Air Force, the Navy and NACA on this project.

Early in 1944, the Development Engineering Branch of the Materiel Division of the USAAF decided to move forward on research. A small team of engineers and aerodynamicists, among whom were Kotcher and von Kármán, began to investigate the propulsion system of such a transonic aircraft: rocket or jet propulsion was the question. A rocket engine was found to offer the best performance for its lighter weight and was proposed for installation in an aircraft still retaining the general configuration of the future Bell X-1.

While various experiments were conducted by NACA with scale models, important meetings took place at Langley between the Army Air Technical Service Command, the Navy Bureau of Aeronautics and NACA. Discussions led to two different approaches to the transonic aircraft project which would eventually materialize as the turbojet propelled Douglas D-558-1 Skystreak (Navy/NACA) and the rocket propelled Bell X-1 (Air Force/ NACA). During the summer of 1944, Kotcher began to look for an appropriate contractor to build the aircraft and move forward on the so-called MX-524 project. This was not an easy task and, after several unfruitful contacts with aircraft manufacturers, Kotcher attracted the interest of Bob Woods and the Bell Aircraft Corp.

An engineering team was set up at Bell with Stanley Smith as chief project engineer. The first specification draft was completed by December 1944 and, on 16 March, 1945, the first contract (No.W33-038-AC-9183) was signed calling for the building of three aircraft (s/n 46-062/064 designated XS-1 (X standing for experimental and S for supersonic; in 1947, with the introduction of the new USAF designation system, the S was eventually deleted) and to be known as Model 44 within Bell but also as the MX-653 project. Little was known about transonic

*The first X-1 (s/n 46-062). (Bell)*

*The shape of the X-1 was based on the .50 calibre bullet.* (Bell)

flight and associated technologies (materials, aerofoil sections, assembly methods. All was new, all had to be invented). As for the fuselage shape, the Bell team took the 0.50 calibre bullet as a reference, because this bullet was known to be one of the few objects capable of supersonic speeds.

After much discussion, it was decided that the aircraft would be air-launched in order to save fuel for the XLR11 rocket engine then under development at Reaction Motors Inc.

The Model 44 full-scale mock-up was inspected on 10 October, 1945, by Air Force and NACA representatives, and construction began in due course. The X-1 was of conventional aluminium stressed-skin construction. The cross-section of the fuselage was circular and the straight cantilever mid-wing had a NACA 65-110 aerofoil of 10 per cent thickness (aspect ratio 6.03; leading edge sweepback 5°2′52″; no dihedral). Control surfaces were not power-boosted and the X-1 had an all-moving stabilizer; elevators and rudder remained conventional however. The cockpit was pressurized but no ejection seat was provided. The powerplant was a single four-chamber Reaction Motors bi-fuel XLR11-RM3 rocket engine giving a maximum thrust of 6,000lb st at sea level for approximately five minutes and using liquid oxygen and diluted ethyl alcohol as fuels.

Aircraft s/n 46-062 was completed in due course and rolled out minus its engine at Wheatfield on 27 December, 1945. It was then mated to the underside of a Boeing B-29 Superfortress mothership (s/n 45-21800) and first flown as such to Pinecastle Field (Florida) on 19 January, 1946. For the first gliding-flight ballast replaced the still unfitted powerplant and this event took place on 25 January, 1946, with Jack Woolams at the controls. Nine gliding flights were to follow until 6 March, 1946, all by Woolams and some involved incidents (undercarriage collapses on fourth and fifth

*The second X-1 was transferred to the NACA and painted white overall. This aircraft flew for the last time on 23 October, 1951. (NASA)*

*The first X-1 (s/n 46-062) seen at Wright Field on 4 June, 1946. The characteristic silhouette of the X-1 is quite apparent as well as the starboard side access door. (P M Bowers)*

landings). It was then decided to transfer the X-1 to Muroc AFB but, due to modifications to the wings, the aircraft was not ready for its next flight before April 1947.

Meanwhile, the second prototype had been completed and arrived in Muroc on 7 October, 1946. The first glide of No.2 aircraft took place on 11 October with Chalmers 'Slick' Goodlin in the cockpit (Jack Woolams had been killed in an accident on 30 August, while flying a P-39 racer). This glide was followed by three others before the first powered flight took place on 9 December, 1946. During this flight, the X-1 climbed to 35,000ft and achieved a speed of Mach .75/ 510mph.

Several subsequent flights were made until aircraft No.1 arrived at Muroc on 5 April. This aircraft accomplished its first powered flight on 11 April with Chalmers Goodlin in the cockpit (a speed of Mach .77 was achieved). Contractor flights were completed in May 1947 and both aircraft were then turned over to the Air Force. Some weeks later the test flight programme was shared between the Air Force and NACA: the Air Force was to explore the transonic and supersonic speed envelope with the first prototype while NACA would explore the transonic stability and control with aircraft No.2. Three Air Force pilots were selected by Col Albert Boyd: Capt Charles E. 'Chuck' Yeager, Lieut Robert A Hoover and Capt Jack Ridley; and NACA assigned Herbert Hoover and Howard Lilly to its own test programme.

On 6 August, 1947, a first gliding flight was accomplished by Yeager, followed on 29 August, by a powered flight during which the speed of Mach .85 was reached. Several powered flights followed at increasing speeds. Mach .997 was reached on 10 October. On Tuesday, 14 October the B-29 mothership launched the X-1, named *Glamorous Glennis* after Yeager's wife, from an altitude of 20,000ft. The bright-orange air-

*The X-1 had a conventional straight wing with ailerons and flaps and the tailplane incidence was adjustable in flight. (Bell)*

*The second X-1 (s/n 46-063) on final approach. The narrow-track undercarriage is evident. (via P M Bowers)*

craft climbed to 40,000ft and reached the fateful Mach number, the machmeter indicating 1.06. For the first time a man had flown beyond the speed of sound. This performance was not publicized immediately and was revealed to the public more than two months later by *Aviation Week* (22 December, 1947). On 14 October 1947, aircraft No.2 made its first flight with Herbert Hoover in the cockpit; Mach .84 was reached at 24,000ft. The two aircraft accomplished several flights to the end of 1947 and in the first months of 1948. On 10 March, Hoover achieved the first NACA supersonic flight with Mach 1.065, and on 26 March, Yeager reached Mach 1.45 (957mph/1,540km/h) at the controls of the first aircraft. Numerous additional flights were accomplished by both aircraft in the course of the following months in order to explore the flight envelope, some of them being aborted due to engine malfunction (with aircraft No.1 on 31 March, aircraft No.2 on 4 April and aircraft No.1 on 26 April).

For the first time, on 5 January, 1949, the B-29 was not used as Yeager took-off from Muroc with aircraft No.1 in a conventional manner and climbed to an altitude of 23,000ft. Maj Frank Everest was soon assigned to the programme with the task of exploring X-1's maximum altitude. Several altitude record attempts were conducted by this pilot: on 25 July, he reached 66,846ft, on 8 August, 71,902ft and on 25 August, 69,000ft but this last flight was aborted due to loss of pressurization. The last flight of X-1 No.1 was accomplished by 'Chuck' Yeager on 5 December, 1950.

Meanwhile, the flight-test programme had been pursued by NACA with aircraft No.2 but not without incident due to several nosewheel collapses. Successive groundings, a major overhaul and an engine change delayed the programme considerably. Nevertheless, several additional flights were logged by John Griffith and Scott Crossfield. The Bell X-1 No.3 (s/n 46-064) was not delivered before April 1951, i.e.

*The X-1B hung in the modified bomb bay of the Boeing B-29 (s/n 45-21800). The limited ground clearance of the X-1 is clearly apparent in this photograph. (J Wegg)*

*The X-1A-BE (s/n 48-1384) had missions logged on the cockpit side. This aircraft was destroyed on 8 August, 1955. (P M Bowers)*

more than three years later than originally expected. This was mainly due to the new steam-driven turbopump's teething troubles and difficulties with funding. The third X-1 differed only in minor details from its two predecessors; it was externally recognizable by the absence of the restraining straps on the canopy. This aircraft completed its first gliding flight on 20 July with Joseph Cannon in the cockpit. The second flight of the prototype had to be aborted en route and the B-29 mothership landed with the X-1 still hung under its fuselage. This was when jettisoning fuel an explosion occurred followed by a second of far more intensity and then several others. The X-1 was completely destroyed in the accident and the B-29 damaged beyond repair but, fortunately nobody was seriously injured.

On 14 November, 1947, Bell had been authorized by the Air Force to undertake the development of an upgraded version of the X-1 under project number MX–984. A contract (No.W33-038-AC-20062) was signed on 2 April, 1948, calling for the construction of four aircraft and the project was put under the direction of Richard Frost. The Model 58, as it was known within Bell, retained the wings, horizontal tail surfaces and powerplant of the X-1 but had an entirely new fuselage. The fuselage was 4ft 6in longer in order to increase fuel capacity, featured a stepped windscreen and had its cockpit equipped with an ejection-seat.

Of the four aircraft ordered only three were eventually built: X-1A s/n 48-1384, X-1B s/n 48-1385 and X-1D s/n 48-1386. These three aircraft were quite similar and differed only in details. In fact, the X-1D was rolled out first; it had a new low-pressure fuel system and slightly increased fuel capacity. This aircraft made its flying début under the Boeing EB-50A s/n 46-006A with the first gliding flight on 24 July, 1951, with Jean Ziegler in the cockpit. Unfortunately, this flight

*The X-1A and X-1B on Edwards dry lake. There were few external differences between the two aircraft. (Bell)*

*The X-1B in NASA markings. This aircraft is preserved in the USAF Museum at Wright Patterson AFB, Ohio. (P M Bowers)*

*The X-1B was primarily used for pilot familiarization. It accomplished its first gliding flight on 24 September, 1954, with Jack Ridley at the controls. (E M Sommerich via P M Bowers)*

*Charles 'Chuck' Yeager with the X-1* Glamorous Glennis. *(Smithsonian Institution)*

ended with a nosewheel collapse on landing. After repairs, the X-1D was readied for a second flight. During this flight a loss of nitrogen pressure was encountered while the aircraft was still mated to the EB-50A but a short while after the decision had been made to abort the flight, the X-1D exploded. The aircraft was immediately released from the EB-50A and crashed.

The X-1A, painted bright-orange overall, arrived at Edwards AFB on 7 January, 1953, made a first gliding-flight on 14 February and successfully completed its first powered-flight on 21 February with Jean Ziegler at the controls. Several flights followed and on 9 December, Charles Yeager flew the airctaft to Mach 1.9 at 60,000ft. On 12 December, Yeager experienced a loss of control (later known as roll-coupling) while flying at Mach 2.4 at 70,000ft but he was able to recover the aircraft and landed safely. The aircraft was then turned to high-altitude test flights with Maj Arthur Murray as test pilot. The highest altitude was achieved on 26 August, 1954, with 90,440ft. The X-1A was passed to NACA during September 1954 and received some modifications in due course among which was the installation of an ejection seat. The first of the NACA flights took place on 20 July, 1955, with Joseph Walker as pilot. On the following flight, an explosion occurred as the X-1A was still mated to the B-29 and, after several attempts to jettison tanks, it was decided to drop the X-1A which crashed on Edwards AFB bombing range. As further investigation would later prove, the Ulmer leather liquid oxygen tank gaskets were the cause of the accident and also of the loss of X-1 No.3, X-1D and X-2. These gaskets were eventually removed from X-2 No.1, the X-1B and X-1E.

The X-1B arrived at Edwards on 20 June, 1954. The first gliding-flight was completed on 24 September and the first powered flight was made by Maj Arthur Murray on 8 October. After several familiarization flights, the aircraft was turned

*The X-1E (s/n 46-63) was the last variant of the X-1 generation. It accomplished its first gliding flight on 12 December, 1955, with Joseph Walker at the controls. It flew for the last time on 6 November, 1958. (P M Bowers)*

*The Douglas Skyrocket-style canopy was a typical feature of the X-1E. The minimal ground clearance of the aircraft is noteworthy in this photograph.*

over to NACA on 3 December. It was flown again after modification on 14 August, 1955, and suffered a nosewheel collapse on landing. Seventeen flights were accomplished with NACA and further modifications to the aircraft were cancelled due to cracks discovered in the liquid oxygen tank. The X-1B would never fly again.

In April 1952, NACA began considering the possibility of modifying the second X-1 (s/n 46-063) with a new 4 per cent thickness/chord ratio wing and a new low-pressure engine turbopump unit. The aircraft, now known as the X-1E, was ready by late November 1955. In addition to the aforementioned modifications, the X-1E had a new cockpit and canopy to accommodate a new ejection seat and was powered by a Reaction Motors RMI-LR-8-RM-5 still rated at 6,000lb st. The X-1E accomplished its first gliding-flight, with Joseph Walker at the controls, on 3 December, 1955. At least twenty-five other flights were to follow with a maximum speed of Mach 2.24 reached on the seventeenth flight (8 October, 1957). At this stage of the programme several minor modifications were incorporated in the aircraft, including the installation of two ventral fins in order to improve directional stability. A few additional flights were logged and the programme came to an end with the 26th flight (6 November, 1958) after cracks had been discovered in the fuel tank.

During the development of the X-1 many solutions were considered such as a butterfly tail like that tested on the P-63 and a swept-wing (Bell Design D-37). The latter being an interim solution between the X-1 and the X-2. On board armament in the form of a single nose-mounted

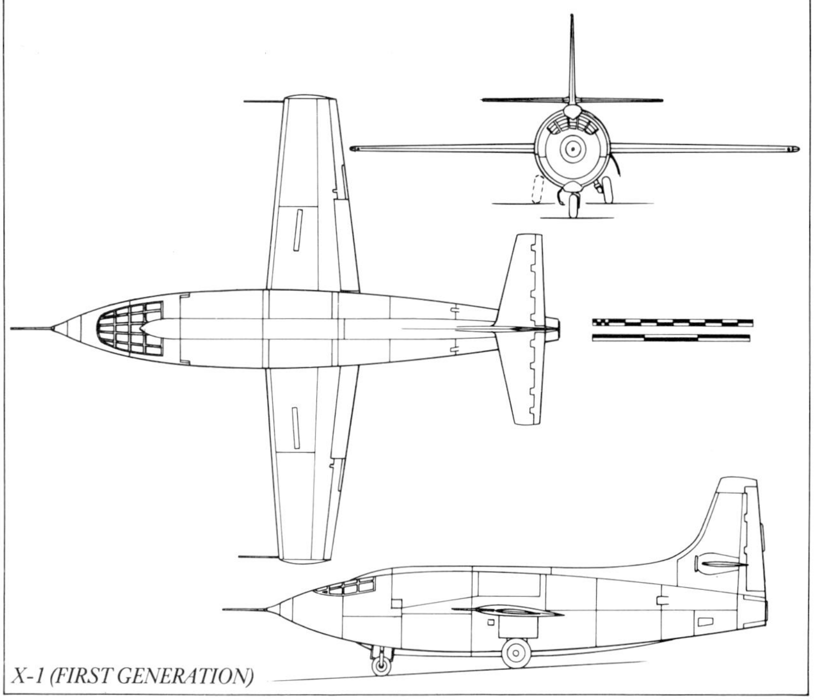

X-1 (FIRST GENERATION)

The X-1A photographed from a chase plane which usually was a North American F-86 Sabre. (Bell)

0.50 cal machine-gun was also considered for installation on the X-1B.

Three X-1s still exist: X-1 s/n 46-062 which is on display at the National Air and Space Museum in Washington, DC; X-1B s/n 48-1385 on display at the US Air Force Museum at Wright Patterson AFB, Ohio, and X-1E s/n 46-063 on display at the Flight Test Historical Museum, on Edwards AFB, California.

## X-1

Span 28ft 0in (8.53m); length 30ft 11in (9.42m); height 10ft 10in (3.30m); wing area 130sq ft (12.08sq m).

Empty weight 7,000lb (3,171kg); gross weight 12,250lb (5,550kg).

Maximum speed Mach 2.44/1,612mph (2,594km/h); maximum altitude 70,000ft (21,330m); endurance 5min.

## X-1A/B/D

Span 28ft 0in (8.53m); length 35ft 8in (10.87m); height 10ft 8in (3.25m); wing area 130sq ft (12.08sq m).

Empty weight 6,880lb (3,117kg); gross weight 16,487lb (7,469kg).

Maximum speed Mach 2.44/1,612mph (2,594km/h); maximum altitude 90,000ft (27,430m); endurance 4min 40sec.

## X-1C

Span 28ft 0in (8.53m); length 35ft+ (10.67m); height 10ft 8in (3.25m); wing area 130sq ft (12.08sq m).

Empty weight 6,880lb (3,117kg); gross weight 16,487lb (7,469kg).

Maximum speed Mach 2.44/1,612mph (2,594km/h); maximum altitude 90,000ft (27,430m); endurance 4min 40sec.

## X-1E

Span 22ft 10in (6.96m); length 30ft 11in (9.42m); height 10ft 10in (3.30m); wing area 115sq ft (10.68sq m).

Empty weight 6,850lb (3,103kg); gross weight 14,750lb (6,682kg).

Maximum speed Mach 2.24/1,450mph (2,333km/h); maximum altitude 75,000ft (22,860m); endurance 4min 45sec.

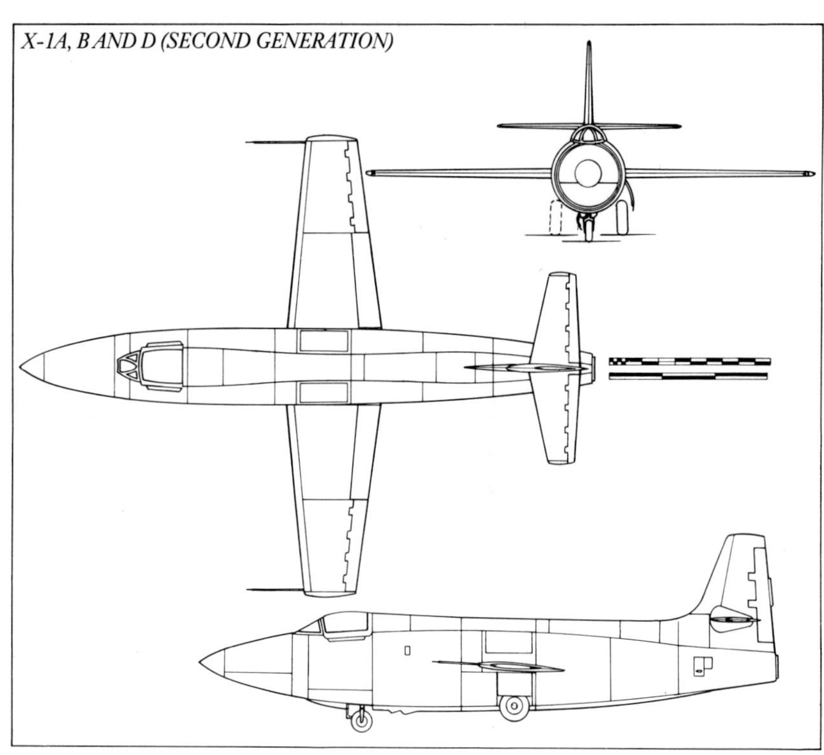

X-1A, B AND D (SECOND GENERATION)

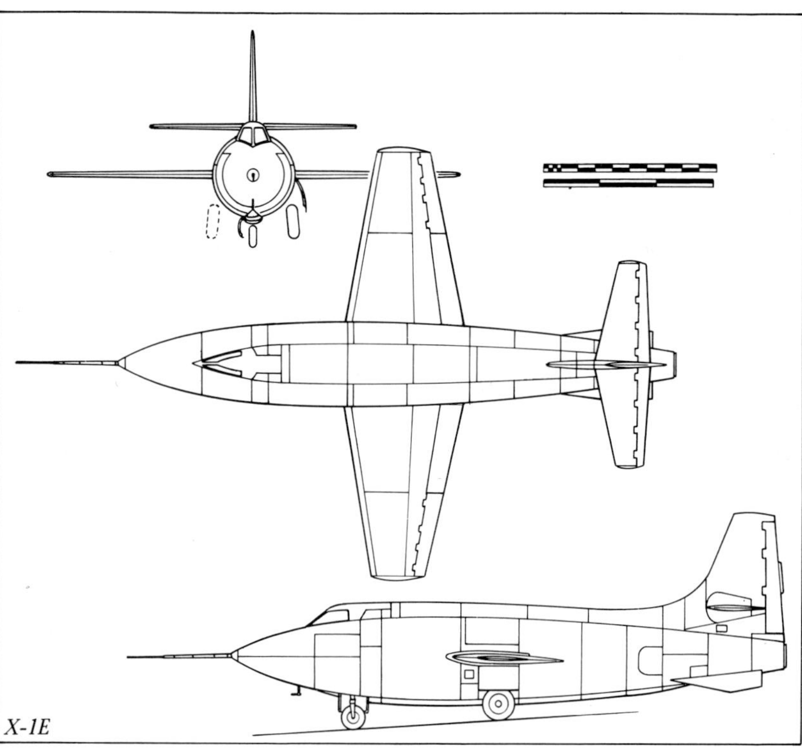

X-1E

# Model 48 R-12/H-12

When in 1946, Bell developed its new general utility helicopter of larger dimensions than the Model 47, the Model 42. The USAAF ordered two prototypes of a military derivative, the Model 48, designated XR-12-BE (s/n 46-214/215) as well as a static test airframe. This contract represented the USAAF's first helicopter procurement from the company and prescribed missions for the XR-12 included personnel evacuation, cargo transport, observation, liaison, general co-operation with ground forces, etc. In fact the Model 48 was quite similar to its civil counterpart; the general configuration was retained with a large two-blade rotor with stabilising

*The first XR-12-BE after roll-out. The Model 48 had a shorter rotor mast than the Model 42. (Bell)*

*A service trials batch YH-12B-BE (s/n 46-225). The classic stabilising bar and its weights are clearly visible. (P M Bowers)*

*The Model 48 was a five-seat general utility helicopter powered by a 550hp Pratt & Whitney R-1340. The first prototype (s/n 46-214) is illustrated. The similarity to the Model 42 is apparent. (Bell)*

*The Bell family in flight: Models 47, 48 and 54. In the foreground is the second XR-12-BE (s/n 46-215) with engine cover and rotor mast fairing removed. (Bell)*

*The first YH-12B-BE (s/n 46-217). The four-wheeled non-retractable undercarriage is shown to advantage. Note the protruding exhaust of the Pratt & Whitney engine. (Bell)*

bar, three-wheel non-retractable undercarriage and streamlined five-seat cabin with car-like windscreen and doors. The engine was a 540hp Pratt & Whitney R-1340-AN-1 Wasp radial mounted horizontally in the rear fuselage with radiator air intake on top. Alternative equipment included flotation gear for water operation (which was tested on aircraft s/n 46-215), rescue hatch and hoist, litters and life rafts.

A first production batch of thirty-four examples (R-12A-BE, s/n 47-491/524) was ordered but never built. This order was cancelled in 1947. Meanwhile, the USAAF had ordered a prototype of an enlarged variant, designated XR-12B-BE (s/n 46-216), able to carry up to ten people. This prototype, known as the Model 48A, was followed by a batch of ten similar service trials YR-12B-BEs (s/n 46-217/226) with the more powerful 600hp Pratt & Whitney R-1340-55 Wasp. The YH-12B was quite different in shape and the undercarriage had four wheels (wheel base 130in; wheel track 84in). The wider cabin had separate doors for the crew and passengers and the nose was nearly all-glazed. Horizontal stabilisers were fitted each side of the tail boom. The anti-torque rotor was now located on the port side of the tail-boom end. At the time, the approximate cost of the YR-12, less government-furnished equipment, was estimated at $175,000.

Initial deliveries of the YR-12s were scheduled for the summer of 1946. However, Bell was faced with serious engineering difficulties with the prototype. The difficulty centred around the main rotor system. Serious blade weaving and rotor governor trouble were encountered. That is why, in April 1946, Bell accepted the assistance of the Propeller Laboratory at Wright Field to overcome these problems. In May 1946, the USAAF considered that the YR-12 'was going to require considerable development and time delay before it was a successful ship' and procurement of the heavier Sikorsky S-51 was then considered. Delivery of the first YR-12 was in September 1946. Flight tests went smoothly but no production batches of the H-12 were ordered. In 1948, the Bell Model 48 and 48A were respectively re-designated XH-12-BE, XH-12B-BE and YH-12B-BE. They were used for a variety of test programmes before being withdrawn from use. None of them is known to have survived.

*The YH-12B was a scaled-up version of the XH-12 capable of carrying five to eight people. (P M Bowers)*

Rotor diameter 47ft 6in (14.48m); fuselage length 39ft 7in (12.06m); overall length 56ft 9in (17.30m); height 11ft 3¼in (3.43m); tail rotor diameter 8ft 6in (2.59m); disc area 1,772sq ft (164.62 sq m).

Loaded weight 6,286lb (2,854kg).

Maximum speed 105mph (168km/h); cruising speed 90mph (145km/h); vertical rate of climb 450ft/min (137m/min); service ceiling 12,800ft (3,960m); absolute ceiling 15,000ft (4,575m); hover ceiling 4,350ft (1,330m); range 300miles (480km).

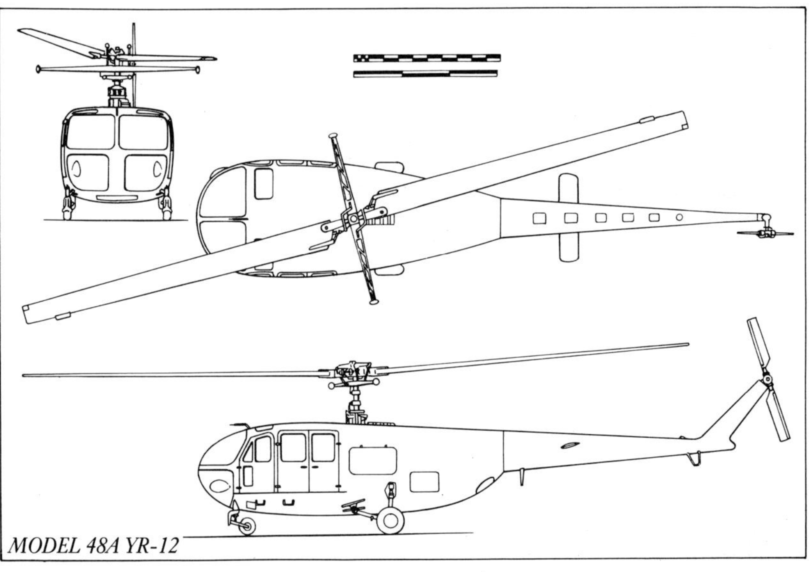

# Model 54 XH-15

By February 1946, action was begun by the USAAF to procure a new type of liaison and observation aircraft. The specification called for a two-seat, single main rotor type of about 3,000lb (1,360kg) gross weight and to be powered by a supercharged engine of approximately 260hp. G & A Aircraft Co (Firestone) of Willow Grove, Pennsylvania, won first place and was awarded a contract for three examples of its 100hp Continental A100 powered XR-14-GA (s/n 46-527/529) which were never built. Bell, with its Model 54 proposal, won only second place in this design competition. But at that time, some AAF personnel advocated a contract with Bell and in May 1946 action was initiated for the building and development of three examples of the Model 54 under the designation

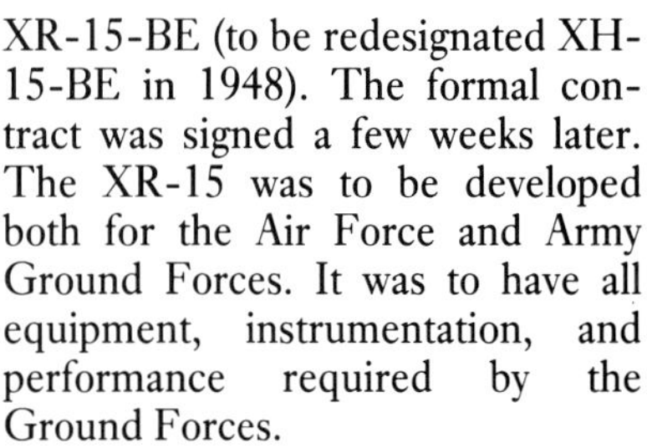

XR-15-BE (to be redesignated XH-15-BE in 1948). The formal contract was signed a few weeks later. The XR-15 was to be developed both for the Air Force and Army Ground Forces. It was to have all equipment, instrumentation, and performance required by the Ground Forces.

The Model 54 was an all-metal four-seat helicopter using the same basic rotor system employed in other Bell models, featuring a two-blade rotor with stabilising bar. Power was provided by one 275hp Continental XO-47-5 engine located at the bottom of the rear cabin. Accommodation was provided for a crew of two seated side-by-side in a largely glazed cabin. It had a semi-monocoque fuselage reinforced with stiffeners and fitted with a horizontal stabiliser, and a tricycle (later quadricycle) non-retractable undercarriage. The two-bladed anti-torque rotor was fitted on the starboard side. Three aircraft were built (s/n 46-530/532) and tested but no production contracts followed. Development of the Model 54 came to a halt at the end of 1950. No XH-15 has survived.

*The XH-15 was a two-seat helicopter intended for observation, liaison, photographic work and communications. Only three prototypes were built. (Bell)*

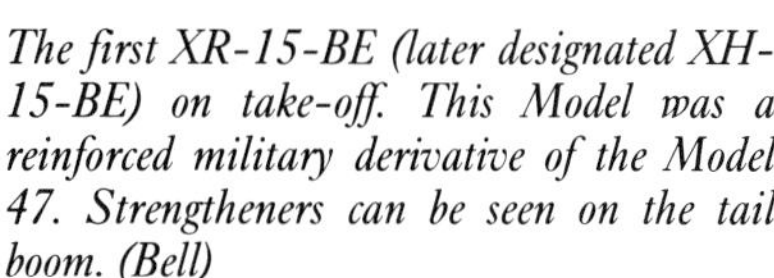

*The first XR-15-BE (later designated XH-15-BE) on take-off. This Model was a reinforced military derivative of the Model 47. Strengtheners can be seen on the tail boom. (Bell)*

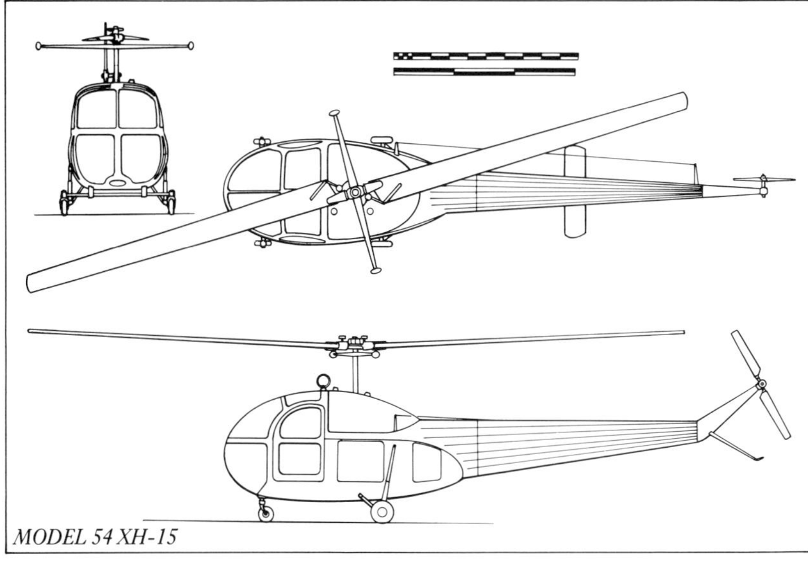

*MODEL 54 XH-15*

Rotor diameter 37ft 4in (11.38m); length 29ft 4in (8.94m); overall length 44ft 9in (13.43m); height 8ft 10½in (2.68m); tail rotor diameter 6ft 5in (1.95m).

Weight 2,800lb (1,268kg).

Maximum speed 105mph (170km/h); absolute ceiling 20,000ft (6,100m); range 200miles (320km).

# Model 60 X-5

On 29 April, 1945, US troops entered Oberammergau, in Bavaria, and situated there was a German research centre totally unknown to allied intelligence services. On 7 May, the Combined Advanced Field Team (CAFT) led by Robert J Woods arrived there to inspect the facility. Among the numerous items discovered was the 80 per cent complete prototype of a single-seat jet aircraft, the Messerschmitt P.1011. This aircraft had been designed early in 1944, at first as a fixed swept-wing fighter, but after withdrawal of the project had been modified by Messerschmitt to explore the behaviour of wings with three fixed sweep angles adjustable on the ground (35, 40 and 45 deg).

*The maximum sweep angle of the X-5 wings was 60 degrees. The entire wing moved fore and aft along the fuselage on rails with changes in wing angle. (Bell)*

The prototype of the P.1011 was completed but its engine, a 1,965lb st Junkers 109-004B turbojet, was unserviceable (originally a 2,870lb st Heinkel-Hirth HeS-011 turbojet had been specified). Nevertheless, the aircraft was disassembled, put into crates and sent to Wright Field. It was not put to any use until it was declared surplus and borrowed by Bell, late in 1948. The first idea of the Bell team was to fly the Messerschmitt with an Allison J35 turbojet and with modified ground-adjustable wings (three positions between 20 and 50 degrees). Unfortunately, the aircraft was badly damaged during delivery preventing the installation of the new engine as well as the inflight variable-geometry device designed by Robert Woods. The team then proposed designing a fighter aircraft of its own using the P.1011 layout as a basis. This proposal was considered more practical and able to give far better results than the war-time Messerschmitt.

Late in 1948, this project was offered to the US Air Force but the USAF's Engineering Division stated that, due to its structure, the aircraft would be unable to carry enough fuel nor the adequate armament required for a good interceptor. As an alternative, Bell proposed building two experimental aircraft (known as Bell Model 60) to prove the validity of Woods' concept. This proposal was accepted with NACA's strong support and, on 26 July, 1949, two Bell X-5 prototypes were ordered under a $2.4 million contract (No.AC-3298), the first of which was to be delivered within a year. Both the NACA and the Wright Field Aircraft Laboratory made a number of suggestions and recommended changes in the design. In fact, the first X-5 (s/n 50-1838) took almost two years to be completed. The full-size mock-up was inspected in December 1949

*The prototype X-5 with wings at intermediate sweep angle. The aircraft flew for the first time on 20 June, 1951, with Jean Ziegler as pilot.*

*The completed Messerschmitt P.1101 with simulated armament painted on the fuselage sides. The original Junkers-Jumo 004B turbojet has been replaced by an Allison J35. (P M Bowers collection)*

*The variable-geometry Messerschmitt P.1101 was taken to the United States at the end of the war. (Bell via P M Bowers)*

and numerous modifications were found necessary. In-depth wind-tunnel tests were conducted at the Langley Laboratories and these led to the introduction of a small ventral fin to increase longitudinal stability. All these improvements and various other technical difficulties resulted in a heavier aircraft than originally expected. The X-5 was powered by a single 4,900lb st Allison J53-A-17 turbojet which was intended to be replaced at a later stage of the development by the more powerful Westinghouse XJ40-WE-2 with afterburner, but this modification never took place. The sweepback angle of the wings could vary from 20 to 60 deg and a 'glove' was designed to assure an optimal airflow at the wing roots. Thanks to Woods' device, the wings moved fore and aft along the fuselage on rails with changes in wing angle in order to maintain stability. Full-span leading-edge slats were fitted and large trailing-edge flaps.

The aircraft was rolled out on 15 February, 1951, and ground testing was begun. The prototype was transported by air to Edwards AFB on 9 June and accomplished its maiden flight on the morning of 20 June with Bell's test pilot, Jean 'Skip' Ziegler, at the controls. During this flight and the three following in July the wings were kept set at maximum span. From the fifth flight (27 July, 1951), sweep-back angle was progressively augmented and maximum sweep-back angle was attained on the ninth flight. The X-5 was officially accepted by the US Air Force on 7 November, 1951, and turned over to NACA which set up an extensive flight-test programme. This programme was found very useful but the various test pilots (J A Walker, A S Crossfield, W P Jones, J P Reeder and S P Butchard of NACA) encountered numerous problems some of them serious. In fact, the Bell X-5 was a difficult aeroplane to fly, being quite unstable under certain circumstances and showing very nasty stall characteristics. But the X-5 provided the engineers with excellent data concerning variable geometry and the Bell white jet also proved to be an excellent chase aeroplane thanks to its flying characteristics.

The second prototype (s/n 50-1839) was delivered at Edwards AFB on 9 December, 1951, and flown the day after by Ziegler. It joined the first aircraft in the flight-test programme a week later after acceptance by the Air Force. On 14 October, 1953, unfortunately, a spin recovery problem led to the loss of the second prototype at Edwards

*The Bell X-5 (s/n 50-1838) with wings at maximum sweep angle. The X-5 was essentially similar to its Messerschmitt forerunner but its structure and systems were much more sophisticated. (Bell)*

*The first X-5 served in the role of chase plane at Edwards AFB for several years before being retired to the USAF Museum. (P M Bowers)*

and caused the death of Maj Raymond Popson. Further tests were made with the surviving example until the autumn of 1955 and on 25 October, 1955, this aircraft was withdrawn from use after completing its 133rd and last flight, with Neil Armstrong at the controls.

## Further development and projects:

For a short period, circa 1949–1951, at the request of Col Victor Haugen, chief of the Aircraft Division, Deputy Chief of Staff for Development, the possibility of developing a fighter variant of the X-5 and modifying both prototypes as such was carefully studied but this project was eventually abandoned. These modifications would have included a redesigned undercarriage, an enlarged cockpit and a strengthened airframe. Derivatives of the X-5 were studied by Bell including several fighter variants. The interceptor variant would have been powered by a 5,200lb st J35-A-17 turbojet and would have flown at 720mph at sea level. Proposed armament consisted of 46 rockets, and there was to have been a nose-mounted AN/APS-19A radar.

Despite its shortcomings, the X-5 research programme could be considered as highly positive. There is no doubt that the huge amount of information gathered during test flights formed an invaluable data basis for the variable-geometry aircraft programmes that were developed in the following years.

The first X-5 prototype (s/n 50-1838) still exists; it is owned by the US Air Force Museum at Wright Patterson (Ohio) where in 1991 it was still in storage awaiting refurbishment.

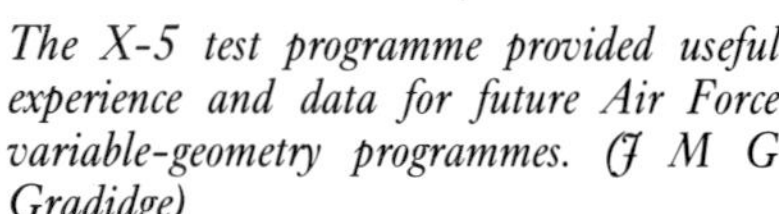

*The X-5 test programme provided useful experience and data for future Air Force variable-geometry programmes. (J M G Gradidge)*

*The first X-5 was retired on 25 October, 1955, after 133 flights. (E M Sommerich via P M Bowers)*

### Messerschmitt P.1101

Span 27ft 0⅜in (8.24m); length 30ft 4⅛in (9.25m); height 9ft 2¼in (2.8m); wing area 170.6sq ft (15.86sq m).

Empty weight 5,733lb (2,600kg); loaded weight 8,974lb (4,070kg).

Maximum speed 609mph at 22,960ft (981km/h at 7,000m); initial rate of climb 4,380ft/min (1,336m/min); service ceiling 45,265ft (13,800m); range 932miles (1,500km).

### Bell X-5

Span maximum 30ft 9⅘in (9.39m), minimum 18ft 7⅕in (5.67m); overall length 33ft 4in (10.16m); height 12ft (3.66m); wing area 175sq ft (16.25sq m).

Empty weight 6,350lb (2,876kg); gross weight 9,892lb (4,487kg).

Maximum speed 705mph (1,134km/h); ceiling 42,000ft (12,800m); range 750miles (1,200km).

# Model 52 X-2

In October 1945 Bell began working on a totally new swept-wing experimental aircraft because a swept-wing version of the Bell X-1 had been found impractical. The initial studies for this new aircraft were made the responsibility of George Ray and led to a contract between the US Air Force and Bell which was signed on 14 December, 1945 (contract No.W33-038-AC-13835). This contract called for the design and construction of two supersonic experimental aircraft designated XS-2. The mission assigned to the XS-2 was to explore very high speeds (Mach 3.5) and altitudes (125,000ft) with the associated compressibility and heat effects.

The swept-wing was then a new concept and almost nothing was known about the behaviour of such a wing configuration on a full-scale aircraft. At the time most of the knowledge consisted of the studies of German and Wright Field engineers. In 1946 a further stage in the understanding of the performance of a swept-wing was achieved with the two L-39 prototypes constructed from P-63 Kingcobra modified airframes in order to study the low-speed performance of the Douglas D-558-2 Skyrocket.

Meanwhile, a design proposal for the Bell Model 52, or X-2 (as the aircraft was now designated), had been proposed to Wright Field in October 1945. For this second aircraft in the 'X' category, various configurations had been considered for the wing position and the fuselage shape, some consideration was given to a variable-sweep wing. Construction of the X-2 began soon after. The airframe structure was designed to sustain the constraints of high speed flight and to fly under 8g manoeuvring load factors. For the first time, new metal alloys were introduced such as K-Monel of which most of the fuselage was made. The wing had 40deg sweepback at 25 per cent chord and a NACA bi-convex aerofoil section (aspect ratio was 4.0 and taper ratio was 0.5; wing dihedral was 3deg). For pilot safety, Bell designed a new system consisting a pressurized, jettisonable nose section. After separation a small parachute was to be deployed to stabilize the capsule and, at an altitude of 20,000ft, the pilot was expected to open the canopy, bale out and use his own parachute. Though originally intended to be powered by a Bell-designed engine, the X-2 was in fact equipped with a single Curtiss-Wright XLR25-CW-1/3 two-chamber rocket unit, developing a continuously variable thrust from 2,500lb to 15,000lb. The 15,000lb thrust rating could be applied for 175 seconds and the 2,500lb thrust rating for 650 seconds.

Ironically, the second X-2 airframe (s/n 46-675) was the first to reach completion. It was rolled out on Saturday, 11 November, 1950, at Bell's Wheatfield minus its rocket engine and prepared for static tests. These tests and preparation for flight took more than eight months. Meanwhile a Boeing EB-50A (s/n 46-011) was prepared to serve as a carrier aircraft. The X-2, now painted white overall, was moved into position and hung under the fuselage of the bomber and both aircraft took off from Buffalo Airport for the first time in July 1951.

After several such captive flights, the X-2 was delivered to Edwards AFB on 22 April, 1952. The first free unpowered flight occurred on 27 June when the X-2 was launched over Edwards AFB with Bell test pilot Jean Ziegler at the controls.

*The X-2 after the main skid strut had been shortened. (Bell)*

*The Bell X-2 on its transport trolley. The X-2 landed on skids and only the front undercarriage unit was equipped with a wheel. (Courtesy P M Bowers)*

Unfortunately the prototype was seriously damaged on landing when the nosewheel collapsed. The test programme had subsequently to be halted for two months. After repairs and modification of the undercarriage, the second free-flight glide took place on 10 October and lasted 6min 46sec. A third flight was made two days later with USAF test pilot Capt Frank Everest in the cockpit (duration 9min 14sec). According to plan, the X-2 was sent back to Bell in order to receive its rocket-engine. Unfortunately, the Curtiss-Wright XLR25 rocket engine was not ready at the time. Numerous technical problems had been encountered and these slowed its development to such an extent that the cancellation of the whole programme was even considered.

Aircraft No.46-674 was completed in turn and joined the unpowered 46-675. As the rocket-engines were still not ready, complementary captive flights were made to check various technical points. At last, a first engine arrived at the beginning of 1953. It was hastily mated to the 46-675 airframe and ground and flight tested during the spring of that year. These first flight-tests were in fact captive flights, the rocket-motor being fired when the aircraft was still under the EB-50A's fuselage. Tragically, on Tuesday, 12 May, 1953, at 18.05, the X-2 exploded, detached from the mothership and fell into Lake Ontario. In this accident Jean Ziegler and Frank Wolko, who was in the bomb-bay, were killed. The cause of this accident was long undiscovered. It was in fact due to the Ulmer leather liquid oxygen tank gaskets.

This accident was obviously a serious drawback to the programme and the second aircraft had now to be readied without delay. This aircraft was ferried to Edwards AFB on 15 July, 1954, and a first glide was made on 15 August with Frank Everest at the controls. This flight showed that the aircraft had a landing instability problem which had to be cured before undertaking any further testing. Once again, the programme was delayed and it was not until late February 1955 that aircraft 46-674 was again ready for flight. A second glide on 8 March ended in a similar way and, once again, the X-2 had to be repaired. The third glide, which was made on 6 April, did not show any significant improvement in the landing behaviour. Bell was asked to find a definitive solution to this problem and, once again, the programme was halted. After several months of research and testing, it was decided to instal a new widened main skid equipped with a 50 per cent shortened oleo-strut, as it has been proved that the high centre of gravity ground attitude was the main reason for the landing instability.

At last, the first powered flight could take place. This happened on 18 November, 1955. During this flight the X-2 reached the speed of Mach .95 (627mph) and an altitude of 32,000ft. A second flight took place on 24 March, 1956 (Mach number reached .91), followed by four others on 25 April (Mach 1.4), 1 May (Mach 1.683), 11 May (Mach 1.8) and 22 May (Mach 2.487), all with Capt Frank Everest at the controls. The seventh powered flight was made by USAF test pilot Capt Iven Kincheloe on 25 May (Mach

*The first prototype X-2. This aircraft logged seventeen flights before being destroyed on 27 September, 1956. The pilot, Capt Milburn Apt, was killed. (Courtesy P M Bowers)*

1.14). At this time, Everest had received a new assignment and Kincheloe became the test pilot in charge of the X-2 flight-test programme. Nevertheless, Everest completed two more flights aboard the X-2: on 12 July, 1956 (8th powered flight; Mach 1.5), and on 23 July (9th powered flight; Mach 2.8706). During the latter, Everest established an unofficial world speed record with a maximum speed of 1,900.34mph. Iven Kincheloe accomplished three more powered flights: the first one took place on 3 August, 1956 (Mach 2.5787), followed five days later by the second (Mach 1.5). The third, in fact the 12th powered flight of the X-2, was on 7 September, 1956, and was the occasion to set a new unofficial world altitude record with 125,907ft. The following flight, which was to be the last of the programme, was accomplished on Thursday 27 September, 1956. This time Capt Milburn Apt was at the controls. An unofficial world speed record was set during this flight (Mach 3.196; 2,094mph), but it came to a tragic end. Following engine shut down, Apt lost control of the aircraft and, after several attempts to recover, decided to jettison the cockpit capsule at an altitude of about 40,000ft. The explosive pistons worked well but, unfortunately, Apt was unable to get out of the capsule and use his parachute. He was killed in the capsule crash. Thus ended the 13th powered flight of the Bell X-2.

Span 32ft 3in (9.83m); length 37ft 10in (11.53m); height 11ft 9in (3.58m); wing area 260.4sq ft (24.19sq m).

Empty weight 12,375lb (5,606kg); gross weight 24,910lb (11,284kg).

Maximum speed Mach 3.196 or 2,094mph (3,369km/h); maximum altitude 126,200ft (38,466m).

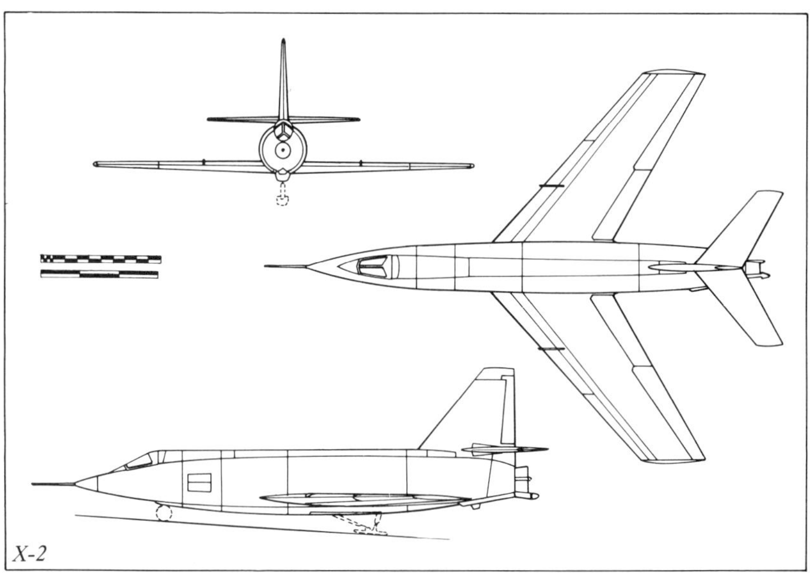

*X-2*

# Model 61 HSL-1

At the end of the 1940s, it became apparent that the helicopters in the Navy's inventory were not of the size to accomplish anti-submarine warfare (ASW) missions. Thus in 1950, the US Navy launched an industry-wide competition for a new helicopter to be designed specifically for the ASW role. In the following June, Bell won this competition and was awarded a contract calling for the building of three prototypes of its Model 61, to be designated XHSL-1 (BuNos 129133/129135). This four-seat machine was the first and would be the only Bell helicopter using the tandem-rotor layout. Nevertheless each of the two rotors were of the basic Bell two blades and automatic stabilising bar. The fore and aft rotors were interconnected and could be folded for carrier operations. Despite the fact that the US Navy would have preferred a twin-engined machine, the Model 61 was powered by a single 2,400hp Pratt & Whitney R-2800-50 engine installed in the centre fuselage and total fuel capacity was 425US gal providing a flight endurance of near-

*A production HSL-1 towing a barge. Note the nose down attitude of the aircraft. (Bell)*

*The first XHSL-1 (BuNo 129133) on flight test. The Pratt & Whitney R-2800-50 engine is clearly visible and the vertical fin has not been fitted. (Bell)*

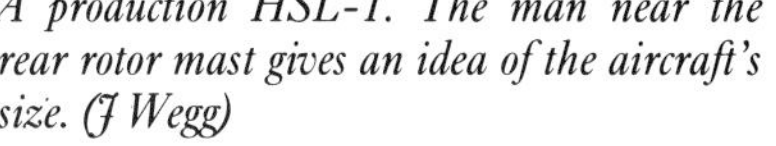
*A production HSL-1. The man near the rear rotor mast gives an idea of the aircraft's size. (J Wegg)*

ly four hours. Armament was intended to include air-to-surface missiles such as the Fairchild AUM-2 Petrel, as well as a dipping ASDIC.

The HSL-1 was equipped with a Bell-developed autopilot which permitted motionless hovering for long

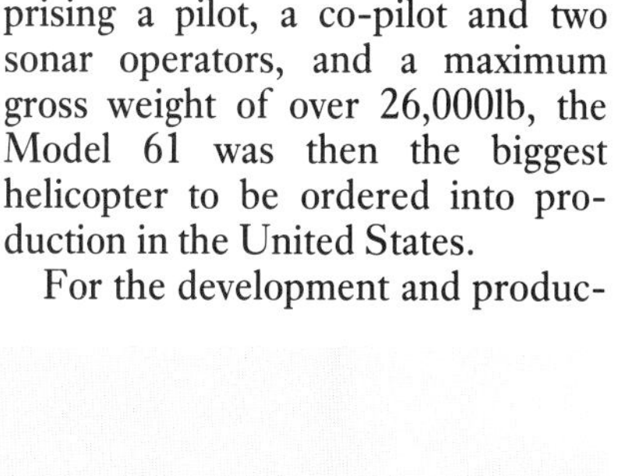
periods. With a crew of four, comprising a pilot, a co-pilot and two sonar operators, and a maximum gross weight of over 26,000lb, the Model 61 was then the biggest helicopter to be ordered into production in the United States.

For the development and production, the Bell Helicopter Division was moved from Buffalo to Fort Worth. The first XHSL-1 flew on 4 March, 1953, but development of the HSL-1 was to be long and difficult. The helicopter suffered many teething troubles, the worst being vibration. After these had been cured, carrier tests were made aboard the escort carrier USS *Kula Gulf* (CVE-108) in March 1955. Even if the HSL performed well in the air, its large size, even with rotor blades folded, was not compatible with the carrier's elevator. Even worse, was its very high level of noise while in stationary flight and this limited the sonar operator's capability of identifying contacts. Due to

*Two production HSL-1s on the flight line of a Naval Air Station. Noteworthy are the stowing frame for the folded rotor blades and the ladders fitted at both ends of the helicopters. (J M G Gradidge)*

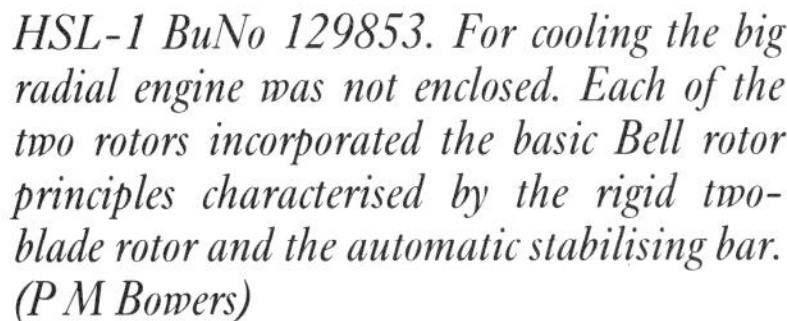
*HSL-1 BuNo 129853. For cooling the big radial engine was not enclosed. Each of the two rotors incorporated the basic Bell rotor principles characterised by the rigid two-blade rotor and the automatic stabilising bar. (P M Bowers)*

*Two prototype XHSL-1s on test. Vertical fins have been fitted to both aircraft in front of the rear rotor mast. In the foreground is XHSL-1 BuNo 129134. (Bell)*

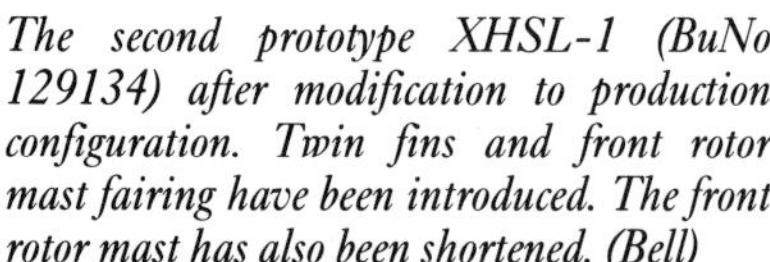

*The second prototype XHSL-1 (BuNo 129134) after modification to production configuration. Twin fins and front rotor mast fairing have been introduced. The front rotor mast has also been shortened. (Bell)*

these shortcomings the first production contract calling for seventy-eight HSL-1s, including eighteen machines under MAP destined for Britain's Fleet Air Arm, was cut back to fifty (BuNo 129154/129168, 129843/129877) in July 1955. A follow-on contract for sixteen more (BuNo 140414/140429) was cancelled. The Navy ordered the Sikorsky HSS-1 Sea Bat instead.

Deliveries to Squadron HU-1 began in January 1957. Production models differed from the prototypes in having stabilising fins at the rear of the fuselage. Nevertheless the HSL-1 programme was not a complete failure because the Bell helicopter demonstrated interesting capabilities in the mine-sweeping role. Six HSL-1s were modified to do this and were operated by the Navy Mine Defense Laboratory in Panama City (Florida), until the end of 1960. The remaining aircraft were used for training or as spares.

A civil variant, the D-116, and two derivatives of the HSL-1 were considered under design numbers D-216 and D-238 but they remained as projects.

Unfortunately, no HSL-1 seems to have survived.

Rotor diameter (both) 51ft 6in (15.7m); length of fuselage 39ft $2\frac{3}{4}$in (11.9m); overall height 14ft 6in (4.4m); width (rotors folded) 11ft $8\frac{1}{2}$in (3.5m); disc area 4,170sq ft (387.4sq m).

Loaded weight 26,500lb (12,020kg).

Maximum speed 115mph (185km/h); cruising speed 96mph (155km/h); range 350miles (563km).

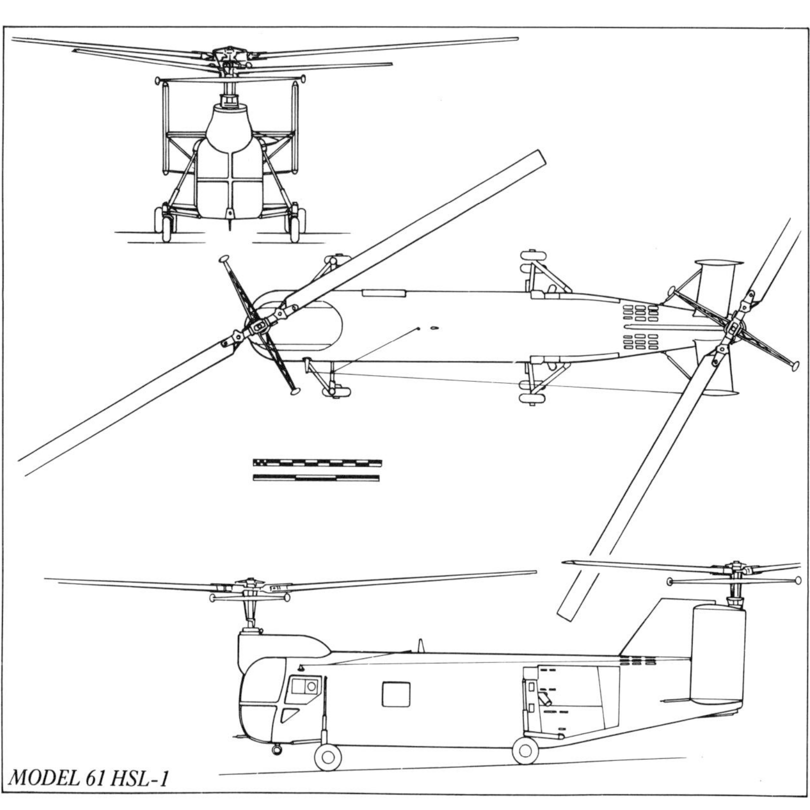

*MODEL 61 HSL-1*

# Model 65 ATV

*The Bell Model 65 in vertical flight. Vertical thrust was provided by two vertically-mounted Fairchild J44 turbojets, each rated at 1,000lb st. (Bell)*

Bell showed interest in VTOL aeroplanes as early as the early 1940s. In January 1941, a patent was taken for a single-engine VTOL tail-sitting fighter with contra-rotating propellers. These studies were followed in 1944 by the design of a twin-engined jet-propelled tail-sitting VTOL tactical aircraft (known as the Young's Convertiplane) which never left the drawing board because the available jet engines were not considered powerful enough.

Studies were taken further when, in 1950, the Bureau of Aeronautics sponsored a competition for a VTOL fighter. Unlike other aircraft manufacturers which proposed a tail-sitting machine (Lockheed XFV-1 and Convair XFY-1), the Bell design team thought that the future VTOL aircraft should remain in a conventional attitude. The XFV-1/XFY-1 programmes were eventually cancelled. In 1952, the Bell proposal for a jet-propelled VTOL fighter led to a feasibility study contract. But the Bell team decided to go beyond that and, as a private venture, initiated the building of a low-cost test vehicle to confirm the viability of their design. The ATV or Air Test Vehicle as it was known (Bell Model 65) was constructed at the lowest cost possi-

*The ATV with flight symbols painted on the nose. The aircraft accomplished only vertical flights and no transitions were ever completed. (J M G Gradidge)*

*The weird shape of the ATV is well in evidence in this side view. This experimental aircraft was built at the lowest cost using existing parts. (J Wegg)*

ble and had a rather weird appearance. The airframe was made of existing parts: wings from a Cessna 170, fuselage from a Schweizer glider and undercarriage from a Bell Model 47. Power came from two 1,000lb st Fairchild J44 lightweight turbojets externally mounted on either side of the fuselage and from an auxiliary Turboméca Palouste turbo-generator which was installed on the back of the fuselage between the two J44s. Its purpose was to deliver compressed air to the attitude control system. Compressed air (2.5lb/sec) was bled in piping through nozzles disposed at the wingtips and tail. Conversions to and from vertical flight were made by rotating the J44 engines 90 degrees.

*A Palouste turbo-compressor, installed between the two J44s, provided compressed air through wingtip and tail nozzles to provide pitch, yaw and roll control. (J M G Gradidge)*

The Model 65 was completed in eight months and, by December 1953, was ready for flight. The first hover flight was made in January 1954 with Dawe Howe at the controls. Unfortunately, a month later, a compressor disc in the starboard engine failed and damaged the fuel lines causing a fire. Dawe Howe escaped uninjured but the machine suffered extensive damage. It was repaired and resumed test flights.

The flight-test programme was terminated in the spring of 1955 by which time the ATV had logged 4½ hours. These comprised only hovering and conventional flights as the ATV never completed any transition from vertical to horizontal flight.

The ATV has survived and is held by the National Air and Space Museum. It was registered N1105V.

Span 26ft (7.93m); length 21ft (6.40m); estimated weight 2,000lb (908kg).

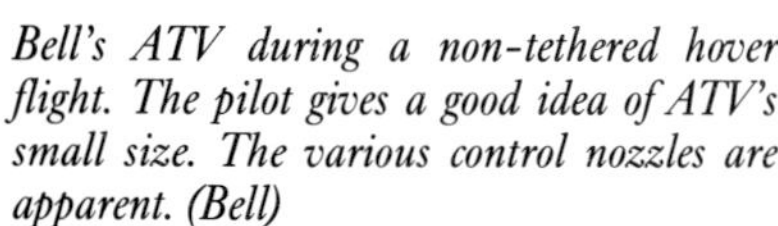

*Bell's ATV during a non-tethered hover flight. The pilot gives a good idea of ATV's small size. The various control nozzles are apparent. (Bell)*

# Model 200 XV-3

In 1943, Larry Bell was quick to realize that a compromise was inevitable between the vertical take-off and landing capabilities of the helicopter and the speed and cruise characteristics of the aeroplane. 'The convertiplane,' he said, 'will open new avenues of aerial transportation that no one dares to dream of now.' Based on this consideration, Arthur Young and Bart Kelley (future Texas Division's chief engineer) began studying various types and flying models of convertiplanes.

In August 1950, a design competition was announced for the development of a practical convertiplane for the Army. And, in 1951, Bell was one of the three companies awarded a joint Army–Air Force contract. The contract was divided into two parts, Phase I and Phase II.

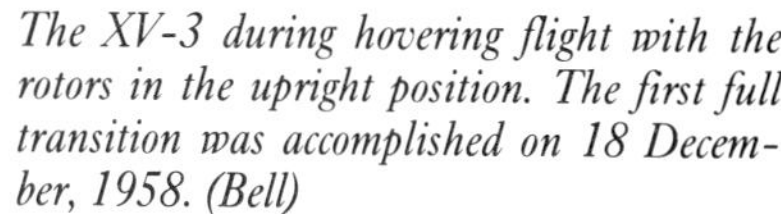
*The XV-3 during hovering flight with the rotors in the upright position. The first full transition was accomplished on 18 December, 1958. (Bell)*

*On the ground the rotor masts of the XV-3 could not be lowered to the fully horizontal position. (Bell)*

Under the Phase I (awarded in May 1951), Bell for the most part devoted its efforts to engineering problems and theory. Following completion of Phase I, a Phase II contract was awarded for the design of the XH-33-BF (later redesignated XV-3-BF) convertiplane which covered further development, prototype construction and testing.

McDonnell presented its Model 82 (designated XL-25-MC, then XH-35-MC and finally XV-1-MC), powered by a 400hp R-975-19 engine, two of which were to be built (53-4016/4017) and Sikorsky its Model S-57 project (designated XV-2-SI).

A mock-up of the Bell Model 200, as it was known by the company, was built and readied for inspection in June 1952, together with a quarter-scale model for wind-tunnel tests which lasted from June to November 1952. A contract for two test aircraft (54-147/148) was awarded in October 1953.

Technically, the Model 200 configuration consisted of a rather conventional fuselage with twin, three-bladed, rotors mounted near the tips of a relatively small wing. Blade section used was a NACA 0015 and blade twist was 18.4deg. The Model 200 was powered by a 450hp Pratt & Whitney R-985-AN-3 nine-cylinder radial engine located behind the four-seat cabin. The rotor mast axis were in the vertical position for helicopter operation and, after a basic speed was reached, the masts were tilted forward, through approximately 90 deg to act as propellers. During the conversion process, which required 10 to 15 seconds, the lift load was transferred from the rotors to the wings. After conversion, a transmission gear shift, similar to an automobile overdrive, was used to reduce rotor speed. In case

*The first complete inflight transition was made at Fort Worth, on Thursday 18 December, 1958, with Bell test pilot Bill Quinlan at the controls. The manoeuvre was described by him as 'smooth and comfortable'. (Bell)*

*The second XV-3 prototype (s/n 54-148) with its two-blade rotor-propellers in the vertical thrust position. A ventral fin has been added under the tail for improved stability. (Bell)*

*The first XV-3 (s/n 54-147) after roll-out. The Pratt & Whitney R-2800 radial engine was installed near the aircraft's centre of gravity. The aeration grids are visible at the fuselage/wing intersection. (Bell)*

of engine failure during 'aeroplane' operation, power-off conversion back to helicopter configuration could be made and the craft merely made a helicopter autorotative landing.

The first aircraft (c/n 1, 54-147) was completed by January 1955 and the three-bladed rotor whirl tests were begun (they would last 100 hours, from January to November 1955) as well as static ground tests (March–August 1955). The second aircraft (c/n 2, 54-148) was completed in April 1955.

The maiden flight of the first prototype took place on 23 August, 1955, at Hurst heliport with chief pilot Floyd Carlson at the controls. This flight lasted approximately five minutes at an altitude of 20ft and Carlson manoeuvred the XV-3 in all directions. The USAAF observers who were present on that day declared themselves quite impressed. The tests were continued for a year until the aircraft was damaged in a crash landing on 23 August, 1956.

New two-bladed rotors were then designed to be mounted on the second prototype. These were tested during 100 hours (April–July 1957) and, after wind-tunnel experimentation (September–October 1957), installed on the second aircraft which flew in January 1958.

After full-scale tunnel tests in October 1958, the first full conversion flight was made on 18 December, 1958, by Bell test pilot Bill Quinlan at Fort Worth. He described the transition as 'smooth and comfortable.'

A three-month preliminary Air Force evaluation, at Edwards AFB, began in January 1959, during which pilots reported that the XV-3 showed considerable flexibility and forgiveness, being capable of comfortable handling at a wide range of airspeeds and configurations. However the most difficult flight regime was hovering the XV-3 in ground effect. Due to marginal power of the engine, the XV-3 was affected by recirculation causing buffeting and thus was less stable than most helicopters. The XV-3 was also found statically and dynamically unstable at speeds below 34.5mph.

*The XV-3 during transition. The rotor masts were tilted by electric motors enclosed in the fairings at each wingtip and movement from horizontal to vertical attitudes was accomplished in 10 to 15 seconds. (Bell)*

*The fuselage of the second prototype XV-3 derelict at Davis Monthan Military Air Disposal Center, Arizona. (B Knowles)*

*The second prototype XV-3 during tests in the 40 by 80ft wind tunnel at the NACA's Ames Research Center, Moffett Field, California. The skids have been discarded for these tests. (NASA)*

First gear shift was made on 13 April, 1959, and the first phase of flight-testing was resumed on 24 April. Robert L Lichten, chief experimental project engineer for Bell Helicopter Corp, was then presented the Dr Alexander Klemin award for the development of the XV-3. A second phase of test flying was then begun. In all a total of more than 250 test flights were made which included 110 full conversions made by nine different test pilots, six of whom converted on their first flight in the aircraft. But flight at the higher speeds indicated some difficulty with the aircraft's flying characteristics and during a wind-tunnel test in 1962 a rotor/pylon instability was encountered.

The XV-3 remained in a hangar from 1962 to 1965, but engineers were working on a solution. Twenty-five additional tests were made in the 40ft by 80ft wind tunnel at NASA's Ames Research Center at Moffett Field in California. Unfortunately, at the conclusion of the test programme, during an investigation at maximum tunnel speed, a progressive failure of the left pylon mounting system caused the loss of that pylon and major damage to the aircraft. Nevertheless, although several technical problems had been found, the general conclusion of the XV-3 programme was that the tilt-rotor configuration demonstrated basic practicability.

The second XV-3A (54-148) survives at the United States Army aviation museum, at Fort Rucker, Alabama.

Rotors diameter 23ft (7.01m); span of fixed wings 31.3ft (9.54m); length of fuselage 30.3ft (9.23m); height 13ft 6in (4.11m); wing area 120sq ft (11.15sq m); disc area 831sq ft (77.2sq m).

Empty weight 3,600lb (1,630kg); loaded weight 4,800lb (2,175kg).

Speed 180mph (290km/h) at 12,000ft (3,660m); initial rate of climb 1,400ft/min (427m/min).

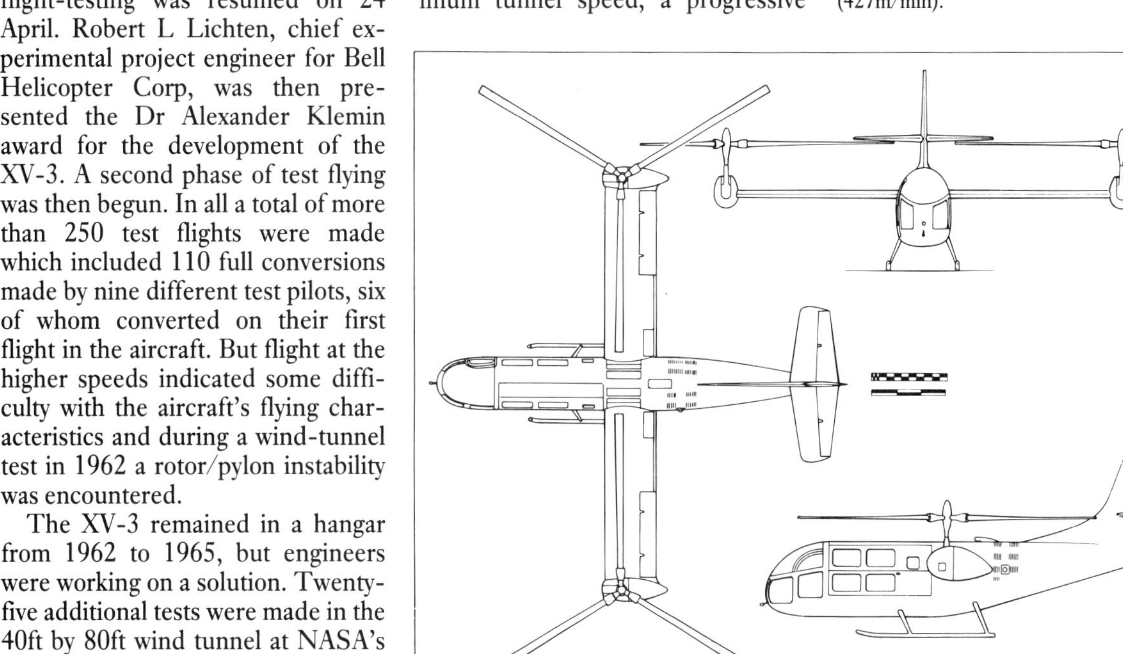

*MODEL 200 XV-3*

# Model 204 H-40 and UH-1A/B/C/E/ F/K/L/M/P Iroquois

The Korean war had shown the great utility of the helicopter in the theatre of operations but it was obvious that its participation would remain limited until more powerful aircraft with greater payload could be developed. That is why, on the basis of a Bell study, the US Army awarded, on 23 February, 1955, a contract for a new utility helicopter to be used primarily for front-line casualty evacuation (Medevac) and with instrument flying training and general duties as secondary roles. The specification for this aircraft was drawn as follows: an 8,000lb payload, a 100 nautical miles mission radius at a speed of 100kt and an hover ceiling outside ground effect of 6,000ft. In addition this aircraft had to be capable of being carried inside a Douglas C-124 Globemaster or a Lockheed C-130 Hercules.

To meet these requirements Bell proposed the Model 204 which was assigned the designation H-40 in the Air Force helicopter category, development of the design being made under the weapon system designation SS443-L. To power the Model 204 the completely new 700shp Lycoming XT53-L-1 free-turbine (turboshaft) was chosen which made the H-40 the first turbine-powered aircraft, either fixed-wing or rotary, ordered by the Army.

Three prototype XH-40-BFs were ordered. These had an all-metal monocoque structure including magnesium parts and the Lycoming engine drove a 44ft diameter two-blade semi-rigid rotor. The classic stabilising bar system remained unchanged. The tail boom incorporated two elevators linked to the cyclic control and the 102in diameter two-blade tail rotor was located on the port side at the top of the fin. The undercarriage comprised two large skids (track 8ft 4in) on which four small wheels could be fitted to facilitate ground movements. The cabin could accommodate up to eight troops or four stretchers in addition to the pilot and co-pilot. The cockpit was spacious and generously glazed ensuring excellent visibility. Empty and gross weights were respectively 3,692lb and 5,650lb.

The first XH-40-BF (c-n 1, s/n 55-4459) was flown for the first time by Bell test pilot Floyd Carlson at Fort Worth on 20 October, 1956, the day that Larry D Bell died and less than 16 months after design work had begun. During the test flights, the Bell helicopter demonstrated a speed range between 124 and 138mph and a service ceiling of 17,500ft.

Before this maiden flight had been achieved, the Army had ordered a service test batch of six YH-40-BFs, and all these were delivered by August 1958. They differed from the prototypes in several respects: they were powered by the 770shp T53 turboshaft and numerous changes had been introduced to the airframe such as a 12in lengthening of the fuselage to increase cabin capacity, reshaped engine cowlings, an increase of ground clearance by four inches, a wider crew door and increased span

*The UH-1B-BF s/n 64-14100 (serialled 115) of Fuerza Aérea Panameña, at Marana Air Park in October 1976. (B Knowles)*

*UH-1M of the 1/18 Cavalry fitted with the M5 turret housing a 40mm grenade launcher and seven-tube M158 rocket launchers. (R J Francillon)*

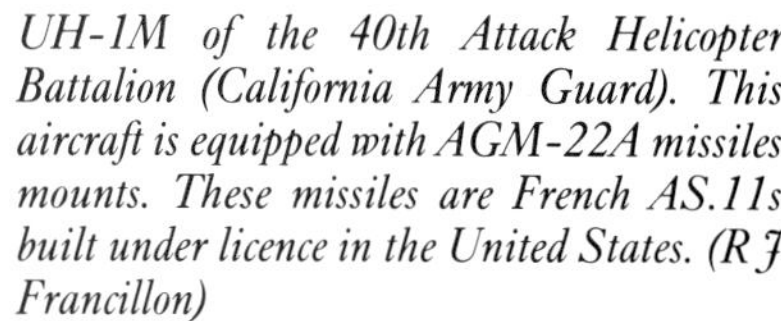
*UH-1M of the 40th Attack Helicopter Battalion (California Army Guard). This aircraft is equipped with AGM-22A missiles mounts. These missiles are French AS.11s built under licence in the United States. (R J Francillon)*

(112in) elevators fitted in a new forward position. Of the six YH-40s, one remained with Bell (together with the XH-40s), one went to Edwards AFB for general evaluation, another went to Eglin AFB for climatic and cold weather testing and the other three were sent to Fort Rucker for Army trials. In 1956, the US Army Aviation introduced a new designation system of its own and the XH-40s and YH-40s were consequently re-designated respectively XHU-1 and YHU-1, the letters HU standing for helicopter utility. Later this HU designation gave birth to the famous nickname Huey, which, although unofficial, was more commonly used than the official name Iroquois. In 1962, the Iroquois became the H-1 in the new tri-Service designation system, with the HU-1A and HU-1B becoming UH-1A and UH-1B respectively.

In 1960, the Bell UH-1 claimed six FAI world records, as follows:

- 19 July, 1960 (with Maj Garrison J Boyle III at the controls); climb to 9,843ft in 3min 29.1sec, and climb to 19,686ft in 8min 7.1sec.
- 22 July, 1960 (with C W O Clifford V Turvey at the controls): speed record on 3km run, at 4,917.42lb, 158.040mph.
- 23 July, 1960 (Col Jack L Marinelli and C W O Clifford V Turvey): speed records over 500km closed-circuit, in E-1 and E-1d classes, 148.481mph.
- 26 July, 1960 (C W O Clifford V Turvey): speed record over 100km closed-circuit, at 4,853.38lb, 142.220mph.

## Production History:

**XH-40-BF:** three prototypes built.

**YH-40-BF:** service test model of which six were built and delivered in 1958. The first one (s/n 56-6723) was later converted to Model 533 high-speed test aircraft to explore compound helicopter configurations.

**HU-1-BF:** pre-production model with 860hp Lycoming T53-L-1A turboshaft. Delivery of the first of these nine pre-production HU-1s was made on 30 June, 1959. Designation changed to UH-1-BF in 1962.

**HU-1A-BF:** first production version initiated in the spring of 1959. These aircraft were generally similar to the YH-40s, with 860hp Lycoming T53-L-1A engines derated to 770shp and incorporated several changes requested as a result of service testing. They are identifiable by their shorter main rotor mast. The US Army order was placed on 13 March, 1959, and deliveries were completed in March 1961. Production totalled 173 aircraft and designation changed to UH-1A-BF in 1962.

**TH-1A-BF:** fourteen HU-1A-BFs were equipped with dual controls and provision for blind flying instrumentation. They were delivered to the Army Aviation School as TH-1A-BF instrument trainers.

**XH-1A-BF:** a single UH-1A-BF (s/n 58-2083) was used for testing various armament installations such as a grenade launcher in the nose.

**YUH-1B-BF:** four prototype aircraft ordered in June 1959 with first flight in April 1960. These aircraft were engined with the Allison T53-L-9 turboshaft. The YUH-1B set an unofficial world's record for helicopters in May 1964, when it flew at 222mph.

*Agusta-Bell AB 204B c/n 3017 serialled 228 in use with 7th Squadron of the Netherlands Naval Air Arm in May 1973. This particular aircraft was previously registered I-MINU. (K Krämer)*

*A UH-1B of the 13th Aviation Battalion at Tan Son Nhut, Vietnam, in February 1966. This aircraft is equipped with the 'Lightning Bug' searchlight, M-21 miniguns and seven-tube 2.75in rocket pod. (US Army photograph)*

**HU-1B-BF:** development of an improved model of the Iroquois began in June 1959 when the Army ordered four prototypes of the YHU-1B. This model was powered by the 960shp Lycoming T53-L-5 engine, or the 1,100shp T53-L-9/9A or T53-L-11 in later batches, and had an enlarged cabin to accommodate a crew of two and seven troops, or three stretchers, two sitting casualties and medical attendant, or 3,000lb of freight. A 13in taller rotor mast and increased-chord rotor blades of honeycomb construction were fitted (21in instead of 14in). These changes made possible a greater all-up weight which now reached 8,500lb and gave the Army a more reliable aircraft. First flight was made on 27 April, 1960, and deliveries began in March 1961. For armed support duties, a rocket pack and an electrically-controlled machine-gun were mounted on each side of the fuselage. Other armament installations included the Springfield Armoury sponsored General Electric M-5 nose-mounted turret with M-75 automatic grenade launcher fed with 107 rounds of 40mm ammunition and the General Electric XM-30 armament system, consisting of two side-mounted XM-140 30mm cannons with central ammunition reservoir and fire-control system. Production continued from March 1961 to 1965, with 1,010 aircraft built. Designation changed to UH-1B-BF in 1962.

*The XM-60 machine-gun on the XM-6 quad mount with 2.75in rockets installed on a UH-1B in Vietnam. (US Army photograph)*

**GUH-1B-BF:** two aircraft (s/n 62-2000 and 64-13960) grounded and used for ground instruction.

**NUH-1B-BF:** one aircraft (s/n 64-18261) built for test purposes.

**UH-1C-BF:** the UH-1Bs were superseded, as the standard Army variant, by the UH-1C improved variant with Model 540 'door-hinge' rotor. In September 1965, Bell introduced the Model 540 rotor with blades of increased (27in) chord, offering some increase in speed and a substantial increase in manoeuvrability through resistance to blade stall. Because of reduced vibration and stress levels, this rotor eliminated previous limitations on maximum level flight speed. In addition the chord of the vertical fin was increased and cambered 7deg to unload the tail rotor during manoeuvres. New elevators were fitted and fuel capacity was increased to 242US gal; overload capacity was now 592US gal. Aerials and the pitot tube were also repositioned. The T53-L-11 engine remained standard and the same armament was carried as on the UH-1B. Deliveries began in September 1965 and production totalled 749. When upgraded with the 1,400shp T53-L-13 engine, the UH-1C was redesignated UH-1M.

**UH-1E-BF:** on 3 March, 1962, Bell won a design competition for an assault support helicopter (ASH programme) for the US Marine Corps, to replace Cessna O-1B/C fixed-wing aircraft and Kaman OH-43D helicopters on VMO squadrons' inventory. Designated UH-1E, this version was generally similar to the UH-1B/C, but had a personnel hoist, a rotor brake, Marine electrical instrument and communication systems, and was of all-aluminium construction. Payload consisted of a pilot and eight troops or 4,000lb of freight. The Model 540 rotor and increased fuel capacity were introduced in 1965.

A small batch of UH-1Bs was ordered in 1962 for evaluation purposes and the first of these flew in February 1963. The first UH-1E (BuNo 151266) was ready in July 1963 and soon entered the evaluation programme and, in December of the same year, carrier qualifications were conducted on board the USS *Guadalcanal*. This aircraft was eventually taken on charge by VMO-1 Squadron (MAG-26) on 21 February, 1964.

Production contracts included several batches: a first batch of forty-eight aircraft was to be deli-

*One of the three XH-40-BF prototypes after roll-out.*

vered during 1964, fifty-two aircraft in 1965 and twenty-seven in 1966; in all a grand total of 192 UH-1Es (c/n 6001/6192) was eventually delivered. On 19 September, 1964, following US involvement in Vietnam, the Chief of Naval Operations requested an armament kit for Marines UH-1Es. Known as TK-2 (Temporary Kit No.2), this included two 0.30 calibre M-60C machine-guns and a bomb rack for a 2.75in rocket pod, mounted on each side of the fuselage. After initial tests and slight improvements, these kits were first delivered to VMO-6 Squadron in Camp Pendleton in January 1965, and more were ordered later. During this period, other armament installations were also successfully tested and ordered such as the twin General Electric 0.50 calibre SM-14 machine-gun pods and the twin M-60 Emerson TAT-101 nose turret originally developed for the experimental Bell Model 207 Sioux Scout. This turret, which contained twin M-60C machine-guns with 1,000 rounds, could swivel through a 220deg arc and could also be deflected 45deg downward and 15deg upward.

**TH-1E-BF**: crew training version of the UH-1E-BF; twenty were built.

**GUH-1E-BF**: one aircraft (s/n 84-0474) grounded and used at Chanute AFB, Illinois.

**UH-1F-BF**: on 7 June, 1963, the Bell Model 204 was selected by the US Air Force in a helicopter design competition for Minuteman and Titan missile site support duties. It was then announced that an initial batch of twenty-five aircraft were to be built. Designated XH-48A in prototype form, this helicopter differed from Army models in being powered by the 1,272shp General Electric T58-GE-3 turboshaft driving a 48ft Model 540 rotor. This new powerplant in an entirely new engine installation and transmission housing had to be redesigned. The XH-48A had provision to handle cargo loads of up to 4,000lb and up to ten passengers could be carried. Normal fuel capacity was of 245US gal and overload capacity was 410US gal. The first flight was made on 20 February, 1964, and the designation was changed to UH-1F. Production totalled 119, with first deliveries to the 4486th Test Squadron at Eglin AFB, Florida, on 23 September, 1964, and the last ones in 1967.

**TH-1F-BF**: instrument and hoist training version of the UH-1F-BF, twenty-seven of which were built for the USAF. First deliveries took place in May 1967.

**GUH-1F-BF**: two grounded aircraft (s/n 65-7922 and 66-1219) based at Kirtland AFB, New Mexico.

**HH-1K-BF**: air-sea rescue version of the UH-1E-BF for US Navy with 1,400shp Lycoming T53-L-13 and revised avionics. A batch of twenty-seven aircraft was contracted (c/n 6301/6327) late in 1968 with deliveries beginning in May 1970.

**TH-1L**: similar to UH-1E-BF but with a 1,400shp T53-L-13 engine and improved electronics, the TH-1L is a training version for the US Navy. A contract was placed for forty-five on 16 May, 1968, with first deliveries in 1969. A total of ninety aircraft was eventually built (c/n 6401/6490).

**UH-1L-BF** utility version of TH-1L-BF for the US Navy with uprated Lycoming T-53-L-13 turboshaft. Eight aircraft were ordered (c/n 6210/6217) on 16 May, 1968, the first of which was accepted on 3 November.

**UH-1M-BF**: small number of modified UH-1C-BFs for the Army in Vietnam. These were fitted with the 1,400shp T53-L-13 turboshaft and with launch rails for six AGM-22A missiles (French AS-11 wire-guided missiles). Some aircraft had the Hughes Aircraft INFANT (Iroquois Night Fighter and Night Tracker) system which used low-light-level TV and searchlights to help aim the side-mounted XM-21 weapons system installation.

*A UH-1B of the 173rd Airborne Brigade equipped with the M-5 40mm grenade launcher. (US Army photograph)*

*UH-1P s/n 63-13165 operated by the 57th Tactical Training Wing at Luke AFB, Arizona, in 1976. Bicentennial markings were applied to this aircraft. (A Pelletier)*

**UH-1P-BF:** psychological warfare variant of the UH-1F-BF. A total of twenty UH-1Fs were converted to UH-1P configuration and used by 1st SOS in Hulburt Field, Florida.

**RH-2:** Research Helicopter 2. One UH-1A-BF was used as a flying laboratory for new instrumentation and control systems. Installations included an electronic control system and high resolution radar in a large fairing above the flight deck, enabling the pilot to detect obstacles ahead of the aircraft in bad visibility.

**HueyTug:** on 3 September, 1968, Bell announced that a UH-1C-BF had been retrofitted with a 2,650shp Lycoming T55-L-7 turboshaft and a 50ft rotor as the prototype of a new flying crane version able to lift a 3-ton external payload (such as a 105mm M101A1 howitzer with ten shells) and hovering out of ground effect at 4,000ft at 14,000lb maximum take-off weight on a 95deg F day. Associated modifications included substitution of a 2,000shp transmission, larger tail rotor (9ft 8in diameter), reinforcement of the airframe (stiffening the boom by riveting external aluminium straps onto each longeron, reinforcing the main rotor pylon and replacing aluminium spar caps with steel caps), fitment of a larger tail boom, and use of a stability control and augmentation system instead of the normal stabiliser bar. These modifications resulted in the aircraft having a gross weight of 14,000lb with external load compared to a maximum loaded weight of 9,500lb for the UH-1C-BF. This new variant, which was named Model 211 HueyTug, had been developed with company funds to demonstrate to the US Army the possibility of modernizing its early-model UH-1s. At the time of announcement, the prototype (registered N6256N) had accumulated more than 200 flying hours in addition to more than 500 hours of testing its dynamic components. The HueyTug made a tour of key Army bases to demonstrate its potential and Bell proposed modifying UH-1B/Cs on inventory as they went through repair and overhaul after combat tours in Vietnam.

**Model 204B:** ten-seat commercial and military export version of UH-1B which received FAA certification on 4 April, 1963. This variant had a 1,100shp T-53-11A turboshaft, tail boom incorporating a 35cu ft baggage compartment, cabin doors with jettisonable emergency exits, and passenger steps on each side, improved outside lights, commercial radio equipment, and fire detection and extinguishing systems. More than seventy were delivered for commercial service (c/n 1501, 2001/2070, 2196/2199).

**Agusta-Bell AB 204B:** following licence-production of the Model 47 under a 1952 agreement, Agusta SpA in Cascina Costa began production of the Bell Model 204B as the Agusta-Bell AB 204B. The Huey 'made in Italy' could be fitted with either a Rolls-Royce Bristol Gnome H.1000/1200 or a General Electric T58-GE-3 turboshaft as alternative to the T-53-11A. It also had standard 242US gal fuel tanks. The first AB 204B flew on 10 May, 1961. Four variant were proposed to customers:

AB 204B-11 with H.1000 engine and 44ft diameter rotor;

AB 204B-12 with H.1000 engine and 48ft diameter rotor;

AB 204B-21 with H.1200 engine

*A camouflaged Norwegian Huey (UH-1B-BF s/n 62-2025) of Squadron Skv 720 belonging to Luftkommando Sor-Norge and stationed at Rygge. (Norwegian Air Force)*

and 44ft diameter rotor;
AB 204B-22 with H.1200 engine and 48ft diameter rotor.

A special ASW version, the AB 204AS which flew for the first time in 1965, was also supplied to the Italian and Spanish navies. Powered by a T58-GE-3, it was designed for individual or dual-role search and attack missions and armed with two Mk.44 homing torpedoes. ASW equipment included a dipping sonar, automatic stabilisation and approach to hover and all-weather instrumentation and an optional AN/APQ-195 search radar. Production of the AB 204B began in 1974 and a grand total of 238 was eventually built, a large number of which were delivered on the Italian civil and military markets.

**Fuji-Bell UH-1B:** on 20 January, 1962, Mitsui & Co Ltd became Bell's Japanese legal licencee in Japan, and Fuji began manufacturing the Model 204B and UH-1B under sub-licence agreement from Mitsui, in its Utsonomiya factory. These aircraft were powered by Kawasaki KT53 engines (assembled from Lycoming-supplied parts) and are recognisable by the tail rotor which is mounted on the starboard side of the tail boom. Initial orders from the Japan Ground Self Defence Force, totalled thirty-six, all of which had been delivered by December 1967. By 31 March, 1969, forty-six UH-1Bs had been delivered to the JGSDF which purchased a further forty-four. A grand total of ninety aircraft (serialled 41501/41590) was eventually delivered to the different Army aviation groups (Homen Kokutai) in Okadama, Kasuminome, Tachikawa, Yao, Metabaru and Fuji. In 1974, six aircraft were evaluated in the attack role being armed with 17mm rocket pods and this successful experiment led to the conversion of twenty aircraft. Deliveries to commercial operators totalled thirty-four Model 204Bs between 1962 and 1973, including three for Asahi Helicopter Co, two for All-Nippon Airways, one for Tokyo Metropolitan Police and one for Japan Domestic Airlines. Several Fuji-built Model 204Bs have also been supplied to Bell in the USA to meet civil orders.

An interesting design was also initiated by Fuji in 1968; this was the XMH which incorporated small wings (span 22ft 3in) and extra stabilising surfaces. Registered JA9009, this experimental aircraft flew for the first time on 11 February, 1970. Flight tests were con-

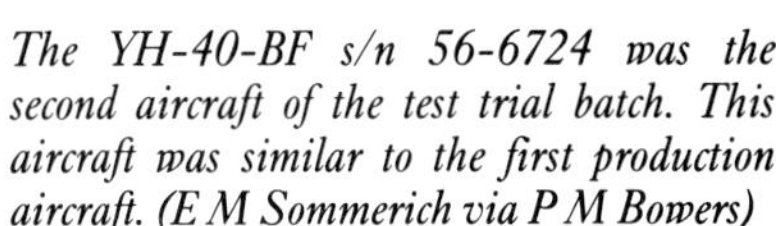
*The YH-40-BF s/n 56-6724 was the second aircraft of the test trial batch. This aircraft was similar to the first production aircraft. (E M Sommerich via P M Bowers)*

*UH-1B-BF s/n 62-1888 in storage at MASDC Davis Monthan, Arizona, in August 1976. This aircraft has since reappeared on the civil register as N5023U. (A Pelletier)*

*UH-1B-BF s/n 62-4612 (c/n 390) of the Royal Australian Air Force operated by No.5 Squadron. The Australian Hueys retained the original constructor's number as serial, here A2-390. This aircraft has since been sold on the US civil market as N345SJ. (M W Prime)*

*The Fuji-built UH-1B s/n 41582 of the Japanese Ground Self-Defence Force (JGSDF) at Kisarazu in May 1973. (Author's collection)*

ducted until 1973 and discontinued after 87 flights. The installation of either two 1,540lb st Teledyne CAE J69S or two 2,645lb st Ishikawa-jimea turbojets was also considered but never adopted.

## Service History

**With the US Army:** the UH-1As were used in the United States within the Aviation and Medical Ambulance Companies and were first sent overseas during the spring of 1960, when two aircraft from the 82nd AD participated in an exercise in the Panama Canal Zone. Early in 1961, the first HU-1As were sent to Korea to serve with the 55th Aviation Company and others were soon deployed to Europe and Alaska.

Bell HU-1As were among the first Army helicopters deployed to Vietnam. The first UH-1As were those of the 57th Medical Detachment (Helicopter Ambulance), which arrived in April 1962 to help in evacuation of ARVN (Army of the Republic of Vietnam) casualties. They were followed, in October, by fifteen armed HU-1As which were operated by Utility Tactical Transport Helicopter Company (UTTCO) from Tan Son Nhut Airport. They had been modified in Okinawa to carry sixteen 2.75in air-to-ground rockets and two 0.30in Browning machine-guns both mounted on the skids. Based in Tan Son Nhut, they soon served as escort to the H-21s from 33rd, 57th and 93rd Helicopter Companies. Reinfored, from November 1962, by eleven HU-1Bs armed with M-6 quad machine-gun systems, they showed good results and in five months of operations (totalling 1,779 combat hours from 16 October, 1962, to 15 March, 1963), only one aircraft was damaged beyond repair due to enemy action. But the Viet Cong soon used heavier weapons against which the armament of the Hueys proved insufficient, as was obvious on 2 January, 1963, during the raid on Ap Bac involving ten H-21s and five Hueys. On that occasion, four H-21s and one Huey were shot down.

In June 1963, the ageing and vulnerable H-21s began to be phased out and replaced by new UH-1Bs. At the end of 1964, 300 Hueys were operating in Vietnam where their prime mission was 'transport of personnel, equipment, supplies, and to serve as an aerial weapons platform'. For the last, a variety of alternative armament installations were developed, the most favoured being the XM-6E-2 (later M-6) flexible quadruple machine-gun mounting (quad mount), with two guns on each side of the fuselage, the XM-3 weapons system comprising a total of forty-eight 2.75in unguided rockets in two packs on the fuselage sides and the M-5 40mm M-75 automatic nose grenade launcher (which was tested at Springfield Armoury, in October 1962). Other armament installations included the XM-16 weapons system with two LAW 54/A rocket launchers containing seven unguided rockets, the M200A-1 rocket pods, the XM-31 gun pod which housed an M24A1 20mm cannon, the M-60CAI 7.62mm machine-gun on Sagami mount, and French SS-11 wire-guided missiles.

Helicopter organisation and use changed throughout the war. In 1964, the Military Assistance Advisory Group (MAAG) decided to form quick response forces known as

*The sole NUH-1B-BF (s/n 64-18261), seen at Lakehurst in August 1974. This aircraft was used for test purposes. (M Cristescu)*

*An armed Huey taking off from a Vietnamese airfield. This aircraft is armed with miniguns and seven-tube 2.75in rocket launchers. A hand operated M60 machine-gun can be seen. (Bell)*

Eagle Flights. These comprised fourteen Hueys (both UH-1Bs and UH-1Cs, commonly known as *Bravo* and *Charlie* models): an armed command and control helicopter, seven ARVN troop carrying ships (commonly known as 'slicks'), five armed Hueys and an Medevac ship. The Eagle Flights could be used at short notice while larger operations (USAF or Air Cavalry) could be set up. Another combat team in use during this period consisted of an Army Huey and an Air Force heavily armed Douglas A-1E Skyraider, acting as a hunter-killer team.

The 1st Cavalry Division (Airmobile) was activated on 1 July, 1965, and settled in An Khe in October. The 1st Cavalry saw major action during the Pleiku campaign in the autumn of 1965 which broke down a North Vietnamese Army offensive in the Ia Drang valley. This huge unit had some 400 helicopters in its inventory. But the number of helicopters operating in Vietnam was still growing and it soon became obvious that a new organisation was necessary. In 1966, under the gunship helicopter programme, this led to the creation of the 1st Aviation Brigade, consisting of seven aviation groups, 15 battalions and four Air Cavalry squadrons. The armed UH-1Bs and Cs were assigned to assault helicopter companies (AHC) within a gun platoon of eight aircraft, five of which were kept at operational readiness.

Among the AHCs engaged in the Vietnam war and which served during most of the Airmobile operations were the 48th, 92nd, 114th, 116th Hornets, 118th Thunderbirds, 119th, 120th Razorbacks, 173rd, 174th, 188th, 197th, 240th Greyhounds and 282nd Black Cats AHCs.

In 1972, three UH-1Bs armed with TOW missiles were sent to Vietnam for operational evaluation. They were eventually used in battle against ARVN mechanized troops during the famous Easter Invasion and the crews of the 12th Combat Air Group claimed not less than 26 tanks destroyed.

**With the US Navy:** when Task Force 116 was established in 1965 with the mission of keeping the Mekong delta free, the need for support helicopters for armed patrol boats (PBR) and Sea-Air-Land (SEAL) commando teams became apparent. But at the time, the Navy lacked such aircraft and eight UH-1Bs had to be loaned from the Army's 197th AvCo. They were formed into four detachments of two aircraft each, the first of which (Det 29) entered action in October 1966. These four detachments were based in Vung Tau, Nha Be, Rung Sat and Vinh Long and became commonly known as Seawolves. Early in 1967, the unit designation was changed to HA(L)-3 (Helicopter Attack [light] squadron) and Seawolves took on charge more Hueys from the 1st Cavalry Division enabling the establishment of three more detachments.

In 1969, as the HueyCobra was entering active service, more Hueys were released to the Navy and thirty-three were on the inventory. Four UH-1Ls and two UH-1Cs were also issued to a special detachment known as the Sealords installed at Binh Thuy. At the end of 1970, the Navy's Huey inventory consisted of twenty-seven UH-1Bs, two UH-1Cs, two HH-1Ks and four UH-1Ls and in the following spring the first UH-1Ms, with T53-L-13 engines, were delivered to HA(L)-3 to replace the Bravo models. HA(L)-3 was deactivated on 26 January, 1972.

In the States, the Navy's UH-1Es and TH-1Ls were operated by HT-18 Squadron of Training Wing 5 stationed at NAS Whiting Field, Florida, and HH-1Ks were flown by HAL-4, HAL-5 (NAS Point Mugu) and HCS-5 (NAS Alameda).

*A sea-air rescue HH-1K (BuNo 157202) of NAS Alameda, California, in October 1975. A total of twenty-seven HH-1Ks was delivered to the US Navy. (J Wegg)*

**With the US Marine Corps:** the first delivery of a US Marine UH-1E to an operational unit (Marine Air Group 26 at New River, North Carolina), was made on 21 February, 1964, and during the spring of 1965, the first armed UH-1Es began to arrive in Vietnam to support Marine ground units. VMO-2 arrived on 3 May, 1965, and VMO-6 in August of the same year; both units were stationed at Marble Mountain, near Da Nang. They flew troop-carrying and escort missions and were usually armed with two fixed 7.62mm M-60 machine-guns on pylons and two rocket pods, each containing seven or eighteen 2.75in rockets, on each side of the cabin. On 27 October, 1965, the Viet Cong attacked Marble Mountain base and destroyed nineteen helicopters of which thirteen were UH-1Es. Several other Hueys were damaged. However, new aircraft were sent to Vietnam. In 1967, two new squadrons were committed in action: VMO-3 which arrived in December and VMO-5 formed for training crews.

After the war the UH-1Es were flown by various Marine units in the States some of the last being HML-771 (MCAS South Weymouth, Washington) and HML-267 (MCAS Camp Pendleton, California).

**With the US Air Force:** first delivery of UH-1Fs to 4486th Test Squadron took place at Eglin AFB, in September 1964. The first UH-1Fs were deployed to South East Asia in 1966 with the 606th ACS based in Nakhon Phanom, Thailand. In June 1967, they were transferred to Vietnam and joined the 20th Helicopter Squadron, which was later (1 August, 1968) renamed 20th Special Operations Squadron. The unit, which flew classified psychological warfare missions ('black' missions), was successively stationed in Nha Trang, Tuy Hoa and Cam Ranh Bay and eventually deactivated in March 1972. This unit operated both armed UH-1Fs and UH-1Ps. The standard weapons system consisted of a pair of LAU-59/A 2.75in rocket launchers and two GAU-2B/A 0.30in mini-guns.

## Foreign Operators

Abroad, the Hueys were operated by the air arms of the following eighteen nations:

**Australia:** this country was the first foreign customer to order the UH-1. From September 1962, the Royal Australian Air Force took delivery of twenty-four UH-1Bs (serialled A2-384/391, A2-714/721, A2-1018/1025) which served with No.9 Squadron in Williamstown and then in Fairbairn. These aircraft were engaged in the Vietnam war and logged 223,487 sorties for the loss of

*Numerous Hueys found their way on to the US civil register. UH-1F-BF s/n 66-1213 (c/n 7109), seen here, was registered N491DF in October 1986. (J Wegg)*

five machines. Some of these aircraft were sold on the civil market in 1990 (A2-388, -390 and -720 becoming N234SJ, N345SJ and N456SJ respectively). The Royal Australian Navy received three UH-1Bs (serialled N9-881/883) as well as four UH-1Cs (N9-3101/3104) which served with No.723 Squadron based in Nowra.

**Austria:** after Italy, Austria was the first foreign customer for the AB 204B. The first AB 204Bs out of a total of twenty-six were delivered in May 1963. The AB 204Bs served with the 3rd Helicopter Squadron and were coded 4D-BA to BZ. All were withdrawn from use in September 1981.

**Colombia:** nine UH-1Bs (serialled 271/279) served with Escuadrón de Helicópteros stationed in Melgar.

**Costa Rica:** the Seguridad Pública used two ex-Panamanean Air Force UH-1Bs (registered TI-SPO and TI-SPP).

**Greece:** the Hellenic Army received three AB 204Bs (coded EΣ -401/EΣ -403).

**Honduras:** four ex-US Army UH-1Bs were delivered.

**Italy:** thirty AB 204Bs delivered to the Air Force were used by No.31 Stormo TS in Rome-Ciampino and the Scuola Volo Elicotteri in Frosinone. Forty-eight AB 204Bs went to Army Aviation serving with No.51 Gruppo Squadroni Elicotteri Multiruolo in Viterbo. Thirty-four AB 204ASs (serialled MM80362/80378 and MM80507/80523) were delivered to the Navy serving with No.2 Grupelicot AMM in Catania-Fontanarossa.

**Norway:** at least thirty-six UH-1B/Cs (using the last three digits of the USAF s/n as code) served with Skv 339 in Bardufoss and Skv 720 in Rygge.

**Panama:** twelve ex-US Army UH-1Bs were delivered in 1976/77 (serialled 102, 111/117).

**Singapore:** thirty ex-US Army UH-1Bs were delivered.

**South Korea:** twenty-five ex-US Army UH-1Bs were delivered.

**Spain:** the army aviation (FAMET) used six UH-1Bs (serialled HU.8-5/10) for training and the Navy four AB 204ASs (serialled Z.8-1/4) for ASW duties, all of which have been withdrawn from use.

**Sweden:** seven AB 204Bs were delivered to the Air Force (designated Hkp 3B and serialled 03421/03427) serving with Flygflottiljer F1 in Västerås-Hässlö, F10 in Ångelholm-Barkåkra and F21 in Luleå-Kallax. Twelve similar AB 204Bs were delivered to the Army Aviation (serialled 03301/03312) and served with Arméflybataljon 1 (AF1) in Boden.

**Thailand:** an unknown quantity of UH-1A and Bs was taken in charge.

**Turkey:** at least twenty AB 204Bs were delivered to the Army and three AB 204ASs to the Navy (coded TCB-31/33) and based in Karamürsel.

**Uruguay:** six ex-US Army UH-1Bs are serving with Grupo de Aviación 5 in Carrasco.

**Venezuela:** a few UH-1Bs serve along with some UH-1Ds and Hs within Escuadrón 42 in La Carlota.

**Yemen:** two AB 204Bs were delivered.

During the Vietnam war the Hueys received numerous modifications other than the described weapons systems. For night surveillance, some *Bravo* models were equipped with a cluster of seven C-130 landing lights and nicknamed 'lightning bugs'. A few *Charlies* also received the INFANT (Iroquois Night Fighter And Night Tracker) remote and direct view image intensifier system. In 1971, a UH-1C and a UH-1M were modified with Helms radar and were designated UH-1 HIMS (Helicopter Integrated Multifunction System) with the scanning antenna mounted in the main rotor blade. Among other modifications, were a Bell UH-1F experimentally equipped with a large suspended radar antenna for the detection of low-flying aircraft. Retraction and rotation of this antenna was performed by two electric motors. But perhaps the most weird looking Huey was the Del Mar DH-2C Whirlymite, designed in 1963 by Del Mar engineering laboratories of Los Angeles. The DH-2C was a radio-controlled target drone fitted with a 7/16-scale replica of the UH-1B. Operatonal trials of this drone were completed in 1965.

Numerous UH-1A/B/C/Fs have been transferred to the US civil

*A UH-1B-BF (s/n 60-3546) of the US Army at Edwards AFB in May 1966. This variant was powered by a 960shp Lycoming T53-L-5. (J P Stewart via J Wegg)*

market and used for forest fire-fighting and crop-dusting (identities of these are given in Appendix VIII). In 1990, US Army Aviation Systems Command (AVSCOM) was given permission to take twenty retired Hueys, overhaul and refurbish them and sell them on the international market. Some 250 more UH-1s of the 400 planned disposals within the next five years may be sold in the same way.

The Huey has become part of aviation history and several aircraft have been preserved in various museums including XH-40 (s/n 55-4459); YH-40 (s/n 56-6723); UH-1As (s/n 58-2091, 59-1625, -1686, -1695 and -1711); UH-1Bs (s/n 60-3553, -3554, -3601, 61-0686, -0693, -0778, -0788, 62-1884, -1920, -2010, -2018, -2099, -12550, -12554, 64-13954, -13986 and -14005); UH-1Es (BuNo 154759, 154760, 154945); UH-1Fs (s/n 63-13141, -13143, 64-15480, -15495, 65-7941, -7946, -7951, -7953, -7956, -7959 and 66-1215); TH-1L (BuNo 157807); UH-1Ms (s/n 65-9446, -12740 and 66-15076); UH-1Ps (s/n 64-15476/15477, -15480, -15493 and -15495).

## UH-1A

Rotor diameter 44ft 0in (13.41m); overall length 53ft (16.15m); height 12ft (3.36m); disc area 1,520sq ft (141.2sq m).

Empty weight 3,791lb (1,719kg); loaded weight 5,800lb (2,631 kg).

Maximum speed 141mph (227km/h); hover ceiling 14,400ft (4,400m); rate of climb at sea level 2,100ft/min (640m/min); normal range 202miles (325km).

## UH-1B

Rotor diameter 44ft 0in (13.41m); fuselage length 39ft 7½in (12.08m); height 14ft 7in (4.44m); disc area 1,520sq ft (141.2sq m).

Empty weight 4,369lb (1,979kg); loaded weight 8,500lb (3,850kg).

Maximum speed 147mph (236km/h); cruising speed 126mph (203km/h); initial rate of climb 2,660ft/min (810m/min); service ceiling 16,900ft (5,150m); range 260miles (418km).

## UH-1C

Rotor diameter 44ft 0in (13.41m); length overall 53ft 0in (16.15m); length of fuselage 42ft 7in (12.98m); height overall 12ft 7¼in (3.84m); disc area 1,520sq ft (141.2sq m)

Empty weight 5,071lb (2,300kg); maximum take-off weight 9,500lb (4,309kg)

Maximum speed at sea level 148mph (238km/h); rate of climb at sea level 1,400ft/min (425m/min); service ceiling 11,500ft (3,500m); hover ceiling in ground effect 10,600ft (3,230m); hover ceiling out of ground effect 10,000ft (3,230m); range 382miles (615km).

## UH-1E

Dimensions as UH-1C: empty weight 5,055lb (2,293kg); maximum take-off weight 9,500lb (4,309kg)

Maximum speed at sea level 161mph (259km/h); maximum cruising speed at sea level 138mph (222km/h); rate of climb at sea level 1,849ft/min (563m/min); service ceiling 21,000ft (6,400m); hover ceiling in ground effect 15,800ft (4,815m); hover ceiling out of ground effect 11,800ft (3,595m); range 286miles (460km).

## UH-1F

Rotor diameter 48ft 0in (14.63m); fuselage length 41ft 5in (12.62m); height 12ft 6in (3.81m); disc area 1,809sq ft (168sq m)

Empty weight 4,430lb (2,009kg); loaded weight 9,000lb (4,077kg)

Maximum speed 138mph (222km/h); cruising speed 123mph (198km/h); initial rate of climb 2,123ft/min (647m/min); service ceiling 22,000ft (6,705m); range 347miles (558km).

## Fuji-Bell Model 204B-2

Rotor diameter 48ft 0in (14.63m); fuselage lenght 40ft 4¾in (12.31m); overall length 44ft 8in (13.61m); height 14ft 6in (4.42m); disc area 1,809sq ft (168sq m)

Empty weight 4,800lb (2,177kg); maximum take-off weight 8,500lb (3,855kg)

Maximum speed 138mph (222km/h); cruising speed 127mph (204km/h); initial rate of climb 1,940ft/min (591m/min); service ceiling 19,000ft (5,790m); hover ceiling in ground effect 15,200ft (4,635m); hover ceiling out of ground effect 10,500ft (3,200m); range 238miles (383km).

# Model 68 X-14

Control of the X-14 was provided by compressed air ejected through wingtip and tail nozzles. (Bell)

Although the ATV had never completed a full transition, it was considered a successful experiment for it proved the feasibility of a jet-powered VTOL aircraft and attracted the interest of the Air Force. Bell then decided to follow on by designing a completely new test-bed aircraft with enlarged capabilities. In July 1955, a new programme was initiated with the awarding of an Air Force contract to Bell for VTOL research which eventually led to the designing of the Bell Model 68 or X-14.

The design team, led by M McEuen, worked fast so that assembly of the unique prototype could be undertaken within three months. The X-14 was an open-cockpit mid-wing monoplane of all-aluminium construction. It was powered by two 1,560lb st Armstrong Siddeley Viper 8 axial-flow turbojets mounted horizontally side-by-side in the forward fuselage. Thrust diverters were mounted behind the engines (in place of the original tailpipes) to deflect the jet thrust towards the ground during take-off and landing. The X-14 was thus able to raise itself vertically off the ground by direct jet lift, with its fuselage still in the horizontal position. At a safe height, the jet thrust was to be deflected slightly rearward to produce a forward thrust in addition to jet lift. When the forward speed was considered sufficient for the fixed wings to provide lift all the thrust was directed aft and the aircraft could fly in a conventional manner. During take-off, landing, hovering and flight at low speeds, directional control was effected by means of compressed-air nozzles located at the wingtips and tail.

Much of the aircraft was assembled from various existing aircraft components. A Beechcraft Model 35 Bonanza provided the wings, parts for the undercarriage and ailerons, and a Beechcraft T-34A Mentor provided the tail section. Ground testing was begun in October 1956 by which time the engines and exhaust nozzle system were under test at All-American Engineering. During the ground test-

*When the Viper turbojets were replaced by J85-5s, the X-14 was redesignated X-14A. (P M Bowers)*

*The X-14 was an experimental VTOL aircraft of simple design using existing components. Thrust was provided by two Armstrong Siddeley Vipers and, at a later date, by two General Electric J85s.*

ing, it was discovered that the arrangement of the exhaust system created a low-pressure area just beneath the aircraft preventing take-off. This problem was overcome by lengthening the undercarriage by two feet.

On 17 February, 1957, just over 18 months after go-ahead, the X-14 (s/n 56-4022), flown by Bell test pilot Dave Howe, completed its first successful hovering flight at Bell's Niagara Falls facility. This maiden flight was followed in June by the first partial transition and by the first complete VTOL cycle on 24 May, 1958. The aircraft was then taken on charge by the Air Force, which turned it over to NASA. The X-14 was received by NASA at Ames Research Center (Moffett Field, California) on 2 October, 1959, but the preliminary flight-test programme indicated that it was seriously underpowered. A modification programme was initiated to increase power: the two Armstrong Siddeley Viper 8 turbojets were replaced by two 2,680lb st General Electric J85-GE-5s, which virtually doubled the available thrust.

Designated X-14A and registered N234NA, the aircraft was back in the flight-test programme in 1961 and began exploring several specific areas such as V/STOL handling qualities and control concepts. The X-14A participated in various research programmes for the next eleven years when its J85-GE-5s were replaced by 3,015lb st J85-

*The X-14 was used by NASA Ames Research Center from 2 October, 1959, until 29 May, 1981, when it was badly damaged in an accident. It has since been transferred to the US Army Museum at Fort Rucker. (P M Bowers)*

*The X-14A became the X-14B when General Electric J85-19 turbojets were installed. The aircraft, registered NASA 704, is seen at Moffett Field in July 1975. (J Whitehead)*

GE-19s and a programmable computer permitting duplication of the flight characteristics of various VTOL aircraft was installed (the X-14A then becoming known as the X-14B and re-registered N704NA). The aircraft flew with its new engines in February 1971 and was used for ten more years. More than 25 test pilots came from around the world to fly the X-14B to gain experience before proceeding to other V/STOL prototypes. Neil Armstrong once flew it as a Lunar lander.

These test flights continued until 29 May, 1981, when the X-14B was victim of a hard landing accident which occurred following loss of roll control while making a ramp hover. The problem was traced to saturation of the VSCAS (Variable Stability Control Augmentation System) autopilot roll servos. The landing caused the collapse of the main undercarriage and ruptured a fuel tank. The tail was seriously damaged in the ensuing fire. Fortunately, the pilot, Ron Gerdes, escaped uninjured.

Following this accident, the X-14B was never flown again and the necessary repairs were never made. It was put into temporary storage at NASA Ames Research Center and, in February 1989, was shipped to the US Army Air Museum at Fort Rucker in Alabama.

A few derivatives of the X-14 were once considered by Bell but never built. Among these were the X-14C with an enclosed cockpit and a retractable undercarriage and the X-14T VTOL trainer.

## X-14B

Span 33ft 9½in (10.30m); length 26ft (7.92m); height 8ft 9½in (2.68m); wing area 179.52sq ft (16.68sq m)

Empty weight 3,173lb (1,437kg); loaded weight 4,269lb (1,934kg)

Maximum speed 172mph (277km/h); ceiling 18,000ft (5,500m); range 300miles (480km).

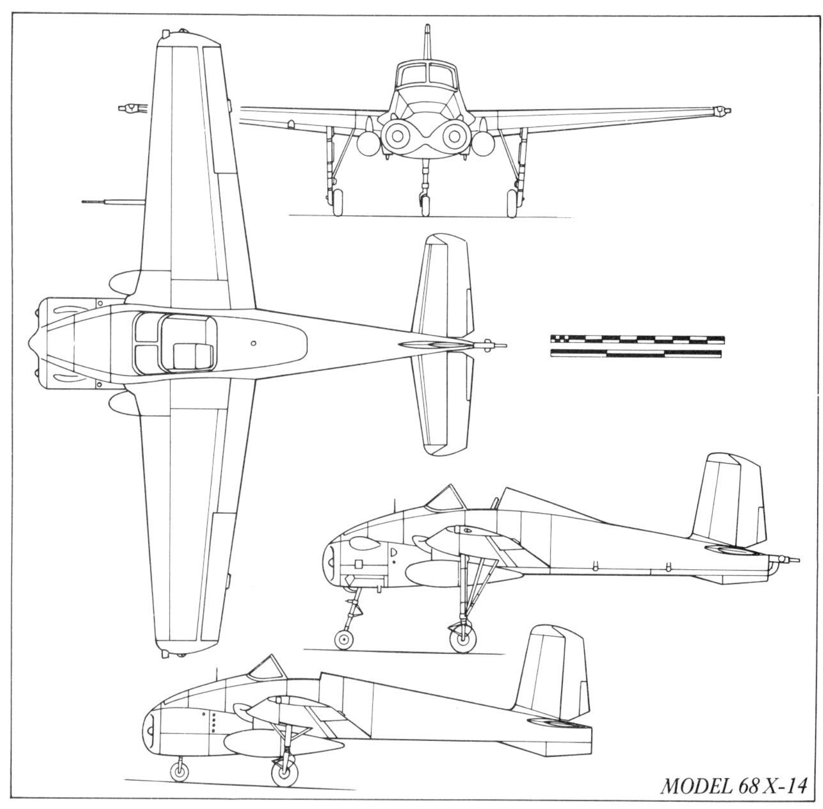

*MODEL 68 X-14*

# Model 205 UH-1D/ H/U/V/X Iroquois

In spite of its successful career debut, the Huey showed limited lifting capacity, especially at high elevations and in hot regions such as those encountered in Vietnam. That is why a contract for a service test batch of seven improved Bell Model 205/YHU-1Ds was announced in July 1960. Among the main improvements, the new Model 205 incorporated a 3ft 5in fuselage stretch, had a 1,100shp Lycoming T53-L-11 turboshaft engine, a 48ft diameter rotor with associated extended tail-boom, a normal fuel capacity of 220US gal and an overload capacity of 520US gal. Relocation of the fuel cells had increased cabin space to 220cu ft, providing room for a pilot and twelve troops, or six stretchers and a medical attendant, or 4,000lb of freight. Among the most discernable external differences from previous Bravo and Charlie models were larger cargo doors, twin cabin windows on each side, a longer transmission housing with twin louvres and a characteristic nose-up attitude in flight.

The first YUH-1D (c/n 701, s/n 60-6028) made its maiden flight on 16 August, 1961, and nine months later, the second aircraft (c/n 702, s/n 60-6029) broke three world records for helicopters:

– on 13 April, 1962, Capt Boyce B Buckner climbed to 19,685ft in 5min 47.4sec.
– on 14 April, 1962, Lieut-Col Leland F Wilhelm climbed to 9,842ft in 2min 17.3sec.
– on 20 April, 1962, Capt William F Gurley broke the speed record over a 621 miles closed circuit with 134.96mph.

The first production UH-1D (c/n 4001, s/n 62-2106) was taken on charge by the US Army on 31 May, 1963, and deliveries of the first Deltas to US Army field units began on 9 August, 1963, when the second and third UH-1Ds (s/n 62-2107 and -2108) went to the 11th Air Assault Division at Fort Benning, Georgia.

Just over a year later, the UH-1D broke an impressive list of world records as follows:

– 14 September, 1964, Maj John A Johnston in a UH-1D, set a speed record over a 621 miles closed circuit at 146.117mph.
– 18 September, 1964, Maj John A Johnston in a UH-1D, set a distance record over a closed circuit at 1,616.028 miles.
– 23 September, 1964, CWO Joseph C Watts in a UH-1D, set a speed record over a 1,243 miles closed circuit at 134.012mph.
– 27 September, 1964, Capt Michael N Antoniou in a UH-1D, set a distance record in a straight line of 1,394.10 miles.
– 27 September, 1964, CWO Joseph C Watts in a UH-1D, set a distance record over a closed circuit at 1,243.099 miles.
– 7 October, 1964, CWO Emery B Nelson in a UH-1D, climbed to 9,842ft in 2min 9.06sec and to 19,685ft in 4min 35.75sec.
– 7 October, 1964, Capt William L Welter Jr in a UH-1D, climbed to 29,527ft in 9min 13.07sec.
– 16 November, 1964, Capt D P Wray in a UH-1D, set a speed record over a 3km base at 173.238mph.
– 20 November, 1964, Maj L R Dennis in a UH-1D, set a speed record over a 15–25km (9–15 miles) base, in the over 6,622lb category at 172.95mph and in the 2,863/6,620lb category at 171.69mph.
– 20 November, 1964, Maj J K Foster in a UH-1D, at 6,622lb, set a speed record over a 62 miles closed circuit at 166.82mph.
– 21 November, 1964, Maj J K Foster in a UH-1D, in the 3,863/6,622lb category, set a speed record over a 62 miles closed circuit at 171.72mph.
– 23 November, 1964, Maj B L Odneal in a UH-1D, in the 3,863/6,622lb category, set a speed record over a 310 miles closed circuit at 178.26mph.
– 23 November, 1964, Capt R A Chubboy in a UH-1D, in the over 6,622lb category, set a speed record over a 310 miles closed circuit at 172.16mph.
– 24 November, 1964, Maj E F Sampson in a UH-1D, in the over 6,622lb category, set a speed record over a 620 miles closed circuit at 165.39mph.
– 25 November, 1964, Capt J F Cromer in a UH-1D, in the 3,863/6,622lb category, set a speed record over a 2 miles base at 180.17mph.
– 11 December, 1964, Maj E F Sampson in a UH-1D, in the 3,863/6,622lb category, set an altitude record at 35,147ft.
– 14 December, 1964, Lieut-Col Richard J Kennedy in a UH-1D, in the over 3,863lb category, set an altitude record at 25,416ft.

*UH-1D-BF s/n 65-10114 (NZ3803) belonging to No.3 Squadron of the Royal New Zealand Air Force stationed at Hobsonville. There is a wire antenna along the tail boom. (RNZAF Official)*

## Production History

### YUH-1D-BF:

ex-YHU-1D-BF, seven service trials aircraft, became UH-1D-BF.

### UH-1D-BF:

ex-HU-1D-BF, production model almost identical to service trials batch machines. Many were eventually brought up to UH-1H-BF standard. The first delivery to a regular unit took place on 9 August, 1963. A grand total of 2,008 were delivered to the US Army.

### CUH-1D:

interim designation of the CUH-1H.

### HH-1D-BF:

rescue conversion of the UH-1D-BF. A contract for thirty HH-1Hs was announced in November 1970 and completed in 1973.

### UH-1H-BF:

even more powerful, the D model had still inadequate engine power and had difficulty hovering in high temperatures (in Vietnam, several hoist missions had to be aborted because the Huey was unable to hover). The replacement of the Lycoming T53-L-11 turboshaft engine by a 1,400shp T53-L-13 gave birth to the H model which had a fuel capacity of 223US gal and overload capacity of 511US gal. Deliveries of this variant began in September 1967. The 4,000th Model 205/205A helicopter delivered was a UH-1H and was completed in March 1969. Deliveries totalled 3,573 for the US Army, followed by another 1,317 to satisfy export orders. Production was halted in December 1980, then restarted to meet a 55-machine order from Turkey (the delivery of which was completed in 1987).

As some 2,700 UH-1Hs are expected to remain on the US Army inventory beyond the year 2000, an improvement programme has been laid down which will consist of the installation of new avionics among which an AN/ALQ-144 infra-red jammer, an AN/APN-209 radar altimeter, an AN/APR-39 radar warning receiver, an AN/ARC-164 UHF/AM radio, an AN/ARN-124 Distance Measuring Equipment, an XM130 chaff/flare dispenser, NOE communications (FM/HF), and communications security. New equipment will also include an infra-red suppressor, a crashworthy auxiliary fuel system, closed-circuit refuelling, an improved main input driveshaft, new composite main rotor blades and improved stabiliser bar.

The UH-1H has also been licence-produced by Agusta in Italy, Fuji in Japan and AIDC in Nationalist China. Total production of the UH-1H was 5,435.

*A Model 205 modified by Conair and used by Frontier for forest fertilisation. The container suspended beneath the helicopter contains 1,500kg of fertiliser. (Conair)*

### CUH-1H:

version of the UH-1H-BF for the Canadian Armed Forces with a batch of ten ordered in 1967 for use by No 403 Helicopter Operational Training Squadron. The first CUH-1H was delivered on 6 March, 1968, the type being redesignated in the CAF system as CH-118.

### EH-1H:

during Fiscal Year 80, a $47 million budget was released to convert several UH-1H-BFs for electronic warfare within Project Quick Fix IA with the new designation EH-1H. These aircraft received additional electronic equipment including an AN/APR-39V2 radar warning receiver, an XM130 chaff/flare dispenser and an AN/ALQ-144 infra-red jammer. With the FY81, $5.1 millions were added to upgrade Quick Fix IA EH-1Hs into Quick Fix IB. Ten aircraft have been so modified and known examples are s/n 68-15578, 69-15145, -15238, -15676, -15858, -15930 and 70-15930.

### HH-1H:

thirty examples of this base rescue version of the UH-1H-BF were delivered to the US Air Force.

### JUH-1H:

the J prefix was given to several aircraft used in special tests. Some of them were used in the SOTAS (Stand Off Target Aquisition System) test programme which consisted of a radar pod intended to be introduced on the Sikorsky EH-60 Black Hawk. Other JUH-1Hs, nicknamed 'Mi-24 surrogates', have been modified and camouflaged to look like Soviet Mil Mi-24 Hinds. Known serial numbers for JUH-1Hs are: 67-17145, -17448, -17691, 68-16103, 69-15532, -15928, 70-15870, 72-21534 and 74-22337.

*Agusta-built AB 205 I–ACUO is operated by Elli Giana. (Agusta s.p.a.)*

### UH-1V:

this designation identifies 220 Medivac UH-1Hs fitted with radar altimeter, distance measuring equipment (AEL AN/ARN-124 DME), glideslope and rescue hoist.

### EH-1X:

some UH-1Hs have been equipped for detecting and jamming enemy radio communications and flown as three-seaters. They are externally identified by the twin Quick Fix dipole aerials on each side of the tail boom, the IR suppression exhaust and a chaff/flare dispenser fitted on each side of the fuselage. Known examples are: s/n 69-15123, -15234, -15335 and -15762.

### Model 205A-1:

15-seat commercial variant of Model 205A, powered by a 1,400shp Lycoming T53-13A turboshaft engine, derated to 1,250shp for take-off. Total cargo capacity is 248cu ft including baggage space in the tail boom. External load capacity in the flying crane role is 5,000lb. The ambulance variant can accommodate six stretchers and one or two medical attendants. Normal fuel capacity is 215US gal and optional capacity is 395US gal.

### Agusta-Bell AB 205:

the Model 205A-1 was produced under licence in Italy by Agusta for military operators. Agusta had built a total of 490 AB 205s by early 1988, mainly for military customers, before the production line was halted. As an attempt to develop a twin-engined version, Agusta designed the AB 205BG powered by two 1,250shp Rolls-Royce Gnome H1200 turboshaft engines (the suffix BG standing for bi-Gnome) and the AB 205TA with two 700shp Turboméca Astazou XII or two Continental 217 or two Pratt & Whitney (UAC) PT6 turboshaft engines.

### Fuji-Bell 204B-2 and HU-1H:

Fuji is manufacturing the Model 205 under sub-licence from Mitsui & Co Ltd. The Fuji-Bell 204B-2 was developed in 1973 and is powered with a 1,400shp Kawasaki-Textron Lycoming KT53-13B turboshaft engine and the first example of this version was delivered at the beginning of 1974. Twenty had been produced by March 1988. Fuji is also producing the HU-1H (Japanese equivalent of the UH-1H) for the Japan Ground Self-Defence Force. The HU-1H is identical to its US counterpart in most respects but is powered by a 1,400shp Kawasaki-Textron Lycoming T53-K-13B turboshaft engine and has a tractor tail rotor. The first aircraft of this variant made its maiden flight on 17 July, 1973, and a total of 107 HU-1Hs has been ordered. Twelve HU-1Hs have been equipped to carry about one hundred mines and plans have been drawn to modify forty more helicopters.

*A Medevac Huey (0-13695), operated by California Army National Guard 126th Medical Company, at Mather AFB in May 1977. (C Waldenmaier)*

### AIDC UH-1H:

between 1969 and 1976, the Aero Industry Development Center (AIDC), in Taiwan, produced 118 UH-1Hs for the Chinese Nationalist Army. These were identical in all respects to the American UH-1Hs.

## Service History

The first production UH-1Ds were released to 11th Air Assault Division in August 1963. Rapidly, UH-1Ds with new armoured seats for the crew accompanied the 1st Cavalry Division in Vietnam. Within a year, more than 300 *Delta* models were operating in South-east Asia. With

*JUH-1Hs are used as aggressor aircraft and modified and painted to look like Russian 'Hind' attack helicopters. Aircraft s/n 68-16103 is seen at Dagget-Barstow Airport, California, in April 1990. (J G Handelman)*

*UH-1V s/n 69-16446 at Camp Roberts, California, in May 1988. (R J Francillon)*

*UH-1H-BF s/n 68-16374 operated by the US Environmental Protection Agency. It has twin pontoons. (B Knowles)*

the decision to use *Bravo* and *Charlie* models as gun ships, most of the *Delta* models were used as transports ('slicks') and for Medevac missions. Nevertheless, numerous aircraft were only armed with two M-60CA1 0.30in machine guns, and only a few Australian and South-Vietnamese Hueys received heavy armament.

When, in July 1967, the 45th Medical Company arrived in Vietnam with its brand new UH-1Hs, the Medevac UH-1Ds were progressively re-allocated to transport missions. By January 1968, no more *Deltas* were used in the Medevac role. They flew air assault missions as troop transports teamed with *Bravo* and *Charlie* gunships. The Huey 'slicks' were involved in most major Airmobile operations such as operations Cedar Falls (January 1967), Junction City (February 1967), Garfield, Fort Smith, Bolling, Pershing, Hickory and Nevada Eagle.

With the policy of 'vietnamization', the 1st Cavalry Division withdrew from Vietnam in 1971, followed by 101st Airborne Division in early 1972. The number of US Army Hueys decreased rapidly and numerous UH-1s were transferred to the South Vietnamese Air Force. Several of them were eventually captured by ARVN troops during the final assault against South Vietnam in 1975. It should be noted that American Hueys were among the very last aircraft to leave Saïgon.

During operation 'Desert Storm' numerous UH-1Hs were operated by US Army Forces (101st Airborne Division, 1st Infantry Division (Mech), 24th Infantry Division, 1st, 2nd and 3rd Armored Divisions, 1st Cavalry Division) and also by the 3rd Squadron of the Sultan of Oman's Air Force and 12th Squadron of the Royal Saudi Air Force.

At the end of the 1980s, the UH-1Ds and Hs were operated by numerous units among which were: 3rd, 25th, 31st, 42nd, 44th, 47th, 158th, 183rd and 193rd AvBats; 6th,

*A UH-1D at Tan Son Nhut in January 1967. This aircraft is equipped with the 'Lightning Bug' searchlight and a .50calibre machine-gun. (US Army photograph)*

25th, 49th, 56th, 62nd, 92nd, 136th, 164th, 180th, 207th, 225th, 285th and 323rd AvCos; 1st, 158th and 227th AvRgts; 11th and 163rd ACRs; 10th, 13th, 122nd, 142nd, 149th and 308th AHBs; 83rd and 88th ARCOMs; 1st, 3rd, 6th and 163rd CavRgts; 24th, 498th and 1150th MedCos and 68th, 236th, 247th, 321st, 347th, 349th and 412th MedDets. They are also operated by most of the US Army National Units throughout the United States. The US Army has four UH-1s in service as aggressors at Fort Irwin, California.

In 1989, a total of twenty-six UH-1Hs had been released by the US Army for use by the State Department's Bureau of International Narcotic Matters to support anti-drug operations in Latin America. For their part, the HH-1Hs are in use with MAC's 37th ARRS (Det3 in Grand Forks, North Dakota, Det4 in Little Rock, Arkansas, Det7 in Minot, North Dakota, and Det9 in Whiteman, Missouri) and AFRes's 304th ARRS in Portland, Oregon, as well as AFSC's 6512th TS at Edwards, California.

## Foreign Military Operators

Abroad, the Model 205s were operated by the following 48 nations:

### Argentine:

four UH-1Ds (serialled H-10/13) and three UH-1Hs (H-14/16) were delivered to the air force and serve with I Escuadrón de Exploración y Ataque stationed at Morón, and more than twenty UH-1Hs (AE-400/424) were taken on charge by the army (Comando de Aviación del Ejército Argentino). These were involved in the Falklands war in 1982. Two of them were destroyed and eight abandoned. Some of them were later ferried to Great Britain and two are now on display there: AE-409 at the Museum of Army Flying at Middle Wallop and AE-422 at the Fleet Air Arm Museum at Yeovilton. A third (AE-413) was flown for three weeks by Sqn Ldr Rob Tierney in support of No.5 Infantry Brigade before being shipped back to the United Kingdom. It was registered to the Benevolent Fund as G-HUEY and raised about £10,000 a year through air show appearances. In September 1990, it remained unsold at the RAF Benevolent Fund's Battle of Britain auction. Another was put back into flying condition and used by the Falkland Islands Government Air Service and registered VP-FBD.

### Australia:

the RAAF received twenty-four UH-1Bs (serialled A2-384/391, -714/721, -1018/1025), two UH-1Ds (A2-085 and -649), twenty-nine newly built UH-1Hs (A2-376/383, -484/490, -505/510, -766/773) and twenty-five ex-US Army aircraft. These served with No.9 Squadron at Amberley and No.5 Squadron at Fairbairn.

The Navy took delivery of three UH-1Bs (N9-881/883) and four UH-1Cs (N9-3101/3104) which serve with No.723 Squadron in Nowra. The RAN is now seeking to acquire eight UH-1Hs that are being phased out by the RAAF.

### Bahrain:

the Bahrain Defence Force Air Wing operates a single Model 205A-1 coded BPS-7.

## Bolivia:

six UH-1Hs were procured from US Army surplus in 1986 and ten in 1988. These are operated by the Grupo Aéreo Mixto 51 stationed at Cochabamba. Bolivia is due to receive six additional UH-1Hs in 1991.

## Brazil:

the Força Aérea Brasileira uses six SH-1Ds and thirty-six UH-1D/Hs (serialled 8530/8568 and 8650/8671) which serve with Grupos de Aviaçao (air groups) No.8, 10 and 11 and with the Centro de Intruçao de Helicópteros.

## Brunei:

the Sultanate of Brunei Air Wing operates three Model 205A-1s (serialled AMDB-100, -102 and -111).

## Burma:

the air force received eighteen UH-1Hs (serialled UB-6201/6218).

## Canada:

the Canadian Armed Forces took delivery of ten CUH-1Hs, designated CH-118 (serialled 118101/118110). They are in use with No.103 Reserve Unit and with the SAR flights stationed at Bagotville, Cold Lake and Moose Jaw.

## Chile:

between 1973 and 1978, the Chilean Air Force (Fuerza Aérea de Chile) received thirteen UH-1Hs (serialled H-80/92) which serve within Grupo de Aviación 10 based at Pudahuel and Grupo de Aviación 6 based at Carlos Ibánez. The army aviation took delivery of three UH-1Hs (serialled 181/183).

## Colombia:

an unknown quantity of UH-1Hs have been delivered to the air force and are flown by the Escuadrón de Helicópteros stationed at Melgar.

## Dominican Republic:

two Model 205A-1s are in use (serialled 3018/3019).

## Ecuador:

the Ecuadorian Air Force uses four UH-1Hs.

## El Salvador:

fourteen UH-1Hs have been initially delivered (serialled in the 200 range) to the Fuerza Aérea Salvadoreña several of which were destroyed during the civil war (six were destroyed during a guerrilla raid against Ilopango base in January 1982). At the end of the 1980s important batches of new equipment were delivered including some eighty-five UH-1Hs, twelve UH-1M gunships and two UH-1Hs modified for special operations.

## Ethiopia:

the army aviation took delivery of six ex-US Army UH-1Hs.

*A newly built Dornier UH-1D (c/n 8500, serialled 73-80) at Oberpfaffenhofen in September 1970. This aircraft was later operated by Light Transport Regiment HFR10 at Celle. (K Krämer)*

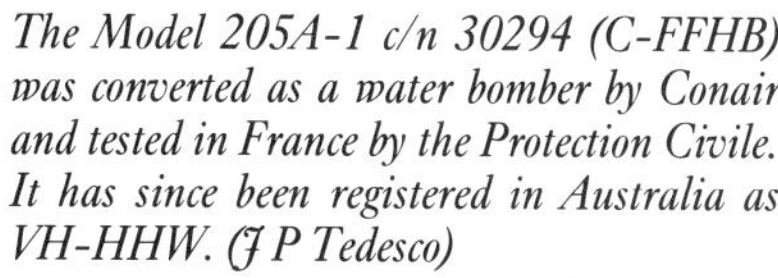

*The Model 205A-1 c/n 30294 (C-FFHB) was converted as a water bomber by Conair and tested in France by the Protection Civile. It has since been registered in Australia as VH-HHW. (J P Tedesco)*

*The Model 205 could carry a wide variety of armament. Here it has 80-mm Oerlikon SURA type rockets mounted on a NATO-type launcher bar. (Oerlikon)*

## Greece:

an unknown quantity of UH-1Hs and forty AB 205As were delivered to the army aviation while the air force received eleven AB 205A-1s which serve with No.359 Mira (squadron) at Dekélia.

## Guatemala:

an unknown quantity of UH-1Ds has been delivered to the air force.

## Indonesia:

an unknown number of Hueys delivered together with sixteen Model 205A-1s.

## Iran:

the Navy took delivery of twenty-four AB 205As.

## Israel:

the IDFAF operates an unknown number of Model 205A-1s and AB 205As.

## Italy:

the army aviation (Aviazione Leggera dell' Esercito Italiano) received one hundred and six AB 205A-1s (serialled MM80439/80461, MM80524/80561, MM80681/80725) while the Corpo Carabinieri took delivery of eight AB 205A-1s (MM80776/80783) and a lone AB 205B (MM80775). The army aviation units flying the AB 205A-1s are squadrons No.521, 522, 531 and 532 in Aosta, No.541, 542, 543, 544 and 545 in Bolzano, No.425 in Veneto, No.551, 552, 553 and 554 in Casarsa della Delizia, No.521 in Cagliari, No.598 in Verona and No.526 in Aurelia.

## Japan:

seventy-three Fuji-Bell UH-1Hs (serialled 41601/41673) were delivered to the Japan Ground Self-Defence Force (JGSDF or Nihon Rikujyo Jieitai) and are flown by the Northern, Northeastern, Eastern, Central and Western army aviation groups (Homen kokutai) and with the aviation school (Koku gakko).

## Kuwait:

the Kuwait Air Force operated eight AB 205As (serialled 909/916).

## Laos:

a dozen UH-1D/Hs are reported in service.

## Mexico:

ten Model 205A-1s serve with the Escuadrón Aéreo 209 stationed at Santa Lucia.

## Morocco:

forty-eight AB 205As are in use (coded CN-AJA-01 to CN-AKV-48).

## New Zealand:

the RNZAF received five UH-1Ds (serialled NZ3810/3805) and ten UH-1Hs (NZ3806/3815) which serve with No.3 Squadron at Hobsonville and the Support Unit at Tengah.

## North Vietnam:

since the conquest of South Vietnam, the Vietnam People's Army Air Force (VPAAF) has maintained some ex-SVNAF Hueys in flying condition.

*Agusta-Bell AB 205A-1 No.221 of the United Arab Emirates Air Force. (J M G Gradidge)*

*Agusta-Bell AB 205A-1 c/n 4241 (serial MM.80709) of the Aviazione Leggera dell' Esercito Italiano. A winch is installed above the starboard door. (A Pelletier)*

### Oman:
Sultanate of Oman Air Force operates twenty-seven AB 205As (serialled 701/727) with its No.3 and 14 Squadrons at Salalah while the Oman Police Air Wing has four AB 205A-1s (registered A40-AM/AQ).

### Pakistan:
the army aviation received six ex-US Army UH-1Hs.

### Panama:
nine UH-1Hs have been delivered.

### Peru:
the air force received at least six UH-1Hs (serialled in the 600 range) while the navy took delivery of six UH-1D/Hs (serialled HC-410/415).

### Philippines:
at least fifty-five UH-1Hs are reportedly in service with seven helicopter squadrons and are used in Mindanao against guerilleros of the New People Army.

*One of the six Agusta-Bell AB 205A-1s operated by the Dubai Defence Force Air Wing before being transferred to the United Arab Emirates Air Force. (J M G Gradidge)*

### Saudi Arabia:
the Royal Saudi Air Force operates twenty-four AB 205A-1s of which one is in VIP transport configuration. They are in use with the 12th and 14th Squadrons at At'Taif.

### Singapore:
at least thirty-four UH-1Hs are in use (serials: 224/270) with 120th Condor Squadron stationed at Changi, Singapore.

### South Korea:
an unknown number of UH-1D/Hs has been received.

### Spain:
seven UH-1Hs (serialled HE.10B-37/39 and 51/54) and fourteen AB 205As (HD.10A-1/14) are in use with the air force with Squadrons 802 and 783, while the army aviation (FAMET) operated sixty UH-1Hs (HU.10B–15/20 and 55/81) from 1975 to 1988 with UHEL IV.

### Tanzania:
at least four AB 205As are in use.

### Taiwan:
one hundred and eighteen UH-1Hs were procured from AIDC for the Chinese Nationalist Army (serialled in the 300 range).

### Thailand:
some thirty UH-1Hs are reported in service with the air force's 203rd Squadron at Lop Buri; the army aviation uses an unknown number of

UH-1D/Hs and the navy four UH-1Hs.

**Tunisia:**
eighteen AB 205As (serialled L81701/81718) have been delivered and are in use with 31st Squadron.

**Turkey:**
at least fifty UH-1D/Hs and an unknown number of AB 205As are in use with the air force (224th Filo based at Etimesgut and various base flights) and the army aviation.

**United Arab Emirates:**
a single Model 205A-1 is in service (coded 111) along with two AB 205A-1s (221/222).

**Uruguay:**
in 1968 this country received two ex-US Army UH-1Hs for operations against the Tupamaros; they were joined by a third aircraft of the same type in 1971. These three UH-1Hs (serialled 50/52) serve with the Grupo de Aviación based at Carrasco.

**Venezuela:**
the air force (Fuerzas Aéreas Venezolanas) operates an unknown number of UH-1D/Hs with Escuadrón 42 at La Carlota, while the army received three UH-1Hs (serialled

*JUH-1H s/n 63-12976 mounted on a trailer at Frankfurt in December 1978. The JUH-1Hs are used in special tests such as the SOTAS programme. (J Wegg)*

*In Spain, the Bell UH-1H is known as the Z.10B. No.68, coded ET-238 of the Spanish Army Aviation or FAMET is illustrated. (J A Cerda)*

*The Royal Thai Air Force UH-1Hs (No.3222 illustrated) are operated by 203rd Squadron of the 2nd Wing based at Lop Buri. (J M G Gradidge)*

EV-7704, -7708 and -7709) and two Model 205A-1s (EV-8016 and 8017).

### West Germany:

the Luftwaffe received one hundred and forty-six UH-1Ds: two built by Bell (serialled 70-01/70-02), four assembled by Dornier (70-37/70-40) and one hundred and forty built by Dornier (70-41/71-80). In addition the army aviation took delivery of two hundred and four UH-1Ds (71-81/73-84). The Heeresfliegerstruppen UH-1Ds will remain in service until at least 2010 through enhancement programmes. In addition, the Federal German Border Security Troops uses thirteen ex-WGAF UH-1Ds. The Luftwaffe Hueys are flown by HTG 64 at Ahlhorn, and Heer's aircraft serve with HFB 6 at Hungriger Wolf, LHFTR 10 at Celle-Wietzenbruch, LHFTR 20 at Kiliansdorf and LHFTR 30 at Fritzlar.

### Yugoslavia:

five AB 205As have been taken on charge.

### Zambia:

unknown quantity of AB 205As (serialled in the AF760 range).

### Zimbabwe:

the air force operates at least twelve AB 205A Cheetahs obtained from Israël which are flown by No.8 Squadron at New Sarum; these are fitted with anti-IR missile exhaust shields.

In Canada, Conair has designed a water-bomber variant known as the Helitanker. Modifications to the original Model 205 include a fixed 360US gal retardant delivery tank, high skid gear, remote-fill system, foam injection systems and rappelling equipment for helicopters in fire control work. Frontier Helicopters Ltd, a wholly owned subsidiary of Conair, operates fifteen Bell Model 205s Helitankers along with eleven Bell Model 206Bs, one Model 212 and one Aérospatiale AS.350B. Since 1987, some Model 205A-1 Helitankers have been rented from Frontier Helicopters Ltd by the French Protection Civile for the 1990 summer fire-fighting season (aircraft c/ns and registrations as follows: 30017/C-GFHD, 30038/C-GFHC, 30086/C-GFHA, 30159/C-GMOR, 30180/SE-HMT, 30195/C-FFHX, 30289/C-GFHM and 30295/C-FFHB).

*The UH-1Hs of the Royal Australian Air Force are operated by No.5 Squadron based at Fairbairn. A2-488 (ex-69-15488) is illustrated. (M W Prime)*

### UH-1D

Rotor diameter 48ft 0in (14.63m); fuselage length 41ft 10¾in (12.77m); length overall 57ft 1in (17.40m); height 14ft 6in (4.42m); disc area 1,809sq ft (168.06sq m).

Empty weight 4,939lb (2,240kg); maximum take-off weight 9,500lb (4,309kg).

Maximum speed at sea level 148mph (238km/h); cruising speed 130mph (209km/h); range 260 miles (418km).

### UH-1H

Dimensions as for UH-1D.

Empty weight 4,973lb (2,255kg); maximum take-off weight 9,500lb (4,309kg).

Maximum speed 127mph (204 km/h); cruising speed 127mph (204km/h); initial rate of climb 1,600ft/min (488m/min); service ceiling 12,600ft (3,840m); hover ceiling in ground effect 13,600ft (3,840m); hover ceiling out of ground effect 4,000ft (1,220m); range 318 miles (511km).

### Model 205A-1

Rotor diameter and disc area same as UH-1D, length of fuselage 41ft 6in (12.65m); overall height 14ft 4¾in (4.39m).

Empty weight 5,082lb (2,305kg); take-off weight 9,500lb (4,309kg); maximum take-off weight 10,500lb (4,763kg).

Maximum speed at sea level 127mph (204km/h); cruising speed at 8,000ft (2,440m) 111mph (179km/h); maximum rate of climb at sea level 1,020ft/min (311m/min); service ceiling 14,700ft (4,480m); hover ceiling in ground effect 10,400ft (3,170m); hover ceiling out of ground effect 6,000ft (1,830m); range at sea level 311 miles (500km).

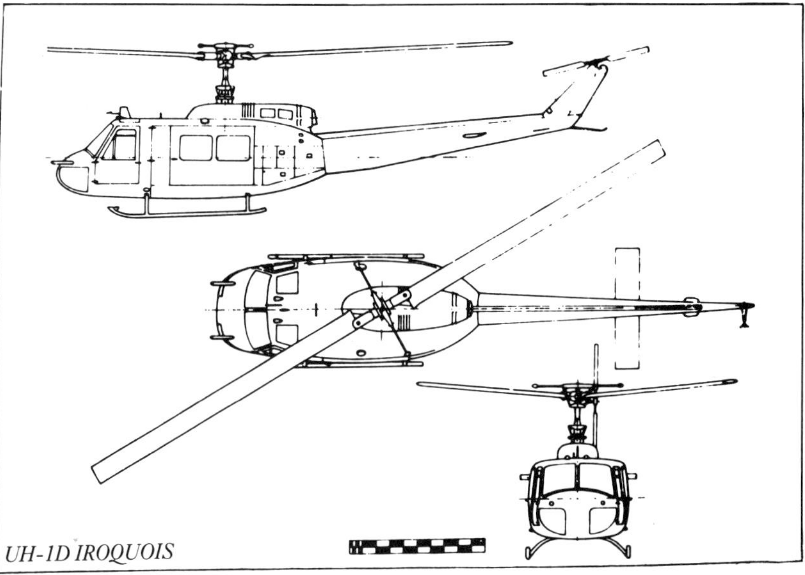

*UH-1D IROQUOIS*

# Model 206A and B JetRanger, OH-58 Kiowa/ TH-57 SeaRanger

In 1960, the US Army launched a design competition for a new four-seat Light Observation Helicopter (LOH) of which it planned to acquire some 3,600 over the next ten years. The new aircraft was to be capable of flying at 120mph with 400lb payload in order to replace the ageing Bell Model 47s, Cessna L-19s and Hiller H-23s on the Army's inventory. Twelve manufacturers submitted designs: Bell, Boeing-Vertol, Cessna, Gyrodyne, Hiller, Hughes, Kaiser, Kaman, Lockheed, McDonnell, Republic and Sikorsky. On 19 May, 1961, after evaluation by a team from Continental Army Command working closely with the US Navy's Bureau of Weapons, three finalists were announced: Bell, Hiller and a newcomer to helicopter production, Hughes. Five prototypes of each project were ordered, respectively designated YHO-4A-BF (Bell design D-250), YHO-5A-UH (Fairchild-Hiller FH.1100) and YHO-6A-HU (Hughes Model 369). In July 1962, these were redesignated OH-4A, OH-5A and OH-6A, in accordnace with the new tri-Service designation system.

The Bell Design D-250 was powered by an Allison T63-A-5 turboshaft engine. The first of the five prototype OH-4As (c/n 001, s/n 62-4202) made its maiden flight on 8 December, 1962, at Fort Worth and received FAA Type approval on 28 April, 1964. All five OH-4As were delivered by 19 March, 1964, three of them went to Fort Rucker, Alabama, and two to Edwards AFB, California. The fourth OH-4A was evaluated in the armed configuration with a twin machine-gun pod on the starboard side and an interchangeable pod for machine-guns or XM-75 grenade launcher on the port side. The comparative tests subsequently conducted by the US Army led to the final selection and production of the Hughes design, on 26 May, 1965. Hughes had won on the basis both of its superior performance and very attractive price.

At that time, in April 1965, Bell's marketing team, led by Dwayne Jose, began studying a possible commercial derivative of the OH-4A. Widening the OH-4A's fuselage was first considered but it soon became obvious that the best thing to do was to design an entirely new fuselage. Unfortunately, at that time Bell had no money to divert for such a programme. All efforts were then turned towards the mass production of the Huey and development of the Cobra. But Jose approached two design firms that were under contract to Bell and asked them to work on different drawings of the commercial OH-4. Costs were hidden and spread over the other contracts. With the help of outside designers, Jose and the marketing team prepared a brand new streamlined fuselage, and a full-scale mock-up was constructed. After inspection, launch of what was now known as the Bell Model 206A was finally approved.

The Model 206A was designed as a turbine-powered general-purpose light helicopter. The powerplant was a 317shp Allison 250-C18A turboshaft engine driving a two-blade semi-rigid see-saw type rotor. Blades were of standard Bell 'droop-snoot' section with constant chord. The stabilising bar originally fitted to the OH-4A's rotor system had been left off and the rotor mast extended. The airframe was of aluminium alloy monocoque construction with accommodation for five people (two seats side-by-side in front and a rear bench for three). The undercarriage consisted of aluminium alloy tubular skids bolted to extruded cross-tubes.

Construction of the prototype (c/n 1, N8560F) began in July 1965 and the machine was completed in August. The aircraft flew for the first time in December and was presented at the HAA convention (Helicopter Association of America) on 10 January, 1966. It received a

*A flight of TH-57A SeaRangers belonging to the US Navy's Training Wing 5. The nearest helicopter is BuNo 157360. (Bell)*

OH-58A-BF s/n 69-16695 armed with an M-21 7.26-mm Minigun. (Bell)

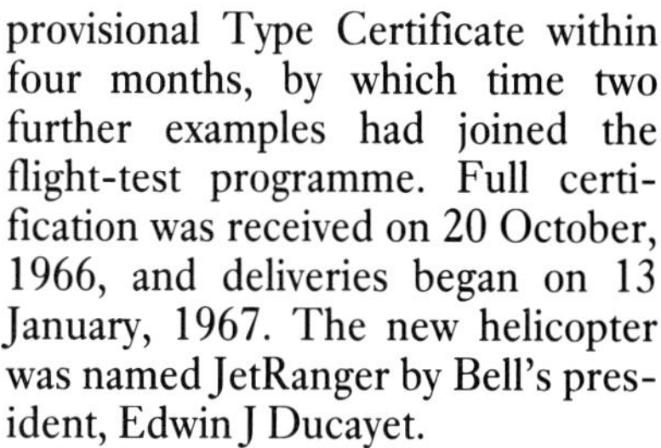

provisional Type Certificate within four months, by which time two further examples had joined the flight-test programme. Full certification was received on 20 October, 1966, and deliveries began on 13 January, 1967. The new helicopter was named JetRanger by Bell's president, Edwin J Ducayet.

By December 1968, a total of 361 commercial examples had been built, excluding JetRangers produced under licence by Agusta in Italy. In the mid-sixties, the production costs of the OH-6A had climbed to such an extent that, in 1967, the US Army decided to re-open the LOH competition and, on 8 March, 1968, named Bell as the winner of this contest with its Model 206A. An initial order for 2,200 aircraft, designated OH-58A, was then placed.

*The Agusta-Bell AB 206B JetRanger c/n 8612 (F-GCTJ) operated by Heli Services at Arromanches in May 1988. (A Pelletier)*

*The Model 206A c/n 60 (N7873S) was brought to 206B configuration. It is now operated by Palm Springs Aviation Inc. (Bell)*

In 1971, an improved variant was introduced, the Model 206B JetRanger II, which received its FAA Type Certificate. The first production JetRanger II (c/n 1) was subsequently delivered to Okanagan Helicopters Ltd of Canada and 1973 saw the delivery of the 1,000th JetRanger and 1976, that of the 2,000th JetRanger, to MacDonald's Corp.

During the summer of 1977, Bell began delivery of another improved model, the Model 206B JetRanger III, which replaced the JetRanger II, 1,619 of which had been produced. The JetRanger III was powered by a 420shp Allison 250-C20J turboshaft engine driving the standard two-blade semi-rigid see-saw type rotor. In 1982, a JetRanger III was used for an unusual record flight. Australian pilot Dick Smith took off from Bell in a JetRanger III to make the first solo flight around the world. On 9 August, Smith landed in the United Kingdom after making the first solo helicopter crossing of the Atlantic and, in 1983, he completed his flight around the world by touching down at Bell. He had flown 35,258 miles without a mechanical problem.

Under a five-year programme, Beech Aircraft produced airframes for both the commercial and military variants of the Model 206A. The work involved manufacture of the fuselage, skid gear, tail-boom, spar, stabiliser and two rear fairing assemblies. The first Beech-produced airframe was delivered to Bell on 1 March, 1968. This work was later gradually taken over by the Canadian factory and the first example was delivered on 20 December, 1986. By January 1988, Bell and its licensees had manufactured over 7,000 Model 206s. In the summer of 1988, the 4,000th JetRanger, a JetRanger III, was delivered to Texas dairy farmer R J Swelley Co.

*Model 206A c/n 474 (VH–AND) operated by Ansett Airlines of Australia. This aircraft was previously registered VH–FVT. It was converted to Model 206B configuration at a later date and sold to NBN Ltd of Newcastle, New South Wales. (M W Prime)*

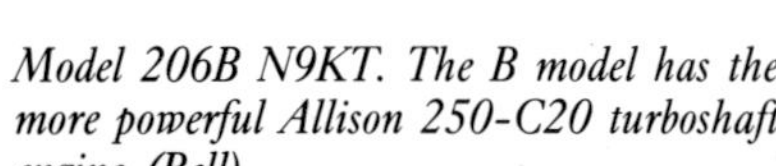

*OH-58A-BF s/n 70-15239 operated by the Nevada Army National Guard from Reno-Stead Municipal Airport in August 1976. (A Pelletier)*

*Model 206B N9KT. The B model has the more powerful Allison 250-C20 turboshaft engine. (Bell)*

## Production History

### OH-58A:

LOH version of the Model 206A. Major differences to the 206A concerned the main rotor, which had an increased diameter, avionics and internal layout (pilot and co-pilot/observer seated in front side-by-side and 40cu ft compartment at the rear). The engine was a 317shp Allison T63-A-700. First aircraft was delivered on 23 May, 1969.

### OH-58B:

designation applied to a batch of twelve helicopters exported to Austria and similar to the OH-58A.

### OH-58C:

in 1976, under US Army contract, Bell began improving the Kiowa through a series of modifications that included installation of an uprated version of the 317shp Allison T63-A-700 together with 'Black Hole' exhaust stacks and hot metal shroud for infra-red suppression. A flat glass canopy was adopted and a number of internal improvements made. Three OH-58As were modified to this configuration and received OH-58C designation. Bell received later a contract from the Army to bring 435 OH-58As to OH-58C configuration. All were delivered by March 1985. Standard armament kit, not always fitted, consisted of the M27 with a 0.30in Minigun.

### OH-58D:

see under chapter Bell Model 406.

### TH-57A:

on 31 January, 1968, the US Navy announced the selection of the Model 206A. Named SeaRanger, the TH-57A is used by the US Navy as a training helicopter. A total of

*The pontoon-equipped Agusta-Bell AB 206B c/n 8049 (VH–BHV) operated by Bristow. (M W Prime)*

*Two OH-58Bs belonging to 2nd Staffel of the Austrian Air Force, stationed at Tulln, flying over a typical Alpine landscape. (Austrian Air Force)*

*The Agusta-Bell AB 206B JetRanger c/n 8168 (D–HARO) as it was displayed at Hannover Air Show in May 1970. It is now operated by Karl Mannheim, of Mülheim-Kärlich. (M Cristescu)*

*Model 206B-1 of No.723 Squadron of the Royal Australian Navy at Nowra in April 1974. (Courtesy B Knowles)*

forty aircraft were ordered to replace the Bell TH-13Ms used by the Naval Air Training Command at Pensacola. All forty were delivered during 1968. The TH-57A was basically similar to the Model 206A but was equipped with naval avionics.

**TH-57B and TH-57C:**
respectively 51 and 89 examples of these were ordered by the US Navy for use with Training Wing 5 (HT-8 and HT-18) stationed at Whiting Field, Florida.

**Model 206A JetRanger:**
first commercial production variant, powered by a 317shp Allison 250-C18A turboshaft engine.

**Model 206B JetRanger II:**
second commercial production variant with more powerful 400shp Allison 250-C20 turboshaft engine. Even a commercial variant, the Model 206B is also proposed to customers as a military helicopter which could be armed with twin MAG Pod machine-guns (0.30 or 0.50cal MGs) or 2.75in (70mm) air-to-ground rocket system (with fourteen folding fin aerial rockets).

**Model 206B JetRanger III:**
last commercial production variant introduced in 1977 with an uprated 420shp Allison 250-C20B turboshaft engine, an enlarged and improved tail rotor and some other minor changes. A retrofit kit was made available to bring earlier JetRangers to JetRanger III configuration.

**Agusta-Bell 206A:**
variant manufactured in Italy under licence from Bell since the end of 1967, virtually similar to its American counterpart.

**Agusta-Bell 206B:**
first delivery of AB 206B JetRanger II in 1972 and of AB 206B JetRanger III at the end of 1978.

*OH-58C-BF s/n 71-20694 in July 1988. The passengers' door has been discarded and the tail is painted day-glo orange. (R J Francillon)*

## Service History

The first delivery of an OH-58A to the US Army took place on 23 May, 1969. Deployment of the OH-58A to Vietnam began in the late summer of 1969, and the type was widely used throughout the combat and thereafter (units: 120th AHC at Bien Hoa; 20th Engineer Brigade at Bien Hoa, responsible for activities with III and IV Corps, and 1st Signal Brigade). Though used as a LOH, the OH-58 saw much more service as a transport. At present the OH-58 is flown by 10th, 13th, 149th, 308th AHBs; 3rd, 4th, 25th, 44th, 47th, 158th, 193rd, 307th AvBat; 25th, 49th, 56th, 62nd, 193rd, 225th, 285th AvCo; 1st, 4th AvRgt; 2nd, 11th ACR; 3rd AvDet; 4th ARC; 83rd, 88th, 97th ARCOM; 3rd, 6th CavRgt; 2/9 Cav, 3/4 Cav; 18th AB; 98th Div; 1st InfDiv; 126th MedCo; AMARC; USAAEFA; USAICS Fort Rucker, Sill, Eustis Alabama; Army National Guards of Arizona, California, Florida, Georgia, Kansas, Louisiana, Michigan, Missouri, Nebraska, North Carolina, Ohio, Oklahoma, Pennsylvania, South Carolina, Utah and Wisconsin.

In July 1989, a US Army team consisting of seven Kiowas and two UH-1Hs as support aircraft won the 6th World's Helicopter Championship held at Chantilly in France. The crew Jon A Iseminger and Rudolph V Hobbs was designated as world champions 1989.

## Foreign Military Operators

Model 206B JetRanger III N49703. The JetRanger III is an improved variant of the JetRanger II and retrofit kits have been made available to JetRanger II owners. (Bell)

### Argentine:

the Army received seven Model 206s.

### Australia:

the Army took delivery of seventy-five Model 206B-1s (of which thirty-four were built by CAC), named 'Kalkadoon' and serialled A17-001/075. The Navy received three Model 206B-1s (serialled N17-013, 025 and 049).

### Austria:

twelve OH-58Bs (coded 3C-OA/OL) and eighteen AB 206As (code 3C-JA/JR).

### Brazil:

seven Model 206As were taken on charge by the air force under designation VH-4 (serials 8570/8572, 8580/8583); in 1974, the Navy received eighteen Model 206Bs designated UH-6/IH-6/IH-6A (serials N5021/5030, N7028/7035, the last batch being previously serialled N5031/5037).

### Brunei:

this Sultanate bought three Model 206As, later converted to 206B configuration, and one Model 206B (codes are AMDB-103, 104, 107 and 109).

### Canada:

seventy-four COH-58As delivered (designated CH-136 and serialled 136201/136274) plus fourteen Model 206Bs (designated CH-139 and serialled 139301/139314). In 1989, plans to select a successor for the CH-136 under Canadian Forces Light Helicopter programme (CFLH) have been postponed for budgetary reasons.

### Chile:

two Model 206Bs were delivered to the army (serialled 151 and 152) and four Model 206As to the air force serialled (31/34).

### Colombia:

ten OH-58As delivered.

### Ethiopia:

six AB 206Bs delivered.

### Finland:

this country uses a lone AB 206A bought in 1968 and coded HB–1.

### Greece:

the Hellenic Air Force received two AB 206As.

### Guatemala:

at least one Model 206 was delivered to the air force.

### Guyana:

the tiny Guyana Defence Force Air Command uses two Model 206Bs registered 8R-GEX and 8R-GEY.

### Indonesia:

two Model 206Bs delivered.

### Iran:

seventeen AB 206A-1s (coded 4-705/721) were delivered to the army as well as twelve AB 206A-1s (101/

*Agusta-Bell AB 206B JetRanger III c/n 8612 (F–GCTJ) operated by the French company Heli Services. (A Pelletier)*

*The YHO-4-BF. The fuselage strengtheners are prominent. (Bell)*

112) to the navy and thirteen AB-206As (201/213) to the gendarmerie. According to Western sources, Iran is currently developing a light combat helicopter using a Model 206 airframe as a basis.

**Italy:**
fifteen AB 206As (MM80562/80577) and 134 AB 206A-1s (MM80578/80650 and MM80858/80918) were delivered to the army; thirteen AB 206A-1s (MM80729/80741) were taken in charge by the police and thirty-nine aircraft by the Corpo carabinieri (four AB 206As serialled MM80919/80922; nine AB 206A-1s serialled MM80923/80931 and twenty-six AB 206B-1s serialled MM80932, 81019/81043).

**Israel:**
unknown quantity of OH-58s/Model 206A and Bs.

**Jamaica:**
three Model 206As (coded JDFH-3/5) and three Model 206Bs (coded JDFH-14 and 15).

**Kuwait:**
two AB 206As (906/907) were used by the air force.

**Libya:**
five AB 206As are used by the army.

**Mexico:**
two Model 206As (serialled EBRE-1162/1163) and five Model 206Bs (EBRE-1001/1005).

**Morocco:**
at least six AB 206Bs (registered CN-AQA/F) delivered.

**Oman:**
this Sultanate uses four AB 206As (601/601).

**Pakistan:**
the army uses an unknown number of Model 206s.

**Peru:**
the air force has taken on charge ten Model 206Bs (serialled 667/676).

**Philippines:**
an unknown number of Model 206As serve with the air force (serialled in the 400 range).

**PLO:**
from Israeli sources, the Palestinian organisation uses several Model 206s of unknown origin from bases located in North Yemen (pilots are reported to have been trained in Libya, Pakistan and both Yemens).

**Saudi Arabia:**
at least twenty-nine AB 206As were delivered to this country (known serials are 1201/1213, 1401/1416).

**Spain:**
the army uses thirteen OH-58Bs (serialled HU.12A-1 and HR.12B-6/17) and the air force four AB 206A-1s (serialled HD.12A-2/5).

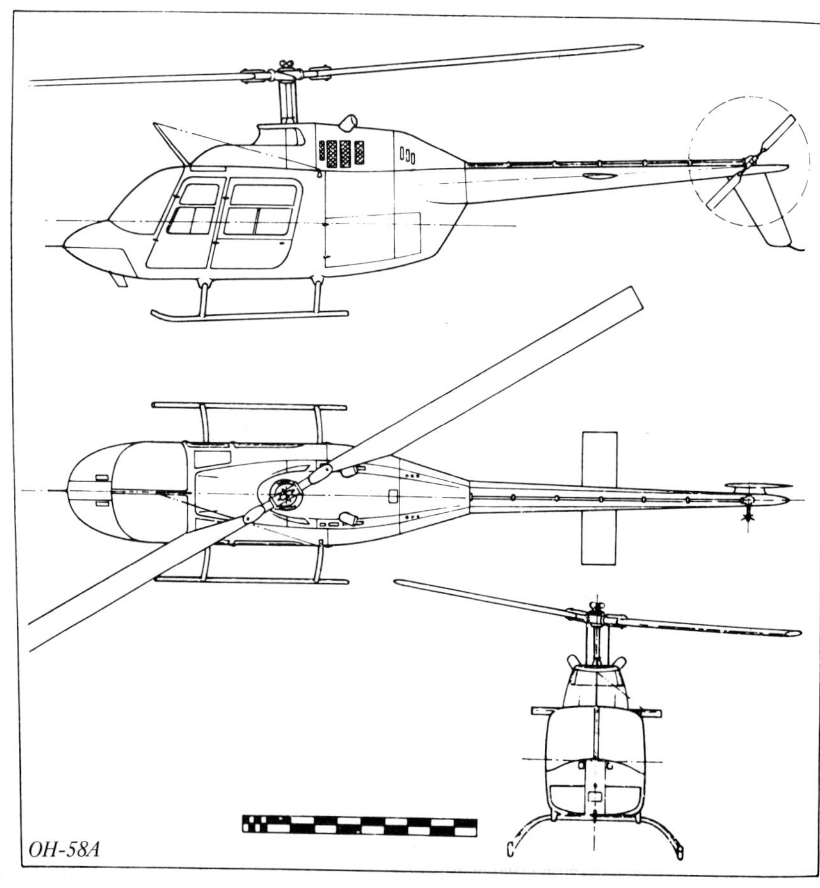

*OH-58A*

### Sri Lanka:

ten Model 206As (serialled in the CH550 range) delivered.

### Sweden:

the army received twenty-two AB 206As under the designation Hkp 6A (serials 06261/06282) and the navy ten AB 206As under the designation Hkp 6B (serials 06044/06053).

### Tanzania:

two AB 206Bs (JW9601/9602) are in use with the air force.

### Thailand:

four Model 206As (0130, 0135, 0141 and 0471) and five Model 206Bs (0872, 2116, 2120, 2124 and 2128) are in use.

### Turkey:

eight AB 206As were delivered to the air force.

### Uganda:

at least two Model 206s (serialled U-708/709) were delivered.

### United Arab Emirates:

a lone AB 206A serialled 123 was delivered.

Modifications to the Model 206A mainly concern accessories such as pontoons or a searchlight under the nose (on the police variant as used by California Highways Patrol and Metro Police). Various options and equipment are available such as infra-red viewers, external cargo hook and loudspeaker.

## Model 206 (OH-4A)

Rotor diameter 33ft 4in (10.16m); length of fuselage 30ft 1in (9.17m); height 8ft 10in (2.69m); disc area 873sq ft (81.1sq m).

Empty weight 1,500lb (680kg); gross weight 2,500lb (1,135kg); maximum weight 2,900lb (1,315kg).

## Model 206A

Rotor diameter 33ft 4in (10.16m); length of fuselage 31ft 2in (9.50m); length overall 39ft 1in (11.91m); height 9ft 6½in (2.91m); disc area 873sq ft (81.1sq m).

Empty weight 1,407lb (638kg); maximum take-off weight 3,000lb (1,360kg).

Performance at 2,600lb (1,179kg): maximum speed at sea level 138mph (222km/h); maximum cruising speed 121mph (195km/h); maximum rate of climb at sea level 1,980ft/min (604m/min); service ceiling 18,500ft (5,640m); hover ceiling in ground effect 12,600ft (3,840m); hover ceiling out of ground effect 8,550ft (2,605m); maximum range at sea level 380 miles (611km).

*OH-58A-BF Kiowa s/n 69-16214 was converted to OH-58C. Noteworthy are the flat windscreen and the fairing around the tail rotor transmission, distinguishing features of this variant. (Bell)*

## OH-58A

Dimensions as Model 206A except: rotor diameter 35ft 4in (10.77m); length overall 40ft 11¾in (12.49m)

Empty weight 1,583lb (718kg); maximum take-off weight 3,000lb (1,360kg).

Maximum speed at sea level 150mph (241km/h); cruising speed 117mph (188km/h); maximum rate of climb at sea level 1,780ft/min (543m/min); service ceiling 19,000ft (5,790m); hover ceiling in ground effect 13,750ft (4,190m); hover ceiling out of ground effect 9,000ft (2,745m); range at sea level 299 miles (481km).

## Model 206B JetRanger III

Rotor diameter, disc area and length of fuselage as Model 206A; length overall 38ft 9½in (11.82m); height 9ft 6½in (2.91m).

Empty weight 1,635lb (742kg); maximum take-off weight 3,200lb (1,451kg).

Maximum speed at sea level 140mph (225km/h); cruising speed 134mph (216km/h); maximum rate of climb at sea level 1,260ft/min (384m/min); service ceiling 13,500ft (4,115m); hover ceiling in ground effect 12,800ft (3,900m); hover ceiling out of ground effect 8,800ft (2,680m); range 419 miles (674km).

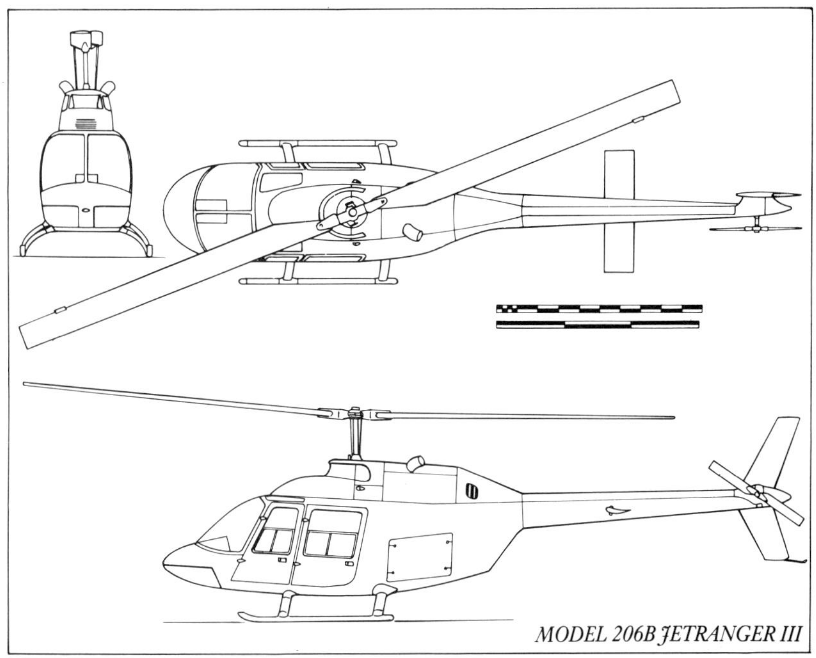

*MODEL 206B JETRANGER III*

# Model 533

In 1959, the TRECOM (United States Army's Transportation Research Command) set up a programme in order to determine various rotor systems and methods of drag reduction for helicopters. As a result Bell modified the first YH-40-BF service test model (s/n 56–6723) as a research test-bed which was known at Bell as the Model 533. A lot of reworking was done on the airframe in order to reduce drag. These refinements included a cambered vertical tail surface to unload the tail rotor, streamlined fairing for the rotor head, flush air intakes located on each side of the new rotor fairing, redesigned cross-tubes for landing skids and new hinges for the doors. The well-known stabilising bar was removed and replaced by a variable-tilt rotor mast in order to maintain the fuselage in low-drag attitude. The 1,400shp Lycoming T53-L-13 turboshaft was retained.

Tests in NASA's Ames wind tunnel showed that the aerodynamics of the airframe had been improved to such an extent that the equivalent flatplane area of the Huey had been reduced from 25sq ft to 11sq ft. Still with its original US Army serial number, the Model 533 made its maiden flight on Friday 10 August, 1962, and flight tests were conducted at Fort Worth in late 1962. In March 1963, the Model 533 flew at 173mph and 188mph was attained in a shallow dive. As the months went by more and more modifications were introduced in this helicopter. Several rotor types were tested (two-blade UH-1B-like rotor and rigid three-blade rotors) and two 1,700lb st Continental J69-T-9 turbojets were installed on each side of the fuselage. Take-off weight of the aircraft was now 8,600lb. On 17 January, 1964, the helicopter achieved a speed of 210mph in level flight using only 780shp from the 1,100shp Lycoming T53-L-9A shaft-turbine, plus 1,260lb st from the J69s.

The next modification consisted of fitting two small sweptback fixed wings to convert the aircraft into a compound helicopter. On 11 May, 1964, it flew at 222mph. The aircraft was then flown to San Antonio to have its J69-T-9s replaced by 1,700lb st J69-T-29s, and, on 15 October, 1964, the Model 533 was the first helicopter to break the 200 knots (230mph) barrier by attaining 236mph. On 6 April, 1965, the Model 533 flew at 250mph in level flight and 254mph in a shallow dive. It showed also its outstanding manoeuvrability in performing 2g turns and 60deg banks at speeds around 200mph, and a Mach number of 0.985 was recorded by the advancing blades of the rotor.

Early in 1968, a subsequent phase of the programme was the installation of two 3,300lb st Pratt & Whitney JT12A-3 turbojets at the end of short stub wings. The first flight in this configuration was made in 1968, the machine gradually recording still higher speeds and, in May 1969, Bell announced that 316mph had been attained.

Rotor diameter 44ft 0in (13.41m); disc area 1,520sq ft (141.2sq m); length of fuselage 42ft 7in (12.98m).
Normal take-off weight 9,200lb (4,173kg).
Maximum speed 316mph (509km/h).

*The fourth YH-40-BF (c/n 4; s/n 56-6723) was converted to become the Bell Model 533 experimental aircraft in order to test various rotor systems. (Bell, courtesy of J Scutts)*

*Late in its career, the Model 533 was fitted with two small wings. On 11 May, 1964, this aircraft flew at 222mph. (Bell)*

# Model 207 Sioux Scout

In July 1962, the experiments with armed helicopters turned to reality as the first Army armed helicopter company was activated in Okinawa for initial deployment in Vietnam. However, the evolution of armed helicopters led to such an increase in weight that the flight capabilities of these machines was severely compromised. Helicopter manufacturers began soon to develop new variants for an interim programme which later became known as AAFSS or Army's Advanced Aerial Fire Support System.

Bell proposed the Warrior and, by December 1962, also modified an OH-13S as an armed helicopter which would combine the desired combat potential with the desired flight performance. The aircraft, known by Bell as Model 207 Sioux Scout embodied several elements which were to become commonplace on future armed attack helicopters, for instance, low drag profile, crew of two seated in tandem with integrated weapons, sighting systems and equipment. A new profiled fuselage was made from a Model 47J-2 rear fuselage mated with an all-new glazed streamlined cockpit with reinforced plastic bubble. The landing gear was of the classic skid-type. As powerplant the Sioux Scout retained the 260hp turbo-supercharged Lycoming TVO-435-A1A and had the rotor system of the OH-13S. The crew was seated in tandem with dual flying controls. The pilot was above and behind the gunner who controlled an Emerson Electric TAT-101 chin-turret armed with two 0.30-in machine-guns. This turret was a privately-funded modified version of the M-60-C gun barbette which, linked to the movement of the gunner's sight, could swivel 200deg in azimuth, and 15deg above and 45deg below the horizon. The Sioux Scout also incorporated stub wings which had been designed to carry auxiliary fuel tanks as well as providing extra lift. Flight tests showed that these wings also improved high-speed turning capability. Several types of wings were evaluated on the Model 207, as well as various types of cowlings, tailboom elevators and fins.

The sole Model 207 prototype (N73927) made its maiden flight on 27 June, 1963, with Al Averill at the controls. This flight lasted ten minutes and by 25 July, the Sioux Scout had logged 18hr 30min flying. At the end of 1963, the aircraft was passed to the US Army for further evaluation by pilots of the 11th Air Assault Division at Fort Benning in Georgia. The Army pilots were surprised at the Model 207's capabilities and asked that such an aircraft but with a more powerful engine be promptly developed.

In fact, albeit a highly promising concept, the Sioux Scout was somewhat limited in true combat capability and had no future. However, it was a major step forward to today's AAHs.

*The Sioux Scout, showing the nose-mounted Emerson Electric TAT-101 gun turret. (Bell courtesy of J Scutts)*

*The Sioux Scout was built from commercial Model 47J-2 parts and featured a new streamlined cockpit as well as short wings. (Bell)*

# Model 208 Twin Delta, Model 212 Twin Two-Twelve and Military Twin

At the beginning of the 1960s, the Bell design team considered that the only way to give the UH-1 more power was to install two engines. In 1964, the conversion of a standard UH-1D to a twin-engined configuration was funded by Bell. Work was done in Fort Worth, and by the spring of 1965, the prototype Model 208 Twin Delta was ready to fly. Its powerplant comprised two Continental T72-T-2 Model 217 turboshafts mounted side by side and driving, via a combining gearbox, a single output shaft. Designated XT67-T-1, this powerplant offered 1,240shp for take-off. Besides offering more power, this arrangement also increased safety, an important factor in off-shore and rescue operations.

The maiden flight was made on 29 April, 1965. The new helicopter aroused interest on the US civil market but the very first orders came from Canada. On 1 May, 1968, Bell announced that the Canadian Government had approved the development of the twin-engined variant of the UH-1. This variant, known as Model 212, was to be powered by a 1,290shp Pratt & Whitney Canada PT6T-3 Twin Pac powerplant driving a two-blade all-metal semi-rigid rotor. The new helicopter could accommodate a pilot and up to fourteen passengers and, in its military variant, armament could include 0.30in MAG pod machine-gun systems, 2.75in air-to-ground rocket launchers (7 or 19 rounds), side-mounted 0.50in or 0.30in machine-guns. The order for a first batch of fifty helicopters was placed by the Canadian Armed Forces (under designation CUH-1N, later modified to CH-135) and the first Model 212 flew in April 1969. More orders soon followed, both civil and military: seventy-nine UH-1Ns for the US Air Force; forty UH-1Ns for the US Navy and twenty-two UH-1Ns for the US Marine Corps; 159 more being ordered later by the US Navy and Marine Corps.

The commercial version (Model 212 Twin Two-Twelve) received its FAA type certification in October 1970 and the FAA Transport Type Category A certification on 30 June, 1971. In June 1977, this Model became the first helicopter to receive FAA certification for single-pilot IFR operations with fixed floats. In June 1980, an improved variant of the PT6T-3, the PT6T-3B, was introduced which besides giving more power (1,800shp), also offered improved single-engine performance.

*Model 212 Twin Two-Twelve PT-HIG of the Brazilian company Lider Taxi Aerea S A operating from an offshore oil platform. (Bell)*

In mid-1988, production of the Model 212 was transferred to Bell's Canadian factory and, at the time of writing, more than 1,000 Model 212/UH-1N/CUH-1Ns have been produced. Among the main operators are Helikopter Service A/S (Norway), the Canada Department of Transport (Ottawa), ERA Helicopters (Anchorage, Alaska), the

*UH-1N BuNo 159703 of USMC Squadron HMM-165 at Kanehoe Bay, Hawaii, in September 1979. (J Wegg)*

*Model 212 (C-FNSA), modified by Conair, picking up water in a Canadian river using a remote system to fill the fuselage tank. (Conair)*

Connecticut National Bank (Hartford) and Grønlandsfly A/S (Greenland).

The Model 212 also entered production with Agusta in Italy under the AB 212 designation. The AB 212 is generally similar to its American counterpart. In addition Agusta developed on its own an ASW naval version, called AB 212AS. The AB 212AS is an extensively modified variant which incorporates a 1,875shp Pratt & Whitney Canada PT6T-6 Turbo Twin Pac powerplant, a strengthened structure protected against corrosion, provision for auxiliary fuel tanks and improved avionics and equipment for ASW missions (such as a Bendix AN/AQS-13B/F low-frequency variable depth sonar). Modifications were also made to the flying controls, fuel and electrical systems. Armament comprises two Motofides 244AS or two Mk.44/46 torpedoes, or two Marte Mk.2 or Sea Skua air-to surface missiles.

## Service History:

The first UH-1N was accepted by the US Air Force at Eglin AFB on 2 October, 1970. The UH-1Ns gradually replaced the UH-1Fs of the 20th SOS 'Green Hornet' stationed at Cam Ranh Bay. These were fitted with weapons systems such as GAU-2B/A, LAU-59/A rocket launchers and XM-94 rapid-fire 40mm hand-operated grenade launchers. 20th SOS UH-1Ns were later absorbed into the 24th Composite Wing based at Howard AFB in Panama.

Production of the UH-1N totalled seventy-nine machines which were deployed in various units of TAC (1st TFW, 24th CW, 57th FWW), MAC (89th MAG, 40th ARRS, 48th ARRS, 67th ARRS, 1550th CCTW), USAFE, PACAF (475th ABW), AFSC (3246th TW), AFRES (304th ARRS) and Air Force Headquarters. Of these, twenty-two were modified for rescue missions and designated HH-1N and ten were used as VIP transports with 89th MAG and designated VH-1N.

Deliveries to the US Navy and US Marine Corps began in 1971 and covered a total of 204 helicopters. The US Navy used the UH-1N with some of its squadrons such as HC-6, HC-16, TW-1, TW-4, VXE-6 and NATC and several Marine Corps units were equipped with the type: HMM-161, HMM-162, HMM-163, HMLA-167, HMLA-169, HMM-266, HMLA-267, HMLA-268, HMLA-269, HMT-303, HMLA-367, HMLA-369, HMH-463, HML-767, HML-771, HML-776, HMX-1 and Base Flights El Toro and Yuma. They were often used aboard amphibious assault ships (LPH). The six VH-1Ns used by HMX-1 were replaced in 1989 by Sikorsky VH-60s.

During the war against Iraq in January/February 1991, sixty UH-1Ns were operated by five USMC squadrons (HMLA-167, -267, -269, -367 and -369), along with the twenty-four UH-1Ns of the 14th Squadron of the Royal Saudi Air Force.

## Foreign Operators

The Model 212 has been delivered to numerous foreign civil operators

*UH-1N s/n 69-6606 belonging to 58th MAS at Ramstein in September 1974. (J Wegg)*

*A Canadian CUH-1N, or CH-135 in the current Canadian terminology, (s/n 135103) of CAF Mobile Command at CFB Trenton in August 1974. (J Gerritsma)*

*UH-1N (BuNo 158282) of HML-767 in the current Marine three-tone camouflage and low-visibility markings. (J Ethell)*

*One of the two Model 212s which were operated by Fuerza Aerea Mexicana. This one, c/n 30517, was sold on the US civil market as N4205Q. (J M G Gradidge)*

as well as more than thirty military operators as follows:

### Argentine:

the Fuerza Aérea Argentina took delivery of eight Model 212s (serialled H-81/H-88) and the Army of two Model 212s (AE-450/451).

### Austria:

the air force (Österreichische Luftstreitkräfte) bought eighteen AB 212s (coded 5D-HA/HR) in 1977 which are operated by Fliegerregiment I in Tulln-Langenlab'n and Fliegerregiment III in Linz-Hörsching.

### Bangladesh:

this country took delivery of at least seven Model 212s.

### Bolivia:

two Model 212s (serialled 101/102) were delivered.

### Botswana:

in 1990 the Botswana Defence Force ordered two additional Model 212s to supplement the three aircraft already in service.

### Brunei:

the Sultanate of Brunei Air Wing received five Model 212s (AMDB-105/106 and 117/119).

### Canada:

fifty CUH-1N/CH-135s (serialled 135101/135150) were delivered. The Canadians took delivery of their first CUH-1N on 3 May, 1971, and the fifty machines were all delivered within a year. They were deployed with Nos.403, 408, 422, 424, 427 and VU-32 Squadrons where they replaced the ageing CH-118.

### Chile:

Grupo 19 operated a single Model 212 which was lost in a crash in the early 1980s.

### Colombia:

the air force use one Model 212 (c/n 30511, serialled FAC002) as a VIP aircraft with Escuadrilla Presidencial stationed at Bogotá.

### Ghana:

the air force uses two Model 212s (serialled G650/651) in a VIP flight at Accra.

### Greece:

the Hellenic Air Force has two Model 212s, (c/n 30763 and 30765) and the army a single AB 212. The Greek navy received sixteen AB 212s among which eight are equipped for anti-submarine warfare and two modified for electronic warfare.

These are stationed in Marathon.

### Guyana:

the Guyana Defence Force Air Command fly three Model 212s (registered 8R-GEO–GEQ and -GEZ).

### Indonesia:

the army uses six Model 212s.

### Iran:

the navy took delivery of fourteen AB 212s (Nos.6-2401/2414). Twelve Model 212s were ordered in 1990.

*Agusta-Bell 212AS (MM.80937) belonging to Aviazione per la Marina Militare Italiana, in June 1978. This variant was developed by Bell's Italian licencee primarily for use by the Italian Navy. (R Farina)*

*The Model 212 Twin Two-Twelve is a versatile aircraft. It is seen here landing on a platform installed on top of a building. (Bell)*

*UH-1N BuNo 160444 from HMLA-167 stationed at New River, North Carolina. (Bell)*

### Israel:

IDFAF received at least two Model 212s.

### Italy:

Italian air force received three AB 212s (serialled MM81072/81074 and coded AWTI-01/03), the army has four AB 212s (MM81117/81120). the police have two AB 212s (MM80742/80743), and the Italian navy has fifty-five AB 212ASs (MM80933/80960 and MM81075/81100) which serve with 4th and 5th Grupelicot AMM aboard Vittorio Veneto and Andrea Doria-class cruisers, Audace-class destroyers and Maestrale and Alpino-class frigates.

### Jamaica:

the air force received three Model 212s (coded JDFH-6/8).

### Lebanon:

the air force flies twelve AB 212s (serialled L-551/562).

### Libya:

the army has two AB 212s (one of which is coded LC-5521).

### Mexico:

the air force operates two Model 212s (coded TPH-01/02) within Escuadrón Aéreo 209 at Santa Lucía.

### Morocco:

the air force took delivery of five AB 212s (registered CN-APA-01/APE-05).

### Panama:

the Fuerza Aérea Panameña operates four UH-1Ns (serialled 001/004).

### Peru:

the air force received at least eighteen Model 212s (serialled in the 600 range) which are operated by Escuadron 341 at Lima-Callao and the navy has six AB 212ASs (serialled HE-470/475) which serve aboard Montero-class frigates.

*A factory-fresh Model 212 dropping hay bales in a flooded region of Africa. (Bell)*

*Model 212 of Fuerzas de Defensa Panama (FAP-120). (Bell)*

## Saudi Arabia:

ten AB 212s are in use with 1st Squadron at Riyadh and 14th Squadron at At'Taif.

## Singapore:

three SAR equipped Model 212s (serialled 210/212) were delivered and are operated by 120th Squadron at Changi.

## Somalia:

the air force received four AB 212s (serialled MM60218/60221).

## South Korea:

the ROKAF took delivery of an unknown quantity of Model 212s.

## Spain:

the Spanish army (FAMET) used AB 212s within its Helicopter unit IV (UHEL IV) stationed at Seville, from 1981 to 1987. They have now been replaced by Aérospatiale AS.332B Super Pumas. The Spanish Navy took delivery of twelve AB 212ASs (serialled Z.18-1/2 and HA.18-3/12) and uses them with Escuadrilla 003.

## Sri Lanka:

two Model 212s (serialled CH543 and 544) were acquired in 1984 and an order for a further twelve has been placed with Bell-Asia together with a contract with Heli Orient for the modification of nine of them with pintle-mounted 12.7mm machine-guns and 2.75in rocket pods. These are operated by the 4th HW at Katunayake.

### Thailand:

the RTAF used two Model 212s in its Royal Flight (replaced by Model 412 in 1982), the army has nine Model 212s and the navy operates eight Model 212s with ASW capability. In early 1990, the Royal Thai Army placed a $118.4 million order for twenty-five Model 212s.

### Turkey:

the Turkish navy received six AB 212ASs (coded TCB-34/39) which are deployed aboard Yavuz-class frigates.

### Uganda:

the air force operates an unknown quantity of Model 212s (serialled in the U-700 range) and the police have four Model 212s (registered AW-1, AW-2, 5X-UWF and 5X-UWG).

### Uruguay:

two Model 212s were delivered early 1980 and are used for VIP and staff transport by Grupo No.5 stationed at Carrasco.

### Venezuela:

the Fuerza Aéreas Venezolanas operates two Model 212s (serialled 0929 and 1972) and the navy has ten AB 212ASs (MP-0301/0310) in the maritime patrol role with Escuadrón MP-03 deployed aboard Lupo-class frigates.

### West Germany:

Border Security Troops operate seven Model 212s (registered D-HAND, D-HARZ, D-HBZS, D-HBZT, D-HEPP, D-HHPP and D-HIPP).

### Yemen:

the air force has a single Model 212 equipped as a VIP transport.

### Zambia:

the Zambian Air Force fly an unknown quantity of AB 212s (serialled in the AF700 range).

In Canada, Conair Aviation Ltd, in Abbotsford, has developed a water-bomber variant of the Model 212 under the designation Bell 212 Helitanker. In addition to the normal passenger and cargo carrying equipment, the Helitanker has a 1,360-litre-retardant delivery belly-mounted tank (which can be removed in fifteen minutes), an extra high skid gear, a tank self-loading system, an off-load system and a foam injection system. The Helitanker has two distinct operational roles. It can be used as an air tanker to deliver fire retardant, foam or water from a ground-based operation to a fire site, or it can be used independently in co-ordination with ground crews on smaller spot fires. The type has been in operation since 1980 in Canada with Frontier Helicopters (a Conair subsidiary) and Australia with the National Safety Council.

## Model 212

Rotor diameter 48ft 2¼in (14.69m); length overall 57ft 3¼in (17.46m); length of fuselage 42ft 4¾in (12.92m); height overall 14ft 10¼in (4.53m); disc area 1,871,91sq ft (173.9sq m).

Empty weight 5,997lb (2,720kg); maximum take-off weight 11,200lb (5080kg).

Maximum cruising speed at sea level 115mph (185km/h); maximum rate of climb at sea level 1,320ft/min (402m/min); service ceiling 13,000ft (3,960m); hover ceiling in ground effect 11,000ft (3,350m); maximum range 261 miles (420km).

## AB 212ASW

Rotor diameter 48ft 0in (14.63m); length overall 57ft 1in (17.40m); disc area 1,809.5sq ft (168.1sq m).

Empty weight 7,540lb (3,420kg); loaded weight (ASW mission) 11,176lb (5,070kg).

Maximum speed at sea level 122mph (196km/h); maximum rate of climb at sea level 1,300ft/min (396m/min); hover ceiling in ground effect 10,500ft (3,200m); hover ceiling outside ground effect 1,300ft (396m); maximum range with auxiliary tanks 414 miles (667km).

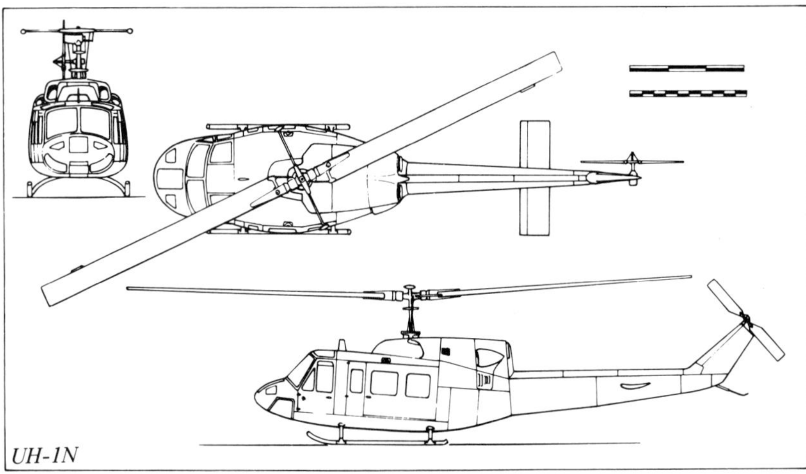
*UH-1N*

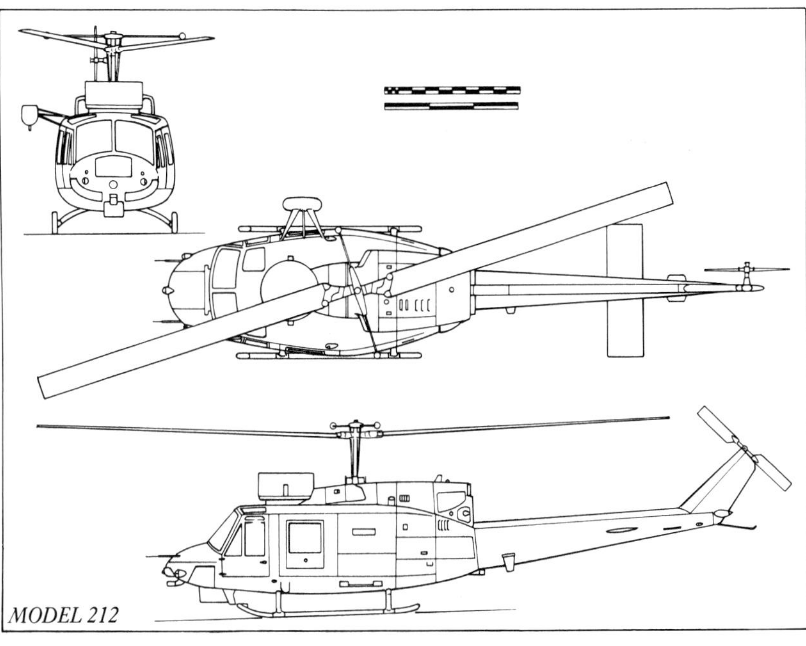
*MODEL 212*

# Models 209/249 and 309 AH-1 HueyCobra, KingCobra, SeaCobra, SuperCobra and Viper

In June 1962, Bell invited US Army officials to the Fort Worth facility to see the mock-up of a highly innovative combat helicopter. Known at the time as the Design D-255 Iroquois Warrior and wearing false s/n 62-00255 (HU-1F), the new aircraft looked like an hybrid between a fighter and a helicopter. Relatively small, the Iroquois Warrior retained several features of the famous Huey and had a low silhouette, narrow profile and a small cross-section forward fuselage. This new streamlined fuselage with retractable skids had been designed for maximum speed, armament payload and crew efficiency. It featured a stepped cockpit configuration (nowadays widespread among the world's combat helicopters) with the gunner placed just in front and below the pilot. Armament included a ball-turret in the nose, a streamlined gun compartment under the fuselage and various external loads (including French SS-11 missiles and 2.75in FFAR rocket pods). Although innovative, the D-255 retained the powerplant as well as the basic transmission and rotor system of the well proven UH-1C in order to reduce maintenance and development time as well as to cut costs.

On 30 August, 1962, the so-called Howze Board, a study group led by Gen Hamilton H Howze, submitted its final report in which recommendations were made for the creation of Air Cavalry Combat Brigades and the design of specific aircraft for that purpose. Bell decided to go further in its company funded attack helicopter research programme but on a reduced cost basis. The first step was to build a flying test-bed by transforming a standard Model 47 into the Model 207 Sioux Scout, described elsewhere in this book. The flight tests were highly successful but the Army pilots called for a larger turbine-engined aircraft.

Bell went back to work on a redesigned scaled-down version of the D-255, known as the D-262, which was entered in the 1964 Advanced Aerial Fire Support System (AAFSS) competition calling for a fast, armoured, heavily-armed helicopter for which Lockheed (with the AH-56A Cheyenne) and Sikorsky (with the Model S-66) were eventually selected. The D-262 had been eliminated to the great disappointment of the Bell team. In any case, the AAFSS programme called for a highly sophisticated aircraft which would require time and large amounts of money to develop (in fact the programme eventually became a nightmare) and at Bell, Charlie Siebel, chief experimental helicopter

*The sixth AH-1G (s/n 66-15249) during a test flight. On this aircraft, the anti-torque tail rotor is on the port side of the tail. (Bell)*

*Spanish AH-1Gs of Escuadrilla 007. These aircraft were later returned to the United States. (Bell)*

projects engineer, was convinced that an interim aircraft would soon be necessary.

In December 1964, without any Army requirement, Bell's staff decided to go ahead with the development of such an aircraft, the Model 209 which soon got the unofficial name of Cobra. At a later date, in a management meeting, it was decided that the Model 209 should be built as quickly as possible (in no more than six months with the first flight occurring no later than 1 October, 1965) for no more than $1 million. In fact the prototype was eventually completed ahead of schedule at a cost of just over a million dollars ($1,040,000). Charlie Siebel was designated to direct the project which was to be kept confidential even within the company.

The project was started on 10 March, 1965, and the mock-up was completed in the same month. The Model 209 silhouette was roughly similar to that of the D-255. It featured the same sleek tandem-seat layout with a semi-monocoque fuselage whose width was only 3ft, to be compared to the 8ft width of the standard UH-1. The new design made use of a 1,100shp Lycoming T-53L-11 turboshaft engine driving a 44ft diameter Model 540 'door-hinge' two-blade rotor with UH-1C transmission unit. The 27in chord blades made of extruded aluminium spars and laminates were turning at between 294rpm and 324rpm, but the traditional rotor stabiliser bar had been abandoned in favour of the Stability Control Augmentation System (SCAS) in order to save weight. Also taken directly from the UH-1C was the tail boom, empennage (with wider chord fin) and 8ft 6in diameter anti-torque rotor. Stub wings, located each side of the forward fuselage, generated some additional lift. Finally, after much discussion, it was decided that the undercarriage would comprise two retractable skids.

Armament consisted of a single GAU-2B/A 7.62mm Minigun housed in an Emerson Electric nose-turret with 4,000 rounds of ammunition and external loads fixed under a hard point located beneath each stub wing. Calculated maximum level speed was 175 knots in clean configuration.

Construction was well advanced when the Army announced what Charlie Siebel had suspected a year before, that is to say that the US Army was seeking an interim gunship to meet immediate combat needs in Southeast Asia within 24 months. Bell was quick to propose its Model 209 and a formal presentation was made on 18 August, 1965. Proposals were also made by four other manufacturers: Kaman, Boeing-Vertol, Piasecki and Sikorsky.

The Model 209 was rolled out on 2 September, 1965, and, at 7.30am, on 7 September, 1965, three weeks ahead of schedule, the helicopter took off on its 12-minute maiden flight with Bill Quinlan, Bell's chief test pilot, at the controls. For the occasion, the Cobra had been painted in US Army olive drab and registered N209J. The prototype was flown again on 8 September and the following day achieved 162 knots in level flight. Manufacturer's tests were conducted over September and October, and these revealed vibrations which were cured in due course. In early November, at the request of the Army, comparative tests were conducted at Edwards AFB between the three remaining contenders, ie the Kaman UH-2 Seasprite, the Sikorsky S-61 and the Bell Model 209 (the Boeing-Vertol Chinook and Piasecki Pathfinder entries having been eliminated). Subsequent tests were conducted at Fort Sill, Oklahoma, and on 11 March, 1966, the Army finally announced that the Model 209 was the winner and its intention to order it into full-scale production. A development contract was awarded on 4 April, 1966, and a production contract for 110 units plus long lead-time spares followed nine days later.

In June 1967, with the Paris Air Show, the Model 209 began a tour of Europe, followed by a tour of the US Army bases in the USA. The Model 209 prototype was used until 1972 for various tests and accumulated some 1,090 flying hours. It has been preserved in the George S Patton Museum of Cavalry and Armor, at Fort Knox, Kentucky, since November 1972.

## Production History:

### AH-1G Cobra:

the development contract for the Model 209 included the construction of two pre-production aircraft (s/n 66-15246 and -15247) which were mostly identical to the Model 209 with the exception of some noticeable modifications such as a

*Model of a projected twin-engined Model 280 wide-body Cobra. (Bell)*

non-retractable undercarriage, a new and larger chin-turret as well as redesigned and reinforced stub wings to satisfy anticipated armament requirements. The first of these was rolled out in October 1966 and accomplished its maiden flight on 15 October with Gene Colvin at the controls. Testing proceeded remarkably rapidly. Armament qualification was conducted at Fort Hood, Texas, during the following February with this aircraft, and the second aircraft flew on 10 March, 1967, with Turpin Gerald in the cockpit. This second aircraft was primarily used to qualify the SCAS. The first production examples followed soon after as they were rolled out in May and the first deliveries to the Army took place in June. The production AH-1G was powered by a 1,400shp (derated to 1,100shp) Lycoming T53-L-13 turboshaft engine, driving a two-blade wide-chord Model 540 'door-hinge' rotor. On later aircraft, the tail rotor was moved from the port to the starboard side of the tail boom to improve directional control. On the armament side, Emerson Electric designed and developed the TAT-102A tactical armament turret, which was faired into the front fuselage and housed a GAU-2B/A Minigun six-barrel 7.62mm machine-gun, with 8,000 rounds. This turret, which was accepted by the Army as an interim system, was later superseded on the AH-1G by the XM-28 subsystem in TAT-141 turret, mounting either two Miniguns with 4,000 rounds each, two XM-129 (similar to the XM-75) 40mm grenade launchers, each with 300 rounds; or one Minigun and one XM-129. Structural provisions had also been incorporated in the airframe to accept a turret sub-system capable of firing the M-61A1 20mm Vulcan gun, the XM-197 three-barrel 20mm gun, or a three-barrel 30mm gun. Four external store attachments under the stub-wings could accommodate various loads, including a total of seventy-six 2.75in rockets in four XM-159 packs, two XM-18 or XM-18E1 Minigun pods or four Hughes BGM-71A TOW wire-guided missiles. In normal operation, the co-pilot/gunner controlled and fired the turret armament, using a hand-held pantograph-mounted sight to which the turret was slaved. The TAT-102 turret could be fired throughout a field of 230deg, 50deg down and 21deg up, and the TAT-141 could be fired throughout 115deg, 60deg and 25deg respectively. The crew was protected by seats and side panels made of NOROC armour, manufactured by the Norton Company, and an armoured windscreen. Other panels protected vital areas of the aircraft such as the engine compressor.

*This project dated 1958 and known as the Bell Model D-245 is the earliest known Cobra concept. The short swept stub-wings are fitted with wingtip pods. (Bell)*

Subsequent contracts raised the total of AH-1Gs on order to 838 by October 1968. Deliveries began in June 1967 and operational deployment in Vietnam was begun in the early autumn of 1967. On 30 January, 1970, 170 additional aircraft were ordered, followed by a further seventy in 1971, bringing the total prouction to 1,126. The last Cobra was delivered in February 1973. As an interim aircraft during development of a twin-engined variant, the Marine Corps ordered a batch of seventy-two AH-1Gs which was eventually cut to only thirty-eight. These helicopters were allocated BuNos 157204/157241 but in fact they retained their original Army serial numbers. The first aircraft were taken in charge by USMC in February 1969 and introduced in

*The Model 249 was converted into a research aircraft for the US Army's Advanced Rotorcraft Technology Integration (ARTI) programme. (Bell)*

*AH-1S s/n 71-20991 belonging to 8th CavCo at Ramstein in June 1987. This aircraft has the TOW launcher with missile tubes installed as well as 19-tube FFAR rocket pod. Noteworthy is the extended exhaust nozzle. (M C Klaver)*

Vietnam as soon as the following April. There, they undertook operational missions until April 1971.

### TH-1G:

some AH-1Gs, such as aircraft s/n 66-15288 and 67-15623, have been modified to TH-1G dual control trainers to include instructor's flying controls and instrument panel.

### JAH-1G:

some AH-1Gs have been converted as test-bed aircraft for various experiments such as Rockwell AGM-114A Hellfire laser-guided missile, General Electric M197 three-barrel 20mm gun with improved rate of fire (1,500rpm to 3,000rpm). The JAH-1Gs included s/n 67-15681 written off on 29 August, 1984, 68-15191 written off on 1 November, 1975, and 71-20985.

### Model 309 KingCobra:

late in 1969, with the US disengagement from Vietnam, the US Army began to be more concerned by the military balance in central Europe. The huge number of tanks deployed by the Warsaw Pact land forces was its prime matter of concern. An attack helicopter with tank-killing capability was considered a high priority. At the time, the Lockheed AH-56A Cheyenne, developed under AAFSS and flown in May 1967, had such a capability but its cost, complexity and teething troubles greatly handicapped its future. The ideal weapon system appeared then to be a combination of the AH-1 Cobra helicopter and the anti-tank TOW missile. Bell decided to build, with company funds, two prototypes of such an aircraft, both in single-engined and twin-engined configurations, known as the Model 309 KingCobra.

Design work was begun by a team led by Joe Tilley and construction started in January 1971. The Model 309 was a scaled-up version of the AH-1G with a gross weight of 14,000lb, a lengthened and stiffened fuselage, a redesigned tail assembly with lower fin for improved longitudinal stability and a considerably modified nose. It also had the transmission, wide-chord two-blade main rotor and drive train of the Model 211 HueyTug.

The single-engine prototype retained the 2,850shp Avco-Lycoming T55-L-7C turboshaft engine of the Model 211 while the twin-engined prototype had the 1,800shp Pratt & Whitney T400-CP-400 turboshaft TwinPac powerplant. The KingCobra incorporated new avionics and systems to fulfill its anti-tank mission (inertial navigation system, APN-198 radar altimeter, fire-control computer, multi-sensor sight, head-up display, helmet sighting system, FL-33 FLIR, low-light level television and, of course TOW guidance system). Armament included provision for sixteen TOW missiles under extended stub wings and a General Electric chin-turret housing a three-barelled 20mm Gatling gun with 1,345 rounds.

The twin-engined Model 309 (c/n 2503, registered N309J) made its maiden flight at Fort Worth on 10 September, 1971, with Gene Colvin at the controls, followed by its single-engined stable mate in January 1972. Unfortunately, the latter was the victim of an accident on 11 April, 1972, and suffered major damage. To meet future Army needs it was decided to convert the twin-engined 309 into single-engined configura-

*AH-1W BuNo 162532 in the three-tone Marine Corps camouflage. Chaff dispensers are mounted on top of each stub wing and eight TOW missiles are carried. (Bell)*

tion. As expected, on 9 August, 1972, the Army finally cancelled the Cheyenne programme and in due course two helicopter manufacturers, Sikorsky and Bell, submitted proposals for a less sophisticated aircraft, the Model S-67 and the Model 309 respectively. Tests and demonstrations were successfully conducted with both aircraft, but the Army set up new requirements and opened a new contest within the Advanced Attack Helicopter programme (AAH) which would eventually lead to the selection of today's MDD/Hughes AH-64 Apache.

The Bell Model 309 (N309J) is now preserved by the US Army Aviation Museum in Fort Rucker, Alabama.

### AH-1E:

following the production of one hundred AH-1S(PROD)/AH-1Ps, new improvements were incorporated in the ninety-eight following production aircraft of Step 2, at first designated AH-1S(ECAS). These improvements mainly concerned the armament (defined under Enhanced Cobra Armament Program or ECAP). The Enhanced Cobra Armament System (ECAS) consisted of an electrically-powered General Electric M79E1 universal turret with an M-197 Vulcan 20mm three-barrelled gun which could be fired throughout a field of 220deg, 20.5deg up and 50deg down, automatic compensation for off-axis gun firing, provision for the XM138 Rocket Management Subsystem and a 10kVA alternator to provide the necessary additional electric power.

In 1987, all AH-1S(ECAS)s were redesignated AH-1E. A total of ninety-eight AH-1Es were produced with the first aircraft delivered in September 1978 and the last in October 1979.

### AH-1F:

Phase II of the ECAP was initiated with the 199th production AH-1S (first designated AH-1S(MC), MC standing for modernized Cobra, and then AH-1F from 1987; not to be confused with AH-1S(MOD)). These modifications were evaluated at first on two prototypes which were converted AH-1Ps (s/n 76-22567 and -22600). The main improvement concerned the introduction of a new fire control subsystem with Kaiser HUD and Rockwell AN/AAS-32 laser rangefinder and tracker linked to a ballistic computer which increased both accuracy and efficiency of the armaments. The AH-1F was also equipped with a low-airspeed sensor, a Doppler navigation system, an IFF transponder, new secure voice communications, an AN/ALQ-144 infra-red jammer and an infra-red suppression exhaust shroud.

The first AH-1F was taken on charge by the Army in November 1979 and the 99th and last one of the first batch was delivered in March 1981. Follow on contracts concerned fifty additional aircraft which were delivered from April 1981, bringing the grand total to 151 AH-1Fs (including the two prototypes).

### TAH-1F:

designation for forty-one training variant examples of the AH-1F.

### AH-1J SeaCobra:

although satisfied with its AH-1Gs in most respects, the Marine Corps was still in need of an attack helicopter more nearly tailored to its requirements, especially in respect of armament, engine configuration (the Corps preferred a twin-engined installation for safety and reliability) and avionics. By the autumn of 1967, after much discussion and controversy, the Marines obtained thirty-eight navalized Cobras incorporating Navy avionics, 20mm gun and rotor brake, but retaining at first a single-engine configuration. This was later changed when, in May 1968, Bell was awarded a $15.5

*The SuperCobra seen carrying eight Hellfire missiles. (Bell)*

million contract for development and production of forty-nine twin-engined AH-1J SeaCobras. The AH-1J differed from the AH-1G in having a 1,800shp Pratt & Whitney Canada PT6T-3 Turbo TwinPac (also designated T400-CP-400) coupled powerplant of the kind specified for the UH-1N. Externally the main modification concerned the engine cowlings. An electrically-driven chin-turret system, developed by the General Electric Company, was faired into the forward fuselage, and housed an M197 three-barrelled 20mm gun (firing rate: 750rpm, but a 16 round burst limiter was incorporated in the firing switch). This turret could be fired throughout a field of 220deg, 18deg up and 50deg down. External stores fitted under stub wings, mainly similar to those for the Army version, included LAU-61, -68 or -69 rocket pods, SUU-11A Minigun pods, Rockwell AGM-114A Hellfire anti-armour modular missile system, CBU-55 fuel-air explosive bombs, M118 smoke grenade dispensers. The avionics featured a navalised package with AN/ARC-51AX UHF command set, AN/ARC-131 FM tactical set, AN/AIC-18 intercom, AN/ARN-52(V) TACAN. Other modifications included the much demanded rotor brake, increased chord tail rotor blades and new push/pull rotor controls.

The first production AH-1J (BuNo 157757) was rolled out and made its initial flight on 14 October, 1969, and, following a complementary order for twenty additional aircraft, the last and 69th left the production line in February, 1975.

## AH-1P:

during 1975, a special study group of the Army's PASS IN Review (Priority Aircraft Subsystem Suitability Review) worked to determine how to improve the Cobra beyond the ICAP/ICAM programmes. The scope of this study was to 'harden' the aircraft against new anti-aircraft defence systems by incorporating new cockpit instrumentation and canopy, better armament and ECM equipment. This modernization programme eventually led to the production of 305 (later 297) aircraft in three versions (or Steps): the AH-1S(PROD) which became designated AH-1P in 1987, the AH-1S (ECAS) which became AH-1E and the AH-1S(MC) which became AH-1F.

Step 1 called for the procurement of one hundred AH-1S(PROD) which were essentially similar to the AH-1S(MOD) with the T53-L-703 engine, new gearboxes and transmissions, push/pull anti-torque controls (from the 67th aircraft) and a newly designed flat-plate low-glint canopy. The AH-1P also incorporated new instrumentation and avionics (improved nap-of-the-earth NOE instrument panel layout, continental United States navigation equipment, radar altimeter . . .). A first $37.3 million contract for forty-four aircraft was awarded on 18 December, 1975, and first production machines were delivered to the Army during the summer of 1977. The first unit to receive this version was the 82nd Airborne Division at Fort Bragg, North Carolina. The 100th and last aircraft was delivered in August 1978. Two US Army AH-1Ps (s/n 77-22785 and -22787) have been acquired for night interception missions by the US Customs Service.

## AH-1Q:

during development and testing of the ill-fated AH-56 and evaluation of Model 309, the Army had in fact not fulfilled its urgent need for an anti-tank helicopter. That is why the Army decided to equip its current AH-1G fleet with TOW and to procure additional Cobras. On 6 March, 1972, the Army awarded Bell a $24 million contract to conduct the Improved Cobra Armament Program (ICAP). This consisted of

*The prototype of the SuperCobra displayed this colourful scheme. It was painted glossy black overall and the fuselage-long snake was gold. (Bell)*

modifying eight AH-1Gs with TOW missile system and Helmet Directed Fire Control subsystem. These aircraft were designated YAH-1Q. Although some strengthening had to be introduced in the airframe following preliminary launching tests, the first YAH-1Q was delivered in February 1973, and a first $59.2 million contract was issued on 31 January, 1974, for the conversion of one hundred and one AH-1Gs to AH-1Q configuration. On 16 December, 1974, 189 additional conversions were required by the Army.

### AH-1R:

the additional weight introduced by the integration of the TOW missile system on the AH-1Q had influenced performance and manoeuvrability of the Cobra to such an extent that this led to a Product Improvement Program consisting of the introduction of an uprated engine and modified drive train. Under Improved Cobra Agility and Manoeuvrability program (ICAM), one AH-1G was modified as the YAH-1R (s/n 70-15936), and one YAH-1Q was so-modified as the the YAH-1S. The uprated engine was developed from the Avco-Lycoming T53-L-13 turboshaft. Known as the T53-L-703, it offered 1,800shp. The airframe also incorporated a new transmission and Model 212 tail rotor. The two development aircraft were completed by December 1974 and taken on charge by the Army for evaluation.

### AH-1S

(see AH-1R section): on 30 June, 1975, following testing of two evaluation aircraft upgraded under the ICAM programme, a contract was initiated by the Army in order to incorporate improvements on seventy-two AH-1Qs still under production and to modify 198 out of the 290 AH-1Gs due to receive TOW and the twenty AH-1Qs yet to be delivered to ICAM standards. These aircraft were known as AH-1S(MOD), 'MOD' standing for 'Modified', and were all modified by February 1979. In addition to an uprated engine, these aircraft incorporated new fibreglass rotor blades. In 1976, the YAH-1R was tested with success with composite rotor blades, and this led to a first short production run of 200 blades which were introduced on some AH-1Ss. There were teething problems with these blades and several modifications had to be introduced before satisfactory blades could be delivered to field units. Early in 1987, all AH-1S(MOD)s became officially known as AH-1Ss.

### TH-1S(MOD):

under the Minuteman programme, a contract was awarded on 26 September, 1984, for the modification of fifteen aircraft to TH-1S(MOD) for the Army National Guard. These aircraft were modified by Northrop's Electro-Mechanical Division under a programme known as 'Night Stalker' and incorporated ICAM modifications and TOW missiles.

### AH-1S(PROD):

first designation of the AH-1P. See under AH-1P.

### AH-1S(ECAS):

first designation of the AH-1E. See under AH-1E.

### AH-1S(MC):

firsat designation of the AH-1F. See under AH-1F.

*The first AH-1J SeaCobra (BuNo 157757) of the US Marine Corps. (Bell)*

*The single-engine KingCobra. It has a Telescopic Sighting Unit associated with the General Electric 20-mm M197 rotary cannon. (Bell)*

### AH-1T SeaCobra:

as the US Army had done for the AH-1G, the Marine Corps soon began seeking to improve the AH-1J, especially its performance. Thanks to the Iran contract for Model 214s and AH-1Js, a more powerful variant of the TwinPac, delivering 1,970shp, and improved transmissions were developed with Irani funds. In 1974, two AH-1Js (BuNos 159228 and 159229) were modified to receive the T400-WV-402 TwinPac as well as a new transmission and the tail rotor of the Model 214A. Congress also insisted that the TOW system be incorporated. After much discussion it was decided that about a half (twenty-four aircraft) of the fifty-five AH-1Ts to be procured would receive the BGM-71A TOW (aircraft designated AH-1T(TOW)). The remaining aircraft were eventually TOW-equipped by a retrofit programme in 1981/83. Externally, the main differences were a 12in fuselage stretch to overcome centre of gravity problems, a re-positioned tail rotor and a ventral tail fin to improve longitudinal stability. Armament remained the same. The first production order was placed in June 1975 and the first AH-1T prtotype (BuNo 159228) made its maiden flight on 20 May, 1976, with Gene Colvin at the controls. Subsequent testing by the Marines proved successful and the first production helicopter (BuNo 160105) was delivered to the Marine Corps on 15 October, 1977.

### AH-1T+:

the AH-1T suffered performance problems, especially in hot conditions, so in 1978, funds were raised for a powerplant improvement programme with procurement of new aircraft and retrofitting of existing AH-1Ts. The modifications comprised the integration of two individual 3,250shp General Electric T700-GE-401 turboshaft engines and gearboxes from the Model 214ST. The Marines sent back one of its AH-1Ts to Bell for modification and the new aircraft flew for the first time in April 1980, with Dick Kjellander at the controls. Further testing showed significant performance improvements. Unfortunately, at the time there were no funds to follow on the project and the modified AH-1T was converted back to its original configuration.

In 1983, sufficient funds could be raised for further testings. Once again, a standard AH-1T (BuNo 161022) was used as test aircraft and flown for the first time on 16 November, 1983. It was then known as the AH-1T+. Flight tests were very encouraging and led to the approval of a first production batch of twenty-two aircraft on FY85, soon followed by a second batch of twenty-two aircraft on FY86. In addition to the new powerplant and gearboxes, several other improvements were introduced in the AH-1T+ such as modified rotor head, new vibration suppression system, upgraded avionics (AN/APR-39 and AN/APR-44 radar warning systems, AN/ALQ-144 IR jammer).

On the armament side, in addition to the standard three-barrelled M-197 20mm gun qualified to fire standard M-50 series or improved PIE 20mm ammunition at 675 shots per minute, the AH-1T+ could carry BGM-71A TOW and AGM-114A Hellfire anti-tank missiles, AIM-9L Sidewinder air-to-air missiles and AGM-122A Sidearm anti-

*The first of the Fuji-built AH-1Fs (s/n 73401) firing a salvo of 2.75-in FFAR rockets. (Bell)*

*One of the AH-1Fs used by the Pakistani Army. This aircraft, serialled 786-007, is armed with eight TOW missile tubes. The GEC M-143 low-speed, omni-directional air data sensor is visible on the right side of the canopy. (Bell)*

radiation missiles, Zuni air-to-ground rockets, 20mm gun pods, bombs, AN/ALE-39 dispensers with chaff, flares and active radio jammers. The Kaiser HUD is compatible with PNVS-5 and ANVIS-6 night vision goggles. Other improvements include enhanced armour protection for crew members and for the fuel system which was able to withstand a direct hit by a 23mm HEI round, as well as special low IR-reflective paint.

### AH-1W SuperCobra:

when the first AH-1T+ (BuNo 162532) was rolled out of Bell's facilities in Fort Worth in 1986, it was almost an entirely new aircraft and not just an upgraded variant. The type was thus redesignated AH-1W SuperCobra. This aircraft was taken on charge by the Marines Air Ground Task Force on 27 March, 1986, and the 44th and last of the first batch was delivered in August 1988. In 1988, a $146.9 million contract for a further thirty AH-1W 'Whiskey Cobras' was awarded to Bell with an option on four additional aircraft. Deliveries of these began in June 1990 and ended in June 1991. Current plans call for the retrofit of thirty-nine AH-1Ts to AH-1W configuration under a separate contract with Naval Air Systems Command (NAVAIR); the first AH-1T (BuNo 160801) entered conversion procedure in June 1987 and all aircraft have been delivered. The USMC Reserves also have indicated a need for forty-two AH-1Ws. Among further improvements under test, noteworthy is the installation of the Model 680 rotor system on an AH-1W (see later). The development of a night targeting sight is being conducted through a contract awarded to Taman jointly funded by the Marines and Israeli Air Force. This sight will provide a FLIR capability as well as laser designation and range finding. Other proposals to enhance the SuperCobra are an improved navigation system which will include a Doppler navigation device and a cockpit control system, and a new wing which will provide two extra armament stations.

### TAH-1W:

designation for a single trainer example of the AH-1W.

### Viper:

in 1987, Bell announced the Viper which is a hybrid aircraft: in fact, an AH-1W mated with the Model 680 bearingless rotor. The Viper has an uprated transmission and a higher maximum gross weight to accommodate more armament, ie eight AGM-114A Hellfire or BGM-71A TOW II missiles, fourteen 2.75in rockets, 20mm M-197 three-barrelled gun with 750 rounds, two AIM-9L Sidewinder or Stinger air-to-air missiles and two AN/ALE-39 dispensers.

Modification programmes are still continuing. The most recent included C-Nite providing capability for detecting, acquiring and engaging targets at night, air-to-air Stinger or ATAS, C-Flex or Cobra fleet life extension featuring Night Fix lighting, rotor improvements, improved TOW test set and radio upgrade, improved SCAS and AN/AVR-2 laser warning.

In addition to the numerous production variants and sub-variants of

*The Model 249 served as test-bed for the Model 412 four-blade rotor. It has a provisional nose-probe. (Bell)*

the Cobra, some aircraft have been modified specifically and were used in various test programmes. One aircraft (s/n 66-15248) has been delivered from the US Army's maintenance depot at Corpus Christie to NASA Langley Research Center. This aircraft has been involved in the investigation of accoustic phenomena as well as a number of programmes concerning rotor aerodynamics and performance. In 1976, this aircraft was transferred to Ames Research Center where it served as a chase aeroplane before being returned to the US Army in 1983. Among other modified aircraft, AH-1s of US Customs Service are worth mention as the nose turret has been replaced by a powerful 'Nitesun' searchlight. In Fort Rucker, the US Army uses some fifteen AH-1Ss fitted with the PNVS of the Apache system to train pilots to take off and land 'blind'. Several projects to enhance the Cobra were also prepared by Bell's design team among which a swept-wing variant, a 'flip-tip' variant with wheeled undercarriage hidden in downward-folding stub wings, and a wide-body variant known as the Model 280.

## Service History

On 29 August, 1967, the first six AH-1Gs were airlifted to Bien Hoa and two days later came the first flight of a Cobra in Vietnam. At first, the aircraft were assigned to the New Equipment Training Team (NETT) of the 1st Aviation Brigade. On 4 September, Maj Gen G P Seneff destroyed a sampan in the Mekong delta using rockets and Minigun, but the first real combat operation took place on 8 October when two Cobras of the 334th AHC successfully escorted ten 'slick' transport Hueys. Thanks to its low silhouette, its speed and its great ability, the Cobra (soon nicknamed the 'Snake') was found ideal for low-level work. It was able to hide when approaching a landing zone

*Mock-up of the Bell D-255. Noteworthy are the ball gun-turret and the double curvature canopy. This mock-up carries the fake serial number 00255. (Bell)*

*The AH-1-4BW (Four-bladed Whiskey) in flight near the Bell Helicopter Textron Flight Research Facility at Arlington, Texas. Exhaust of the T700 engines is visible on this view. (Bell)*

(LZ) and was a much harder target to hit than the Iroquois.

During its presence in Southeast Asia, the Cobra proved highly successful escorting troop carrying Hueys as well as in accomplishing close fire support missions. The AH-1G arrived just in time as the Viet-Congs launched their now famous 'Tet' offensive in January 1968. It was also the spearhead of the operation code-named Lamson 719 which began on 8 February, 1971, and lasted till 9 April. The scope of this operation was to strike North Vietnamese bases and infiltration routes in Laos. During this campaign the 'Snakes' proved once again their excellence and for the first time engaged tanks. Their heyday took place on 24 March when the Cobras sighted sixty-six enemy PT-76 tanks and destroyed six of them, but one helicopter was shot down. With the Hueys the Cobras were among the very last American aircraft to leave Vietnam.

On 30 September, 1976, the

*The NASA Ames Research Center has been operating YAH-1S s/n 70-15979 (N736NA) since November 1987. This aircraft was acquired from Fort Rucker, Alabama. (J L Sherlock via J Wegg)*

*AH-1T of the USMC Squadron HMM-365 stationed at MCAS New River, North Carolina, seen here at San Juan, Majorca, Spain. (J A Cerda)*

Army had one hundred and forty-eight AH-1Q/S TOW/Cobras on its inventory, most of which were deployed in Europe with USAREUR. The first AH-1P was delivered to the Army on 16 March, 1977, and the first unit to operate the type was the 82nd Airborne Division at Fort Bragg. By the end of 1977, about two hundred and thirty TOW/Cobras were stationed in Europe.

The first AH-1F was delivered to the US Army in November 1979 and issued to field units, and later to Army National Guard (April 1981). The first AH-1G(MOD) was accepted by the US Army on 27 May, 1986.

Among today's units equipped with AH-1G/S/Fs are: 8th and 47th AB; 2nd and 11th ACR; 101st AirDiv; 4th ARC; 193rd and 307th AvBat; 21st, 150th and 285th AvCo; 1st, 3rd, 4th and 127th AvRgt; 10th, 13th, 122nd, 149th, 224th and 308th AHB; 6th and 163rd CavRgt; 2/9 Cav; 1st InfDiv; 2-3, 3-3 Avn; California, Florida, Missouri, New York, North Carolina, Ohio, Texas, Utah and Washington ARNG.

The first Marine AH-1Gs arrived in Vietnam on 10 April, 1969, and were assigned to VMO-2 based near Da Nang and the first combat mission occurred on 18 September. The AH-1J SeaCobras began to be turned over to the Marines (VMO-1 Squadron in New River) in July 1970 and entered operation with HML-367 in Vietnam at the end of the following February. During the war the Marine SeaCobras accomplished missions which differed litte from those of the Army, escort, reconnaissance and fire support. Like them, they also participated in operation Lamson 719. The Cobra-equipped Marine squadrons ceased combat on 26 May, 1971, and were eventually redeployéd at New River,

*An AH-1S during a test flight. This aircraft is armed with TOW wire-guided missiles and its chin gun-turret has no fairing. Note the extended infra-red suppressing exhaust nozzle and the dorsal mount for the AN/ALQ-144 infra-red jammer. (Bell)*

*The AH-1W BuNo 162532 flying low over a bayou. This aircraft is armed with two AGM-114 Hellfire missiles and Zuni rocket launchers. (Courtesy of Rockwell International)*

*AH-1G-BF s/n 70-16000 displaying a rather aggressive shark's mouth at Büchel, West Germany, in September 1973. (P Zastrow via J Wegg)*

North Carolina. Other units to receive AH-1Js were HMA-269 (formed July 1971) and HMA-169 (formed late 1971).

The first AH-1T was delivered to the Marines on 15 October, 1977, and the HMA-269 received its first aircraft in December 1978. The type later saw combat during operation 'Urgent Fury' led by American forces in Grenada from 24 October to 2 November, 1983. Four AH-1Ts of HMM-261 were operated from the assault ship USS *Guam* in attack and assault support missions.

The first production AH-1W was delivered to the Marines on 27 March, 1986, and the first aircraft was taken in charge by the HMLA-169 (MAG-39, MCAS Camp Pendleton) in the following October. Marines units currently operating AH-1J/T/Ws are: HMA-169, 269, 369 and 773, HMT-303, HMLA-167, 169, 267, 269, 367 and 369, HMM-161, 162, 169, 261, 264, 266, 268 and 269, HML-167.

In January/February 1991, during the war against Iraq (operation 'Desert Storm') numerous AH-1Ss were deployed in Saudi Arabia by Aviation Battalions of the 101st Airborne Division, the 82nd Aviation Brigade, the Aviation Brigade of the 1st Infantry Division (Mech), the Aviation Regiment of the 24th Infantry Division, the 501st Aviation Battalion of the 1st Armoured Division and the 503rd Aviation Battalion of the 3rd Armoured Division.

Some sixty AH-1Ws belonging to the US Marine Corps Squadrons HMLA-167, -267, -269, -367 and -369 were also used during the Gulf conflict against Iraq.

## Foreign Operators:

### Iraq:

a few captured Iran AH-1Js were in use with the Iraqi Air Force (Al Quwwat al Jawwiya al Iraquiya).

### Iran:

a total of two hundred and two AH-1Js were delivered to the Imperial Irani Army Aviation (IIAF) of which 140 were basic AH-1Js (serialled 3-4401/4540) and the remainder were AH-1J(TOW)s (serialled 3-4541/4602). Aircraft s/n 3-4402, 4412 and 4484 were converted to AH-1J(TOW) to serve as evaluation aircraft. Irani AH-1Js differed from the Marines AH-1Js by having a larger diameter main rotor, a repositioned anti-torque rotor and a 1,970shp T400-WV-402 TwinPac powerplant. Today, the number of flyable examples currently in service in the Iran Islamic Revolutionary Air Force remains difficult to assess.

### Israel:

the exact number of Cobras in service with the IDFAF remains unknown, a first batch concerned forty-two AH-1Gs which were delivered between 1977 and 1985, these being later converted to AH-1Qs then to AH-1Ss. A second batch of aircraft consisted of six AH-1Es and thirty AH-1Fs.

### Japan:

the first AH-1Es imported into Japan (c/n 21507 and 21508) were ordered by Bell licensee Mitsui & Co in 1977/78. Following extensive evaluation, an agreement was signed for the production of the AH-1S/TOW in Japan by Fuji Heavy Industries in Utsunomiya as well as T53-K-703 engines by Kawasaki.

*An AH-1S (s/n 76-22568) on a test flight. This aircraft has TOW missile mounts but lacks its 20-mm M197 gun in the chin turret. (Bell)*

The Fuji-Bell AH-1S correspond to the US Army AH-1F version. The first Japanese-built aircraft (serialled 73401) flew for the first time on 2 July, 1984, and was taken on charge by the JGSDF during the following December. The first AH-1F equipped anti-armour squadron is based at Obihiro on Hokkaïdo, and the second at Hachinohe. The third squadron was formed in 1989 at Metabaru and a fourth is being commissioned. A fifth anti-armour helicopter unit will be formed in 1994. Fuji intends to manufacture a grand total of eighty-eight AH-1Fs.

## Jordan:

through a $156.8 million contract twenty-four AH-1Fs were ordered in 1982 (serialled 1001/1012, 1213/1224) for the Royal Jordanian Air Force (Al Quwwat al Jawwiya al Malakiya al Urduniya). They are operated by No.7 Squadron stationed at Amman-King Abdullah Air Base along with Alouette IIIs, Hughes 500s and Sikorsky S-76s.

## Pakistan:

two batches of ten AH-1Fs each (serialled 786-001/020) were ordered in 1986 by the Pakistan Army Aviation with deliveries beginning in October 1984. These helicopters entered service in March 1985 and aircraft of the second batch arrived early in 1986. In 1990 a proposal was made to furnish the Pakistan Army with a further ten AH-1Fs armed with TOW missiles and M65/C-NITE system under an $89 million contract. A fourth batch of ten machines is expected later.

## South Korea:

eight AH-1J(TOW)s were delivered to the Republic of Korea between December 1976 and April 1977. The Aviation Brigade of the Republic of Korea Army is to receive a further twenty TOW-armed AH-1Fs under a $197 million contract.

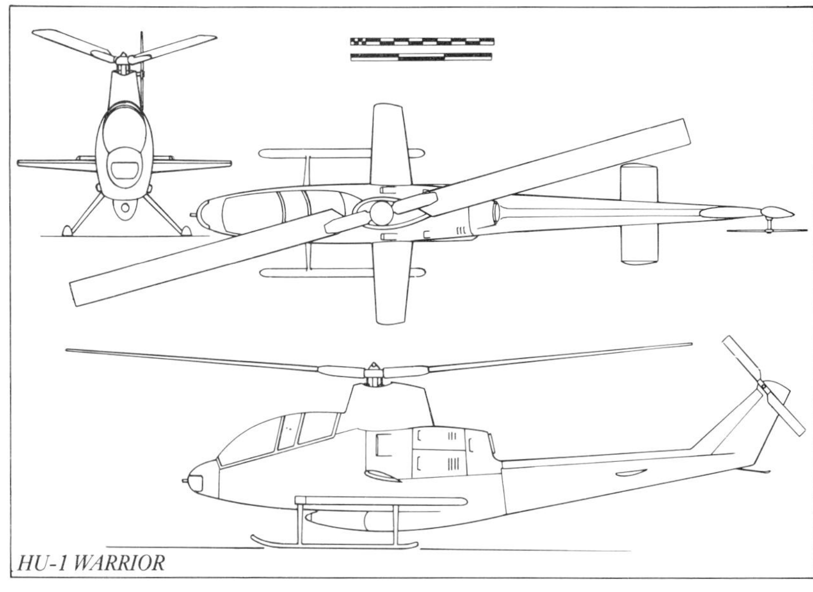

*HU-1 WARRIOR*

Forty-two similar helicopters were ordered in two batches in 1985 and 1987.

### Spain:

during 1971/72 a small batch of seven AH-1Gs (serialled HA.14-1/8) was supplied to the Spanish Naval Air Arm (Arma Aérea de la Armada Española) under US Military Assistance Program and an eighth example was purchased outright. These were operated by the Escuadrilla 007 stationed at Rota and aboard the aircraft carrier *Dédalo*. Four of these helicopters were written off in accidents and, in 1985, three of the surviving examples were returned to the US Army which converted them to TAH-1F trainers. The fourth helicopter is still in store at Rota.

### Thailand:

the Royal Thai Army has received a first batch of four AH-1Fs and was scheduled to receive a second batch of four AH-1Fs in 1990.

### Turkey:

Turkey ordered five examples of the AH-1W which were delivered in 1990. These aircraft were sold to Turkey by the USMC under the US Government's Foreign Military Sales (FMS) programme. Initial pilot qualification and maintenance technician qualification training were conducted at Bell's Customer Flight Academy in Fort Worth.

### HU-1 Warrior (Lycoming T53-L-9)

Rotor diameter 44ft 0in (13.41m); wing span 14ft 4in (4.37m); fuselage length 42ft (12.80m); height overall 12ft (3.66m); disc area 1,520.4sq ft (141.2sq m)

Empty weight 5,385lb (2,440kg); gross weight 8,000lb (3,624kg).

Maximum speed at sea level 189mph (304km/h); hover ceiling outside ground effect 8,100ft (2,470m).

### AH-1G

Rotor diameter 44ft 0in (13.41m); wing span 10ft 4in (3,15m); overall length 52ft 11½in (16.14m); length of fuselage 44ft 5in (13.54m); height overall 13ft 5½in (4.10m); disc area 1,520.4sq ft (141.2sq m).

Operating weight 6,096lb (2,765kg); maximum take-off weight 9,500lb (4,309kg).

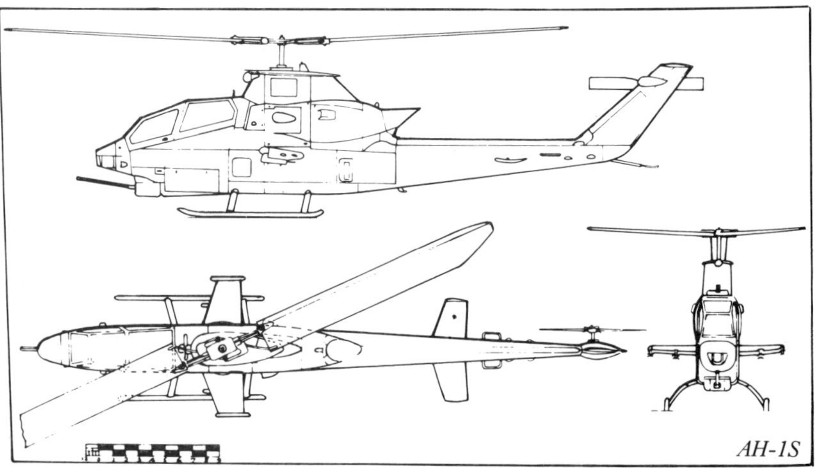
AH-1S

Maximum diving speed 219mph (352km/h); cruising speed 166mph (267km/h); rate of climb at sea level 1,680ft/min (512m/min); hover ceiling in ground effect 10,800ft (3,290m); range 362 miles (582km).

### AH-1F

Dimensions as for AH-1G except overall length 53ft 1in (16.18m).

Empty weight 6,598lb (2,993kg); operating weight 9,975lb (4,524kg); maximum take-off weight 10,000lb (4,535kg).

Maximum speed (with TOW) 141mph (228km/h); initial rate of climb 1,620ft/min (494m/min); service ceiling 12,200ft (3,720m); hover ceiling in ground effect 12,200ft (3,720m); range 315 miles (507km).

### AH-1J

Dimensions as for AH-1G except overall length 53ft 4in (16.26m); length of fuselage 44ft 7in (13.59m); height overall 13ft 7in (4.14m).

Operating weight 6,926lb (3,140kg); maximum take-off weight 10,000lb (4,530kg); mission weight 9,624lb (4,365kg).

### AH-1S

Dimensions as for AH-1G except overall length 53ft 1in (16.18m); height overall 13ft 5in (4.09m).

Empty weight 6,598lb (2,993kg); maximum take-off weight 10,000lb (4,535kg).

Maximum level speed 141mph (227km/h); maximum rate of climb 1,620ft/min (494m/min); service ceiling 12,200ft (3,720m); hover ceiling in ground effect 12,200ft (3,720m); range 315 miles (507km).

### AH-1W

Rotor diameter 48ft 0in (14.63m); wing span 10ft 7in (3.23m); overall length 58ft 0in (17.68m); length of fuselage 45ft 6in (13.87m); height overall 14ft 2in (4.32m); disc area 1,809.56sq ft (168.11sq m).

Empty weight 10,200lb (4,627kg); maximum take-off weight 14,750lb (6,690kg).

Maximum speed at sea level 175mph (282km/h); cruising speed 173mph (278km/h); service ceiling 14,000ft (4,270m); hover ceiling in ground effect 14,750ft (4,495m); hover ceiling outside ground effect 3,000ft (914m); range 395 miles (635km).

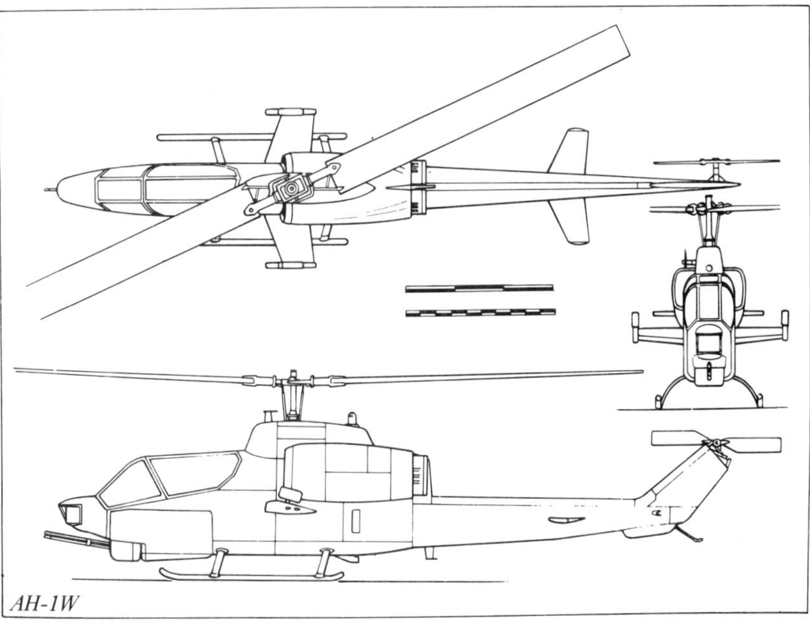
AH-1W

# Design D-2127 X-22

In the early 1950s, Bell was exploring VTOL flight and aircraft in various directions. A new and unconventional method of achieving this involved the study of the ducted-fan configuration. In 1953, the US Navy sponsored a one-year study of a VTOL assault transport equipped with tilting ducted propellers. This programme led to several very interesting designs (see Appendix IV) among which was the promising Bell Design D-190 sea-air-rescue (SAR) utility aircraft, which eventually reached the full-scale mock-up stage. Several configurations of the D-190 were studied, one of them being a variant capable of being carried under the fuselage of a specially modified Lockheed C-130 Hercules. Another related design was the D-2005 which appeared in 1959 and which evolved into the D-2022. Design D-2022 was intended to be used as an assault transport to meet the US Marines' VTOL Assault Transport System Requirement and the Army's ASR 3-60 study. The D-2022 was to be powered by four Lycoming T55-L-5 turboshaft engines, have a gross weight of 28,500lb and accommodate up to 30 armed troops and a crew of two. But like its relatives, this remained a project.

Early in 1961, a competition was held for a tilt-wing VTOL aircraft answering the Tri-Service Transport Aircraft Specification TS-152. To meet this Bell teamed up with Lockheed to propose the Design D-2064 with ducted-fan configuration. The D-2064 was not chosen and the competition was won by the Vought-Hiller-Ryan team with the tilt-wing Vought XC-142A which never went beyond the prototype stage. But, fortunately for Bell, this Tri-Service programme was subsequently extended to include the testing of a research aircraft of the ducted-fan type. Consequently, on 30 November, 1962, a 42-month contract was awarded to Bell for the building of two examples of the smaller Design D-2127, this proposal having been chosen in preference to the Douglas design in competition.

These two experimental aircraft, which were to become the last aircraft built at Niagara Falls, were designated X-22A. During the design phase, Bell researches focused on three aspects: a wide range of centre of gravity movement during hover and transition, sufficient control forces for precise control in hover and transition, and a low empty weight to attain maximum operational payload. These three requirements led to a configuration that consisted of two pairs of interconnected ducted fans. With such an arrangement, large pitch trim and control forces could be attained by varying blade pitch differentially.

From February 1963, Bell conducted numerous tests in wind tunnels with eight separate scale models both at NASA Ames and NASA Langley: a 1/20th scale model was used for spinning tests; a 1/6th scale model was used to collect basic aerodynamic data; a 1/5th scale model was used for performance and stability dynamic data; a 1/3rd scale powered duct model and a full-scale powered duct model were prepared for propeller performance investigation; a 0.0032-scale ground effect model was used to examine hover characteristics; a 0.018 scale flight model was tested by NASA for transition characteristics. The eighth model was an elevon effectiveness model. In addition several test-beds for the major dynamic components were used and a full-scale mock-up of the cockpit was built and formally approved in September 1963. Meanwhile, in Bell's Niagara Falls facility, the first of the two prototypes (which had received US Navy Bureau Number 151520 in spite of its tri-Service purpose) was nearing completion. The official roll-out took place on 25 May, 1965, and preparation began for flight trials. The Bell X-22A was powered by four 1,250shp General Electric YT-58-GE-8D shaft-drive turbines rated at 19,500rpm and mounted in pairs in streamlined nacelles fitted to each side of the rear fuselage. Each pair of engines was connected to a gearbox driving a transmission shaft itself connected to the two rear ducted propellers. This shaft also drove, through a 'T' gearbox, another transmission shaft linked to the two forward ducted propellers. This arrangement was fail-safe; the failure of one engine was not critical because the three remaining operative engines could still drive the four propellers but, in this case, performance was degraded. The propellers were four three-bladed 7ft diameter Hamilton Standards. Take-off rpm was 2,590. The cockpit arrangement included two zero-zero ejection seats set side-by-side, full conventional instrument displays (plus a master tachometer for propeller revolutions and a duct angle indicator)

*This view of the first protoype X-22 reveals the rather crude aerodynamic form of the fuselage. (J M G Gradidge)*

*The tri-Service Bell Aerospace Textron X-22A first prototype (BuNo 151520) on a hovering flight. This aircraft had a short flying career, being damaged beyond repair on 6 August, 1966. (Courtesy P M Bowers)*

duplicated for each pilot. Engine controls were gathered on the central console. It should be noted that the X-22A had no conventional ailerons, flaps or rudder, but nevertheless the pilots' controls remained conventional. In addition, a collective pitch lever, duct rotation switches and a variable stability system (VSS) developed by the Cornell Aeronautical Laboratory were fitted. As part of the pre-flight tests, pilot evaluation of the handling characteristics of the aircraft were made on a six-degree-of-freedom analogue simulator.

Roll-out of the second aircraft (BuNo 151521) took place on 30 October, 1965, ie, seven months after the first prototype. After half a year of static tests, a first 10-minute hover flight was made with the first aircraft on 17 March, 1966. For this flight, Bell test pilots Stanley Kakol and Paul Miller were at the controls. Unfortunately, the first X-22A had a relatively short career. On 8 August, 1966, it was damaged beyond repair when a dual hydraulic system failure caused the aircraft to make a hard landing. The crew escaped safely and the salvaged components were eventually used by Calspan Corporation to set up a VTOL flight simulator and other parts were used as spares for aircraft BuNo 151521. The test programme was thus continued with the remaining prototype which accomplished its maiden flight on 26 January, 1967, with Stanley Kakol and Richard Carlin in the cockpit, the first transition being successfully made on 3 March.

For two full years, the X-22A was involved in a flight-test programme with Bell and the NASA. During this period some 220 flights and 110 flying hours were logged. This phase was followed, in January 1968, by a first military preliminary evaluation during which the X-22A was ex-

*A rare view showing the X-22A with its undercarriage fully retracted. Noteworthy is the absence of fairings in front of the jet engine air intakes. (Bell)*

The second prototype X-22A (BuNo 151521) at altitude with its undercarriage extended. Teething troubles encountered with this undercarriage led to keeping it permanently locked down. (Courtesy P M Bowers)

amined by pilots and engineers of the three Services and accomplished fourteen flights. A second military evaluation took place at the beginning of the following April. During this period, the X-22A demonstrated good performance such as a sustained hover at an altitude of 8,020ft. On 19 May, 1968, the X-22A was officially taken on charge by the US Navy which turned it over almost immediately to Calspan Corp responsible for the test programme on behalf of the Navy. The prototype had been equipped with an automatic flight control system known as LORAS (Linear Omnidirectional Resolving Airspeed System). This programme, which was broken down into several tasks, totalled 273 flights, 279.9 flying hours, 130 VTOL take-offs and 236 VTOL landings. The aircraft was flown until the autumn of 1984 when flight testing was considered terminated. Even this programme did not lead to a production contract, but it contributed to a great extent in better knowledge of VTOL technologies, especially the ducted fan-configuration.

## Projects

Some derivatives were studied such as an armed variant known as the X-22A-1 with redesigned forward fuselage; a 1,400shp T58-GE-5 powered general purpose X-22B and the X-22C, an enlarged cargo variant with rear ramp and 2,650shp T55-L-7 turboshaft engines.

### X-22

Span (rear wing) 39ft 3in (11.96m); span (forward ducts) 23ft (7.01m); overall length 39ft 7in (12.06m); overall height 19ft 8in (5.9m).

Empty weight 11,458lb (5,190kg); gross weight for VTOL, one engine out, 14,600lb (6,622kg); gross weight for VTOL, all engines running, or STOL, 18,016lb (8,161kg).

Maximum speed 255mph (410km/h); cruising speed 290mph (467km/h); absolute ceiling 27,800ft (8,475m); range 445 miles (716km).

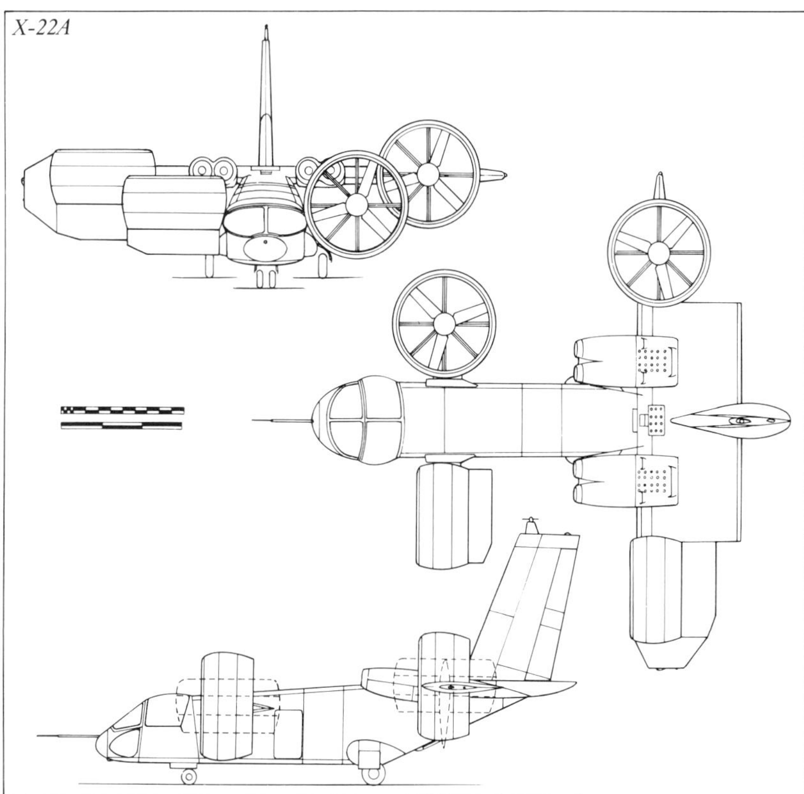

# Models 214 and 214ST Super Transport

At the beginning of the 1970s, Bell was still busy improving the performance of its workhorse, the UH-1. A more powerful variant of the Model 205 (UH-1H) had been studied in which a 1,900shp Lycoming T53-L-702 turboshaft had replaced the standard 1,400shp T-53-L13 unit. The newcomer, designated Model 214 HueyPlus also retained the main rotor and tail rotor drive systems and the larger two-blade rotor of the Model 309 KingCobra, these offering better high speed and weight performance as well as reduced noise. The airframe was also strengthened including the pylon structure and fuselage.

The Model 214 prototype flew for the first time at Arlington in October 1970. Development of the HueyPlus progressed steadily until 1972 when Iran approached Bell for the design of a UH-1 derivative which could be operated in hot and high conditions. Several hundreds of this new type of helicopter would be delivered together with some two hundred AH-1J Cobras. A $500 million contract for 287 machines was signed on 22 December, 1972, by the US Army, acting on Iran's behalf.

During the first phase of this programme, Bell built three additional prototypes of the Model 214. These were powered by 2,050shp Avco Lycoming T55-L-7C turboshafts, and in August 1972, one of them was shipped to Iran for evaluation. The tests were considered successful and Bell moved on to the Model 214A which was the production model. On this variant, power was increased further by the installation of a 2,930shp Avco Lycoming LTC4B-8D turboshaft which permitted operation at a greater gross weight. Three prototypes of the Model 214A were prepared by Bell (c/n 27001/27003), the first of them (N214J) making its maiden flight on 13 March, 1974. The second prototype flew in April 1974 and the third in May. Flight testing and certification were resumed in the following year.

The first production Model 214A (c/n 27004) was taken in charge by the Iran Imperial Army Aviation (IIAA) on 26 April, 1975. Three days later, on 29 April, this aircraft with Maj-Gen Manouchehr Khosrowdad, commander of the IIAA, and Clem A Bailey, Bell's assistant chief production test pilot, at the controls, established five new world records in the FAI Class E-1e. The helicopter reached a maximum altitude of 29,760ft and sustained a horizontal altitude of 29,560ft for 30 seconds. It also climbed to 9,843ft in 1min 58sec; to 19,686ft in 5min 13.2sec and to 29,529ft in 15min .05sec.

The last Model 214A of the first batch was completed on 19 December, 1975. A second batch comprising thirty-nine examples of a modified variant tailored specifically to SAR missions (Model 214C) was ordered in February 1976, and delivered between January 1977 and March 1978. A third batch of six Model 214As was ordered in March 1977 and this order was completed by the autumn of 1978.

The whole contract was so huge that a separate division of Textron Inc had to be founded to handle the programme with Maj-Gen Delk M Oden as president. The partnership between Bell and Iran would have led to the building of a factory in Isfahan for the production of a further 400 helicopters (Model 214As and 214STs), but all the contracts were cancelled because of the Islamic revolution in December 1978.

Today, Model 214s are still operated by the Iran Islamic Revolutionary Air Force, but the actual numbers of aircraft in service are not known. Limited stocks of spares, and quality of maintenance are likely to ground a large number of aircraft.

As for the majority of its products, Bell also prepared a commercial derivative of the Model 214A (with

*One of the prototypes of the Model 214 which was originally known as the HueyPlus. It was initiated in 1970 as a progressive development of the Model 205. (Bell)*

*Model 214ST c/n 28108 (N704H) is operated by Aramco Associated Company of Houston, Texas. It is seen here during a rescue exercise aboard a supertanker. (Bell)*

*The Model 214ST received FAA Type certification for VFR and IFR operations in 1982. Typical IFR radius is 100 nautical miles with 18 passengers. (Bell)*

Avco Lycoming T5508D turboshaft with the same ratings as LTC4B). Known as Model 214B BigLifter, this helicopter received FAA type certification on 27 January, 1976, but saw limited success and no more than seventy were produced. The Model 214B was externally similar to the Model 214A with the exception of an additional window in the side sliding door. Other differences included a fire-fighting system and new avionics. The Model 214B-1 variant was certificated under a different weight specification.

In its Isfahan plant, Iran intended to produce a larger and more powerful variant of the Model 214A capable of carrying up to 16 people. A Model 214A was modified by Bell with the installation of two 2,250shp General Electric T700/T1C turboshafts and tested in Iran in February 1977. The definitive Model, known as Model 214ST (ST stood for 'Stretched Twin', but this was later modified to 'Super Transport'), had its fuselage stretched by 8ft. Bell assembled three prototypes (two for commercial certification and one of the military variant, c/n 18401/18403). Under the agreement, Iran would have paid up to 50 per cent of the launching programme cost, but with the withdrawal of the United States from Iran, Bell decided to fund the Model 214ST programme alone and initiated the production of a first batch of 100 aircraft in November 1979. The first prototype (c/n 18401, N214BH) flew on 21 July, 1979. The production examples were powered by 2,930shp Avco Lycoming LTC4B-8Ds driving a large five-blade rotor with Noda-Matic head. In 1982, the Model 214ST received FAA and CAA type certification for VFR and IFR operations. A version with wheel undercarriage was certificated in March 1983.

Production began in 1981, deliveries started in 1982 and by the beginning of 1984, some twenty

*The Model 214's certification for VFR and IFR operations proves very useful when flying in extreme conditions such as those encountered near the oil platforms in the North Sea. (Bell)*

*The Model 214B-1 c/n 28040 (N2673Q) as operated by Wright Airlift International, at Long Beach in December 1982. This aircraft has since been acquired by B & G Helicopter Corp of Grand Rapids, Michigan. (J Wegg)*

*Model 214ST c/n 28109 (G-BKFN) is operated by British Caledonian Helicopters Ltd of Aberdeen. It serves off-shore platforms in the North Sea. (Bell)*

machines were in service and seventy-eight had been delivered by early 1988. Among the first operators were British Caledonian Helicopters (c/n 28109/28110; G-BKFN and G-BKFP) which operated offshore in the North Sea and People's Republic of China. At the time of writing, some two hundred Model 214STs have been sold. The bulk of the Model 214ST production has found its way on to the civil market and only a few have been delivered to military customers: Brunei (one), Peru (eleven), Thailand (nine) and Venezuela (four) and Sultan of Oman's Air Force which operated eight Model 214B/STs from Salalah during the war against Iraq in January/February 1991.

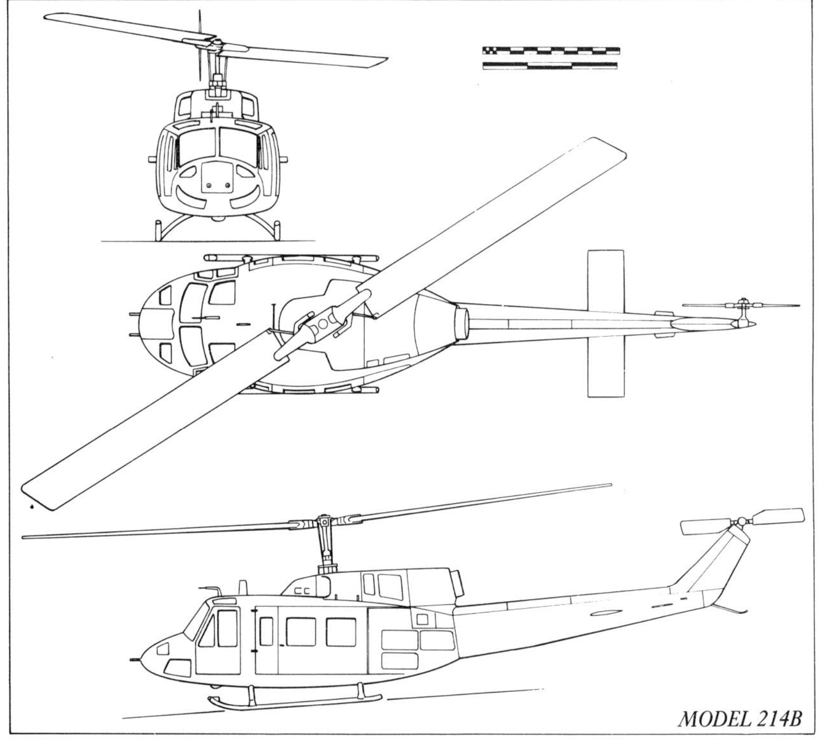

*MODEL 214B*

## Model 214A

Rotor diameter 50ft 0in (15.24m); length overall 60ft 9in (18.52m); length of fuselage 49ft 3in (15.01m); height 15ft 0in (4.57m).

Empty weight 7,460lb (3,384kg); take-off weight 11,480lb (5,208kg).

Maximum cruising speed 161mph at sea level (259km/h); maximum rate of climb 2,240ft/min (684m/min); service ceiling 20,000ft (6,100m); hover ceiling outside ground effect 11,700ft (3,565m); maximum range 215 miles (346km).

## Model 214ST

Rotor diameter 52ft 0in (15.85m); length overall 62ft 2¼in (18.95m); length of fuselage 49ft 3½in (15.02m); height 15ft 10½in (4.84m); disc area 2,123.7sq ft (197.3sq m).

Maximum take-off weight 17,500lb (7,938kg).

Normal cruising speed at sea level 161mph (259km/h); cruising speed 159mph at 4,000ft (256km/h at 1,220m); maximum rate of climb at sea level 1,780ft/min (543m/min); hover ceiling in ground effect 6,400ft (1,950m); range 505 miles (813km); ferry range with auxiliary fuel 633 miles (1,019km).

# Model 206L LongRanger and TexasRanger

The Model 206L LongRanger was announced by Bell on 25 September, 1973. The purpose of this new helicopter was to fill the existing gap between the small five-seat JetRanger and the much larger fifteen-seat Model 205. The Model 206L incorporated a lengthened fuselage with an 83cu ft cabin volume with accommodation for seven passengers and increased fuel capacity. The engine retained was the 420shp Allison 250-C20B turboshaft driving a larger two-blade rotor. Flight testing with the prototype (c/n 45001, N206L) began on 11 September, 1974, and deliveries began a year later, in October 1975.

## Production History

### Model 206L-1 LongRanger II:

in 1977, an improved variant, the Model 206L-1 LongRanger II, was announced at the annual National Business Aircraft Association Convention (NBAA). This new variant had a 500shp Allison 250-C28B turboshaft engine. By 1978, the LongRanger II received FAA Type Certificate as well as certification for single-pilot IFR operations and replaced the original Model 206L on the production lines. Other improvements included a redesigned rear cabin to provide more headroom for passengers, new cowlings, firewall, engine mountings, freewheeling unit and input shaft. Deliveries began in due course and the type gained publicity thanks to some outstanding performances. In 1980, a LongRanger II piloted by two German pilots, Karl Wagner and Werner Roschlau, accomplished the first transatlantic light helicopter crossing (5,100 miles). Two years later, in 1982, another LongRanger II, named *The Spirit of Texas* and piloted by Ross Perot Jr and Jay

*The first Model 206L-3 LongRanger (c/n 51001, N1083G) was owned by North Central Texas Services of Dallas, Texas. (Bell)*

*The Model 206L LongRanger III is the stretched version of the 206B, seating up to seven people. The Model 206L-1 c/n 45777 (N713ML) illustrated was operated by Action JetRanger Helicopters and later owned by Mel Larson of Las Vegas, Nevada.* (Bell)

*Model 206L-3 c/n 51055 (N318OL) of the California Highway Patrol of Sacramento, at Beale in June 1987. It has a searchlight under the forward fuselage. (J Wegg)*

Coburn, accomplished a round-the-world flight in less than a month, arriving in Dallas, Texas, on 30 September, 1982.

### Model 206L-3 LongRanger III:

further improvements were made with the Model 206L-3 LongRanger III which was developed and entered production in 1981. This helicopter used the 650shp Allison 250-C30P turboshaft and Bell's Noda-Matic cabin suspension system which reduced substantially vibration and noise levels. Several other refinements were also introduced including double doors on the port side to provide a 5ft opening.

The first LongRanger III (c/n 51001, N1083G) was delivered to North Central Texas Services and by January 1986, a total of 960 LongRanger I/IIIs had been delivered to numerous civil operators (especially to emergency medical services, because its spacious cabin was regarded as ideal for the job), but there were also a few military customers such as Bangladesh which took delivery of two Model 206L-1s (c/n 45484 serialled 45-484 and c/n 45557 serialled 45-557).

Production in Canada, by Textron Canada Ltée, in Québec, began in January 1987 with deliveries beginning in the following May and so far production of the Model 206L has totalled some 1,150 aircraft among which more than 300 are of the L-3 variant (c/n 51001/51338).

### TexasRanger:

in October 1980, a multi-role military variant of the Model 206L-1 LongRanger II for the export market was announced as the TexasRanger. It was powered by a 650shp Allison 250-C30P turboshaft. Configured for quick-change, the TexasRanger had provision for four TOW missiles, 0.30/0.50in machine-gun pods or 2.75in air-to-ground rocket system. Armoured crew seats were fitted and missile control electronics were housed in the rear cabin. The prototype completed a successful TOW missile firing programme in the Mojave desert and undertook sales tours throughout the world but without drawing much interest up to now.

Several experimental variants have been developed on the LongRanger airframe. A LongRanger was modified to become the Model 406LM which was an experimental test-bed for the dynamic components to be incorporated in the US Army's OH-58D and the Model 400 TwinRanger. These components included a four-blade main rotor system, a new tail rotor with composite blades, improved transmission and tail rotor gearbox.

In 1990, a twin-engined conversion of the Model 206L-3 was planned by California-based Tridair and known as the Gemini ST. Using a Soloy Conversion twin-turboshaft 870shp Dual Pac, this aircraft will have two Allison 250-C20R engines in place of the single 650shp 250-C30P. First flight of the prototype was expected by the end of the year and Tridair has taken options with Bell on fifty LongRangers.

Another modification was proposed in Chile by Dr Carlos Cardoen Cornejo of Industrias Cardoen. This aircraft was a multi-role attack helicopter based on the LongRanger III. On the prototype, which was the first helicopter to be built in Chile, the classic two-pilot cabin has been replaced by a single-seat flat-plate

canopy nose section, and armament is carried under fuselage hardpoints. This prototype flew in mid-1989 and had logged 100 flying hours before being flown to Fort Worth to undergo FAA certification.

## Model 206L LongRanger

Rotor diameter 37ft 0in (11.28m); length overall 42ft 8½in (13.02m); height 9ft 6¼in (2.90m); disc area 1,075.2sq ft (99.89sq m).

Empty weight 1,861lb (844kg); maximum take-off weight 3,900lb (1,769kg).

Maximum speed 144mph (232km/h); cruising speed at sea level 136mph (229km/h); hover ceiling in ground effect 8,200ft (2,500m); hover ceiling outside ground effect 2,000ft (610m); range 390 miles (628km).

## Model 206L-1 LongRanger II

Dimensions as for Model 206L; empty weight 2,160lb (980kg); maximum take-off weight 4,050lb (1,837kg).

## Model 206L-3 LongRanger III

Dimensions as for Model 206L; empty weight 2,200lb (998kg); maximum take-off weight 4,150lb (1,882kg).

Maximum speed at sea level 150mph (241km/h), at 5,000ft (1,525m) 153mph (246km/h); maximum rate of climb at sea level 1,340ft/min (397.6m/min); service ceiling 20,000ft (6,100m); hover ceiling in ground effect 16,500ft (5,030m); hover ceiling outside ground effect 5,400ft (1,645m); range at 5,000ft (1,525m) 414 miles (666km).

## Model 206L TexasRanger

Dimensions as for Model 206L; maximum take-off weight (with external load) 4,250lb (1,928kg).

Maximum cruising speed 131mph (211km/h); maximum rate of climb 1,360ft/min (397.8m/min); hover ceiling in ground effect 12,000ft (3,658m); maximum range 356 miles (573km).

*The Model 206L-3 c/n 51089 (N206NS) is operated by Summers Air Charters of Fort Worth, Texas. (Bell)*

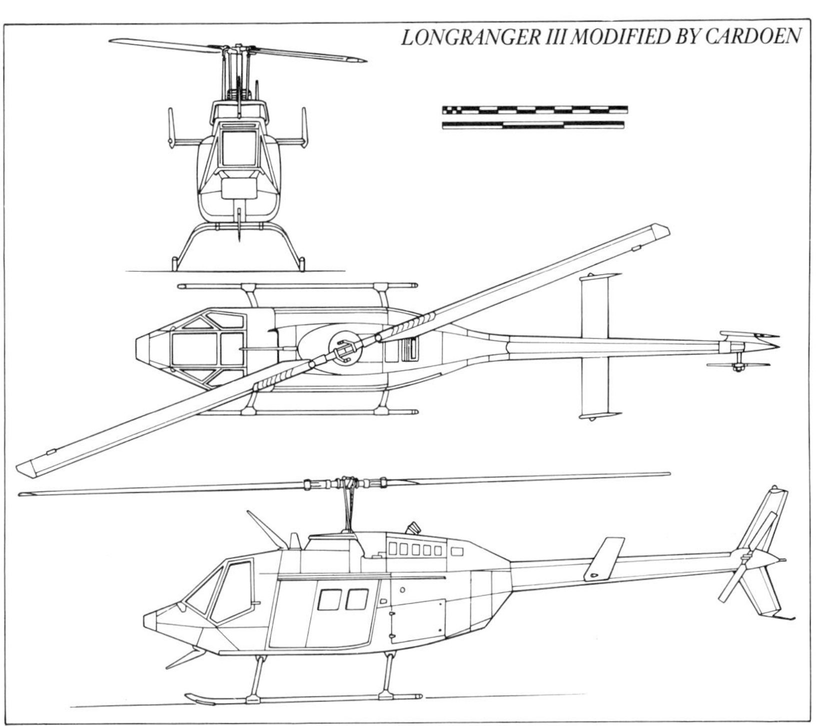

# Model 409 YAH-63

Full-size mock-up of the YAH-63 with fake serial number 74409. The aircraft has a three-tone camouflage and is seen armed with the 30mm turret, TOW missiles and FFAR rocket pods. (Bell)

Two prototypes of the YAH-63A-BF. The YAH-63 had wide-chord rotor blades with separated spars to provide 23mm hits survivability. (Bell)

YAH-63A-BF s/n 73-22246. The I tail unit had no movable surfaces and was designed to enhance stability. Note the upward angle of the gun. (Bell)

In November 1972, after abandoning the Lockheed AH-56A Cheyenne programme as well as the Sikorsky S-67 and Bell Model 309 replacement proposals, the US Army created an Advanced Attack Helicopter (AAH) Task Force which issued a new set of specifications. The key objectives for the future aircraft were the ability to operate by day or night and in adverse weather, to strike the enemy with great accuracy, to have superior flight performance, to survive battle damage (no single hit by a 12.7mm round was to cause a mission to be aborted and maximum invulnerability to 23mm rounds was required) and to be easily maintained in the field. As far as performance was concerned, the cruising speed at 4,000ft was to be 145kt, the vertical rate of climb with eight Hellfire missiles and 320 rounds of 30mm ammunition was to be 450ft/min and endurance was to be 1hr 50min.

Submissions were received from Boeing-Vertol, Lockheed, Sikorsky, Hughes and Bell. The Bell Model 409, designated YAH-63, was one of the two designs selected by the US Army in June 1973 for competetive evaluation for selection, its competitor being the Hughes Model 77 (YAH-64). A contract was awarded to Bell on 22 June, 1973, for design, construction and qualification (Phase 1) of two flying prototypes (YAH-63A-BF) and a ground test vehicle (GTV). The Bell YAH-63 embodied a tandem cockpit with flat-plate canopy for reduced glint detection in combat. The pilot was now positioned in the forward cockpit for better visibility while flying nap-of-the-earth. The two-blade tail rotor and drive train were supported and protected by the tail boom and an I tail. This I tail played an important role in stabilty and control; it also prevented inadvertent ground strikes. The YAH-63 also had a high flotation tricycle wheeled undercarriage with oleo struts equipped with 'strut cutter' crash energy absorber to meet the design impact velocity of 42ft/sec. Power was provided by two widely separated 1,500shp General Electric YT700-GE-700 turboshafts driving wide-chord, two-bladed semi-rigid main and tail rotors. Main rotor blade chord was 42.6in and an FX-69-H-083 aerofoil was used. The wide-chord had been selected mainly because it met performance requirements, permitted the spar separation required for 23mm survivability and was less complex by a factor of two. The 'flat-pack' transmission had large slow turning herringbone gears for increased survivability, reduced noise and a 30-minute fly-dry capability. The main rotor mast quickly retracted into the transmission for air transport. The weapon systems consisted of a turret-mounted triple-barrel 30-mm XM-188 rotary cannon (fire rate 600 to 1,800rpm) mounted ahead of the stabilised sight to minimize damaging muzzle blast effects, and up to sixteen Rockwell AGM-114A Hellfire air-to-ground missiles or seventy-six 2.75in FFAR rockets could be carried on the four wing stores.

The first protoype YAH-63 (s/n 73-22246) began its flight-test programme on 1 October, 1975, and the second prototype (s/n 73–22247) followed it into the air two months later. On 4 June, 1976, the first prototype experienced a heavy emergency landing and suffered minor damage. It was repaired in time to take part in the evaluation of the two contenders which was made at the Army Engineering Flight Activity (AEFA) from June to September 1976. The comparative tests between YAH-63 and YAH-64 led eventually to the selection of the Hughes design on 10 December, 1976. All flight testing with the YAH-63 then ceased and plans were made to continue work with the T700 powerplant.

One Bell YAH-63 (s/n 73-22247) survives today and is preserved by the US Army Aviation Museum, at Fort Rucker, Alabama.

*A YAH-63A firing salvos of 2.75in rockets from four FFAR pods on a gunnery range. Up to 76 of the rockets could be carried under the stub wings. (Bell)*

Rotor diameter 51ft 6in (15.7m); tail rotor diameter 9ft 6in (2.89m); wing span 17ft 10¾in (5.45m); overall length 69ft 8½in (21.24m); height 12ft 2½in (3.72m); disc area 2,083sq ft (193.5sq m).

Loaded weight 15,000lb (6,795kg); maximum gross weight 19,255lb (8,722kg).

Maximum speed (estimated) 173kt (322km/h) at 4,000ft (1,220m); maximum cruising speed 178mph (286km/h); maximum range 300 miles (483km)

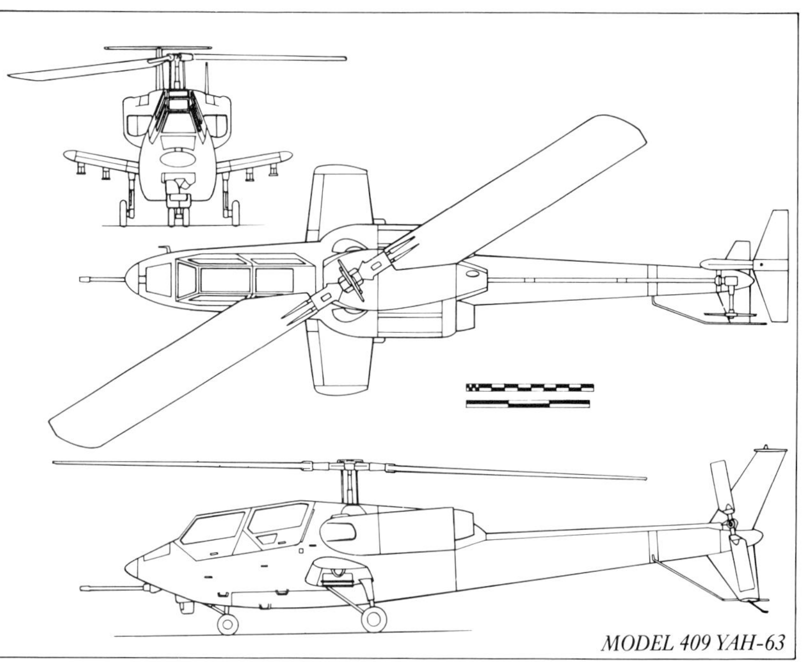

# Model 222

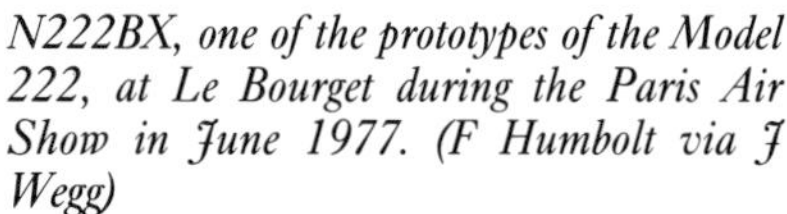

*N222BX, one of the prototypes of the Model 222, at Le Bourget during the Paris Air Show in June 1977. (F Humbolt via J Wegg)*

In March 1974, in view of the rapidly growing market for business and utility helicopters (especially in the oil related work), Bell decided to commit its own resources to the development of a new twin-turbine, ten-seat helicopter. This helicopter was evolved from studies begun in the late 1960s which had led, in 1973, to the Design D-306, a twin-turboshaft helicopter. The engines were to be either the 500shp Allison 250-C28, the 590shp Lycoming LTS-101 or the 650shp Pratt & Whitney Canada PT7B driving the Bell classic two-blade main rotor. The D-306 could accommodate two pilots and eight passengers (four passengers in executive configuration).

In January 1974, a full-scale mock-up of the D-306 was displayed at the Helicopter Association of America (HAA) convention in order to study the market potential and to gather the would-be customers remarks in order to upgrade the project.

The reactions were so promising that, on 20 April, 1974, Bell announced its decision to go ahead. This gave birth to the Model 222, five prototypes of which were to be built and which were quite similar to the D-306 (the windscreen was improved and the fuselage lengthened by a few inches). The Model 222 was the first completely new Bell design to reach production status since the JetRanger and the Model 222 was described then as 'the first American made light twin-turbine helicopter'. It had a semi-monocoque light alloy fuselage with a hydraulically retractable tricycle undercarriage. The two Avco Lycoming turboshafts drove a two-blade main rotor through a gearbox with two spiral bevel reductions and one planetary reduction.

The maiden flight of the prototype was expected by the end of 1975 but, in fact, the first prototype (c/n 47001, N9988K) got into the air on Friday 13 August, 1976, with Donald Bloom at the controls. Certification by the FAA under FAR Part 29 was received on 16 August, 1979, followed by approval for VFR operation on 20 December of the same year. On 15 May, 1980, the Model 222 received FAA approval for single-pilot IFR operation.

During flight tests several improvements were introduced on the prototypes, the most discernible of these being a completely new tail configuration. With the fourth prototype (c/n 47004, N680L) a new tail layout was adopted: the T tail was replaced by tailplanes and end-plate fins fixed forward of the rear fuselage. The fifth prototype (c/n 47005, N222BX), representative of the production aircraft, was presented at the Paris Air Show in June 1978. In fourteen months, the five prototypes logged more than 600 flying hours and by December, 1977, the figure of 700 hours was reached.

Production was launched with a backlog of orders for some 140 aircraft and Bell had to boost its planned production from 125 machines the first year to 137. On 16 January 1980, Petroleum Helicopters Inc (New Orleans) received the first of its sixteen machines soon followed by Schiavone Construction which received an aircraft in executive configuration. Heliflight Systems (Houston), Aerogulf Sales Co (Dubai), Bemor Agencies (Bermudas), CSE Aviation Ltd (UK) and Astra Helicopters (South Africa) were among the main customers. On 18 January 1981, Bell Helicopters delivered its 25,000th helicopter, a Model 222, to Omniflight Helicopters. Several versions have been developed:

### Model 222 and 222A:

first production variants powered by two 592shp Avco-Lycoming LTS 101-650C-3 engines.

*The fourth Model 222 (c/n 47004, N680L) was modified with the four-blade Model 680 advanced rotor system. (Bell)*

*Model 222UT c/n 47522 (N77UT) in the white and red livery of the University of Tennessee Research Center and Hospital of Knoxville. This variant is recognisable by the replacement of the wheeled retractable undercarriage by skids. (Bell)*

## Model 222B:

this was the second main production variant with accommodation for seven to nine passengers. The Model 222B incorporates numerous improvements such as a taller main rotor mast, increased diameter narrow-chord blades, larger tail rotor and lengthened tail boom. The powerplant consists of two 684shp Textron Lycoming LTS 101-750C-1 turboshafts. The fuel is contained in five crash resistant tanks located in the fuselage as well as in the sponsons, with a total capacity of 187.5US gal.

The Model 222B Executive is the luxury variant for five or six people with complete systems and avionics such as IFR, Sperry coupled automatic flight control system and VOR/LOC. Luxury equipment includes automatic temperature control, fluorescent and reading lights and window curtains. A stereo system and refreshment cabinet are optional.

In 1982, the Model 222B became the first transport category helicopter to be certificated by the FAA for single-pilot IFR flight without stability augmentation.

*Model 222UT c/n 47539 (N101MM) in the livery of the Massachusetts Mutual Life Insurance Company, of Springfield. (Bell)*

## Model 222U and 222UT:

the Model 222UT (UT for Utility Twin) variant is externally recognisible by its tubular skid undercarriage in place of the usual retractable wheels. It can accommodate up to eight passengers and could have a fuselage mounted flotation system. The powerplant is the same as for the Model 222B but fuel capacity has been increased to 246US gal. This variant received VFR and single-pilot IFR certification during the spring of 1983.

First deliveries of the Model 222UT were in September 1983. Among the main operators are the New York City Police Department, the Port Authority of New York, Michigan State Police, West Virginia State Police and Lloyd Helicopters.

From 1982, the fourth prototype (N680L) served as test bed for the Model 680 four-blade composite bearingless rotor system, designed to improve performance and reduce noise. On 10 November, 1987, this Model 222 flew with a digital control system developed by Bell and Lucas Aerospace which gave the engine the ability to adapt its characteristics in flight.

To date, one hundred and fifty-six Model 222Bs and seventy-two 222UTs have been delivered, mainly on the civil market. Only two aircraft are known to have been taken on charge by military customers: one by the Uruguayan Air Force and the other by the Uruguayan Navy.

*The Model 222B c/n 47138 (N153CD) operated by Corwin D Denney of Beverly Hills, California. (Bell)*

*The luxury accommodation of the Bell 222B. (Bell)*

*The elegant lines of the Model 222 are shown to advantage in this view of Model 222B N3187H. (Bell)*

## Model 222X:

at the end of 1988, a multi-mission variant of the Model 222, called Model 222X, was proposed among several contenders in order to replace the CH-136 and CH-139 of the Canadian Armed Forces but no decision had been taken by early 1991.

## Model 222A

Rotor diameter 42ft 0in (12.80m); length of fuselage 39ft 9in (12.12m).

Empty weight 4,577lb (2,076kg); maximum take-off weight 7.650lb (3,470kg).

Maximum cruising speed at sea level 150mph (241km/h); maximum cruising speed at 8,000ft (2,400m) 146mph (235km/h); maximum rate of climb 1,730ft/min (527m/min); hover ceiling in ground effect 10,300ft (3,135m); hover ceiling outside ground effect 6,400ft (1,940m); range (no reserves) 450 miles (724km).

## Model 222B

Rotor diameter 42ft 0in (12.80m); tail rotor diameter 6ft 10½in (2.10m); length of fuselage 42ft 2in (12.85m); length overall 50ft 4¾in (15.36m); height overall 11ft 6in (3.51m); disc area 1,385.4sq ft (128.7sq m).

Empty weight 4,900lb (2,223kg); maximum take-off weight 8,250lb (3,742kg).

Never-exceed speed at sea level 172mph (278km/h); economic cruising speed 161mph (259km/h); maximum rate of climb at sea level 1,680ft/min (512m/min); service ceiling 15,800ft (4,815m); hover ceiling in ground effect 7,100ft (2,165m); hover ceiling outside ground effect 6,400ft (1,950m); maximum range at sea level 294 miles (472km); maximum range at 4,000ft (1,220m) 330 miles (532km).

## Model 222UT

Dimensions as for Model 222B; empty weight 4,874lb (2,210kg); maximum take-off weight 8,250lb (3,742kg).

Never-exceed speed at sea level 172mph (278km/h); economic cruising speed 153mph (246km/h); maximum rate of climb at sea level 1,680ft/min (512m/min); service ceiling 15,800ft (4,815m); hover ceiling in ground effect 7,100ft (2,165m); hover ceiling outside ground effect 6,400ft (1,950m); maximum range at sea level 429 miles (691km); maximum range at 4,000ft (1,220m) 380 miles (610km).

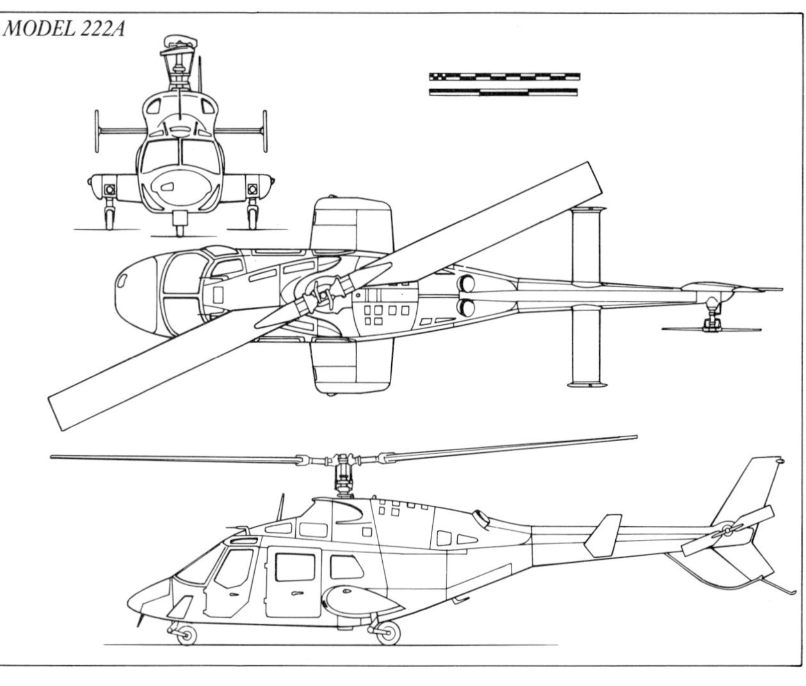

# Model 301 XV-15

*The prototype XV-15 landing aboard* USS *Tripoli (LPH-10). Small electric motors in each engine nacelle provided back-up tilt capability. (Bob Lawson)*

In 1973, Bell Helicopter was chosen as prime contractor on a joint NASA/US Army Air Mobility Research and Development Laboratory research programme to prove the concept of tilt-rotor technology. The purpose of this research programme was to explore the benefits that might be derived from vehicles that combined both helicopter and aeroplane characteristics. With the experience gained with its Model 200/XV-3, the Bell team designed and proposed the Model 301 to meet this requirement. Complementary US Navy funding was provided in 1979 and 1980, and two prototypes were eventually ordered.

Designated XV-15, the Model 301 looked like a high-wing monoplane with two wingtip-mounted 1,550shp Avco Lycoming LTC1K-4K turboshafts, each fitted with 25ft diameter three-blade propeller-rotors able to be tilted from vertical take-off configuration to high-speed forward flight mode. Limiting rotor speed in forward flight was 458rpm and in hovering flight 565rpm. Transition took 12 seconds and the vehicle was designed to accelerate from hover to 240kt in less than 30 seconds. Driveshafts were interconnected to permit single-engined operation in case of a failure.

In April 1974, Rockwell International (Tulsa Division) received a contract for the construction of the fuselage and the tail assembly of the two XV-15 airframes. On 2 October, 1975, components of the first prototype were delivered to Bell Helicopter in Fort Worth where final assembly would be undertaken. Aircraft No.1 (c/n 00001, N702NA) was rolled out, at Arlington, on 22 October, 1976. Before tiedown dynamic tests simulating all flight modes, the XV-15 No.1 underwent an extensive integration checkout.

On 3 March, 1977, the first simulated transition was a complete success and the first free flight took place on 3 May, 1977, at Fort

*The first prototype XV-15 during a demonstration flight over Washington in 1987. (Bell)*

*The XV-15 landing on* USS Tripoli *(LPH-10) during initial shipboard evaluation near San Diego, in August 1982. The aircraft had been painted Navy grey overall. (Bob Lawson)*

Worth. The prototype was then tested for six weeks in the large wind tunnel of the Ames Research Center at Moffett Field, California. During these tests various configurations of the aircraft were evaluated including forward flight up to 180kt, vertical flight up to 123kt, autorotation up to 80kt etc.

The XV-15 No.1 was followed into the air by aircraft No.2 (c/n 00002, N703NA) on 23 April, 1979, with Ron Erhart and Dorman Cannon, Bell's XV-15 project pilot, at the controls. This maiden flight was followed by the first complete free transition on 24 July. On 21 April, 1980, No.2 prototype reached 302mph at 8,300ft and, in one year of testing, aircraft No.2 logged 40 hours flying. All these flights proved that the basic behaviour of the aircraft was good and that transition could be made within a large range of speeds. The first prototype was then evaluated by NASA and US Army pilots in order to sample operational applications and, in October 1981, the second aircraft began flying at the NASA Ames Dryden Research Center at Moffett Field to expand the flight envelope.

Under the new JVX programme (Joint Services Advanced Vertical Lift Aircraft Program) the XV-15 served as test-bed. In direct relation to the JVX programme, XV-15 No.1 was tested in Fort Huachuca to evaluate its ability to accomplish SEMA missions (Special Electronics Mission Aircraft); the aircraft was sent to China Lake to measure its radar signature and, on 2-5 August, 1982, off San Diego, Lieut-Cdr John Ball and Dorman Cannon conducted the initial shipboard evaluation on board the amphibious assault ship USS *Tripoli* (LPH-10). This evaluation included vertical and short rolling take-offs, hovering flights and vertical landings. On this occasion, one of the 54 XV-15 landings was the ship's 60,000th. The aircraft was then sent back to Fort Worth to undergo a complete overhaul and to receive several modifications. By the end of August 1982, the two prototypes had logged 289 hours of flight testing.

The two XV-15s were then used in a research programme to explore the limits of the operational flight envelope and assess its application to military and civil transport needs. Late in 1987, the XV-15, piloted by Dorman Cannon and Don Borge, demonstrated its capabilities in the civil transport role at Washington and Chicago. The Chicago demonstration was conducted from Miegs Field in the very heart of the city.

*The XV-15 prototype shortly after roll-out. The span between the outer portion of the arcs of the two propeller/rotors is 52ft 2in. (Bell)*

From November 1987, XV-15 No.2 was tested with new rotor blades made of composite materials (glass and carbon fibres) built by Boeing Helicopters Company. New advanced technology rotor blades, built of carbon fibre and Nomex,

*The XV-15 during a transition from vertical to horizontal flight. Transition took 12 seconds. The aircraft was designed to accelerate from hover to 240 knots in less than 30 seconds. (Bell)*

and developed by Boeing Helicopters as part of the V-22 Osprey programme, were first flown on the second XV-15 on 13 November, 1987. Some 30 hours of flight-testing were planned in 1988.

Span over engine nacelles 35ft 2in (10.72m); rotor diameter 25ft 0in (7.62m); width overall 57ft 2in (17.42m); length overall 42ft 1in (12.82m); height (engines vertical) 15ft 4in (4.67m); disc area (each) 490.9sq ft (45.60sq m); wing area 169.0sq ft (15.70sq m).

Empty weight 9,570lb (4,341kg); maximum weight (VTOL) 13,000lb (5,897kg); maximum weight (STOL) 15,000lb (6,804kg)

Maximum level speed at 17,000ft (5,180m) 382mph (615km/h); maximum cruising speed at 16,300ft (4,970m) 349mph (561km/h); rate of climb 3,150ft/min (960m/min); service ceiling 29,000ft (8,840m); hover ceiling in ground effect 10,500ft (3,200m); hover ceiling outside ground effect 8,650ft (2,635m); maximum range 512 miles (824km).

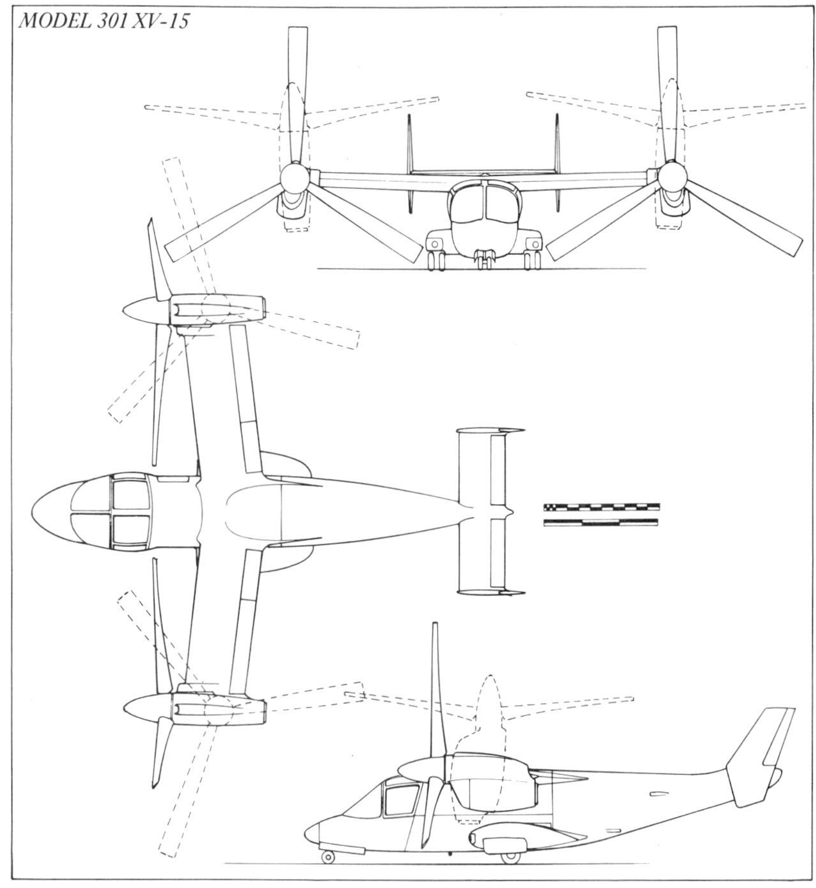

# Model 412

On 8 September, 1978, Bell announced its intention to develop a four-bladed variant of its twin-turbine Model 212. Designated Model 412 (the figure 4 in the designation standing for 4-blade), this helicopter was the first four-blade rotor helicopter to be produced by Bell (multi-bladed aircraft already having been flown by Bell but only for research purposes). The new four-blade rotor improved the performance of the aircraft in many respects, first being the reduction of noise and vibration levels. The rotor head had elastomeric bearings that eliminated both mechanical hinges and viscous dampers. In mid-1984, the internal vibration level was further lowered by the introduction of a pendulum damper kit on production aircraft, but this was also available independently for retrofit to earlier machines.

Creation of the new Model was made on two newly built Model 212 airframes without costly redesign. Both aircraft served as development prototypes and for the certification programme. The Model 412 retained the same powerplant as the Model 212, the Pratt & Whitney Canada PT6-3B-1 Turbo Twin Pac delivering 1,400hp for take-off and 1,130hp for continuous operation. The first modified helicopter made its maiden flight in early August 1979, followed by the second machine in December of the same year. FAA type approval was given on 9 January, 1981, and IFR certification came on 13 February, 1981. Meanwhile, the first deliveries had taken place. On 18 January, 1981, ERA Helicopter Inc of Anchorage received its first aircraft (c/n 33001, N412EH), this company eventually acquiring up to nine Model 412s (c/n 33004/N164EH, 33007/ N414EH, 33009/N415EH, 33011/ N416EH, 33043/N419EH, 33068/ N422EH, 33069/N524EH and 33072/N356EH) to be operated alongside some sixteen Model 212s and fifty-two other Bell helicopters.

*A Nigerian Police Model 412 carrying the double registration N9B and 5N-AQS. (Bell)*

By the end of 1987, a total of 145 Model 412s had been delivered and, at the time of writing, some 200 machines have been manufactured.

Although the Model 412 is available in both civil and military configurations, up to now the majority of the operators are civil. Only a few machines have been sold to military customers: two aircraft to Bahrain Defence Force Air Wing with codes BPS-03 and 04; two to the Venezuelan Air Force (one is c/n 33013);

*Model 412 c/n 33126 (N539KG) of the New York City Police Aviation Unit, Brooklyn. There is a searchlight under the forward fuselage. (Bell)*

three to the Botswana Defence Force (with two more on order); one to Panama (c/n 33091, serialled FAP-1101); four to Sri Lanka's armed forces; two to the Nigerian Police Air Wing; an estimated seven to the Bangladesh Air Force and some aircraft to Peru to equip Escuadron 341 and Escuadrilla Presidencial.

An improved variant, know as the Model 412SP (SP for Special Performance), was later introduced. This Model had increased maximum take-off weight, a 55 per cent increase in fuel capacity and new interior seating options. This variant is also available to customers in both civil and military configurations. Up to now, several military operators have ordered Model 412SPs:

*Agusta developed a specific armed variant of the AB 412 known as the Griffon. The prototype (c/n 25507, I-DACB) is seen here when displayed at the Paris Air Show in June 1983. (A Pelletier)*

*The Model 412AH (c/n 33119) is the armed variant of the commercial Model 412. This aircraft is armed with a 600 rpm 0.50 cal machine-gun in a Lucas Aerospace undernose turret guided by a Sperry Head Tracker helmet sight. (Bell)*

*Model 412SP c/n 33111 (N911AR) of Metro Dade County Fire Rescue operating from Miami, Florida. It has loudspeakers and a searchlight under the nose. (Bell)*

Model 412SP c/n 33042 (N2071C) operated by Air Logistics of Lafayette, Louisiana. (Bell)

Bahrain (the Public Security Flying Wing operates two), Botswana (five aircraft to be supplemented by two more in 1991), Honduras (ten), Nigeria (the Police Air Wing received two aircraft), Sri Lanka (four), Venezuela (two) and Norway (eighteen). Norway is assembling seventeen out of the eighteen machines ordered in Helikopter Services A/S workshops at Stavanger. These machines are due to replace ageing Bell UH-1Bs operated by 339 and 720 Squadrons.

In June 1986, Bell proposed an armed version of the Model 412SP: the Model 412AH (AH standing for Attack Helicopter). The demonstrator aircraft (c/n 33119, N412AH) is equipped with a 0.50in machine-gun (carrying 875 rounds) in a Lucas Aerospace undernose turret aimed through a Sperry Head Tracker helmet sight system (as on the AH-1S) and had provision for nineteen air-to-ground rockets on each side of the cabin.

Model 412SP c/n 33017 (N20703) operated by St Mary's Hospital of Grand Junction, Colorado. It has a side fairing. (Bell)

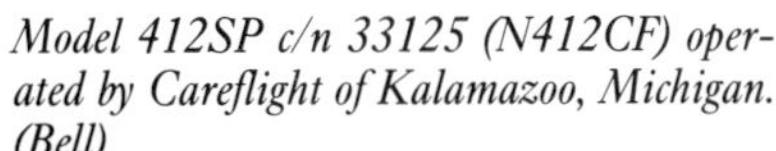

Model 412SP c/n 33125 (N412CF) operated by Careflight of Kalamazoo, Michigan. (Bell)

The Bell Model 412 is under production by Bell Helicopter Textron in Canada (production was transferred in January 1989), and also by Industri Pesawat Terbang Nusantara (IPTN) in Bandung, Indonesia, and by Agusta in Italy. In November 1982, a licence agreement was signed with IPTN for the partial manufacture and complete assembly of more than one hundred Model 412s. The first of these Indonesian-built aircraft (designated NBell-412) flew for the first time in April 1986. Among the customers are the Indonesian armed forces and several private operators. Agusta began production of the Model 412 in 1981 and has since developed its own military variant designated AB 412 Griffon. This variant includes a high-energy-absorbing undercarriage, energy attenuating seats and crash resistant self-sealing fuel tanks. Armament can include a wide range of external weapons such as an 0.50in (12.7mm) gun and 25mm Oerlikon cannon under a swivelling turret, four to eight TOW missiles, 2.75in rocket launchers, air-to-air missiles and air-to-surface Sea Skua missiles. The Griffon prototype flew for the first time in August 1982 and deliveries began in the following January. Among military customers for the AB 412 are the Italian Army, Carabinieri and Special Civil Protection, Capitanerie di Porto (four AB 412SP for coastal patrol and SAR duties), Dubai Central Military Command (three aircraft), Finnish Coast Guards (two), Ugandan Army and Zimbabwe Air Force (ten). A version for SAR and maritime surveillance is under development.

*NBell-412 PK-XFA built by Bell's Indonesian licencee IPTN. (IPTN)*

*OH-HVD, an Agusta-Bell AB 412SP of Rajavartiolaitos. (Agusta S.p.a.)*

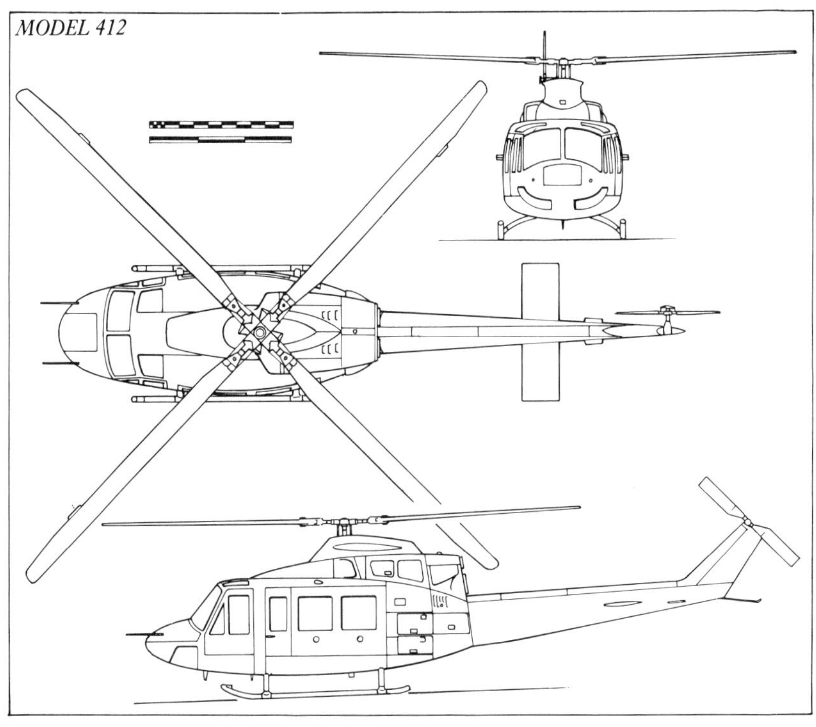


## Model 412SP

Rotor diameter 46ft 0in (14.02m); length overall 56ft 0in (17.07m); length of fuselage 42ft 4¾in (12.92m); disc area 1,661.9sq ft (154.40sq m).

Empty weight 6,470lb (2,935kg); maximum take-off weight 11,900lb (5,397kg).

Maximum speed at sea level 161mph (259km/h); maximum cruising speed at sea level 143mph (230km/h); maximum rate of climb at sea level 1,350ft/min (411m/min); service ceiling 16,300ft (4,970m); hover ceiling in ground effect 10,800ft (3,290m); hover ceiling outside ground effect 7,100ft (2,165m); maximum range at sea level 408miles (656km).

# Model 680 rotor

From the late 1970s, Bell concentrated on the use of composite materials in the development of advanced rotor hubs and blades. In the early eighties, Bell began the development (under Independent Research and Development programme) of a composite bearingless and hingeless research rotor system which began to be tested in flight on 27 May, 1982. Known as Model 680, this rotor system is 15 per cent lighter than today's production rotor systems, has 50 per cent fewer parts and provides a jet smooth ride with appreciably lower sound levels. It consists of a one-piece glassfibre yoke with inboard flapping flexures and outboard feathering elements. Most of its components are made of composite materials.

The Model 680 was first tested in four-blade form on the fourth Bell Model 222 (c/n 47004, N680L) and had logged 375 hours by May 1985. The Model 222 had been chosen as test aircraft because it was in the medium-size range of the product line and provided the desired performance capability for the evaluation. During the tests the modified Model 222 accomplished split-S manoeuvres with dives exceeding 210kt as well as +2.8g to -0.1g manoeuvres. On 10 November, 1987, the same Model 222 began flying with an adaptive engine control and a digital control system. In addition the first Bell AH-1T loaned to Bell by the USMC, was modified to AH-1W configuration (BuNo 161022), received in turn a four-blade Model 680 rotor as well as a fourth generation digital automatic flight control system (DAFCS). This aircraft, designated AH-1-4BW (Four-Bladed Whiskey) began test flying on 24 January, 1989, at Arlington Flight Research Facility with Tom Warren as test pilot. During these test flights the aircraft achieved a speed of 208mph and made aerobatic flights with high-g manoeuvres including maximum rate roll reversals, hammerhead stall, rolls, loops, one-half Cuban 8s and split S turns. Then, the aircraft was shown in a series of demonstration flights in order to draw the attention of USMC representatives. These were enthusiastic about the capabilities of the 680 rotor system and Bell initiated an IR&D programme to develop a larger, advanced bearingless rotor for

*Close-up showing the Model 680 rotor hub which is a bearingless, hingeless design with 50 per cent fewer parts than conventional hubs. (Bell)*

*The Model 222B equipped with the 680 rotor completed a series of flight tests involving numerous manoeuvres normally only done with high performance fixed-wing aircraft, including loops, rolls and split-S turns. (Bell)*

the AH-1W. The USMC and Bell are now working on a programme to introduce the Model 680 rotor into the Marine Corps fleet of AH-1Ws. Industrial co-operation was also established with Dornier to develop a higher-thrust variant of the Model 680 known as the 'Rotor 90' which comprised only six basic parts. The Model 680 programme was also an important part of the LHX programme as the future Army helicopter will incorporate such a rotor system.

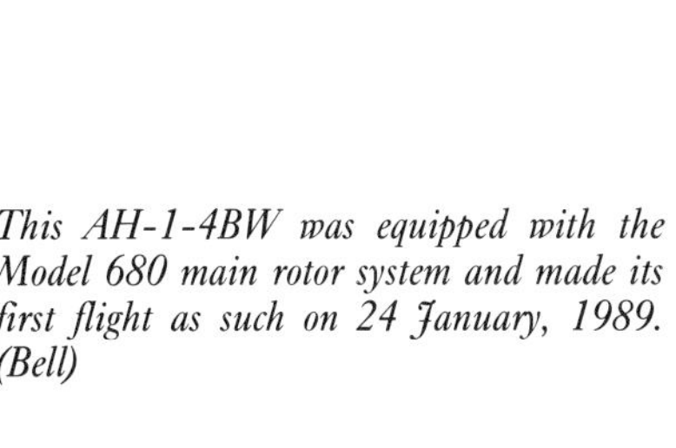

*This AH-1-4BW was equipped with the Model 680 main rotor system and made its first flight as such on 24 January, 1989. (Bell)*

# Model 400A/440 TwinRanger

In February 1983, Bell announced the first of a new helicopter family, both commercial and military, single and twin-engined, the Model 400 TwinRanger. This seven-seat aircraft was in the 4,000-6,000lb gross weight class. The Model 400 was powered by two 443shp Allison 250-C20R turboshaft engines, had a four-blade soft-in-plane main rotor, an advanced technology transmission and drive system with 'run-dry' capability (similar to those of the Model 406).

*The Model 400 was to have been produced by the Bell facility in Canada under a contract with the Canadian Government. (J P Tedesco)*

*The Model 400 TwinRanger was a multi-purpose seven-seat light helicopter but market demand was considered too low to launch production. (Bell)*

The aircraft entered development in 1983 with wind-tunnel testing with a one-quarter scale model and

*The Model 400 had enlarged tail surfaces and modified skids. (Bell)*

*Artist's impression of a Model 440 flying over Quebec. (Bell)*

flight testing of the dynamic components on a specially modified Model 206LM LongRanger (c/n 45003, N206N) which served as test-bed and flew in March 1983. This aircraft had the four-bladed OH-58D AHIP rotor, a strengthened tail boom, a ring guard tail rotor and a deepened fuselage to increase fuel capacity.

The first prototype of the Model 400 (c/n 48001, N3185K) accomplished its maiden flight on 30 June, 1984. Three pre-production Model 400 TwinRangers (c/n 48002/48004) were built, the first of which (N3185L) flew for the first time on 4 July, 1985, the second (N3185U) in May and the third (N400BH) in June 1985. The first aircraft was later used as a ground test vehicle.

It was expected that the Canadian factory, at Mirabel, Montreal, would undertake production of the Model 400. Initially, the rotor heads, rotor blades, transmission and other components would have been manufactured at Fort Worth and shipped to Canada. The Canadian plant being responsible for the airframe, final assembly, flight testing and delivery. The first production example was expected to be rolled out during the final quarter of 1985 and certification was scheduled for August 1986 with first deliveries occurring in due course. Bell planned then to produce a hundred TwinRangers during 1986–87. In addition the Canadians were due to develop and manufacture the Model 400A, a variant of the Model 400 powered by a single 1,000shp Pratt & Whitney Canada PW209T turboshaft engine, and the Model 440 which would have employed major composites components. The Model 440 was due to fly in 1988 with deliveries to customers in 1989. As for all previous Bell models, military variants of the Models 400/440 would have been developed to satisfy foreign customers.

Unfortunately, this programme has been suspended indefinitely pending a market situation that would support an annual sales rate of about 120 aircraft. The four existing aircraft have been cancelled from the register and put in storage by Bell Helicopter Textron Canada, at Mirabel.

Rotor diameter 37ft 1in (11.30m); overall length 43ft 11in (13.39m); length of fuselage 36ft 2in (11.02m); height overall 11ft 8in (3.56m); disc area 1,080.1sq ft (100.34sq m).

Empty weight 3,146lb (1,427kg); maximum take-off weight 5,500lb (2,495kg).

Maximum speed 172mph (278km/h); maximum cruising speed 152mph (244km/h) at 5,000ft (1,525m); initial rate of climb 1,521ft/min (464m/min); service ceiling 20,000ft (6,100m); hover ceiling outside ground effect 10,200ft (3,110m); hover ceiling in ground effect 14,300ft (4,360m); maximum range 518 miles (834km).

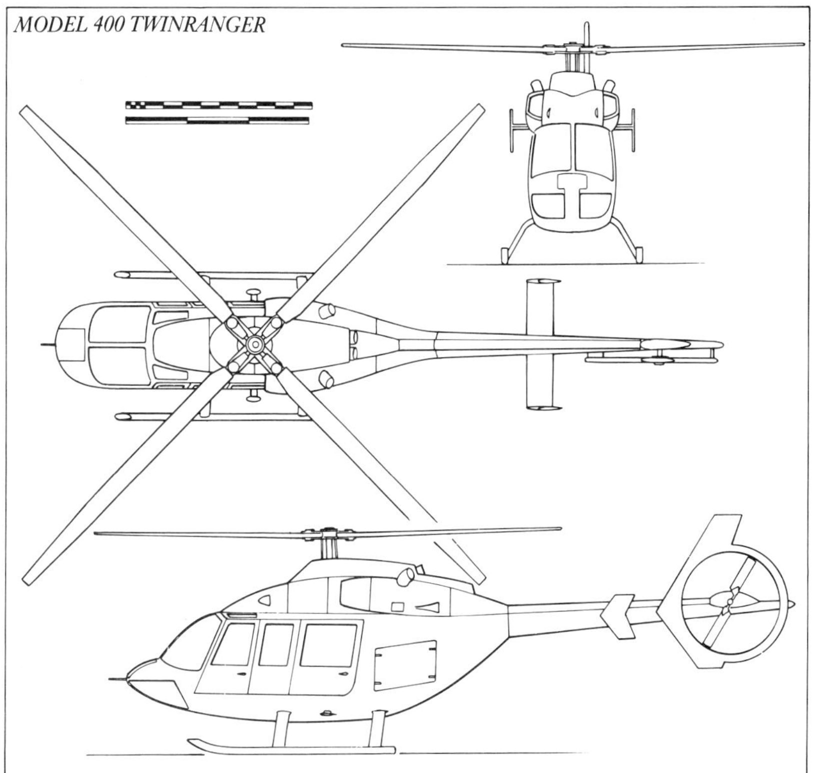

*MODEL 400 TWINRANGER*

# Model 406 (AHIP), OH-58D Advanced Scout and Kiowa Warrior, and Model 406CS Combat Scout

At the end of the 1970s, the US Army set up the Army Helicopter Improvement Program (AHIP) to provide a near-term scout helicopter (NTSH) as an interim aircraft pending development of a new design (in fact the LHX). After several proposals had been examined, Bell's Model 406 proposal was declared the winning contender in the AHIP competition and, on 21 September, 1981, the US Army announced that the Model 406 had been selected. A $151 million contract called for Bell to design, modify and test five prototype aircraft. The dynamic components were tested in March 1983 on the Model 206LM LongRanger c/n 45003 (N206N). The first of these five prototypes flew on 6 October, 1983, and was used for manual validation and training. The second and fifth prototypes were employed in flight testing at Bell's Flight Research Center in Arlington, while the third prototype was equipped with the mast mounted sight and sent to Yuma for mission equipment package evaluation. The fourth aircraft was used for avionics and electro-magnetic compatibility.

The qualification programme was completed by June 1984 and operational tests were conducted at Yuma and Edwards in February 1985 and completed by March of the same year.

The Model 406 incorporated several refinements: a new powerplant, advanced avionics and systems as well as extended armament capa-

*The first OH-58Ds were shipped to the Persian Gulf where they were stationed protecting vital sea lanes for the world's oil supply. (Northrop)*

*The Mast-Mounted Sight (MMS) is an electro-optical fire control system the heart of which is a Northrop sensor system package. MMS is being built by McDonnell Douglas for the AHIP programme. (Bell)*

bilities. The powerplant was a 650shp Allison 250-C30R (T703-AD-700) turboshaft driving a four-blade soft-in-plane rotor, in place of the 420shp Allison T63-A-720 turboshaft driving the classic two-blade rotor of the OH-58C. The OH-58D, as it was officially designated, was equipped with a McDonnell Douglas/Northrop mast-mounted sight (MMS) capable of operating in day/night and limited visibility and with a Honeywell Sperry cockpit control and display subsystem. The MMS brings together a lot of sophisticated technology. It is a combination of television camera, thermal imaging sensor, boresight system and laser range finder/designator. Automatically, the system focuses and tracks the area and points targets. This system provides commanders with a survivable real time combat information, command and control, reconnaissance, security, aerial observation and target acquisition/designation system to operate with attack helicopters, air-cavalry and field artillery units during day, night and reduced visibility. The MMS enhances survivability by allowing the crew to accomplish its mission while hovering behind trees and hilltops. By day, the MMS provides long-range target acquisition with television in a 2deg by 8deg field of view, and at night with thermal imaging in a 3deg by 10deg field of view. It also provides laser designation at stand-off ranges for Hellfire, M172 Copperhead and other Army and Air Force laser guided munitions (LGM).

Armament of the OH-58D includes four FIM-92A Stinger air-to-air missiles, or four Hellfire air-

*The Model 406CS seen armed with TOW 2 anti-armour missiles. The 406CS is a versatile helicopter powered by a 650shp Allison 250-C30 turboshaft engine. (Bell)*

*The OH-58D could carry a large variety of armament. This one is armed with two Hellfire missiles and a 12.7mm gun pod. (Bell)*

*The first of fifteen Bell 406CSs for the Royal Saudi Arabian Land Forces Army Aviation (RSALAV) was officially accepted in May 1990. This photograph shows the aircraft armed with four TOW 2 anti-armour missiles. (Bell)*

to-surface missiles, or two rocket pods, or two 0.50in machine-gun pods, mounted on outriggers on the cabin sides. Qualification tests for these armaments were conducted during November and December 1987.

Under the AHIP programme, 578 OH-58Ds were expected to be procured over the 1985–91 period at an estimated cost of $2,000 million. An initial batch of 171 aircraft had been funded during FY88, in five lots (16, 44, 39, 36 and 36 aircraft). A further thirty-six aircraft have been requested in FY89. In 1987, deliveries totalled eighty-seven OH-58Ds among which several were of the armed version. Responding to the Army's desire to field an initial armed helicopter, Bell modified fifteen OH-58Ds to the attack configuration known as Kiowa Warrior or simply Warrior. By July 1987,

sixty-four were on the US Army inventory and the first shipment to units stationed in Europe began on 11 June, 1987, when twelve OH-58Ds were loaded on board a single Lockheed C-5A Galaxy.

Deliveries of the armed version began during the spring of 1988 to the 18th Airborne Corps Brigade at Fort Bragg. The Warriors were shipped to the Persian Gulf where they were stationed to protect the vital sea lanes for the world's oil supply. Because of the success of the Persian Gulf operation, the Secretary of the Army ordered that 243 OH-58Ds be reconfigured to the armed Warrior version. Eighty-one of these aircraft will also be equipped as the Multi-purpose Light Helicopter (MPLH), capable of carrying troops externally, litter patients or cargo on a sling. First operational deployment of the US Army OH-

*Responding to the Army's desire to field an initial armed reconnaissance light attack helicopter, Bell began to modify several Army OH-58Ds and an extremely compressed test and modification schedule yielded the first aircraft delivered to the Army in December 1987. (Bell)*

*The Model 406CS prototype seen armed with two French 20mm M621 gun pods. (GIAT)*

58Ds occurred during operation 'Desert Storm' when aircraft were deployed by the Aviation Battalion of the 101st Airborne Division and the 82nd Aviation Brigade of the 82nd Airborne Division.

## Model 406CS Combat Scout

On 21 May, 1984, Bell announced development of the Model 406CS Combat Scout which was a simplified derivative of the Model 406/AHIP retaining the dynamics and drive train, having a four-blade soft-in-plane rotor, folding rotor blades and a collapsible undercarriage. The Model 406CS was designed to accept any of the roof-mounted sights in production or under development, with growth provisions for laser target designation, FLIR and video thermal tracker. It also has a quick-change weapon system which can receive a large variety of armaments: TOW 2 missiles, General Dynamics Stinger air-to-air missiles, Rockwell Hellfire anti-tanks missiles, Hydra-70 anti-armour 2.75in rocket pods, 7.62mm gun pods, French 20mm M621 GIAT cannon pods (firing 750rpm), 7.62mm miniguns, and 50mm machine-gun in undernose turret.

The prototype of the Model 406CS flew for the first time in June 1984. In 1987, a helicopter of this type conducted air-to-air combat manoeuvring tests at NAS Patuxent River, Maryland. For this test, which proved highly successful, the helicopter was equipped with a Lucas Aerospace chin gun turret and a laser designator. But, at the time of writing, there are still few military customers for the Model 406CS. After a competition conducted over an 18-month period, Saudi Arabia ordered a total of fifteen aircraft at the end of 1987 for its Land Forces Army Aviation (RSALAV) fleet under an \$86 million contract. The weapons system of these helicopters included 0.3in and 0.5in podded machine-guns, 2.75in FFAR rocket pods and TOW 2 missiles. The first aircraft reached Saudi Arabia in July 1990. The Singapore Air Force is to receive twenty Model 406CSs in knock-down form. But the Israel Defence Force (IDF/AF) has cancelled its plans to procure four Bell OH-58Ds due to budget cuts.

*The Model 406CS was designed to accept any of the roof-mounted sights in production or development. (Bell)*

### Model 406

Rotor diameter 35ft 0in (10.67m); length of fuselage 33ft 10in (10.31m); length overall 42ft 2in (12.85m); height overall 12ft 9½in (3.90m); disc area 962sq ft (89.37sq m).

Empty weight 2,825lb (1,281kg); maximum take-off weight 4,500lb (2,041kg).

Maximum speed 147mph at 4,000ft (237km/h at 1,220m); economic cruising speed 127mph at 4,000ft (204km/h at 1,220m); maximum rate of climb at sea level 500ft/min (152m/min); service ceiling 12,000ft (3,660m); hover ceiling in ground effect 12,000ft (3,660m); hover ceiling outside ground effect 11,200ft (3,415m); maximum range 345miles (556km).

### Model 406CS

Dimensions as for Model 406; empty weight 2,271lb (1,029kg); maximum take-off weight 5,000lb (2,265kg).

Maximum speed 143mph (230km/h); maximum cruising speed 138mph (222km/h); hover ceiling in ground effect 20,500ft (6,250m); hover ceiling outside ground effect 14,500ft (4,420m); maximum range 250miles (402km).

*The prototype Model 406CS was demonstrated in desert sand camouflage. It is seen here armed with twin-7.62mm gun pods. (J P Tedesco)*

# Design D-292 ACAP

Under the Army's Advanced Composite Airframe Program (ACAP), Bell Helicopter Textron was one of the two manufacturers (the other being Sikorsky) awarded a contract to design and develop a prototype of an all-composite helicopter. Phase I of this programme, which consisted of the engineering design and design support testing, was completed by the end of 1982. The construction and testing of three airframes (Phase II), began in October 1982. The first airframe was a tool-proofing article (TPA) used for repairability demonstrations and ballistic testing, while the second airframe became the flight-test vehicle (FTV) and accomplished its initial hover flight on 30 August, 1985.

*The all-composite Bell Design D-292 ACAP. (Bell)*

In addition to 15 hours of ground running and 50 hours of flight testing, which were completed in October 1985, the D-292 was used for shake testing and controls proof loading. A five-phase militarisation test and evaluation programme (MT&E) began in 1985 and was completed in 1988, following evaluation of undercarriage crashworthiness, lightning protection system, internal acoustics and additional repairability demonstrations. This programme included dropping the helicopter airframe from 42ft in September 1987 at the NASA Langley Research Centre to demonstrate the capability of meeting stringent military crash survivability requirements. This included a 50ft/sec impact velocity at an aircraft attitude of ten degrees roll and ten degrees nose up pitch without any apparent serious injuries to the four dummy occupants (this impact velocity was comparable to a free fall from a three-storey building). Another major advancement demonstrated by the Bell ACAP design during these tests was the fuel system which totally contained the fuel during the drop test, thus reducing the risk of post-crash fires. But the main purpose of the ACAP programme was to achieve the US Army's goal of reducing weight and cost, as well as improving military helicopter characteristics, by demonstrating the application of advanced composite materials. In this sphere, the Bell D-292 featured a weight reduction of 22 per cent in the airframe structure, a 17 per cent saving in cost, survivability in a vertical crash, and reduced radar signature. These comparisons were made possible because Bell and Sikorsky each also designed a duplicate aircraft of current conventional metal construction.

Thus the ACAP programme proved successful in meeting its objectives to demonstrate the use of advanced composites in a fully militarized airframe. This fruitful experience was to be used in the development of the future LHX light attack/armed reconnaissance helicopter.

*A crash test with one of the ACAP airframes. (Bell)*

# Bell/Boeing V-22 Osprey

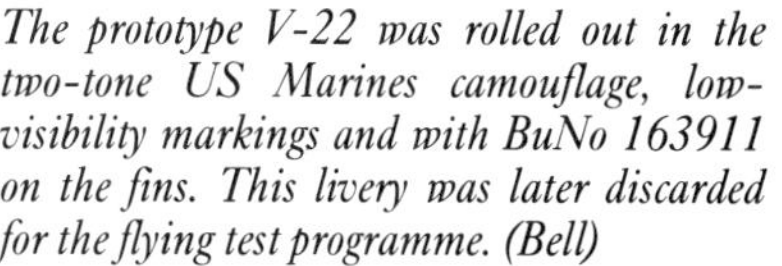

*The prototype V-22 was rolled out in the two-tone US Marines camouflage, low-visibility markings and with BuNo 163911 on the fins. This livery was later discarded for the flying test programme. (Bell)*

At the beginning of the 1980s, the Department of Defense (DoD) drew up a specification for a Joint Services Vertical Lift aircraft. The so-called JVX programme was initiated in December 1981 with the start of the technology validation phase (which established Milestone 0) during which a tilt-rotor configuration derived from the XV-15 was considered as the ideal answer. In April 1982, Bell and Boeing joined to form the Bell/Boeing Tiltrotor Team and began preliminary design. The JVX programme began as an Army-led programme (Army needs were evaluated as 231 aircraft) but it was transferred to the US Navy in January 1983. In February 1983, a preliminary design proposal was submitted and on 26 April, 1983, a 24-month preliminary design contract was awarded by NAVAIR.

In January 1984, Bell began a simulated V-22 flight-test programme using data from wind-tunnel tests and analyses. Boeing built a two-thirds scale rotor/wing model, a fuselage mock-up and critical structural components for test. In all ten different scale models accumulated more than 8,000 hours in eight wind tunnels. In May 1984, Stage II of preliminary design was awarded and in January 1985, the selected aircraft was named V-22 Osprey. In February 1985, a Full-Scale Development (FSD) proposal programme was submitted by the team. This FSD began in June 1985. Boeing-Vertol was responsible for the aircraft's tail unit, overwing fairings, fuselage and avionics integration. Bell was responsible for the wing, nacelles, transmissions, rotor, hub assemblies and the integration of the engines.

In September 1985, the V-22 programme got the approval of the Department of the Navy System Acquisition Review Council (DNSARC). In December 1985, Navy Secretary John Lehman announced that Allison Gas Turbine Division of General Motors has been awarded a $76.4million contract for FSD and qualification testing of its 6,000shp 501-M80C turboshaft engine. The Allison engine, which received the Service designation T406-AD-400, had been chosen over the General Electric GE-27 and the Pratt & Whitney PW-3005 turboshafts. This powerplant was a derivative of the T56 that powers the Grumman E-2C/C-2A and Lockheed C-130/P-3.

The V-22 was a cargo and troop carrying aeroplane, with full-width rear cargo ramp, able to accommodate twenty-four combat equipped troops or twelve stretcher cases with

*This view of the first V-22 prototype reveals the wide span as well as the wide track undercarriage. (Bell)*

*The one-piece overhead wing of the first prototype V-22 was assembled in special jigs. Extensive use of graphite-epoxy solid laminates in both wing-nacelle structures reduces airframe weight and improves combat survivability and repair. This wing has four single-slotted flaperons, two on each side. (Bell)*

*The forward fuselage of the first V-22 prototype during final assembly. (Bell)*

medical attendants. The aircraft had a cantilever two-spar torsion box high-wing. At each wingtip was a streamlined nacelle housing a 6,150shp T406 turboshaft engine connected to a transmission. This gearbox drove a helicopter rotor head to which was attached a three-bladed graphite/glassfibre rotor. The entire nacelle could be tilted from vertical to horizontal by a screwjack actuator. Safety mechanisms allowed the rotors to return to the helicopter mode in case of actuator failure. Flight control in the aeroplane mode was accomplished by means of flaperons, elevators and rudders. The V-22 had fully computerized digital and fly-by-wire flight control systems. Completely designed by computer, the V-22 had an airframe almost entirely made of composite materials (mainly graphite-epoxy); metal in the structure accounted for only 1,000lb.

On 2 May, 1986, the 'Air Vehicle FSD' contract was awarded. The Government approved a $1.714 billion fixed price incentive award to the Bell-Boeing team. The primary goal of this seven-year FSD programme was to build and flight-test six prototypes and to construct three additional vehicles for static, fatigue and ground tests, with first flight scheduled for June 1988 and initial deliveries beginning in December 1991. The first two flight-test aircraft would be assembled at Bell (one by Bell's personnel, the other by Boeing's personnel). Of the remaining four prototypes, Bell and Boeing would assemble two each at their respective facilities. Aircraft No.1 and No.3 would be used to explore the flight envelope and structural limitations. Aircraft No.2 would determine flight control and

*The third prototype V-22 (c/n 90003, BuNo 163913) on its maiden flight. (Bell)*

propulsion characteristics. No.4 would be used by the Air Force for propulsion studies and for operational tests and evaluations. Nos. 5 and 6 would be used by the Navy and Marine Corps for operational tests and evaluations and for avionics and mission systems assessment.

The static test article (STA) assembled by Boeing was a complete airframe which was tested at Boeing Helicopters' facilities near Philadelphia to demonstrate the structural integrity of the all composite airframe. It was completed by a ground test article (GTA) assembled

A dramatic view of the first prototype V-22 taking off. The fly-by-wire flight-control system of the Osprey has triple primary flight-control system (PFCS) processors and triple automatic flight-control system (AFCS) processors. (Bell)

by Bell consisting of a wing, two nacelles with engine and rotor, the interconnecting drive system and the flight control system. This was operated on an elevated ramp so that the systems could be thoroughly checked in both helicopter and aeroplane modes before test flights.

The six all-composite fuselages and tail units were assembled at Boeing Helicopters' Philadelphia facility, meanwhile the wing/nacelle assemblies were built at Bell Helicopter Textron's Fort Worth factory. The first of the six FSD aircraft (c/n 90001, BuNo 163911) was rolled-out during a ceremony at Arlington on 23 May, 1988. For the occasion,

The fourth V-22 prototype, assembled by Boeing, (c/n 90004, BuNo 163914) during its maiden flight on 21 December, 1989, at Philadelphia. (Bell)

The first two V-22s during final assembly. The all-composite fuselages are fabricated with integral stiffeners, greatly reducing the number of fasteners required. (Bell)

*The propeller-rotor assembly was ground tested in October 1988. The Ground Test Article (GTA) consisted of a wing, two nacelles, each with propeller-rotor gearbox and an Allison T-406 engine, interconnect drive system and flight control system. Operated on an elevated ramp, systems were thoroughly checked in both helicopter and aeroplane modes before flight tests. (Bell)*

*The first two V-22 prototypes. In the foreground is aircraft No.2 in hover configuration with, in the background, aircraft No.1 in horizontal flight configuration. (Bell)*

the aircraft had received a temporary camouflage scheme and Marines/Navy/Air Force/Army markings. This first YV-22A accomplished its maiden flight at Bell Helicopter Textron's Flight Research Center at Arlington, on 19 March, 1989, at 10.56am. During this flight, which lasted nearly 15 minutes, top speed was limited to 20kt and altitude to 30ft. After a six-week grounding for the introduction of some minor modifications, aircraft No.1 entered Phase 2 of the flight-test programme on 18 July, 1989. During this phase the Osprey was due to make the first conversions from helicopter to aeroplane mode. First flight with retracted undercarriage (16th flight) took place on 8 August and the first conversion was accomplished on 14 September. The second prototype (c/n 90002, BuNo 163912) began flight tests on 9 August, 1989.

By 24 August, 1990, the four development aircraft had flown 202 times and logged 209.3 flying hours. During these tests, the aircraft had flown at altitudes up to 15,000ft, achieved 247kt true airspeed in level flight, pulled a 2.3g load factor, achieved a speed of nearly 350kt in dives up to 5,000ft per minute and performed normal aeroplane stalls.

On 21 December, 1989, the V-22 No.4 became the third Osprey prototype to fly at Philadelphia where it was joined by No.2 transferred from Bell's Arlington facility. The first flight of V-22 No.5 took place at New Castle County Airport on 11 June, 1991, but ran into difficulty, the aircraft crashed and was damaged beyond repair. The crew survived.

*An artist's impression of the armed variant of the JVX. The aircraft was then fitted with an inflight refuelling probe and armed with a Vulcan cannon and Stinger missiles. (Bell)*

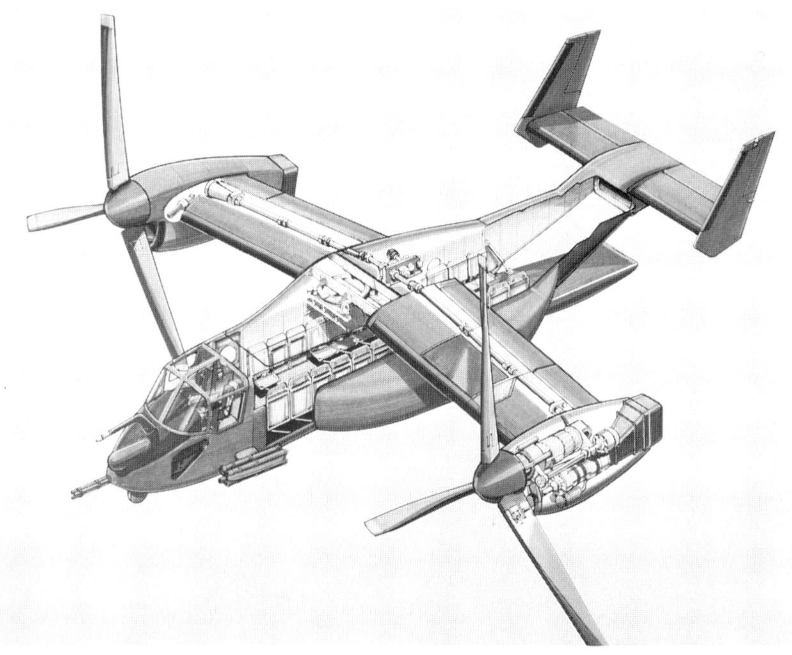

## Production History

During 1989, the V-22 was a subject of controversy. The Pentagon proposed cancelling the programme as an effort to cut down the FY90 defence budget, but the House of Representatives and the Senate maintained fundings.

### CV-22A:

variant for the USAF for long-range Special Operations Forces missions (SOF). Initial procurement called for eighty aircraft but has been reduced to fifty-five. The CV-22A has accommodation for twelve troops.

### HV-22A:

variant for US Navy for combat and SAR activities. Initial procurement calls for fifty aircraft which will replace Sikorsky HH-3 helicopters.

### MV-22A:

major production variant for the US Marine Corps for combat assault, assault support, logistic resupply and medical evacuation (medevac). Initial procurement is for 552 aircraft which will replace the Boeing-Vertol CH-46 Sea Knight and Sikorsky CH-53 Sea Stallion. The Marine Corps will be first Service to have combat ready aircraft. The MV-22A is designed to carry twenty-four combat equipped marines at a speed of 288mph over an operational radius of 230 miles. The US Army had an initial requirement for 231 Ospreys in USMC configuration for medevac duties but his requirement has been withdrawn.

### SV-22A:

variant for the US Navy to replace carrier based ASW aircraft (Lockheed S-3 Viking). The SV-22A will be equipped with an AN/APS-137 radar, a sonar, external fuel tanks, FLIR, anti-shipping and self-defence missiles. Development of this variant has been deferred. Initial procurement: 300 aircraft.

Production orders are as follows: twelve pre-production aircraft ordered in Fiscal Year 1990, forty-five production aircraft in FY91 and sixty-one aircraft in FY92.

The market for derivative rotor aircraft, both large and small, had been explored by Bell-Boeing. The FAA had implemented a plan to approve provisional certification of the V-22 as a civil tiltrotor. In 1988, Bell and Boeing signed an agreement with two Japanese trading companies (C. Itoh and Mitsui) to assess the military tilt-rotor marketplace in Japan. Similar agreements have also been signed with Dornier and British Aerospace.

Several configurations have been designed for the V-22 among which are an Airborne Early Warning (AEW) variant with a large fixed radome over the fuselage and a tanker variant. Derivatives and other projects are covered in Appendix I.

Wing span 46ft (14.02m); rotor diameter 38ft (11.58m); span overall 84ft 6¾in (25.78m); fuselage length 57ft 4in (17.47m); overall height (nacelles vertical) 20ft 10in (6.35m); disc area, each 1,134sq ft (105.4sq m).

Empty weight 30,850lb (13,993kg); normal take-off weight (vertical take-off) 47,500lb (21,545kg) (short take-off) 55,000lb (24,947kg).

Maximum cruising speed at sea level, helicopter mode 115mph (185km/h), aeroplane mode 316mph (509km/h); service ceiling 26,000ft (7,925m); range with vertical take-off at 46,619lb (21,146kg) gross weight, 1,382miles (2,224km).

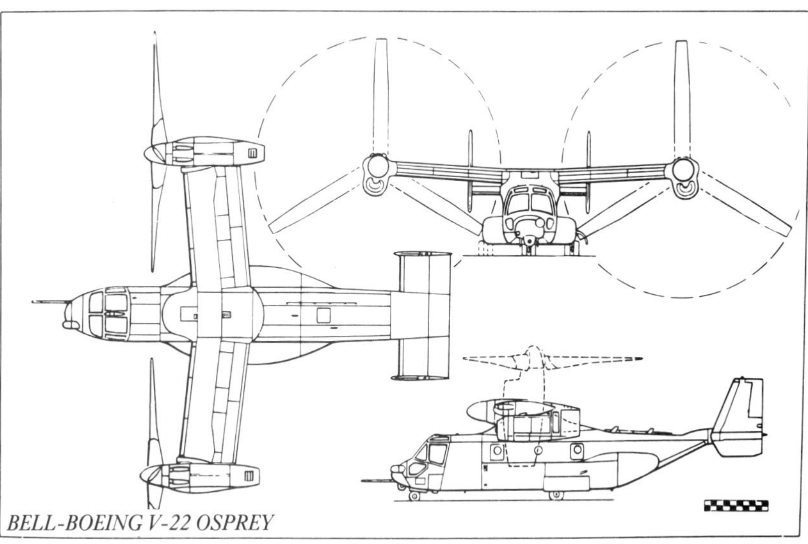

*BELL-BOEING V-22 OSPREY*

# Model 230

During the autumn of 1989, Bell announced its intention to develop an improved variant of its Model 222. Powered by two 700shp Allison 250-C30-G2 turbines driving an advanced design two-blade rotor, the Model 230 could carry up to ten people in a 135cu ft passenger compartment. Internal fuel capacity had been increased to 246US gal with a maximum of 359gal with optional fuel tanks. A fixed skid undercarriage is also available and, from the 51st production aircraft, Bell will offer a variant powered by Lycoming LTS101-750 turbo-shafts. This helicopter is to be built at the company's facility in Canada. Two prototypes have been built at the Mirabel factory near Montreal and the first of these (registered C-GEXP) accomplished its maiden flight on 12 August, 1991 with certification expected during the first quarter of 1992. An initial order for twenty has been placed by Bell's Japanese representative Mitsui & Co, in Tokyo, with first deliveries due in August 1992.

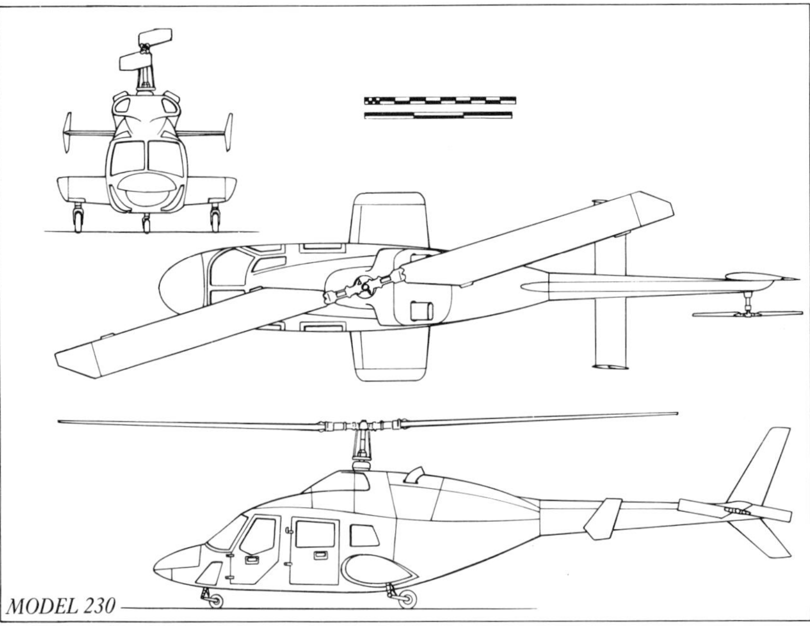
MODEL 230

Empty weight 4,903lb (2,224kg); maximum weight 8,250lb (3,742kg).

Maximum speed 140kt (259km/h); range 420nautical miles (780km), with a maximum of 359gal (1,359litres) with optional fuel tanks.

# Appendices

## Appendix I

# Selected Bell Projects

During its existence Bell Corporation worked on a large number of projects and preliminary designs. Some of them reached the full-scale mock-up stage, but the vast majority did not leave the drawing board. Due to space limitations, only a small number of these projects have been selected for publication.

## Model 3

The Bell Model 3 was one of the two preliminary proposals (the other being Model 4 which led to the P-39 Airacobra) submitted by Bell in response to the Army Air Corps specification No. X-609 issued on 19 March, 1937, for a single-seat fighter. This aircraft had a rather conventional layout with the engine forward of the cockpit but as near as possible to the centre of gravity. Such an installation required a 61in extension shaft and reduction gear (ratio 2:1). The engine was a 1,150hp Allison V-1710E-2 driving a 120in diameter three-blade Curtiss Electric propeller and equipped with a General Electric Model B-10 turbo-supercharger. Like the Model 4, the Model 3 had a tricycle undercarriage (wheelbase 9ft 6in) and a bubble canopy. The wing had NACA aerofoils (NACA 23018 at the root and NACA 23009 at the tip). Armament would have consisted of a single 25mm cannon and two 0.50in machine-guns (or four 0.50in MGs) in the forward fuselage in the space left between the reduction gearbox

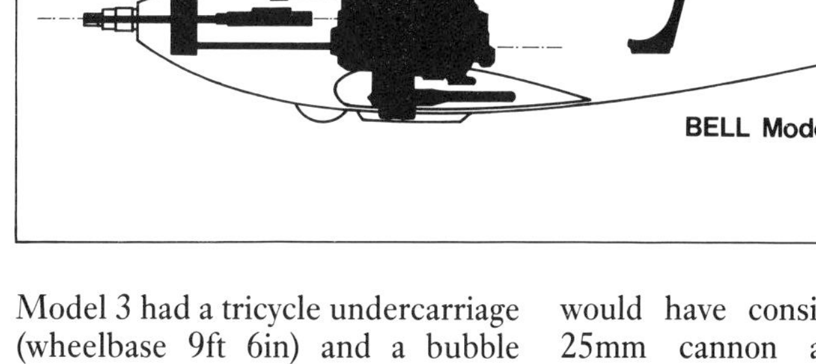


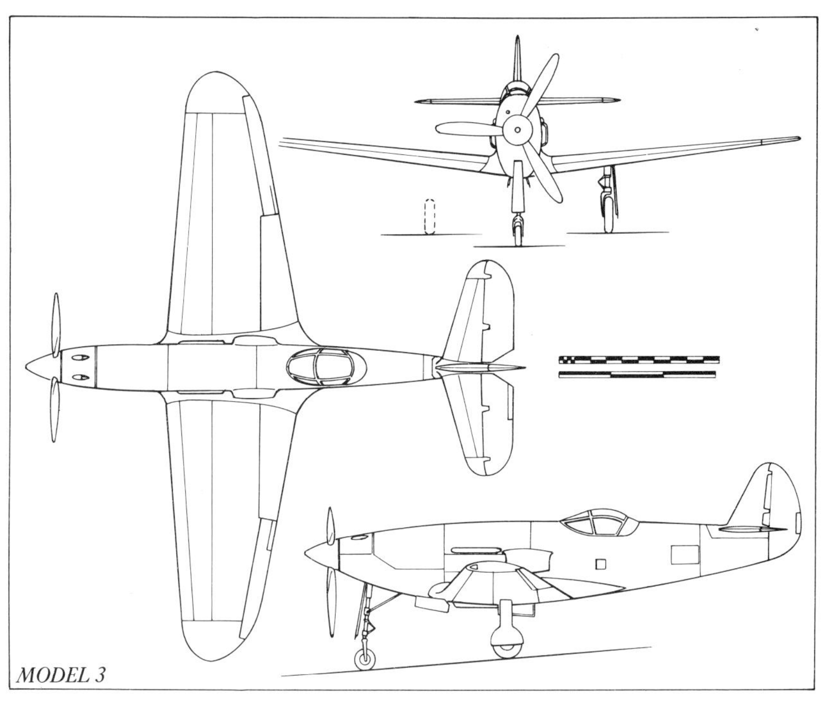

*Mock-up of the Model 240 UTTAS. (Bell)*

and the engine. This project did not go beyond the full-scale mock-up stage but is known to have later greatly influenced the design of the Model 32/XP-77.

Known specification for Model 3: Span 35ft (10.67m); length 29ft 8in (9.04m); height 11ft 10in (3.61m); wing area 299sq ft (27.78sq m); loaded weight 5,400lb (2,446kg).

## Model 16 (XP-52)

In 1941, Bell proposed a number of unorthodox and interesting aircraft during the immediate prewar days. These were in the tradition of the Airacuda and Airacobra. Among these was the Model 16 (XP-52) which was a single-seat fighter of twin-boom pusher configuration. Unfortunately, like Curtiss's XP-53, it had been conceived with the Continental XIV-1430 engine which was never produced.

Characteristics of the XP-52: One 1,250hp Continental XIV-1430-5 engine; span 35ft 0in (10.67m); length 34ft 9in (10.59m); loaded weight 8,200lb (3,714kg); armament: two 20mm cannon in the nose and six 0.50in machine-guns at the forward end of the booms.

## XP-59

Because the Continental XIV-1430 engine was not to be available the XP-52 was re-engined on the drawing board and thus became the XP-59. This fighter had swept wings and tricycle undercarriage. This type was never built and for security reasons, the same designation was retained for the Airacomet.

Characteristics of the XP-59: one 2,000hp Pratt & Whitney R-2800-23 driving Hamilton contra-rotating propellers; span 40ft 0in (12.19m); length 37ft 3in (11.35m); loaded weight 10,463lb (4,740kg); estimated maximum speed 450mph (724km/h); armament: two 20mm cannon and six 0.50 machine-guns.

## Bomi

In 1951, following the research of the German engineers Eugene Sänger and Walter Dornberger, Bell initiated the study of the problems associated with long-range high-altitude aircraft. During 1952, the company offered the Air Force a hypersonic-glide bomber-missile known as the Bomi. The Bomi foreshadowed today's space shuttle principle and consisted of a large two-manned delta-winged five-rocket engine booster attached to a small delta winged three-rocket engine bomber mounted atop the booster. After having boosted the bomber to high altitude by rocket propulsion, the booster would have turned back to its base, completed its mission in a glide and was intended to be fully reusable. The manned rocket bomber, armed with a nuclear bomb, would have continued its flight to the target. An orbital variant of the Bomi was also proposed. After Air Force evaluation, a contract was awarded for the study of a new weapons system, known as the MX-2276, able to fly at 15,000mph at 259,000ft! A later project, dated 1955, concerned a two-stage rocket reconnaissance aircraft known as System 118P, which eventually evolved into the reconnaissance system 459L (or Brass Bell). In 1956, Bell studied a hypersonic bombardment system, known as the rocket-bomber or Robo, and in 1957, designed a passenger variant of the Bomi. Of course, none of these projects ever left the drawing boards but they undoubtedly influenced the later development of the Rockwell Space Shuttle, and were gathered in a single programme, the Dyna-Soar programme.

Characteristics of the Bomi: booster dimensions: span 60ft (18m) and length 100/120ft (30/36m); bomber dimensions: span 35ft (10m) and length 60ft (18m), gross weight 600,000/800,000lb (272,000/362,000kg), maximum speed Mach 4 at 100,000ft (30,500m), range 3,000miles (4,800km).

## Design D-190

Designed in 1959, the D-190 was to be an Air Rescue System using the ducted-fan concept. It was to be fitted under a specially modified Lockheed C-130 Hercules launch aircraft. Derivatives under consideration were designs D-196 and D-2004.

## Model 67 (X-16)

In the early 1950s, with the Soviet threat becoming ever more intense, the need to develop new intelligence tools had become urgent, especially in the matter of aerial reconnaissance. What was then needed was an aircraft with extra-long range and high altitude capabilites in order to undertake missions over most of the USSR at such an altitude that the Soviet fighters would be unable to intercept and destroy it. Preliminary specifications for such an aircraft were prepared and issued by the US Air Force on 27 March, 1953. They called for a single-seat aircraft

*The wooden mock-up of the Bell X-16. (Bell)*

weapon system having an operational radius of 1,500 nautical miles (1,725 statute miles), capable of conducting pre- and post-strike reconnaissance missions during daylight in good visibility and having an operating altitude above 70,000ft. Powerplants were to be current production engines with modifications. No defensive armament was required. On 1 July, 1953, Bell Aircraft Corporation, Fairchild Aircraft Corporation and Martin Aircraft Company were awarded a six-month contract for the study of what was known as the Weapon System MX-2147 under project code-name *'Bald Eagle'*. Two of these three medium-sized aircraft manufacturers, Bell and Fairchild, had been chosen because they were known to have innovative engineers and also because the production batches were to be very limited (a few dozens). Martin, for its part, had been asked to produce a specially modified variant of its B-57 twin-engined bomber. Early in 1954, all three manufacturers submitted their respective projects: Martin the Model 294, Fairchild the Model 195 and Bell the Model 67. And, by March 1954, after careful study of the three contenders by Wright Field engineers, Martin and Bell designs were chosen. The easiest to produce, the Martin Model 294, was considered as an interim aircraft during full development of the Bell design. The Bell Model 67 had been designed in Bell's Niagara Falls facility by a team led by Richard Smith. To assume complete secrecy, a special building had been erected to hide the full-scale mock-up of the new aircraft. The Model 67 had also received an official designation in the X series to conceal its role, X-16.

In fact, the X-16 had a strange silhouette. It consisted of a thin cylindrical monocoque fuselage with a pressurized cockpit to which very-high-aspect-ratio swept wings had been mated. Sweepback was 15deg and anhedral was 2deg. Under each wing was a large engine nacelle which contained a 10,000lb st Pratt & Whitney J57-PW-31 turbojet. A B-47-like mono-track undercarriage was chosen with a small outrigger at each wingtip. However, the structure, very light and flexible, had limited manoeuvre capabilities (+3g/-1g).

Operational payload would have included four KA-1 or K-38 cameras and various electromagnetic sensors.

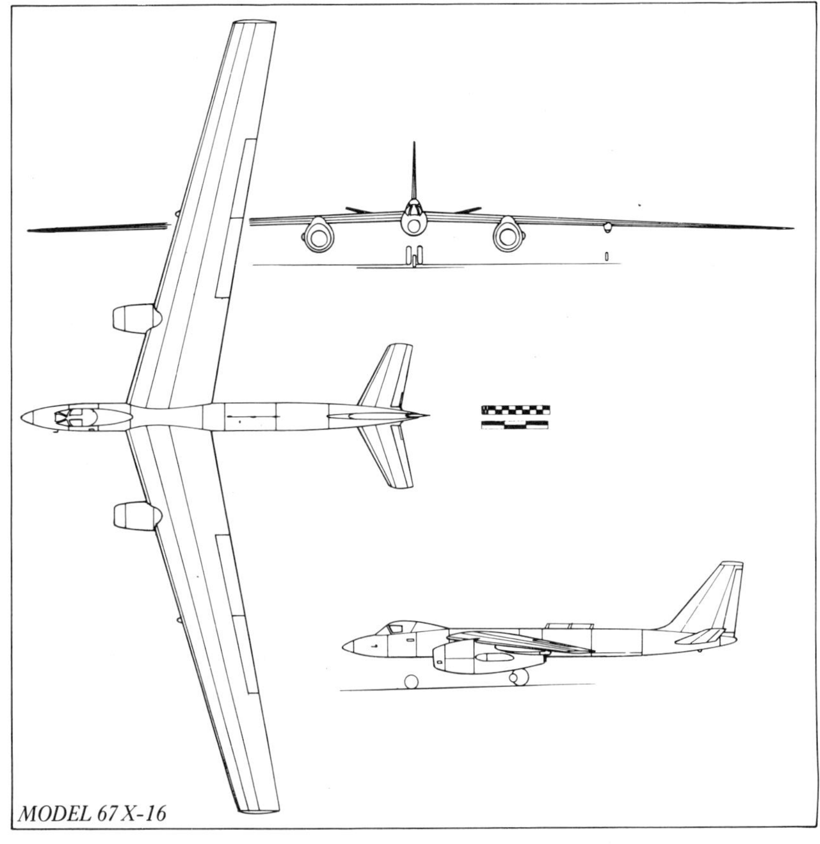

*MODEL 67 X-16*

Construction of the first prototype began in September 1954 with a first flight expected in March 1956 and a first batch of twenty-eight production machines was ordered by the US Air Force. Meanwhile, Lockheed in the person of its designer of genius, Clarence 'Kelly' Johnson, had heard about the 'Bald Eagle' project and, although not selected, had decided to produce a project of its own. Thus, Johnson designed and presented in May 1954 a high-altitude reconnaissance version of the XF-104 (the CL-282) powered by a 9,300lb st General Electric J73-GE-X52 turbojet. Lockheed's proposal was rejected, first, because two manufacturers were already working on the project and, second, because the aircraft was not powered by a J57. But Johnson was not defeated. Instead of giving up, he continued working hard on his project until mid-1954 when all projects were re-examined by a special advisory group which was very impressed by the project and recommended that funding be provided. After recommendations had been made to the Secretary of Defense and Director of CIA, and then to President Eisenhower, $35 million were budgeted for the delivery of thirty aircraft. Meanwhile, Bell had been unaware of Kelly Johnson's forceful lobbying and his guarantee to complete a prototype within eight months, nor of the CIA involvement. Parallel development and production of both aircraft was now unthinkable and in October 1955, the X-16 programme was officially cancelled. The first aircraft was then 80 per cent complete.

Data and calculated performance of the X-16 were: span 114ft 10¼in (35m); length 60ft 10¼in (18.55m); height 16ft 8½in (5.09m); wing area 1,100sq ft (102,2sq m); empty weight 23,330lb (10,568kg); loaded weight 36,200lb (16,398kg); maximum speed 550mph (885km/h); maximum altitude 72,000ft (21,945m); range 3,300miles (5,310km).

## Design D-188A

Between 1956 and February 1959, $14,500,000 were spent on preliminary studies of a common Navy/Air Force fighter designated D-188A. This aircraft was a Mach 2 VTOL fighter powered by no less than eight General Electric J85-GE-5 turbojets. Two of these turbojets were articulated at each wingtip and could be tilted from the horizontal to vertical position. Two more turbojets were set in a vertical position just aft of the cockpit and the two remaining engines were installed in a more conventional position at the rear of the fuselage. A full scale mock-up of the D-188A was built for inspection and designated XF-109 with serial 92109. In fact the XF-109 designation was never accepted by the USAF and the serial 59-2109 was that of a Bomarc missile. The programme was abandoned at the beginning of the sixties when full priority had been given to the TFX programme. A very similar design, but simplified, was later used by the Germans in the Entwinklungsring-Süd VJ-101C. This latter aircraft did not have the horizontally fitted engines and used four tilting Rolls-Royce RB.145 turbojets. Two prototypes were built, the first flying on 31 August, 1963. Development of the VJ-101C was later halted.

*Bell's D-188A US Air Force V/STOL fighter mock-up. This programme was abandoned circa 1961. (Bell)*

## Designs D-2005/D-2022

Designs D-2005 and D-2022 were two operational variants of a four ducted-fan VTOL aircraft designed in 1959 and having a layout comparable to the X-22. They were intended to be used as assault transports for thirty soldiers.

## Design D-246A

Design D-246A was a tactical military transport using the tilting rotor principle. Propulsion was to be provided by two 2,200shp Lycoming

*The D-188 was unofficially designated XF-109. The serial 59-2109 was actually that of a Boeing IM-99B Bomarc missile. (Bell)*

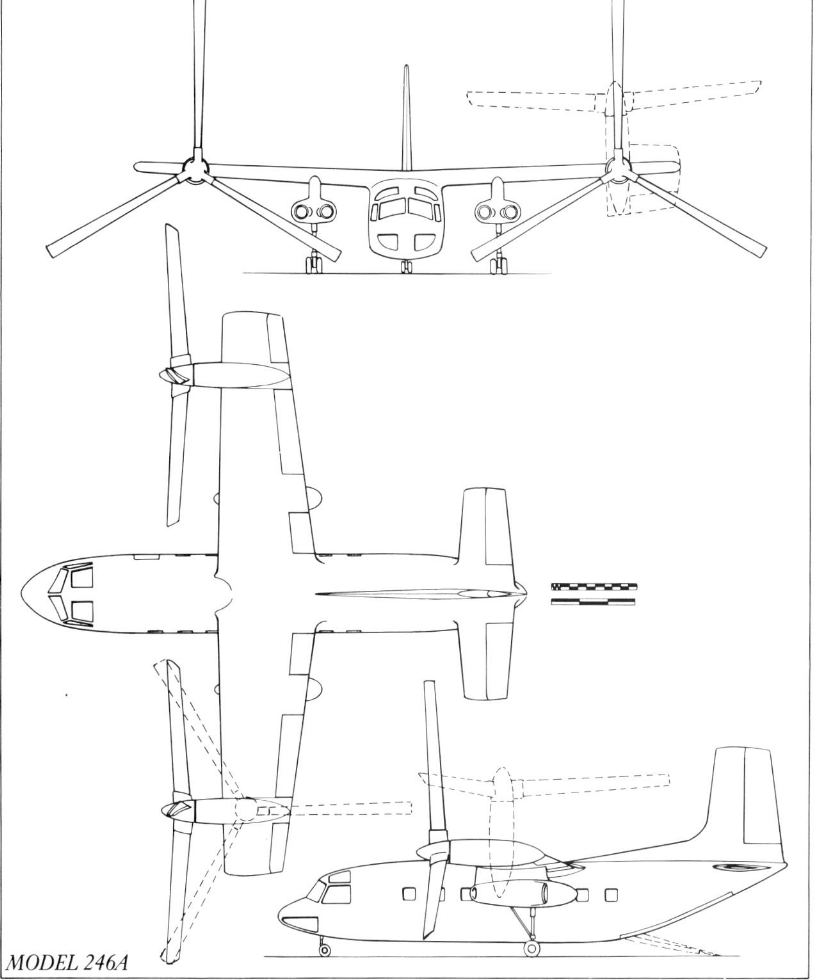


T55-L-55 turboshafts driving two 39ft 6in three-blade rotors, but these rotors were not located at the wingtips. The tilting nacelles were designed with a fixed outboard wing panel with aileron so that this panel tilted with the rotor. Extra power in level flight would have been provided by four turbofans arranged in pairs in nacelles under the wing (these nacelles also housed the retractable main undercarriage). At the rear of the fuselage, a large cargo ramp would have permitted the loading of oversize loads and light vehicles in a 26ft 8in long cargo compartment.

Known characteristics: span (excluding rotors) 64ft 0in (19.50m); length 59ft 7in (18.16m); height overall 24ft (7.31m); wing area 602sq ft (55.9sq m); rotor diameter 39ft 6in (12.00m); disc area 2,450sq ft (227.6sq m); empty weight 22,636lb (10,254kg); loaded weight 38,000lb (17,214kg).

## Design D-266

In 1966, Bell submitted a composite research aircraft project to the US Army Aviation Materiel Laboratories at Fort Eustis, Virginia, for competitive evaluation. The Model 266, as it was known, used the tilting rotor principle. Streamlined nacelles at each wingtip contained two T64 engines as well as reduction gearboxes driving three-bladed semi-rigid rotors. Blades were of constant chord but tapered rapidly in thickness to provide maximum strength inboard and minimum drag outboard. Rotor hubs and controls were completely enclosed within a removable spinner fairing. Nacelle conversion was controlled by two synchronized, hydraulically-operated screwjacks. A spanwise driveshaft interconnected the gearboxes so that one engine could drive both rotors.

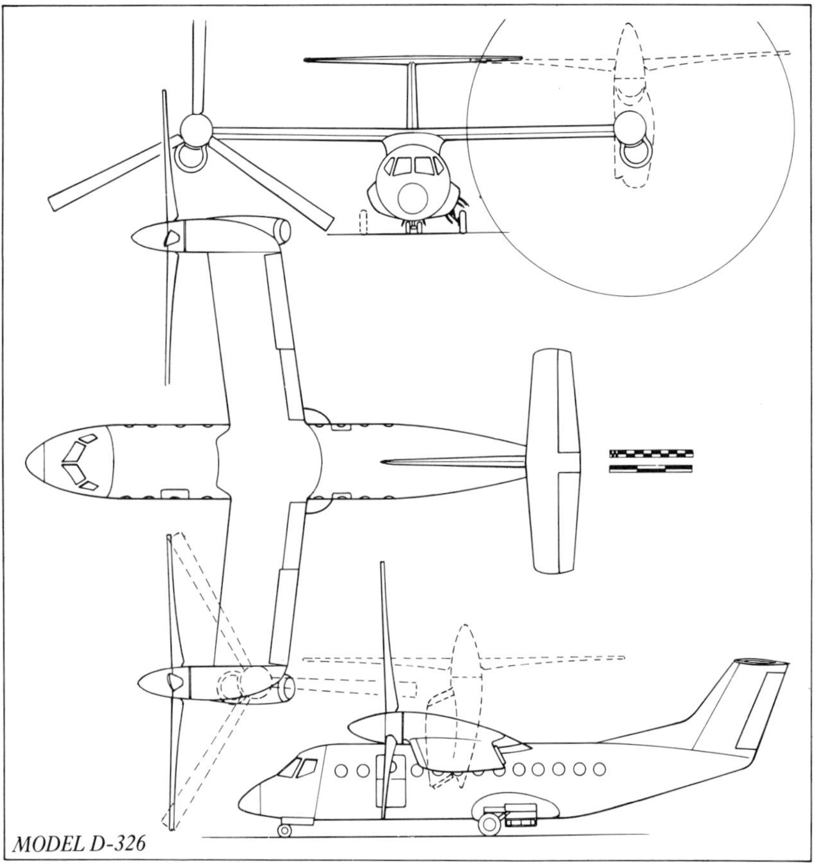
MODEL D-326

## Model 240 UTTAS

In October 1965, a Qualitative Material Development Objective was approved by the DoD for what became known as the Utility Tactical Transport Aircraft System (UTTAS) in order to replace the ageing UH-1s. The specification called for an aircraft able to carry a crew of three and eleven troops, a 7,000lb slung load, at a cruising speed of 145–175kt. Other requirements included a 450–550ft/min vertical climb rate, a 2.3 hours endurance, and a 5,000ft single-engine ceiling. Requests for proposals were issued to the US industry on 5 January, 1972, submissions being made in due course by Bell, Boeing-Vertol and Sikorsky. The three companies submitted five proposals and Boeing-Vertol and Sikorsky were selected to proceed to prototype construction, contracts being placed on 30 August, 1972.

Bell's proposal was the Model 240, a twin-engine, fourteen-seat helicopter, larger than the UH-1, with four-blade main and tail rotors. Among the most significant design features were the two 1,500shp General Electric T700-GE-700 turboshafts, a fail-safe modular transmission, a four-bladed swept-tip gimbaled rotor with a new Wortmann aerofoil for enhanced aerodynamic efficiency.

## Design D-303

At the 1981 Paris Air Show, Bell officials unveiled a three-engined design which was to be a growth variant of the XV-15. Designated D-303, this tilt-rotor aircraft was proposed in both civil and military versions and offered 16/20-passenger capability. For this project, Bell selected three General Electric T700 engines in order to comply with FAA and CAA one-engine inoperative requirements. Two of these engines were used to drive the three-blade tilting rotors, the third one was on the back of the fuselage in a horizontal position.

Maximum speed 260kt (480km/h); service ceiling 16,000ft (4,880m).

## Design D-326 Clipper

Following the successful flight testing of the XV-15, the Bell design team evolved several tilt-rotor aircraft for a large range of missions. The Design D-326 Clipper was aimed at the off-shore oil support market. The large fuselage would have provided accomodation for thirty passengers. The inverted swept-wing would have carried a 5,000shp General Electric CT64 propeller-turbine under streamlined fairings.

Overall width 87ft (26.52m); overall length 60ft (18.29m), maximum height 23ft 8in (7.21m); main rotor diameter 38ft 6in (11.73m); empty weight 24,740lb (11,222kg); maximum vertical take-off weight 37,000lb (16,783kg); maximum short take-off weight 50,000lb (22,680kg); maximum speed 330kt (611km/h) at 20,000ft (6,100m); maximum range with 16 passengers 1,330 nautical miles (2,464km).

## BAT

In 1984, the Bell Advanced Tilt Rotor (or BAT) was a lightweight advanced, single seat, tilt-rotor aircraft proposed by Bell in response to the US Army's Light Helicopter Experimental programme (LHX) Development of the BAT had to be abandoned due to new LHX requirements, especially in the matter of weight (LHX had to be under 7,000lb). The BAT was a small aircraft, with a butterfly tail unit, that would have had the following characteristics:

Gross weight 8,000lb (3,624kg); maximum speed 350mph at 14,000ft (563km/h at

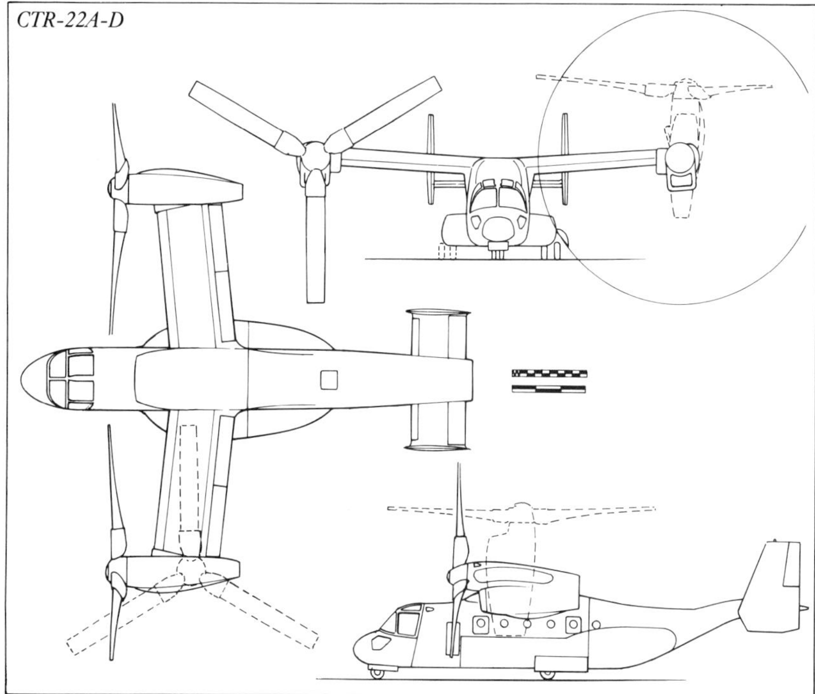


*Full-scale mock-up of the Bell Advanced Tilt Rotor, known as the BAT. The rotor blades have been sawn off and actual blades would have been a half-span longer. (Bell)*

4,270m); hover ceiling outside ground effect 10,000ft (3,050m); ferry range 2,100 nautical miles (3,890km); armament four Hellfire and four Stinger missiles.

## CTR-22A and B

In 1983, the FAA-sponsored National Rotorcraft Program sought to identify improvements to the United States interurban transport networks and determined that conventional helicopters did not have the potential to satisfy requirements because of a lack of capacity, high operational costs and high noise levels. Tilt-rotor aircraft, it was felt, offered better potential to improve interurban air transport service. In 1985, FAA administrator D D Engen proposed a joint civil tilt-rotor study with NASA and DoD that would capitalize on development of the military Bell-Boeing V-22 and document the potential of the commercial tilt-rotor transport market. This study, conducted by Boeing Commercial Airplane Company teamed with Bell-Textron and Boeing-Vertol, led to several de-

*The CTR-22A/B. (Bell)*

*The CTR-22C. (Bell)*

signs: CTR-22A/B/C and D, CTR-800, CTR-1900 and CTR-7500. The CTR-22A and B were direct civil derivatives of the V-22. With minimum change (all military equipment, including cargo ramp, removed), the CTR-22B provided seating for 31 passengers and included typical amenities. With an uprated transmission for higher horsepower (6,805shp Allison T406 engines), the CTR-22B would achieve the 600 nautical miles design range. The CTR-22A did not meet this civil design range requirement.

Data and calculated performance for the CTR-22B: wing span 45ft 9½in (13.96m); rotor diameter 38ft (11.58m); overall span 84ft 7¼in (25.75m); overall length 57ft 3½in (17.46m); height (rotors in upward position) 21ft 7½in (6.58m); take-off gross weight 45,120lb (20,440kg); cruising speed 276mph (445km/h); range 600 nautical miles (1,110km).

## CTR-22C

The CTR-22C is a 39-passenger derivative of the V-22. This aircraft uses the V-22 wing and propulsion system with a new pressurized fuselage. Engines are two 6,805shp Allison T406s.

Data and calculated performance: Dimensions as CTR-22B except overall length 68ft 7½in (20.9m); take-off gross weight 46,230lb (20,942kg); cruising speed 325mph (522km/h); range 600 nautical miles (1,110km).

## CTR-22D

The CTR-22D was developed to evaluate higher capacity and more efficient fuselage cross-section. It

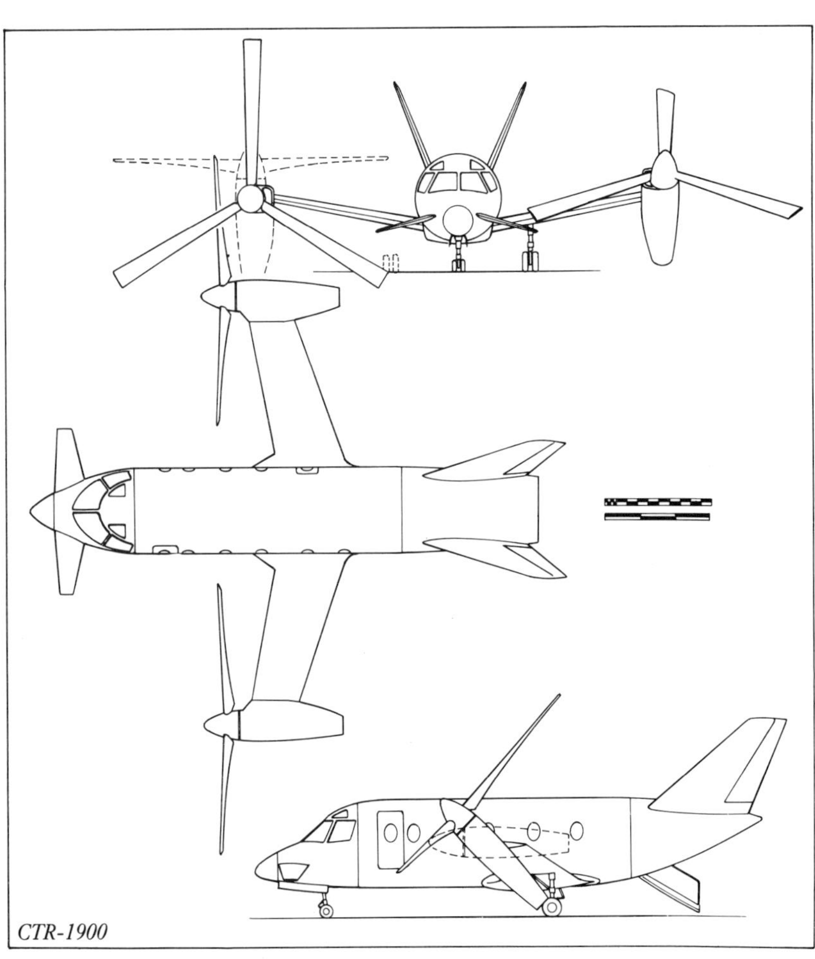

*CTR-1900*

*The CTR-1900. (Bell)*

expands the CTR-22C's three-abreast fuselage to four-abreast to hold 52 passengers. Engines would be two growth 7,312shp Allison T406s. Fully loaded, the CTR-22D's design range is 280 nautical miles. With increased gross weight and approximately 15 per cent increased engine thrust, the 600 nautical miles requirement could be met with 52 passengers.

Data and calculated performance: wing span 48ft (14.63m); rotor diameter 38ft (11.58m); overall span 86ft (26.21m); overall length 71ft 8½in (21.85m); take-off gross weight 49,260lb (22,315kg); maximum cruising speed 325mph (522km/h); range 280 nautical miles (518km).

## CTR-800

This configuration is based on the XV-15 tilt-rotor and could carry eight passengers. It has a pressurized fuselage and uprated 2,100shp Rolls-Royce/Turboméca RTM-322 engines.

*The CTR-800. (Bell)*

Data and calculated performance: wing span 32ft 2½in (9.81m); rotor diameter 26ft (7.92m); overall length 41ft 6in (12.65m); take-off gross weight 15,750lb (7,135kg); cruising speed 314mph (506km/h); range 600 nautical miles (1,110km).

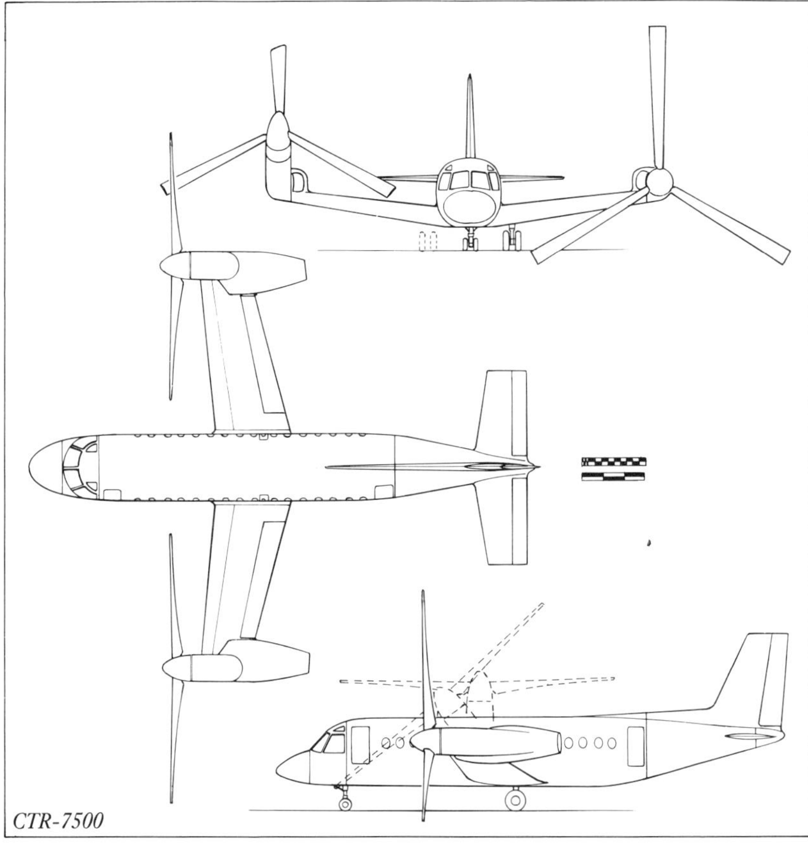

*CTR-7500*

## CTR-1900

The CTR-1900 is an all-new 19-passenger design. It is the result of a trade study comparing the V-22 high-wing and H-tail configuration and new configurations (low-wing and conventional tail or low-wing, V-tail and canard). The CTR-1900 with the V-tail and canard had the lowest drag and weight. This aircraft would use 3,440shp Rolls-Royce/ Turboméca RTM-322 engines.

Data and calculated performance for the CTR-1900 are: wing span 37ft (11.28m); rotor diameter 28ft (8.53m); overall length 46ft 7½in (14.20m); take-off gross weight 22,800lb (10,328kg); cruising speed 325mph (524km/h); range 637 nautical miles (1,180km).

*The CTR-7500. (Bell)*

## CTR-7500

The CTR-7500 is also an all-new 75-passenger design. Propulsion is to be assumed by the largest projected growth version of the Allison T406 engine delivering up to 12,883shp (16,100shp for 30 seconds).

Data and calculated performance: wing span 63ft (19.20m); rotor diameter 46ft (14.02m); overall length 83ft 8½in (25.51m); take-off gross weight 79,820lb (36,158kg); cruising speed 345mph (555km/h); range 600 nautical miles (1,110km).

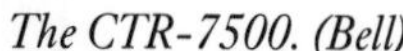

*The CTR-7500. (Bell)*

## Bell Helicopter Textron/ McDonnell Douglas LHX

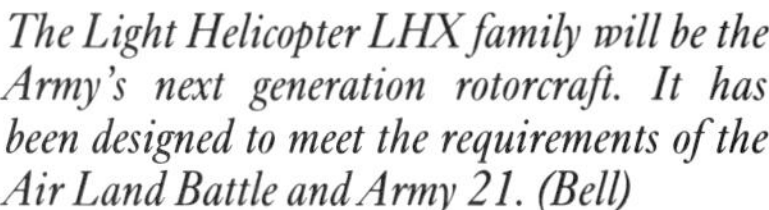

*The Light Helicopter LHX family will be the Army's next generation rotorcraft. It has been designed to meet the requirements of the Air Land Battle and Army 21. (Bell)*

In 1982, the US Army invited aircraft manufacturers to submit design concepts for its Light Helicopter Experimental (LHX) programme to meet the requirements of the Air Land Battle and Army 21, the Army's blue-print for waging and winning conflicts in the 21st century. The LHX will be a lightweight (8,000lb plus or minus 500lb) highly reliable and easily maintained weapons system that will achieve a high degree of standardization and reduced support costs.

In January 1983, the US Army announced plans to field up to 4,500 LHX helicopters with first deliveries taking place in the 1990s. In July 1983, McDonnell Douglas Helicopter Co received a $205,000 preliminary design study award from the US Army Aviation Systems Command to explore LHX mission-oriented design alternatives. A month later, the US Army announced initial plans to develop ARTI (Army-funded Advanced Rotorcraft Technology Integration which allows virtual 'hands-off' flying) as a first phase of the LHX programme effort. In September 1983, McDonnell Douglas received $1.7 million to determine the company's best technical approach for the LHX programme. MDD Helicopter Co was teamed with Hughes Aircraft Co and Honeywell Inc on the ARTI phase of the LHX programme, then, in March 1984, MDD Aircraft Co joined the LHX development team. In November of the same year, modifications were introduced on a prototype of the MDD AH-64 Apache helicopter for use as an ARTI demonstrator and this flew for the first time in October 1985. In March 1985, the US Army stipulated that the LHX will be a conventional helicopter and will replace four existing helicopter types (Bell UH-1, AH-1, OH-58 and Hughes OH-6).

One year later, in April 1986, the LHX 'SuperTeam' was announced in Washington led by McDD Helicopter Company, Bell Helicopter Textron and MACAIR. William Randy McDonnell of MDD Helicopter Co was named director of the SuperTeam with Walter Sonneborn of Bell Helicopter Textron as deputy director. Preliminary design began and, in April 1987, the SuperTeam announced the selection of the Bell Model 680 Rotor system and the MDD NOTAR anti-torque system for inclusion in the LHX design. In May 1987, the DoD ordered two independant studies of potential airframe designs for application to LHX requirements (utility and SCAT), including a minimum

*The LHX is a lightweight highly reliable and easily maintained weapons system that will achieve a high degree of standardisation. (Bell)*

*The Bell/McDonnell Douglas proposal for the LHX programme. This aircraft would have carried its weapons inside a wing/sponson. (Bell)*

weight conventional helicopter with a 1,200shp engine, a new development helicopter not restrained by engine power, a tilt-rotor aircraft and an upgraded variant of the AH-64 Apache. Two competing teams (Bell-MDD and Boeing-Sikorsky) worked to create a winning design during a 23-month demonstration/validation phase.

As development was progressing steadily, the US Army announced in January 1988 a 'refocused' LHX programme as an integral part of a comprehensive Army Aviation modernisation plan which called for production of 2.096 armed reconnaissance/light attack combat aircraft with weight and cost goals of 7,500lb and $7.5 million, respectively. By October 1988, the Army had selected the Allison-Garrett LHTEC T-800 engine to power the LHX. Otherwise, the LHX is expected to have a 1.8-g composite airframe, a protected anti-torque system, an advanced-technology rotor, a pilot night vision system with helmet mounted wide-field-of-view display, a digital fly-by-wire flight-control system, a second generation FLIR, an electro-optical target acquisition and designation subsystem (EOTADS), a mission processing subsystem (MPS), a night vision pilotage subsystem (NVPS) and integrated aircraft stabilisation equipment.

On the armament side, in accordance with US Army specifications, the LHX will be designed to fire up to ten laser-guided Hellfire and four heat-seeking Stinger missiles, Hydra 70 2.75inch folding-fin rockets and will have a 20mm turreted chin-gun provision with 500 rounds. This armament will be supported by the helmet integrated display and sight subsystem (HIDSS) developed by SuperTeam, Hughes and Honeywell. This is a helmet-mounted wide-field-of-view display, using a specially designed visor which provides a quick reaction sighting system to the crew member for directing the gun, missiles and rockets.

After more than two years evaluating the two proposals, it was finally announced on 5 April, 1991, that the Boeing-Sikorsky First Team had been chosen in preference to Bell-MDD's proposal.

The first flight of the LHX prototype is expected in August 1993 and equipment of the first Army unit should take place in December 1995. A grand total of 2,096 aircraft is expected to be procured by the US Army and produced at the maximum rate of 216 aircraft a year.

## LHX provisional data

Rotor diameter 41ft (12.5m); disc area 1,320sq ft (122.7sq m).

Empty weight 7,500lb (3,402kg); gross weight 11,000lb (4,990kg).

Cruising speed 170kt or 195mph (315km/h); ferry range 1,260 nautical miles or 1,450 statute miles (2,334km); endurance 2½hr.

*The Bell/MDD LHX would have used the no-tail-rotor (Notar) ducted exhaust system of yaw control. (Bell)*

# Appendix II

# Miscellaneous Types

## Boeing B-29 Superfortress

During the Second World War it was found that Boeing could not carry the full load of the B-29 Superfortress production. Bell Aircraft and Glenn L Martin were then selected to produce this long-range heavy bomber at newly constructed Government financed plants. The Bell plant was located in Atlanta, Georgia, and was the sole manufacturer to produce the B-29B variant which was powered by four 2,200hp Wright R-3350-51 engines and had its armament reduced only to the tail guns (aimed and fired automatically by an AN/APG-15B radar fire control system). Maximum speed of the B-29B was increased to 364mph at 25,000ft. The first employees arrived at the plant in March 1943 and production of the first bomber began in the following October. The first two aircraft were delivered by the end of 1943. The Bell-Atlanta plant produced 357 Superfortresses. At the end of the war, the plant was shut down and unfinished aircraft were scrapped.

### Bell-built Boeing B-29s

| *Models* | *S/n* | *Remarks* |
|---|---|---|
| B-29-1-BA | 42-6222 | c/n 3356 |
| | 42-6224 | c/n 3358 |
| | 42-6233 | c/n 3367 |
| | 42-6235 | c/n 3369 |
| | 42-6237 | c/n 3371 |
| | 42-63352/63365 | |
| B-29-5-BA | 42-63366/63381 | |
| B-29-10-BA | 42-63382/63401 | |
| B-29-15-BA | 42-63402/63451 | |
| B-29-20-BA | 42-63452/63501 | |
| B-29-25-BA | 42-63502/63551 | |
| B-29-30-BA | 42-63552/63580 | |
| B-29-40-BA | 42-63737 | |
| | 42-63744 | |
| | 42-63750 | |
| | 44-83894 | |
| B-29-45-BA | 44-83900 | |
| | 44-83904 | |
| | 44-83908 | |
| | 44-83911 | |
| | 44-83914 | |
| | 44-83917 | |
| | 44-83920 | |
| | 44-83923 | |
| | 44-83926/83940 | (even numbers) |
| | 44-83945/83957 | (odd numbers) |
| | 44-83960 | |
| | 44-83962 | |
| B-29-50-BA | 44-83964/84008 | (even numbers) |
| B-29-55-BA | 44-84010/84056 | (even numbers) |
| B-29-60-BA | 44-84058/84102 | (even numbers) |
| B-29-65-BA | 44-84104/84148 | (even numbers) |
| | 44-84152/84156 | |
| B-29B-30-BA | 42-63581/63621 | |
| B-29B-35-BA | 42-63622/63691 | |
| B-29B-40-BA | 42-63692/63736 | |
| | 42-63738/63743 | |
| | 42-63745/63749 | |
| | 42-63751 | |
| | 44-83890/83893 | |
| | 44-83895 | |
| B-29B-45-BA | 44-83896/83899 | |
| | 44-83901/83903 | |
| | 44-83905/83907 | |
| | 44-83909/83910 | |
| | 44-83912/83913 | |
| | 44-83915/83916 | |
| | 44-83918/83919 | |
| | 44-83921/83922 | |
| | 44-83924/83925 | |
| | 44-83927/83939 | (odd numbers) |
| | 44-83941/83944 | |
| | 44-83946/83958 | (even numbers) |
| | 44-83959/83961 | (odd numbers) |
| B-29B-50-BA | 44-83963/84007 | (odd numbers) |
| B-29B-55-BA | 44-84009/84055 | (odd numbers), 44-84043 converted to XB-29G-BA |
| B-29B-60-BA | 44-84057/84103 | (odd numbers), 44-84061 converted to YB-29J |
| B-29B-65-BA | 44-84105/84149 | (odd numbers), 44-84111 converted to EB-29B-BA |
| | 44-84151 | |
| | 44-84155 | |

*Bell-built Boeing EB-29B-50-BA Superfortress s/n 44-83965. Absence of armament characterised the B model. (P M Bowers)*

*An unidentified Bell-built Boeing TB-29B of the 8th Air Force in July 1946. The aircraft is* The Challenger. *(Courtesy P M Bowers)*

*The Bell VB-13 Tarzon bomb. (USAF)*

## Bell VB-13 Tarzon

Work on a United States-built variant of the British 12,000lb Tallboy bomb was initiated on 26 February, 1945. This bomb, built by Bell Aircraft in its Georgia plant, and later at Niagara Falls, was a free-falling weapon guided both in range and azimuth. Designated VB-13, later (Y)ASM-1A, the Tarzon bomb was cigar shaped with two lift shrouds, one annular around the centre of gravity, the other octagonal at the end (similar to the Second World War German Fritz-X bomb). The Tarzon had a rudder and elevator controlled by radio and four ailerons gyro-stabilised by pneumatic controls. The guidance system consisted of an AN/URW-2 radio-set connected to an AN/ARW-38 radio-transmitter located in the launch aircraft. The aircraft type used to deliver Tarzon was the Boeing B-29 Superfortress. At least three aircraft (s/n 45-21745, -21746 and -21748) were modified to accomodate this weapon which was carried half-buried in the fuselage. From December 1950, 19th Bomb Group used these bombs, with moderate success, against bridges in Korea. Technical problems were commonplace and the last mission against Sinuiju bridges, on 29 March, 1951, was a complete disaster.

Length 21ft (6.40m); body diameter 3ft 2in (0.96m); lift shroud diameter 4ft 6in (1.37m); weight 12,000lb (5,436kg).

## Bell Model 59/X-9 Shrike

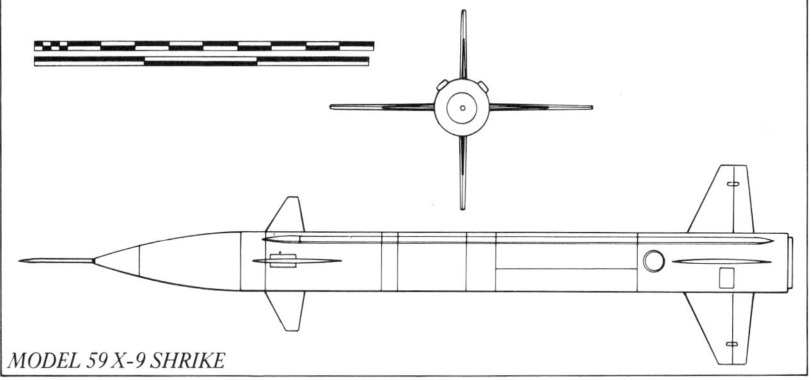
*MODEL 59 X-9 SHRIKE*

Considering the heavy losses sustained by the long-range bombers during the war, the Air Force soon showed interest in weapons that could be launched while the carrier aeroplane was still out of range of enemy fire. Such projectiles were called 'stand-off' weapons. The first specification for such a weapon was published in July 1946. Bell Aircraft was among the companies which received an Air Force contract for preliminary studies of a supersonic missile. In May 1947, a revised contract was signed with Bell for the project MX-776 concerning a missile that could be launched from a Boeing B-29 Superfortress. After several changes in the requirements, it was decided to create a test-bed (known as MX-776A, later MX-774, Bell Model 59 and officially designated RTV-A-4, later X-9) in order to gather the various data (aerodynamic, propulsion, guidance data, etc) necessary in the development of the full-scale missile (MX-776B) which was to become the GAM-63 Rascal. After a free glide flight, the first powered launch was on 17 May, 1950, and the whole test programme was considered very successful in comparison with other missile programmes.

In due course, Bell presented the Air Force with a production armed variant of the X-9 which was not adopted because of poor performance. The last launch of the X-9 took place on 23 January, 1953. All launches were made from Boeing B-50A s/n 46-062 and B-50D s/n 48-069. An estimated total of thirty-one X-9s was eventually built and none are believed to have survived.

Length 22ft 9in (6.98m); wingspan 7ft 9½in (2.38m); diameter 1ft 9½in (0.55m); wing area approx 70sq ft (6.5sq m); empty weight 2,125lb (962kg); loaded weight 3,495lb (1,583kg); maximum speed Mach 1.5 to 2.0; maximum altitude 65,000ft (19,800m); range 50 miles (80km).

## Bell GAM-63 Rascal

The GAM-63 was a rocket-powered air-to-surface stand-off guided missile. It was of aluminium construction with cantilever mid-wing and full-span trailing-edge ailerons. It was powered by a Bell liquid-propellent (liquid oxygen and alcohol) rocket motor, made up of three vertical in-line chambers, each developing a thrust of 4,000lb at 4,000ft. The guidance system consisted of a radar command system developed by Bell Avionics, Radio Corporation of America and Texas Instruments. The warhead was to be either atomic or thermonuclear. On 30 September, 1952, an XGAM-63 was launched for the first time from a specially modified Boeing DB-50D (s/n 48-75); the missile being guided to the target from the aeroplane by a controller. In 1953, a Boeing B-47B Stratojet (s/n 51-2186) was modified to YDB-47B-BW configuration to carry the Bell XGAM-63 Rascal. In January 1954, two additional B-47Es (s/n 51-5219 and -5220) were converted to YDB-47E-BW for service tests and development of the GAM-63. The missile was suspended from the

*The Rascal was flight-tested using converted Boeing B-47 Stratojet bombers. YDB-47E-BW s/n 51-5219 is illustrated. (Boeing)*

starboard side of the fuselage. It was guided to the target by radio control from the YDB-47E. During tests, missiles of the service trials batch (XGAM-63-BC) scored four consecutive direct hits on targets at the Air Force Missile Development Center, in New Mexico. Formal acceptance of the first production GAM-63 took place at Pinecastle AFB, Florida, on 30 October, 1957, but the Rascal never saw operational service. Although this weapon was accurate and effective, it was overtaken by new developments in the air-launched missile field and cancellation of the programme was announced on 9 September, 1958.

Span 14ft (4.27m); length 32ft (9.75m); body diameter 4ft (1.22m); launching weight 13,000lb (5,890kg); cruising speed Mach 1.6; maximum range 100miles (160km).

*A Bell GAM-63 Rascal stand-off missile fitted to the B-47 fuselage side. (Courtesy P M Bowers)*

## Bell 'Pogo' vehicles

In the early 1960s, Bell Aerosystems began the development of several light flying platforms in order to evaluate various configurations for Earth and Lunar Flying Vehicles. These platforms were designed to carry either one or two men and were known as 'Pogo' vehicles. They were powered by a 600lb st hydrogen peroxide propulsion system. The one-man 'Pogo' vehicle weighed approximately 80lb and had a 300lb st propulsion system. The two-man 'Pogo' vehicle had two propulsion systems. Later, Bell evaluated a one-man kinesthetically-controlled 'Pogo', which flew for the

*The GAM-63 Rascal weighed 13,000lb and had to be transported on special trolleys.*

*The Air Cushion Landing Gear, or ACLG, was tested on a modified Lake LA-4 flying-boat. (Bell)*

first time late in 1968. As a follow-up to the one-man rocket-belt device, Bell developed a two-man vehicle which consisted of a platform mounted on four castoring wheels and carrying two rocket-belt propulsion systems. The operator stood on the rear of the platform and controlled the rocket nozzles with hand, arm and shoulder movements. By mid-June 1967, this vehicle had logged 27 flights. In 1968, Bell received a $250,000 contract from NASA for preliminary design of a Lunar Flying Vehicle for the transport of astronauts on exploration missions.

Data for the two-man 'Pogo'. Length 3ft 9½in (1.16m); width 1ft 10½in (0.57m); height 5ft 0in (1.52m); empty weight 147lb (67kg).

## Bell ACLG and ACLS

In December 1963, Bell Aerosystems initiated the development of an air cushion undercarriage (ACLG) using its own funds. In 1966, a $99,000 USAF Systems Command's Flight Dynamics Laboratory contract was awarded for wind-tunnel testing. Three further contracts, totalling $264,500 covered feasibility study, model test and flight-test programme. A Lake LA-4 four-seat flying-boat was modified to receive the ACLG. A small auxiliary engine was installed in the rear fuselage which drove a fan to inflate an air cushion bag fixed to the hull of the aircraft, providing a pressure of 50lb/sq ft. In flight, the auxiliary engine could be shut down or its airflow diverted through louvres located in the sides of the fuselage to provide additional thrust. Flight tests with Lake LA-4 N1015L began in 1969 and lasted for three months. During these tests, the aircraft logged 18½ flying hours and operated on snow, ice, concrete and grass surfaces. In August 1969, other tests were successfully conducted on water and led to preliminary studies that established that this concept was applicable to both the booster and orbiter stages of the Space Shuttle.

In November 1970, Bell Aerospace undertook Phase I of a joint US/Canadian programme to adapt the ACLS for military transport aircraft. It was decided to use a de Havilland Canada CC-115 Buffalo (s/n 115451) loaned by the Canadian Department of National Defence as a test-bed aircraft. This aircraft made its maiden flight at Downsview during the summer of 1973 and tests were conducted with reasonable success. The programme was completed in 1977 and the CC-115 was restored to its original configuration and returned to RCAF No.424 Squadron.

## Bell LLRV and LLTV

In the spring of 1964, as part of the Apollo lunar programme, Bell Aerosystems delivered two Lunar Landing Research Vehicles (LLRV) to NASA. These vehicles, equipped

*The Bell Lunar Landing Research Vehicle, or LLRV. (NASA)*

*Astronaut Charles Conrad Jr, commander of the Apollo 12 lunar mission, flying the LLRV at Ellington AFB in October 1969. (NASA)*

with a variable stability control system, were used at Edwards to provide a realistic simulation of landing on the moon and to gather data for the designers of the LEM. The LLRV was designed to reach altitudes of up to 4,000ft and to fly horizontally at speeds of up to 60ft/sec (40.9mph). It consisted of a platform fitted with four welded aluminium alloy truss legs and was powered by a 4,200lb st General Electric CF700-2V turbofan as well as by eight Bell Aerosystems hydrogen peroxide rockets. In addition sixteen Bell reaction control rockets were mounted for attitude control. The first LLRV made its maiden flight on 30 October, 1964, with NASA project pilot Joseph A Walker at the controls. Later, the LLRVs were transferred to Houston (Manned Spacecraft Center) for the training of the astronauts. On 6 May, 1968, one of the two LLRVs crashed at Ellington AFB due to an inflight failure. Fortunately, its pilot,

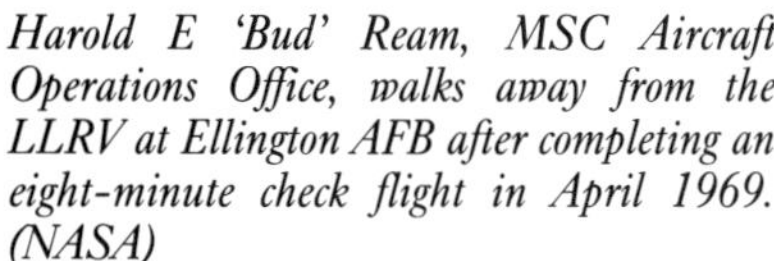

*Harold E 'Bud' Ream, MSC Aircraft Operations Office, walks away from the LLRV at Ellington AFB after completing an eight-minute check flight in April 1969. (NASA)*

*The Bell LLTV. (NASA)*

Neil A Armstrong, managed to eject and was unhurt.

Late in 1967, three examples of a new vehicle were delivered. These were called LLTV (Lunar Landing Training Vehicles), the first flight of an LLTV being made on 3 October, 1968, at Ellington. With Joseph S Algranti, chief aircraft operations officer, Manned Spacecraft Center, at the controls, the LLTV flew for 8 minutes reaching a height of about 50ft. The LLTV was powered by a 4,200lb st General Electric CF700-2V turbofan. Two 500lb st Bell hydrogen peroxide rockets provided additional thrust during take-off and landing. Six additional 500lb st rocket motors were installed in case of failure of the main engine and sixteen reaction control rockets were mounted for attitude control.

Twelve test flights were made before the aircraft was made available for astronaut training. Afterwards, several astronauts flew the LLTV, among whom were Charles Conrad Jr and Alan B Shepard Jr. On 11 December, 1968, one LLTV was lost in an accident but the pilot ejected safely.

### LLRV

Height 10ft (3.05m); width 13ft 4in (4.06m); gross weight 3,710lb (1,683kg); maximum horizontal velocity 60ft/sec (18m/sec); maximum vertical velocity 100ft/sec (30m/sec); maximum altitude 4,000ft (1,220m).

### LLTV

Height 11ft 4in (3.45m); width 13ft 4in (4.06m); normal take-off weight 4,051lb (1,837kg); operating horizontal speed 60ft/sec (18m/sec); vertical velocity 30ft/sec (9m/sec); service ceiling 1,000ft (305m).

## Bell Jet Flying Belt

Under a $3 million contract from DoD's Advanced Research Projects Agency, Bell developed for the US Army an experimental one-man back-pack flying system. The Jet Flying Belt, as it was commonly known, was powered by a single 430lb st Williams Research Corporation WR-19 high-bypass miniature turbojet and flight control was achieved through manually actuated controls. Free flight tests began on 7 April, 1969, and, on 26 January, 1970, Bell announced that a licence to manufacture the Jet Flying Belt as well as other small lift device systems had been granted to Williams Research.

Empty weight 124lb (56kg); gross take-off weight 365lb (165kg); maximum speed 100mph (160km/h); range 30miles (48km); duration 25 minutes.

## Bell-Boeing Pointer RPV

In 1986, Bell and Boeing decided to spend $700,000 of internal research and development funds to build a tilt-rotor RPV weighing less than one per cent of the V-22 Osprey on which it was to be patterned. Thanks to the vertical take-off and landing mode, this unmanned vehicle could carry more delicate loads than conventional RPVs. It could cruise at high speeds, loiter in an orbital pattern and hover for hours over a fixed position. Also the risks of damaging the RPV during recovery are far lower. The powerplant chosen for the Pointer was a 95hp Suzuki snowmobile engine due to its light weight. Boeing constructed the fuselage and flight-control system and Bell built the propeller/rotors and drive system. The Pointer is of all-composite construction.

The Pointer, which made its first public appearance at Farnborough in September 1988, flew for the first time at the end of November 1988.

Wingspan, spinner centerlines 10ft 8in (3.25m); width, blades turning 18ft 5in (5.61m); length of fuselage 13ft 4in (4.06m); height, top of spinner 5ft 5½in (1.67m); rotor diameter 7ft 9in (2.36m); empty weight 409lb (185.5kg); loaded weight 550lb (250kg); maximum speed 185mph (297km/h); cruising speed 162mph (260km/h); hover ceiling in ground effect 9,000ft (2,750m); hover ceiling outside ground effect 7,500ft (2,300m); endurance 7+hr; radius 115miles (185km).

*The Bell/Boeing Pointer RPV performing a target designation. (Boeing)*

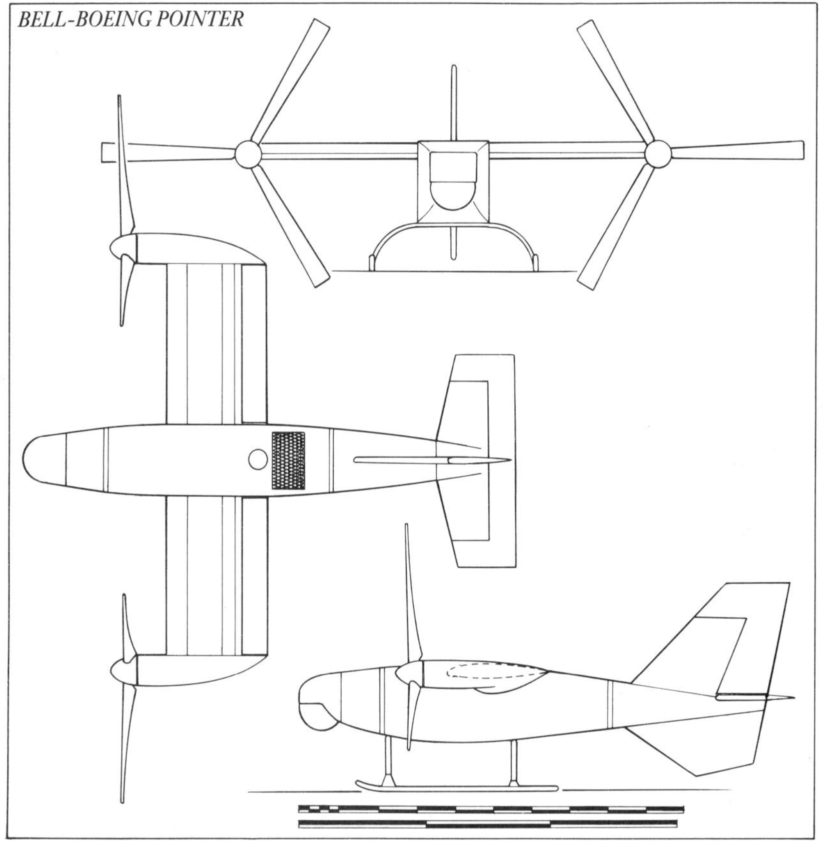

# Appendix III

# Milestones in Bell History

### 1935

Bell Aircraft Corporation is legally founded with 56 employees (10 July).

### 1936

Bell Aircraft Corporation received contract from Consolidated for 146 PBY-2/3 wing panels (28 January).

Bell Aircraft Corp has 167 employees (25 March).

### 1937

First flight of XFM-1 Airacuda (1 September).

### 1938

First flight of XP-39 (6 April).

### 1939

First production contract signed for Model 13/P-39C (12 October).

### 1940

First flight of the XFL-1 Airabonita (13 May).

First flight of Model 12/YP-39 (13 September).

### 1941

Bell agrees to produce a twin-jet fighter (5 September).

Development begins on the first helicopter by Arthur Young; Young proves his invention is workable (1 November).

### 1942

Gardenville becomes the site to produce a full-size vertical take-off aircraft.

First flight of Model 27/XP-59A Airacomet (1 October).

First flight of Model 33/XP-63 (7 December).

### 1943

The Model 30 helicopter is flown successfully for the first time by Floyd Carlson.

### 1944

A Bell helicopter accomplishes the first indoor flight in the United States.

First flight of Model 32/XP-77 light fighter (1 April).

### 1945

First demonstration of emergency medical use of a helicopter.

First flight of XP-83 long-range jet-powered fighter (25 February).

### 1946

First unpowered flight made by the Bell X-1 (10 January).

The Model 47B is awarded the world's first commercial helicopter licence (8 March).

First flight of L-39 swept-wing experimental aircraft (23 April).

Bell establishes the first flight training school for commercial helicopter pilots (1 July).

Bell's test pilot Jack Woolams is killed while flying a P-39 Airacobra (30 August).

First powered flight made by X-1 (9 December).

The first production-line helicopter is delivered to the US Army (December).

### 1947

The X-1 is the first aircraft to exceed the speed of sound in level flight (14 October).

### 1948

Larry Bell, John Stack, and Charles E Yeager receive the Collier's Trophy for their achievement with the Bell X-1.

### 1949

A Bell helicopter sets a new altitude record of 18,550ft (5,654m).

A new speed record for a helicopter is established when an XH-12 flies at 133.9mph (215.4km/h).

### 1950

A Model 47D-1 becomes the first helicopter to fly over the Alps.

First powered flight of a Model 59/X-9 missile (17 May).

### 1951

The US Army announces that the Model 47D-1 has broken all records for speedy evacuation of wounded troops in Korea.

Groundbreaking for first Bell helicopter plant in Texas (21 May).

First flight of the X-5 variable-wing geometry aircraft (20 June).

### 1952

Elton J Smith sets the world's record for helicopter distance in a straight line when he flies a Model 47D-1 nonstop from Hurst to Buffalo, 1,217.137miles (1,958.373km).

First launching of a GAM-63 Rascal missile (30 September).

### 1953

The 1,000th helicopter rolls off the Bell assembly line (April).

A world record is established when the XH-15 autorotates from 16,000ft (4.877m).

First flight of the ASW helicopter HSL. Bell X-1A flies at Mach 2.435 (12 December).

### 1954

Bell Model 65 Air Test Vehicle makes first hover flight (January).

The XH-13F is the first turbine helicopter to fly.

### 1955

First flight of the Model 200/XV-3 (11 August).

UH-1 wins competition for first Army turbine helicopter (23 February).

**1956**

Army pilots set an unofficial world's record for helicopter endurance flight when an H-13H is kept aloft for 57hr and 50min.

The Bell X-2 is destroyed in an accident (27 September).

Death of Lawrence Dale Bell (20 October).

Death of Robert J Woods (3 November).

**1957**

Bell Helicopter Corporation is founded as a wholly-owned subsidiary of Bell Aircraft Corporation.

The 2,000th Model 47 is rolled off the assembly line.

The X-14 makes its first hovering flight (19 February).

**1958**

First transition is made by the X-14 (24 May).

The Rascal programme is terminated (November).

The XV-3 makes the first conversion of a tilting propeller-rotor aircraft (18 December).

**1960**

Textron Inc purchases the defence activities of Bell Aircraft Corp and sets up Bell Aerospace Corp as a wholly-owned subsidiary (2 July).

Six world and one national rotary-wing records are established by an HU-1.

**1961**

Model 47s establish eight new world records.

The HTL-6 sets the unofficial world record for helicopter flight endurance of 72hr 2min.

**1962**

A Bell helicopter flies without a pilot aboard for 72min (19 November).

**1963**

A UH-1B flies at more than 170mph (273km/h).

FAA certificates Model 204B (April).

First flight of Model 207 Sioux Scout (27 June).

First helicopter flight to South Pole: UH-1B (4 February).

**1964**

Eleven world records are claimed by the UH-1D, making a total of 21 for the Iroquois model and a total of 27 records held by Bell helicopters.

**1965**

The YUH-1B flies at 250mph (402km/h).

Two new models are unveiled: the HueyCobra and the JetRanger.

First flight of Model 208 Twin-Delta (29 April).

**1966**

First flight of the JetRanger.

Bell receives the largest contract awarded by the US Army for 2,115 UH-1s.

**1967**

Bell announces Model 205A.

**1968**

The US Navy selects the JetRanger.

JetRanger wins the Light Observation Helicopter (LOH) competition.

The 10,000th Bell helicopter is rolled off the assembly line.

Bell announces the Model 212.

A Bell LLRV crashes and is destroyed at Ellington AFB, its pilot is able to eject safely (8 December).

**1969**

Bell's compound research helicopter attains a speed of 316mph (508km/h) in level flight, an unofficial world record (15 April).

US Army accepts its first OH-58A Kiowa.

**1970**

Model 212 Twin receives its FAA Type Certificate.

First flight of Model 214 (October).

**1971**

The JetRanger II receives its FAA Type Certificate. The mayor of Forth Worth proclaims Bell Week in honour of Bell's 20th year in Texas.

**1972**

Bell submits a proposal for the UTTAS programme which is not adopted.

**1973**

The 1,000th JetRanger is delivered.

Bell Helicopter International Inc is formed as a separate division of Textron to conduct business in Iran.

Bell announces the development of the LongRanger.

**1974**

Bell commemorates the delivery of its 20,000th helicopter (23 April).

Model 206L makes its first flight (11 September).

**1975**

The LongRanger receives FAA certification.

An Irani Model 214A sets five world records (29 April).

**1976**

The company adopts a new name: Bell Helicopter Textron Inc.

Bell marks its 25th anniversary in Texas.

Model 214B receives FAA Type Certificate.

First flight of Model 222.

Delivery of the 2,000th JetRanger.

Roll-out of the XV-15 at the Arlington Flight Research Center.

**1977**

US Army accepts the initial production model of the AH-1S.

Development of the JetRanger III.

Bell announces the development of the Model 214ST.

First hover flight of the XV-15 (3 May).

US Marines accepts its first AH-1T (15 October).

**1978**

Bell announces the Model 412.

Construction of the 135,000sq ft Bell Technical Center at the Hurst Plant.

The LongRanger II receives its FAA Type Certificate.

**1979**

First flight of the XV-15 No.2.

The Model 222 receives FAA Type Certificate.

Construction begins of 270,000sq ft Manufacturing Center at Hurst Plant.

First flight of Model 214ST (21 July).

First flight of Model 412 (August).

**1980**

XV-15 flies at 346mph/557km/h (17 June).

A LongRanger makes the first trans-Atlantic light helicopter crossing (5,100 miles/8,206km).

Bell 222 receives FAA single-pilot certification (15 May).

**1981**

Delivery of the 25,000th Bell helicopter, a Model 222.

Bell receives contract for Army's Advanced Composite Airframe (ACAP) programme (31 March).

Bell is selected as winner of the AHIP industry competition (21 September).

**1982**

The Model 214ST receives FAA Type certification for VFR and IFR operations.

Bell announces Model 222B.

The Bell-Boeing Tilt Rotor team is created to compete in the JVX competition.

First flight of Model 680 advanced rotor (27 May).

First solo helicopter trans-Atlantic flight, by Dick Smith in a JetRanger III (19 August).

First round-the-world helicopter flight, by Perot and Coburn in a LongRanger (completed 30 September).

US Navy accepts its first TH-57 advanced trainer (16 November).

**1983**

Development of Model 400 is announced.

The Model 222 Utility Twin receives FAA Type certification.

The AHIP prototype makes its first flight.

First flight of AH-1T+ SuperCobra.

Establishment of Bell Helicopter Asia (Pte) Ltd (26 October).

Bell-Boeing team awarded V-22 preliminary design contract (26 April).

Dick Smith in JetRanger completes first solo flight around the world (22 July).

Bell is selected to establish a helicopter industry in Canada (7 October).

**1984**

Bell teams with Texas Instruments, Sperry Flight Systems and Honeywell for the LHX and ARTI programmes.

First flight of Model 406 Combat Scout.

**1985**

First flight of D-292 ACAP helicopter (30 August).

**1986**

US Marines accept its first AH-1W (27 March).

Bell-Boeing is awarded V-22 full-scale development contract (2 May).

XV-15 pilot Dorman Cannon receives Harmon International Trophy (29 May).

**1987**

US Army accepts its first armed OH-58D (22 December).

**1988**

Bell-Boeing V-22's roll-out (23 May).

Bell-Canada delivers its 100th helicopter (1 September).

**1989**

First flight of Bell-Boeing V-22 No.1 (19 March).

First flight of V-22 No.2 (9 August).

Bell announces its new Model 230.

First flight of V-22 No.4 (21 December).

**1990**

First flight of V-22 No.3 (February).

First flight of V-22 No.5 (June).

# Appendix IV
# Bell Model Designations

| *Model* | *Year* | *Type, engine, designation* |
|---|---|---|
| 3 | 1937 | Single-seat fighter, project. |
| 4 | 1937 | Single-seat fighter, project. |
| 5 | 1940 | Single-seat shipborne fighter, XV-1710-6, USN designation XFL-1 Airabonita (1 built). |
| 11 | 1937 | Single-seat fighter, V-1710-17, USAAF designation XP-39 and XP-39B (1 built). |
| 12 | 1939 | Single-seat fighter, V-1710-37, USAAF designation YP-39 (13 built). |
| 13 | 1939 | Single-seat fighter, V-1710-37, USAAF designation P-39C Airacobra (20 built). |
| 14 | 1940 | Single-seat fighter, V-1710-35, USAAF designation P-400 Airacobra (675 built). |
| 15 | 1939 | Single-seat fighter, V-1710-35, USAAF designation P-39D Airacobra (1,171 built). |
| 15B | 1940 | Single-seat fighter, V-1710-35, USAAF designation P-39F and P-39J Airacobra (282 built). |
| 16 | *c*1940 | Single-seat pusher fighter, project, XIV-1430-5, USAAF designation XP-52. |
| 26 | 1940 | Single-seat fighter, proposed version, never produced, USAAF designation P-39G. |
| 26A | 1941 | Single-seat fighter, V-1710-63, USAAF designation P-39K Airacobra (217 built). |
| 26B | 1941 | Single-seat fighter, V-1710-63, USAAF designation P-39L Airacobra (261 built). |
| 26C | 1942 | Single-seat fighter, V-1710-85, USAAF designation P-39N-5-BE and N-6-BE Airacobra (779 built). |
| 26D | 1941 | Single-seat fighter, V-1710-83, USAAF designation P-39M Airacobra (248 built). |
| 26E | 1942 | Single-seat fighter, V-1710-85, USAAF designation P-39Q, USN designation XTDL-1 (5,078 built). |
| 26F | 1941 | Single-seat fighter, V-1710-85, USAAF designation P-39N-0-BE to N-3-BE, N-6-BE Airacobra (1,768 built). |
| 27 | 1942 | Single-seat jet fighter, J31-GE-3, USAAF designation P-59 Airacomet (66 built). |
| 30 | 1942 | Experimental helicopter, Franklin, (3 built). |
| 32 | 1944 | Experimental single-seat light fighter, XV-770-7, USAAF designation XP-77 (2 built). |
| 33 | 1941 | Experimental single-seat fighter, USAAF designation XP-39E, proposed production version designated P-76; single-seat fighter, V-1710-93, USAAF designation XP-63, P-63A/C/D/E/F Kingcobra (3,213 built). |
| L39 | 1946 | Experimental aircraft with swept-wings, V-1710-93 (2 built). |
| 42 | 1946 | Transport helicopter, R-985, (3 built). |
| 44 | 1946 | Experimental aircraft, XLR-11-RM-3/5, USAF designation XS-1 then X-1 (3 built). |
| 47 | 1945 | 2-seat general purpose helicopter, Franklin, (11 built). |
| 47A | 1947 | 2-seat general purpose helicopter, O-335-1, USAF designation YR-13 (28 built), USN designation HTL-1. |
| 47B | 1947 | 2-seat general purpose helicopter, 6V4-178-B3, (78 built). |
| 47B-3 | 1948 | 2-seat general purpose helicopter, open cockpit, 6V4-178-B32. |
| 47D | 1948 | 3-seat general purpose helicopter, O-335-3, USAF designation H-13B/C Sioux (65 built), USN designation HTL-2 (12 built). |
| 47D-1 | 1949 | 3-seat general purpose helicopter, O-335-5, USAF designation H-13D/E Sioux (577 built), USN designation HTL-4/5 (82 built). |
| 47E | 1950 | 3-seat general purpose helicopter, USN designation HTL-3 (12 built). |
| 47F | 1951 | 3-seat general purpose helicopter, O-335-5. |
| 47G | 1953 | 3-seat general purpose helicopter, O-335-5, USAF designation H-13G Sioux (265 built), USN designation HTL-6 (48 built). |
| 47G-2 | 1955 | 3-seat general purpose helicopter, VO-435-A1B, USAF designation H-13H Sioux (470 built). |
| 47G-2A | 1960 | 3-seat general purpose helicopter, VO-435-A1B. |
| 47G-3 | 1959 | 3-seat general purpose helicopter, 6VS-335. |
| 47G-3B | 1961 | 3-seat general purpose helicopter, TVO-435, USAF designation OH-13S Sioux (265 built). |
| 47G-3B1 | 1963 | 3-seat general purpose helicopter, TVO-435-B1A. |
| 47G-3B2 | 1968 | 3-seat general purpose helicopter, TVO-435-G1A, USAF designation TH-13T Sioux (411 built). |
| 47G-3B2A | 1969 | 3-seat general purpose helicopter. |
| 47G-4A | 1964 | Trooper, 3-seat general purpose helicopter, VO-540-B1B3 (269 built). |
| 47G-5 | *c*1964 | 3-seat general purpose helicopter, low-cost variant of 47G-4A, VO-435-B1A (336 built). |
| 47H-1 | 1955 | 3-seat general purpose helicopter, de-luxe variant of 47G-4A. |

| | | |
|---|---|---|
| 47J | 1956 | 4-seat general purpose helicopter, VO-435. |
| 47J-1 | 1956 | 4-seat general purpose helicopter, VO-435A, USAF designation H-13J Sioux (2 built), USN designation HUL-1/1C/1M, HTL-7. |
| 47J-2 | 1964 | 4-seat general purpose helicopter, VO-540-B1B, metal rotor blades. |
| 47J-2A | 1964 | 4-seat general purpose helicopter, Agusta variant. |
| 47J-3 | *c*1965 | 4-seat general purpose helicopter, Agusta variant. |
| 47J-3B | *c*1965 | SuperRanger, 4-seat general purpose helicopter, VO-540 derated. |
| 47J-3B1 | *c*1965 | 4-seat general purpose helicopter, high altitude Agusta variant. |
| 47K | *c*1965 | General purpose helicopter, USN designation HTL-7 (18 built). |
| 47L | *c*1965 | General purpose helicopter, USN designation HUL-1M (2 built). |
| 48 | 1946 | 5-seat general purpose helicopter, R-1340, USAF designation XR-12/YR-12B (14 built). |
| 52 | 1952 | Experimental aircraft, XLR25-CW-3, USAF designation XS-2 then X-2 (2 built). |
| 54 | 1946 | 4-seat helicopter, XO-470-5, USAF designation XH-15 (3 built). |
| 58 | 1953 | Experimental aircraft, XLR-11-RM-5, USAF designation X-1A/B/D (3 built). |
| 59 | 1946 | Test-bed version of GAM-63 Rascal missile, USAF designation X-9; Aerojet engineering/Solar engines. |
| 59A | 1946 | Same as Model 59 but with Bell engines. |
| 60 | 1951 | Experimental aircraft, J53-A-17, USAF designation X-5 (2 built). |
| 61 | 1953 | Tandem-rotored ASW helicopter, R-2800-50, USN designation XHSL-1 (53 built). |
| 65 | 1954 | ATV, VTOL test-bed for X-14, J44, (1 built). |
| 67 | 1956 | High altitude reconnaissance aircraft, project, J57-PW-37A, USAF designation X-16. |
| 68 | 1956 | Vectored jet thrust VTOL experimental aircraft, J85, USAF designation X-14/A/B (1 built). |
| 200 | 1951 | Tilt-wing experimental VTOL, R-985, USAF designation H-33, became XV-3 (2 built). |
| 201 | 1955 | Experimental helicopter, XT51-T-3, USAF designation XH-13F (1 built). |
| 204 | 1956 | 10-seat transport helicopter, T-53-L, USAF designation XH-40, YH-40, XH-1A, UH-1A/B/C/E/F/L, HH-1K, TH-1F/L Iroquois, USN designation RH-2. |
| 204B | 1959 | Civil market and military export variant of Model 204, T5311A (70 built). |
| 204B2 | *c*1960 | Fuji-Bell variant, KT53. |
| 205 | 1967 | 15-seat general purpose helicopter, lengthened fuselage, T53-L-11, USAF designation YUH-1D, UH-1D/H, JUH-1D, HH-1H, EH-1H, Canadian designation CUH-1H. |
| 205A-1 | *c*1968 | 15-seat commercial helicopter, T5313A, built under licence as AB 205. |
| 206 | 1961 | General purpose helicopter, T-63-A-720, USAF designation HO-4 then H-4 then OH-58 Kiowa. |
| 206A | 1965 | JetRanger, 5-seat light transport helicopter, T63-A-700, USAF designation OH-58A Kiowa, USN designation TH-57A SeaRanger. |
| 206B | 1971 | JetRanger II, 5-seat light transport helicopter, 250-C20. |
| | | JetRanger III, 5-seat light transport helicopter, 250-C205. |
| 206L | 1973 | LongRanger, 7-seat transport helicopter, 250-C30P. |
| | | TexasRanger, 7-seat multi-role helicopter, 250-C30P. |
| 206L-1 | 1977 | LongRanger II, 7-seat transport helicopter, 250-C28B. |
| 206L-3 | 1983 | LongRanger III, 7-seat transport helicopter, 250-C30P. |
| 206LM | *c*1977 | Experimental test-bed for Model 412 (1 built). |
| 207 | 1963 | Sioux Scout, ground support helicopter, TVO-435-A1A, experimental (1 built). |
| 208 | 1965 | Twin Delta, experimental helicopter, XT67-T-1, (1 built). |
| 209 | 1965 | 2-seat attack helicopter, T53-L, US military designation AH-1G, JAH-1G, TH-1G, AH-1J/Q/R/S/T/T+/W. |
| 211 | 1968 | Huey Tug, 3-ton lift capability UH-1, T55-L (1 built). |
| 212 | 1969 | Twin Two-Twelve, 15-seat transport, PT6T-3, US military designation UH-1N/VH-1N, Canadian designation CUH-1N. |
| 214 | 1970 | Huey Plus, 16-seat utility helicopter, T55-L-7C. |
| 214A | 1974 | BigLifter, 16-seat utilitary helicopter, LTC4B-8D (296 built). |
| 214B | 1975 | BigLifter, commercial variant of Model 214A, T5508D (70 built). |
| 214C | 1977 | Search and Rescue variant for Iran (39 built). |
| 214ST | 1977 | Super Transport, 20-seat commercial helicopter, CT7-2A. |
| 222 | 1976 | 6/10-seat commercial helicopter, LTS101-650C, (90 built). |
| 222B | 1978 | 8/10-seat commercial helicopter, LTS101-750C-1, larger main rotor (26 built). |
| 222UT | 1983 | Utility Twin, 10-seat commercial helicopter, LTS101-750C. |
| 222X | 1988 | Projected variant for Canadian Armed Forces. |
| 230 | 1989 | Improved variant of Model 222, 250-C30-G2. |
| 240 | 1972 | UTTAS programme, twin-engined troop carrier helicopter, T700-GE-700, project. |
| 249 | 1979 | 2-seat attack helicopter, T53-L-703, US military designation AH-1S and AH-1T. |
| 280 | *c*1980 | AH-1J variant with wide-body fuselage, project. |
| 294 | 1952 | High altitude strategic reconnaissance aircraft, project, J57-P-37A, USAF designation X-16. |

| | | |
|---|---|---|
| 301 | 1973 | Experimental tilt-rotor aircraft, LTC1K-4K, USAF designation XV-15 (2 built). |
| 309 | 1971 | KingCobra 2-seat attack helicopter, T55-L-7C (2 built). |
| 400 | 1984 | TwinRanger, 7-seat general purpose helicopter, Allison 250-C20P (4 built). |
| 400A | *c*1984 | TwinRanger, 7-seat general purpose helicopter, Pratt & Whitney 209T, project. |
| 406CS | 1983 | Combat Scout, support helicopter, 250-C30R, US military designation OH-58D. |
| 409 | 1975 | 2-seat attack helicopter, AAH programme contender, T700-GE-700, USAF designation YAH-63 (3 built). |
| 412 | 1979 | 15-seat utility transport helicopter, PT6T-3B-1, multi-purpose military variant produced by Agusta as the AB 412 Griffon. |
| 412SP | 1987 | Special Performance, 15-seat commercial helicopter, PT6T-3B. |
| 440 | *c*1984 | Identical to Model 400 but with major use of composites, project. |
| 504 | 1957 | Flexbeam rotor. |
| 533 | 1962 | High-performance research helicopter, J69-T-29 (1 built). |
| 540 | 1965 | 'Door-hinge' rotor system. |
| 680 | 1982 | Four-blade composite bearingless rotor system. |

## Bell Design Numbers

| | | |
|---|---|---|
| D-6 | 1944 | XP-77 light fighter, *see* Model 32, also referred to as Tri-4. |
| D-37 | 1946 | Project, X-1 with swept wings. |
| D-116 | 1950 | Variant of XHSL-1. |
| D-181 | 1965 | Four-ducted-fan VTOL air-sea-rescue aircraft. |
| D-182 | 1965 | Twin-ducted-fan VTOL air-sea-rescue aircraft. |
| D-188 | 1956 | VTOL fighter project, USAF designation XF-109. |
| D-190 | 1959 | Air Rescue System to be fitted under a modified C-130 Hercules. |
| D-201 | 1951 | Variant of Model 47. |
| D-216 | 1957 | HSL-1 derivative. |
| D-223 | 1956 | Tilt-rotor transport aircraft. |
| D-238 | 1958 | HSL-1 derivative. |
| D-245 | 1959 | Combat reconnaissance helicopter. |
| D-246A | 1959 | Tilt-rotor transport aircraft, project. |
| D-250 | 1962 | Project of Model 206. |
| D-252 | 1961 | Low-wing tilt-rotor transport aircraft. |
| D-253 | 1961 | Cobra's project. |
| D-255 | 1962 | Iroquois Warrior, Cobra's first project. |
| D-261 | 1964 | AAFSS programme submission. |
| D-262 | 1964 | AAFSS programme submission. |
| D-266 | 1966 | 3-engine tilt-rotor variant of Model 301. |
| D-267 | 1967 | Tilt-rotor aircraft. |
| D-292 | 1981 | ACAP programme, 3 built. |
| D-303 | 1981 | Tilt-rotor transport aircraft, project. |
| D-306 | 1973 | Project, led to Model 222. |
| D-326 | 1980 | Clipper. Tilt-rotor aircraft project. |
| D-400 | 1958 | X-14 variant with retractable undercarriage. |
| D-2004 | c1958 | Air Rescue System variant with tip turbine drive ducts. |
| D-2005 | 1959 | VTOL assault transport project for USMC. |
| D-2020 | c1960 | Diminutive D-2022. |
| D-2021A | c1960 | Diminutive D-2022. |
| D-2022 | 1960 | VTOL assault transport project for US Army. |
| D-2064 | c1962 | Tilt-wing aircraft with ducted fan configuration. |
| D-2064A | c1962 | Improved variant of D-2064. |
| D-2127 | 1966 | X-22A, experimental VTOL, YT58-GE-8D (2 built). |
| D-2172 | 1966 | Ducted-fan transport derived from the X-22. |

# Appendix V

# Production Details

* C/n not confirmed

## XFM-1/YFM-1 Airacuda

| | |
|---|---|
| XFM-1 | 36-351 |
| YFM-1 | 38-486/491 |
| YFM-1A | 38-492 (not completed) |
| YFM-1 | 38-493/495 |
| YFM-1A | 38-496/498 |

## Models 11/12/13/15/26/33/P-39 Airacobra

| | | | |
|---|---|---|---|
| XP-39-BE | | | 38-326, became XP-39B-BE |
| YP-39-BE | | | 40-27/39, 40-39 became YP-39A-BE |
| P-39C-BE | | | 40-2971/2990 (40-2981, -2983 and -2984 to RAF as DS173/175) |
| P-39D-BE | c/n | 1/60 * | 40-2991/3050 |
| P-39D-1-BE | c/n | 61/180 * | 41-6722/6841 |
| P-39D-1-BE | c/n | 181/391 * | 41-6842/7052 |
| P-39D-1-BE | c/n | 396/397 * | 41-7057/7058 |
| P-39D-1-BE | c/n | 419/454 * | 41-7080/7115 |
| P-39D-1-BE | | | 41-28257/28406 |
| P-39D-1-BE | | | 41-38220/38404 |
| P-39D-1-BE | | | 41-38563 |
| P-39D-2-BE | | | 41-38405/38562 |
| P-39D-3-BE | | | 26 modified P-39D/D-1-BE |
| P-39D-4-BE | | | 11 modified P-39D-1-BE |
| XP-39E-BE | | | 41-19501/19502, 42-71464 |
| P-39F-1-BE | c/n | 455/683 * | 41-7116/7344 |
| P-39F-2-BE | | | 27 modified P-39F-1-BE |
| TF-39F-BE | | | 1 modified P-39F-1-BE |
| P-39G-BE | | | 42-4244/5043, became P-39K/N |
| P-39G-BE | | | 42-8727/9726, became P-39K/N |
| P-39J-BE | c/n | 392/395 * | 41-7053/7056 |
| P-39J-BE | c/n | 398/418 * | 41-7059/7079 |
| P-39K-1-BE | | | 42-4244/4453 |
| P-39K-2-BE | | | 42-4244, 4273, 4352, 4387, 4433, 4437 |
| P-39K-5-BE | | | ex P-39K-1-BE, became P-39N |
| P-39L-1-BE | | | 42-4454/4703 |
| P-39L-2-BE | | | 42-4457, 4461/4462, 4465/4466, 4470/4471, 4476, 4489, 4553, 4630 |
| P-39M-1-BE | | | 42-4704/4923 |
| P-39M-2-BE | | | 42-4704/4706, 4710, 4712, 4751, 4795, 4824 |
| P-39N-0-BE | | | 42-4944/5043 |
| P-39N-0-BE | | | 42-8727/9126 |
| P-39N-1-BE | | | 42-9127/9726 |
| P-39N-1-BE | | | 42-18246/18545 |
| P-39N-2-BE | | | 128 modified P-39N-1-BE |
| P-39N-3-BE | | | 35 modified P-39N-0-BE |
| P-39N-5-BE | | | 42-18546/19240 |
| P-39N-6-BE | | | 85 modified P-39N-5-BE |
| P-39N | | | 42-19241/19445, cancelled |
| P-39Q-1-BE | | | 42-19446/19595 |
| P-39Q-2-BE | | | 5 modified P-39Q-1-BE |
| P-39Q-5-BE | | | 42-19596/20545, 42-19976 to USN as XTDL-1 (became F2L-1K) |

| | |
|---|---|
| P-39Q-6-BE | 148 modified P-39Q-5-BE |
| P-39Q-10-BE | 42-20546/21250, 42-20807 to USN as XTDL-1 (became F2L-1K) |
| P-39Q-11-BE | 8 modified P-39Q-10-BE |
| P-39Q-15-BE | 44-2001/3000 |
| P-39Q-20-BE | 44-3001/3850 |
| P-39Q-20-BE | 44-3859/3860 |
| P-39Q-20-BE | 44-3865/3870 |
| P-39Q-20-BE | 44-3875/3880 |
| P-39Q-20-BE | 44-3885/3890 |
| P-39Q-20-BE | 44-3895/3900 |
| P-39Q-20-BE | 44-3905/3910 |
| P-39Q-20-BE | 44-3915/3919 |
| P-39Q-20-BE | 44-3937/3940 |
| P-39Q-21-BE | 44-3851/3858 |
| P-39Q-21-BE | 44-3861/3864 |
| P-39Q-21-BE | 44-3871/3874 |
| P-39Q-21-BE | 44-3881/3884 |
| P-39Q-21-BE | 44-3891/3894 |
| P-39Q-21-BE | 44-3901/3904 |
| P-39Q-21-BE | 44-3911/3914 |
| P-39Q-21-BE | 44-3920/3936 |
| P-39Q-21-BE | 44-3941/4000 |
| P-39Q-22-BE | 44-3879, 3885/3887, 3889, 3895, 3897, 3905/3906, 3908, 3917/3918 |
| P-39Q-25-BE | 44-32167/32666 |
| P-39Q-25-BE | 44-70905/71104 |
| P-39Q-30-BE | 44-71105/71504 |
| P-400 Airacobra I | AH570/739 |
| P-400 Airacobra I | AP264/384 |
| P-400 Airacobra I | BW100/183 |
| P-400 Airacobra I | BX135/434 |

## Model 5/XFL-1 Airabonita

| | |
|---|---|
| XFL-1 | BuNo 1588 |

## Model 33/P-63 Kingcobra

| | | | |
|---|---|---|---|
| XP-63-BE | | | 41-19511/19512, prototypes |
| XP-63A-BE | | | 42-78015, prototype |
| P-63A-1-BE | | | 42-68861/68910 |
| P-63A-5-BE | | | 42-68911/68930 |
| P-63A-6-BE | c/n | 33-1 to 33-130 * | 42-68931/69060 |
| P-63A-7-BE | c/n | 33-1 to 33-150 * | 42-69061/69210 |
| P-63A-8-BE | | | 42-69211/69410 |
| P-63A-9-BE | | | 42-69411/69860 |
| P-63A-10-BE | | | 42-69861/69879 |
| | | | 42-69975/70685 |
| RP-63A-11-BE | | | 42-69647, 69654, 69769, 69771, 69801 |
| RP-63A-12-BE | | | 42-69880/69974, ex P-63A-10-BE |
| TP-63A-BE | | | ex P-63A-BE |
| P-63C-1-BE | | | 42-70686/70860 |
| | | | 43-10893/10932 |
| P-63C-5-BE | c/n | 33-1 to 33-585 * | 43-11133/11717 |
| | c/n | 33-586 to -1012 * | 44-4001/4427 |
| RP-63C-2-BE | | | 43-10933/11132, became QF-63C-2-BE |
| TP-63C-BE | | | ex RP-63C-2-BE |
| P-63D-BE | | | 43-11718 |
| P-63E-1-BE | | | 43-11720/11721 |
| | | | 43-11725/11735 |
| P-63F-1-BE | | | 43-11719, 11722 |

| | | | |
|---|---|---|---|
| RP-63G-1-BE | | | 43-11723/11724, became QF-63G-1-BE |
| | | | 45-57283/57312 |
| XP-63H-BE | | | ex-P-63E-1-BE |
| XP-63N | | | 45-57300 and one other ex RP-63G-1-BE |
| XF2L-1 | | | Bu90060/90061 not delivered |

## Model 27/P-59 Airacomet

| | | | |
|---|---|---|---|
| XP-59A-BE | c/n | 27-1 to 27-3 | 42-108784/108786 |
| YP-59A-BE | c/n | 27-4 to 27-16 | 42-108771/108783, 108778/779 to USN as BuNo 63960/63961 |
| P-59A-1-BE | c/n | 27-17 to 27-36 * | 44-22609/22628 |
| P-59B-1-BE | c/n | 27-37 to 27-66 * | 44-22629/22658, 44-22651, 22656/22657 to USN as BuNo 64100, 64108/64109 44-22659/22708, cancelled |

## Model 30

| | | | |
|---|---|---|---|
| | c/n | 1 to 3 | NX41867, NX41868 and NX41869 |

## Model 32/XP-77

| | | | |
|---|---|---|---|
| XP-77-BE | c/n | 1 to 3 * | 43-34915/34916 |
| XP-77-BE | | | 43-34917/34920, cancelled |

## XP-83

| | | | |
|---|---|---|---|
| XP-83-BE | c/n | 1 and 2 * | 44-84990/84991 |

## Model 42

| | | | |
|---|---|---|---|
| | c/n | 1 to 3 | NX33540, NX42063 and one other |

## Model 47

| | | | |
|---|---|---|---|
| 47 | c/n | 1 to 11 | |
| 47/YR-13-BE | c/n | 1 to 28 | 46-227/254, 10 to USN as BuNo 122452/122461 (c/n 10, 11, 16/18, 23/25, 27 and 28). |
| 47B | c/n | 1 to 78 | |
| 47D, G, etc | c/n | 1 to 3850 | (966/975 completed as 665-1/665-10) |
| H-13B-BE | c/n | 101 to 104 | 48-796/799 |
| | | 80 to 100 | 48-800/820 |
| | | 105 to 144 | 48-821/860 |
| YH-13C-BE | | | |
| H-13C-BE | | | ex H-13B-BE |
| H-13D-BF | c/n | 184 to 327 | 51-2446/2531 |
| H-13D-BF | | | 51-16642 |
| H-13E-BF | c/n | 328 to 600 | 51-13742/14014 |
| H-13E-BF | c/n | 725 to 1006 | 51-14015/14231 |
| H-13F-BF | | | ex H-13D-BF |
| H-13G-BF | c/n | 1007 to 1016 | 51-14232/14241 |
| H-13G-BF | c/n | 1017 to 1167 | 52-7790/7940 |
| | | 1181 to 1204 | 52-7941/7964 |
| | | 1213 to 1222 | 52-7965/7974 |
| | | 1243 to 1252 | 52-7975/7984 |
| | | 1263 to 1271 | 52-7985/7993 |
| H-13G-BF | c/n | 1168 to 1180 | 53-3654/3666 |
| | | 1205 to 1212 | 53-3667/3674 |
| H-13G-BF | c/n | 1223 to 1242 | 53-3785/3804 |
| | | 1253 to 1262 | 53-3805/3814 |
| H-13H-BF | c/n | 1326 and 1327 | 55-3355/3356 |
| H-13H-BF | c/n | 1642 to 1662 | 55-4613/4633 |

| | | | |
|---|---|---|---|
| H-13H-BF | c/n | 1873 to 1956 | 56-2161/2244 |
| H-13H-BF | c/n | 2030 to 2113 | 57-1792/1875 |
| H-13H-BF | c/n | 2132 to 2173 | 57-6203/6244 |
| H-13H-BF | c/n | 2261 to 2316 | 58-1497/1552 |
| H-13H-BF | c/n | 2317 to 2408 | 58-5304/5395 |
| H-13H-BF | c/n | 2479 to 2493 | 58-6984/6998, MDAP |
| H-13H-BF | c/n | 2494 to 2555 | 59-4911/4972 |
| H-13H-BF | c/n | 2682 to 2693 | 60-6035/6046 |
| H-13J-BF | c/n | 1575 and 1576 | 57-2728/2729 |
| H-13K-BF | | | ex H-13H-BF |
| OH-13S-BF | c/n | 2958 to 3107 | 63-9072/9221 |
| OH-13S-BF | | -- | 63-9372/9523, cancelled |
| OH-13S-BF | c/n | 3168 to 3185 | 63-13668/13685 |
| OH-13S-BF | c/n | 3186 to 3300 | 64-15318/15432 |
| TH-13T-BF | c/n | 3411 to 3470 | 64-17845/17903 |
| TH-13T-BF | c/n | 3471 to 3513 | 65-8038/8080 |
| OH-13S-BF | c/n | 3901 to 3906,<br>3915, 3916,<br>3909 to 3914,<br>3907 and 3908 | 65-13005/13020 |
| TH-13T-BF | c/n | 3514 to 3539 | 66-4273/4298 |
| TH-13T-BF | c/n | 3540 to 3630 | 66-8040/8130 |
| OH-13S-BF | c/n | 3917 and 3918 | 66-15998/15999 |
| OH-13S-BF | c/n | 3919 to 3957 | 67-15870/15908 |
| TH-13T-BF | c/n | 3631 to 3684 | 67-15912/15965 |
| TH-13T-BF | c/n | 3685 to 3700 | 67-17003/17008 |
| | | 3726 to 3850 | 67-17009/17143 |
| TH-13T-BF | | | 67-17882/17885 |
| 47G-3B-1/OH-13S | c/n | 3958 to 3969 | 69-16380/16391 |
| 47G-3B-1/OH-13S | c/n | 3970 to 4013 | 69-19590/19633 |
| HTL-2 | c/n | 59 to 70 | BuNo 122952/122963 |
| HTL-3 | c/n | 165 to 173 | BuNo 124561/124569 |
| HTL-4 | c/n | 182, 189, 190,<br>195/197, 202/205,<br>208/211, 218/219 | BuNo 128621/128636 |
| HTL-4 | c/n | 223/286 range | BuNo 128887/128916 |
| HTL-5 | c/n | 403 to 410 | BuNo 129942/129949 |
| | | 449 to 476 | BuNo 129950/129977 |
| HUL-1 | c/n | 1419, 1594/1601 | BuNo 142364/142372, became UH-13P |
| HTL-6 | c/n | 1331 to 1333 | BuNo 142373/142375 |
| | | 1339 to 1341 | BuNo 142376/142378 |
| | | 1343 to 1345 | BuNo 142379/142381 |
| | | 1383 to 1386 | BuNo 142382/142385 |
| | | 1389 to 1397 | BuNo 142386/142394 |
| | | 1509 and 1510 | BuNo 142395/142396 |
| HUL-1 | c/n | 1602 to 1615 | BuNo 143134/143147, became UH-13P |
| HTL-6 | c/n | 1663 to 1686 | BuNo 143148/143171 |
| HTL-3 | | | BuNo 144693/144695, MAP |
| HTL-7 | c/n | 2114 to 2131 | BuNo 145837/145854 |
| HUL-1 | | | BuNo 147578/147581, becam UH-13P |
| HUL-1 | | | BuNo 148277, became UH-13P, MAP |
| HUL-1M | c/n | 1832 to 1833 | BuNo 149838/149839, became UH-13R |
| 47G-3B-1/2/2A | c/n | 6501 to 6871 | |
| 47G-3B-1 | c/n | 7401 to 7418 | |
| 47G-4A | c/n | 7501 to 7769 | |
| 47G-5 | c/n | 7800 to 7976 | |
| 47G-5/5A | c/n | 25001 to 25160 | |
| Agusta 47G/G-2 | c/n | 001 to 304 | |
| Agusta 47J | c/n | 1001 to 1152 | |
| Agusta 47G-2/G-3 | c/n | 1501 to 1643 | |
| Agusta 47J-2/J-3 | c/n | 2001 to 2123 | |

| | | |
|---|---|---|
| Agusta 47G-4 | c/n | 2501 to 2559 |
| Westland 47G-3B-1 | c/n | WA310 to WA459 |
| | c/n | WA505 to WA527 |
| | c/n | WA564 to WA611 |
| | c/n | WA699 to WA731 |
| Kawasaki 47G-2 | c/n | 101 to 280 |
| Kawasaki 47G-2A | c/n | 501 to 533 |
| Kawasaki 47G/D | c/n | 0000 |
| | c/n | 1001 to 1024 |
| Kawasaki 47G-3B | c/n | 2000 to 2210 |

## Bell L-39

| | |
|---|---|
| L-39-1 | BuNo 90060 |
| L-39-2 | BuNo 90061 |

## Model 44/X-1

| | |
|---|---|
| X-1-BE | 46-62/64 |

## Model 48/R-12/H-12

| | | | |
|---|---|---|---|
| XR-12-BE | c/n | 1 and 2 * | 46-214/215 (became XH-12-BE) |
| R-12A-BE | | | 47-491/524 (cancelled) |
| XR-12B-BE | | | 46-216 (became XH-12B-BE) |
| YR-12B-BE | | | 46-217/226 (became YH-12B-BE) |

## Model 60/X-5

| | |
|---|---|
| X-5-BE | 50-1838/1839 |

## Model 200/XV-3

| | | | |
|---|---|---|---|
| XV-3-BF | c/n | 1 and 2 * | 54-147/148 |

## Model 52/X-2

| | |
|---|---|
| X-2-BE | 46-674/675 |

## Model 54/XH-15

| | | | |
|---|---|---|---|
| XR-15-BE | c/n | 1 to 3 * | 46-530/532 (became XH-15-BE) |

## Model 58/X-1A/B/D

| | |
|---|---|
| X-1A-BE | 48-1384 |
| X-1B-BE | 48-1385 |
| X-1C-BE | 48-1387, cancelled |
| X-1D-BE | 48-1386 |

## Model 61/HSL-1

| | | | |
|---|---|---|---|
| XHSL-1 | c/n | 1 to 3 | BuNo 129133/129135 |
| XHSL-1 | | | BuNo 129136, cancelled |
| HSL-1 | c/n | 4 to 8 | BuNo 129154/129158 |
| | | 9 to 16 | BuNo 129161/129168 |
| | | 17 and 18 | BuNo 129159/129160 |
| HSL-1 | c/n | 19 to 53 | BuNo 129843/129877 |
| HSL-1 | | | BuNo 129878/129941, cancelled |
| HSL-1 | | | BuNo 135622/135717, cancelled |

| | | | |
|---|---|---|---|
| HSL-1 | | | BuNo 138569/138576, cancelled |
| HSL-1 | | | BuNo 140414/140429, cancelled |

## Model 68/X-14

| | | | |
|---|---|---|---|
| X-14-BE | | | 56-4022, became X-14A-BE |

## Model 67/X-16

| | | | |
|---|---|---|---|
| X-16-BE | | | 56-552/579, cancelled |

## Model 204/UH-1

| | | | |
|---|---|---|---|
| XH-40-BF | c/n | 1 to 3 | 55-4459/4461, became XHU-1-BF |
| YH-40-BF | c/n | 4 to 9 | 56-6723/6728, became YUH-1B-BF |
| HU-1A-BF | c/n | 10 to 18 | 57-6095/6103, became UH-1A-BF |
| HU-1A-BF | c/n | 19 to 34 | 58-2078/2093, became UH-1A-BF |
| HU-1A-BF | c/n | 35 to 65 | 58-3017/3047, became UH-1A-BF |
| HU-1A-BF | c/n | 66 to 175 | 59-1607/1716, became UH-1A-BF |
| HU-1A-BF | c/n | 176 to 191 | 60-3530/3545, became UH-1A-BF |
| YHU-1B-BF | c/n | 192 to 195 | 60-3546/3549, became YUH-1B-BF |
| HU-1B-BF | c/n | 196 to 265 | 60-3550/3619, became UH-1B-BF |
| HU-1B-BF | c/n | 266 to 383 | 61-686/803, became UH-1B-BF |
| UH-1B-BF | c/n | 384 to 391 | 62-4606/4613 (RAAF A2-384/391) |
| UH-1B-BF | c/n | 392 to 625 | 62-1872/2105 |
| UH-1B-BF | c/n | 626 to 665 | 62-4566/4605 |
| UH-1B-BF | c/n | 666 to 700 | 62-12515/12549 |
| YHU-1D-BF | c/n | 701 to 707 | 60-6028/6034, became UH-1D-BF |
| UH-1B-BF | c/n | 708 to 713 | 62-12550/12555 |
| UH-1B-BF | c/n | 714 to 721 | 63-9784/9791 |
| UH-1B-BF | c/n | 722 to 780 | 63-8500/8658 |
| UH-1B-BF | c/n | 881 to 883 | 63-12953/12955 (RAN N9-881/883) |
| UH-1B-BF | c/n | 884 to 963 | 63-8659/8738 |
| UH-1B-BF | c/n | 964 to 1013 | 63-12903/12952 |
| UH-1B-BF | c/n | 1014 to 1017 | 63-13086/13089 (Norway 086/089) |
| UH-1B-BF | c/n | 1018 to 1025 | 63-13586/13593 (RAAF A2-018/025) |
| UH-1B-BF | c/n | 1026 to 1224 | 64-13902/14100 |
| UH-1C-BF | c/n | 1225 to 1315 | 64-14101/14191 |
| UH-1B-BF | | -- | 64-14192/14201, cancelled |
| UH-1B-BF | | | 64-14420, MAP |
| UH-1C-BF | c/n | 1316 to 1464 | 65-9416/9564 |
| UH-1C-BF | c/n | 1465 to 1471 | 65-12738/12744 |
| UH-1C-BF | c/n | 1472 | 65-12772 (RAN N9-472) |
| UH-1C-BF | c/n | 1473 to 1727 | 66-491/745 |
| UH-1C-BF | c/n | 1728 to 1973 | 66-15000/15245 |
| NUH-1B-BF | c/n | 2048 | 64-18261 |
| UH-1C-BF | c/n | 3101 to 3103 | 64-17621/17623 (RAN N9-101/103) |
| UH-1C-BF | c/n | 3104 | 65-12846 (RAN N9-104) |
| UH-1C-BF | c/n | 3105 to 3110 | 65-12759/12764 |
| UH-1C-BF | c/n | 3111 to 3114 | 65-12853/12856, MAP |
| UH-1C-BF | c/n | 3115 | 66-15358 |
| UH-1C-BF | c/n | 3116 to 3117 | 66-15360/15361 |
| SH-1D-BF | c/n | 3202 to 3207 | Brazil |
| UH-1D-BF | c/n | 4001 to 4008 | 62-2106/2113 |
| UH-1D-BF | c/n | 4009 to 4030 | 62-12351/12372 |
| UH-1D-BF | c/n | 4031 to 4151 | 63-8739/8859 |
| UH-1D-BF | c/n | 4152 to 4198 | 63-12956/13002 |
| UH-1D-BF | c/n | 4199 to 4608 | 64-13492/13901 |
| UH-1D-BF | c/n | 4609 to 5179 | 65-9565/10135 |
| UH-1D-BF | c/n | 5180 to 5183 | 65-12773/12776 |
| UH-1D-BF | c/n | 5184 to 5189 | 65-12847/12852 |

| | | | |
|---|---|---|---|
| UH-1D-BF | c/n | 5190 to 5228 | 65-12857/12895 |
| UH-1D-BF | c/n | 5229 to 5693 | 66-746/1210 |
| UH-1D-BF | c/n | 5694 to 6000 | 66-16000/16306 |
| UH-1E | c/n | 6001 to 6034 | BuNo 151266/151299, USMC |
| UH-1E | c/n | 6035 to 6082 | BuNo 151840/151887, USMC |
| UH-1E | c/n | 6083 to 6106 | BuNo 152416/152439, USMC |
| UH-1E | c/n | 6107 to 6134 | BuNo 153740/153767, USMC |
| TH-1E | | | BuNo 154730/154749 |
| UH-1E | c/n | 6135 to 6165 | BuNo 154750/154780, USMC |
| UH-1E | c/n | 6166 to 6192 | BuNo 154943/154969, USMC |
| UH-1E | c/n | 6193 to 6223 | BuNo 155337/155367, cancelled |
| UH-1L | c/n | 6210 to 6217 | BuNo 157851/157858, US Navy |
| HH-1K | c/n | 6301 to 6327 | BuNo 157177/157203, US Navy |
| TH-1L | c/n | 6401 to 6445 | BuNo 157806/157850, US Navy |
| TH-1L | c/n | 6446 to 6490 | BuNo 157859/157903, US Navy |
| UH-1E | | -- | BuNo 157935/157976, cancelled |
| UH-1F-BF | c/n | 7000 | 62-5434 |
| UH-1F-BF | c/n | 7001 to 7025 | 63-13141/13165 |
| UH-1F-BF | c/n | 7026 to 7051 | 64-15476/15501 |
| UH-1F-BF | c/n | 7052 to 7106 | 65-7911/7965 |
| UH-1F-BF | c/n | 7107 to 7120 | 66-1211/1224 |
| TH-1F-BF | c/n | 7301 to 7326 | 66-1225/1250 |
| UH-1H-BF | c/n | 8501 to 9338 | 66-16307/17144 |
| UH-1D-BF | c/n | 9339 to 9342 | 66-8574/8577 |
| UH-1H-BF | c/n | 9343 to 10057 | 67-17145/17859, 22 to RAN |
| UH-1H-BF | c/n | 10058 to 10060 | 67-18411/18413 |
| UH-1H-BF | c/n | 10061 to 10080 | 67-18558/18577 |
| UH-1H-BF | c/n | 10081 to 10143 | 67-19475/19537 |
| UH-1H-BF | c/n | 10144 to 10708 | 68-15214/15778 |
| UH-1H-BF | c/n | 10709 to 11287 | 68-16050/16628 |
| UH-1H-BF | c/n | 11288 to 12247 | 69-15000/15959 |
| UH-1H-BF | c/n | 12248 to 12268 | 69-16650/16670 |
| UH-1H-BF | c/n | 12269 to 12309 | 69-16692/16732 |
| UH-1H-BF | c/n | 12310 to 12484 | 70-15700/15784 |
| UH-1H-BF | c/n | 12485 to 12504 | 70-15913/15932 |
| UH-1H-BF | c/n | 12505 to 12823 | 70-16200/16518 |
| UH-1H-BF | c/n | 12824 to 13163 | 71-20000/20339 |
| UH-1H-BF | c/n | 13164 to 13348 | 72-21465/21649 |
| UH-1H-BF | | | 72-22068/22071, MAP |
| UH-1H-BF | c/n | 13349 to 13548 | 73-21661/21860 |
| UH-1H-BF | c/n | 13549 to 13618 | 73-22066/22135 |
| UH-1H-BF | c/n | 13619 to 13868 | 74-22295/22544 |
| UH-1H-BF | c/n | 13869 to 13890 | 76-22651/22672 |
| UH-1H-BF | c/n | 13891 to 13907 | Singapore |
| UH-1H-BF | c/n | 13908 to 13914 | 76-22685/22691 |
| UH-1H-BF | c/n | 13915 to 13934 | 77-22911/22930 |
| UH-1H-BF | | | 77-22955, 22959, 23175, 23177 |
| UH-1H-BF | c/n | 13997 to 14003 | 78-23180/23186 |
| UH-1H-BF | c/n | 16001 to 16004 | Korea |
| UH-1H-BF | c/n | 16028 to 16040 | Thailand |
| UH-1H-BF | c/n | 16041 to 16054 | 79-23402/23415, Thailand |
| UH-1H-BF | c/n | 17001 to 17016 | 68-15779/15794 |
| UH-1H-BF | c/n | 17017 to 17025 | 69-16671/16679 |
| HH-1H-BF | c/n | 17101 to 17130 | 70-2457/2486 |
| UH-1D-BF | | | 70-4507/4510, MAP |
| UH-1N-BF | c/n | 31001 to 31005 | 68-10772/10776 |
| UH-1N-BF | c/n | 31006 to 31076 | 69-6600/6670 |
| UH-1N-BF | c/n | 31077 to 31079 | 69-7536/7538 |
| UH-1N | c/n | 31401 to 31430 | BuNo 158230/158259 |
| UH-1N-BF | c/n | 31442 to 31443 | 73-22054/22055, Tunisia |
| UH-1N | c/n | 31601 to 31632 | BuNo 158260/158291 |

| | | | |
|---|---|---|---|
| UH-1N | | | BuNo 158438/158452, cancelled |
| UH-1N | c/n | 31633 to 31635 | BuNo 158548/158550 |
| VH-1N | c/n | 31636 to 31639 | BuNo 158551/158554 |
| UH-1N | c/n | 31640 | BuNo 158555 |
| VH-1N | c/n | 31641 to 31642 | BuNo 158556/158557 |
| UH-1N | c/n | 31643 to 31647 | BuNo 158558/158562 |
| UH-1N | c/n | 31431 to 31440 | BuNo 158762/158771 |
| UH-1N | c/n | 31648 to 31661 | BuNo 158772/158785 |
| UH-1N | c/n | 31662 to 31685 | BuNo 159186/159209 |
| UH-1N | c/n | 31441 | BuNo 159565 |
| UH-1N | c/n | 31687 to 31691 | BuNo 159680/159683 |
| UH-1N | c/n | 31694 to 31711 | BuNo 159684/159703 |
| UH-1N | c/n | 31444 and 31712 to 31714 | BuNo 159774/159777 |
| UH-1N | c/n | 31715 to 31729 | BuNo 160165/160179 |
| UH-1N | c/n | 31730 to 31753 | BuNo 160438/160461 |
| UH-1N | c/n | 31755 to 31759 | BuNo 160619/160624 |
| UH-1N | c/n | 31445 to 31456 | BuNo 160827/160838 |
| CUH-1N | c/n | 32001 to 32050 | Canada |
| UH-1H | | | 82-24044/24053 |
| GUH-1E | | | 84-0474 |
| Dornier UH-1D | c/n | 8051 to 8066 | German Police |
| | c/n | 8101 to 8240 | Luftwaffe (70-41/71-80) |
| | c/n | 8301 to 8504 | Heer (71-81/73-84) |
| 204B | c/n | 1501 | |
| | c/n | 2001 to 2070 | |
| | c/n | 2196 to 2199 | |
| Agusta 204 | c/n | 3001 to 3238 | |
| Fuji 204B | c/n | 3001 and 3002 | |
| | c/n | CH-1 to CH-57 | |

## Model 205

| | | |
|---|---|---|
| 205A-1 | c/n | 30001 to 30332 |
| Agusta 205 | c/n | 4001 to 4477 |
| | c/n | 4500 to 4512 |

## Model 206

| | | | |
|---|---|---|---|
| YHO-4-BF | c/n | 001 to 005 | 62-4202/4206, became OH-4A |
| 206/OH-4A | c/n | 1 to 8 | 62-4207/4214 |
| 206A-1 | c/n | 39998 to 39999 | N4782R and N4783R |
| OH-58A-BF | c/n | 40001 to 40300 | 68-16687/16986 |
| OH-58A-BF | c/n | 40301 to 40600 | 69-16080/16379 |
| OH-58A-BF | c/n | 40601 to 41200 | 70-15040/15649 |
| OH-58A-BF | c/n | 41201 to 41726 | 71-20350/20865 |
| OH-58A-BF | c/n | 41727 to 42126 | 72-21061/21460 |
| OH-58A-BF | c/n | 42127 to 42200 | 73-21861/21934 |
| OH-58A-BF | c/n | 42201 to 42223 | Israël |
| OH-58A-BF | c/n | 42224 to 42235 | Spain |
| OH-58A-BF | c/n | 42236 to 42238 | Turkey |
| OH-58A-BF | c/n | 42239 to 42250 | Austria |
| COH-58A-BF | c/n | 44001 to 44074 | 71-20866/20939 (Canada 136201/136227) |
| OH-58A-BF | c/n | 44501 to 44056 | Australia |
| OH-58D | | | 85-24690/24733 |
| OH-58D | | | 84-24129/24144 |
| OH-58D | | | 86-8901/8939 |
| OH-58D | | | 87-0729/0760 |
| TH-57A | c/n | 5001 to 5040 | BuNo 157355/157394 |
| TH-57B | | | BuNo 161695/161701 |
| TH-57C | | | BuNo 162013/162067 |

| | | | |
|---|---|---|---|
| TH-57C | | | BuNo 162666/162686 |
| TH-57B/C | | | BuNo 162803/162823 |
| TH-57B | | | BuNo 163312/163347 |
| 206A/B | c/n | 1 to 4168 | |
| 206L/L-1 | c/n | 45001 to 45790 | |
| | c/n | 46601 to 46617 | |
| 206L-3 | c/n | 51001 to 51472 | |
| Agusta 206 | c/n | 8001 to 8716 | |
| Agusta 206A-1 | c/n | 9001 to 9170 | |

## Model 309

| | | | |
|---|---|---|---|
| 309 | c/n | 2503 and 2504 | |

## Model 409/YAH-63

| | | | |
|---|---|---|---|
| YAH-63A-BF | | | 73-22244/22247 |

## Design D-2127/X-22A

| | | | |
|---|---|---|---|
| X-22A | | | BuNo 151520/151521 |

## Model 212

| | | | |
|---|---|---|---|
| 212 | c/n | 30501 to 30999 | |
| | c/n | 31101 to 31310 | |
| | c/n | 32101 to 32142 | |
| | c/n | 32201 to 32262 | Iran |
| | c/n | 35001 to 35014 | |
| Agusta 212 | c/n | 5501 to 5724 | |
| Agusta 212ASW | c/n | 001 to 040 | |

## Model 214

| | | | |
|---|---|---|---|
| 214A | c/n | 27000 to 27003 | |
| 214A | c/n | 27004 to 27295 | Iran (6-4651/....) |
| 214B | c/n | 28001 to 28070 | |
| 214C | c/n | 17201 to 17239 | Iran |
| 214ST | c/n | 18401 to 18403 | |
| | c/n | 28101 to 28195 | |

## Model 209/Huey Cobra

| | | | |
|---|---|---|---|
| AH-1G-BF | c/n | 2600 | 64-7015 |
| AH-1Q | c/n | 19291 to 19296 | Israël |
| AH-1G-BF | c/n | 20001 | 64-7016 |
| AH-1G-BF | c/n | 20002 to 20113 | 66-15246/15357 |
| AH-1G-BF | c/n | 20114 to 20533 | 67-15450/15869 |
| AH-1G-BF | c/n | 20534 to 20747 | 68-15000/15213, 4 to Spain |
| AH-1G-BF | c/n | 20748 to 20841 | 68-17020/17113 |
| AH-1G-BF | c/n | 20842 to 20879 | 69-16410/16447 |
| AH-1G-BF | c/n | 20880 to 21049 | 70-15936/16105, 20963 to YAH-1S |
| AH-1G-BF | c/n | 21050 to 21053 | 71-15090/15093 |
| AH-1G-BF | c/n | 21054 to 21123 | 71-20983/21052 |
| AH-1G-BF | c/n | 21124 to 21127 | 72-21461/21464, to Spain |
| AH-1E | c/n | 21501 to 21506 | Israël |
| AH-1E | c/n | 21507 to 21508 | Japan |
| AH-1F | c/n | 21701 to 21708 | 23167/23174, to Israël |
| AH-1F | c/n | 21709 to 21712 | 79-23390/23393, to Israël |
| AH-1F | c/n | 21713 to 21716 | 80-23522/23525, to Israël |

| | | | |
|---|---|---|---|
| AH-1F | c/n | 21717 to 21728 | 83-24188/24199, to Israël |
| AH-1F | c/n | 21729 to 21730 | Israël |
| AH-1E-BF | c/n | 22101 to 22148 | 77-22763/22810 |
| AH-1E-BF | c/n | 22149 to 22198 | 78-23043/23092 |
| AH-1F-BF | c/n | 22199 to 22231 | 78-23093/23125 |
| AH-1F-BF | c/n | 22232 to 22297 | 79-23187/23253 |
| AH-1F-BF | c/n | 22298 to 22309 | 80-23510/23521, ANG |
| AH-1F-BF | c/n | 22310 to 22324 | 81-23526/23540, ANG |
| AH-1F-BF | c/n | 22325 to 22336 | 82-24065/24076, ANG |
| AH-1F-BF | c/n | 22337 to 22347 | 83-24189/24199, ANG |
| AH-1F | c/n | 22501 to 22510 | 82-24055/24064, to Pakistan |
| AH-1F | c/n | 22511 to 22520 | Pakistan |
| AH-1F | c/n | 22601 to 22624 | 82-24077/24100, to Jordan |
| AH-1P-BF | c/n | 24001 to 24044 | 76-22567/22610 |
| AH-1P-BF | c/n | 24045 to 24066 | 76-22692/22713 |
| AH-1P-BF | c/n | 24067 to 24100 | 77-22729/22762 |
| AH-1J | c/n | 26001 to 26049 | BuNo 157757/157805 |
| AH-1J | c/n | 26050 to 26069 | BuNo 159210/159229 |
| AH-1T | c/n | 26070 to 26079 | BuNo 160105/160114 |
| AH-1T | c/n | 26080 to 26086 | BuNo 160742/160748 |
| AH-1T | c/n | 26087 to 26116 | BuNo 160797/160826 |
| AH-1T | c/n | 26117 to 26124 | BuNo 161015/161022 |
| AH-1W | c/n | 26201 to 26245 | BuNo 162532/162576 |
| AH-1J | c/n | 26501 to 26640 | Iran (3-4401/4540) |
| AH-1T/AH-1W MOD | c/n | 26901 | BuNo 160801 |
| AH-1J (TOW) | c/n | 29001 to 29062 | Iran (3-4541/4602) |
| AH-1J (TOW) | c/n | 29063 to 29070 | Korea |
| Fuji AH-1F | c/n | 73401 to ..... | Japan (JG-3401/....) |

## Model 301/XV-15

| | | | |
|---|---|---|---|
| XV-15 | c/n | 0001 and 0002 | N702NA/N703NA |

## Model 222

| | | |
|---|---|---|
| 222 and 222A | c/n | 47001 to 47089 |
| | c/n | 47099 |
| 222B | c/n | 47131 to 47156 |
| 222UT | c/n | 47501 to 47574 |

## Model 412

| | | |
|---|---|---|
| 412 | c/n | 33001 to 33209 |
| 412 | c/n | 36001 to 36028 |
| Agusta 412 | c/n | 25501 to 25571 |

## Model 400

| | | |
|---|---|---|
| 400 | c/n | 48001 to 48004 |

## Model 533

| | | | |
|---|---|---|---|
| 533 | c/n | 4 | 56-6723, ex YH-40-BF |

## Bell/Boeing V-22

| | | | |
|---|---|---|---|
| YV-22A | c/n | 90001 to 90006* | BuNo 163911/163916 |

## Missiles

### Model 59/X-9 Shrike

| | |
|---|---|
| X-9 | 52-2166/2209 |

### B-63/GAM-63 RASCAL

| | |
|---|---|
| XGAM-63-BC | 51-17581/17625 |
| | 52-10984/10986 |
| | 53-8195/8196 |
| | 53-8198/8199 |
| | 53-8210/8229 |
| | 53-8231/8236 |
| GAM-63-BC | 53-8208/8209 |
| | 53-8230 |
| | 53-8237/8256 |
| GAM-63A-BC | 53-8197 |
| | 53-8200/8207 |
| | 53-8257/8259 |
| | 56-4448/4469 |

# Appendix VI

# Bell Aircraft used By NASA

### NASA Wallops Flight Facility, Wallops Island, Virginia (WFF)

| *Reg'n* | *Type* | *C/n* | *S/n* | *From* | *Until* | *Remarks* |
|---|---|---|---|---|---|---|
| N415NA | UH-1B | 920 | 63-8695 | 25.04.87 | 2:90 | Acquired from Kennedy Space Center, Florida. |
| N424NA (1) | UH-1B | 1031 | 64-13907 | 11.12.72 | 07.03.74 | Destroyed in accident. |
| N424NA (2) | UH-1B | 1145 | 64-14021 | 08.03.74 | current | Replaced c/n 1031. |
| N950NS | 206B | 508 | – | 10.12.84 | 05.88 | Acquired from JSC. Transferred to US Forestry Service, Boise, Idaho. |

### NASA Kennedy Space Flight Center, Florida (KSC)

| | | | | | | |
|---|---|---|---|---|---|---|
| N414NA | UH-1B | 428 | 62-1908 | 15.02.80 | circa 85 | Salvaged at KSC. |
| N415NA(1) | UH-1B | 920 | 63-8695 | 18.10.81 | 25.04.87 | Transferred to WFF. |
| N415NA(2) | UH-1H | 5129 | 65-10085 | 2.90 | – | Replaced c/n 920 |

| *Reg'n* | *Type* | *C/n* | *S/n* | *From* | *Until* | *Remarks* |
|---|---|---|---|---|---|---|
| N416NA | UH-1B | 584 | 62-2064 | 27.10.81 | current | Acquired from US Army, Fort Rucker, Alabama. |
| N417NA | UH-1M | 1509 | 66-0608 | 30.11.85 | current | Acquired from US Army, Edgewood Arsenal, Maryland. |
| N418NA | UH-1M | 1646 | 66-0664 | 30.01.86 | current | Acquired from US Army, Morristown, New Jersey. |
| N419NA | UH-1H | 4752 | 65-09708 | 10.90 | current | |
| N420NA | UH-1H | 5148 | 65-10104 | 10.90 | – | |

Note: all KSC aircraft are hangared and maintained at Patrick AFB, Florida.

## NASA Jet Propulsion Laboratories, Pasadena, California (JPL)

| | | | | | | |
|---|---|---|---|---|---|---|
| NASA12 N12NA | 206B | 508 | – | 01.70 | 01.10.70 | Replaced two 47Js on lease. Transferred to JSC. |
| N3261 | 47J-2 | – | – | 12.63 | 08.65 | Leased. Flown by JPL pilots. |
| N8490E | 47J-2 | – | – | 12.63 | 08.65 | Leased. Flown by JPL pilots. |
| N73232 | 47G-3B | – | – | 12.63 | 30.06.67 | Leased. Based out of Goldstone Tracking Station, Fort Irwin (CA) |
| N256PH | 47J-2A | – | – | 08.65 | – | Leased. Flown by JPL pilots. |
| N257H | 47J-2A | – | – | 08.65 | – | Leased. Flown by JPL pilots. |
| N8550F | 47J-2A | – | – | – | 01.70 | Leased. Replaced N256PH |
| N8581F | 47J-2A | – | – | – | 01.70 | Leased. Replaced N257PH |

## NACA/NASA Lewis Research Center, Cleveland, Ohio (LeRC)

| | | | | | | |
|---|---|---|---|---|---|---|
| – | P-63A-1 | – | 42-68864 | 10.43 | 06.45 | Modified with under fuselage glycol cooler scoop and large caburettor intake. |
| – | P-63A-1 | – | 42-68868 | 02.45 | 07.45 | Exhaust flame suppression research. |
| – | P-59B-1 | 27-58 | 44-22650 | 09.45 | 01.49 | Jet thrust performance and augmentation research. |
| – | L-39-1 | – | 90060 | 12.12.49 | – | Swept wing research. |
| – | L-39-2 | – | 90061 | 12.12.49 | – | Swept wing research. |

## NASA Johnson Space Center, Houston, Texas (JCS)

| | | | | | | |
|---|---|---|---|---|---|---|
| N2490B | 47G | – | – | 02.07.63 | 06.09.63 | Leased. Flew 31 hours |
| NASA930 | TH-13N | 2118 | 145841 | 10.02.64 | 02.02.68 | |
| NASA931 | OH-13H | 2136 | 57-6207 | 06.07.65 | 14.02.68 | Transfered to LaRC as NASA537. |
| NASA946 | 47G-3B1 | 6663 | – | 05.12.67 | 02.08.69 | Destroyed in accident Pilot: Gibson. |
| NASA947 N947NA | 47G-3B1 | 6665 | – | 11.12.67 | 23.01.71 | Destroyed in accident Pilot: Astronaut Gene Cernan |
| NASA948 N822NA | 47G-3B1 | 6670 | – | 10.01.68 | 11.01.73 | Transferred to Dryden as NASA822. |

| *Reg'n* | *Type* | *C/n* | *S/n* | *From* | *Until* | *Remarks* |
|---|---|---|---|---|---|---|
| NASA948<br>N948NA | 47G-3B2 | 6752 | – | 29.10.69 | 06.83 | |
| N950NS | 206B | 508 | – | 01.10.73 | 10.12.84 | Acquired from JPL as N12NA. Transferred to WFF. |

## NACA/NASA Ames Research Center, Moffett Field, California (ARC)

| *Reg'n* | *Type* | *C/n* | *S/n* | *From* | *Until* | *Remarks* |
|---|---|---|---|---|---|---|
| – | P-39D-1 | – | – | 31.12.42 | – | |
| – | P-39D-1 | – | 41-28268 | 04.01.43 | 05.01.43 | |
| – | P-39D-1 | – | 41-28328 | 05.01.43 | 06.01.43 | |
| – | P-39N-1 | – | 42-18476 | 10.05.43 | 11.05.43 | |
| – | P-39N-0 | – | 42-8849 | 11.05.43 | 17.05.43 | |
| – | P-39Q-10 | – | 42-20790 | 07.01.44 | 30.01.44 | |
| – | P-63A | – | 42-68892 | 17.02.44 | – | |
| – | P-63A-6 | – | 42-68941 | 27.01.45 | 18.06.46 | |
| – | XV-3 | 2 | 54-148 | 04.08.57<br>16.09.58<br>12.08.59 | 28.10.57<br>29.10.58<br>09.06.65 | 40 × 80 wind tunnel tests<br>40 × 80 wind tunnel tests<br>Flight tests |
| NASA234<br>N704N4 | X-14A/B | – | 56-4022 | 02.10.59 | 29.05.81 | Damaged in accident 29 May '81. Pilot: Ron Gerdes Transferred to US Army Museum, Fort Rucker. |
| – | HU-1 | 13 | 57-6098 | 04.01.61 | 23.10.61 | 40 × 80 wind tunnel tests. |
| N732NA | UH-1B | 428 | 62-1908 | 14.10.70 | 10.02.80 | Transferred to KSC as N414NA |
| N733NA | UH-1H | 11519 | 69-15231 | 04.05.74 | current | |
| N734NA | UH-1H | 4335 | 64-13628 | 01.03.78 | current | Acquired from LaRC as N544NA |
| N736NA | AH-1G | 20004 | 66-15248 | 01.03.78 | 23.05.85 | Acquired from LaRC as N541NA |
| N730NA | JAH-1S | 22105 | 77-22768 | 08.05.85 | current | |
| N736NA | YAH-1S | 20933 | 70-15979 | 10.11.87 | current | Acquired from Fort Rucker |
| N702NA | XV-15 | 0001 | – | 23.03.78 | – | |
| N703NA | XV-15 | 0002 | – | 30.10.80 | – | |

## NACA/NASA Langley Research Center, Hampton, Virginia (LaRC)

| *Reg'n* | *Type* | *C/n* | *S/n* | *From* | *Until* | *Remarks* |
|---|---|---|---|---|---|---|
| – | XP-39 | – | 38-326 | 06.06.39 | – | |
| – | YP-39 | – | – | 06.02.41 | 27.07.44 | |

| *Reg'n* | *Type* | *C/n* | *S/n* | *From* | *Until* | *Remarks* |
|---|---|---|---|---|---|---|
| – | P-39D-1 | – | 41-28378 | 05.01.43 | 23.04.43 | |
| – | P-63A-1 | – | 42-68861 | 26.07.43 | 25.11.43 | |
| – | P-63A-1 | – | 42-68889 | 04.02.44 | 27.08.45 | |
| – | P-63A-1 | – | 42-68881 | 10.05.44 | 46 | |
| – | L-39-1 | – | 90060 | 22.08.46 | 12.12.49 | Transferred to LeRC. |
| – | L-39-2 | – | 90061 | 11.12.46 | 12.12.49 | Transferred to LeRC. |
| – | H-13B | 123 | 48-839 | 26.05.49 | 18.04.50 | |
| – | RP-63G-1 | – | 45-57300 | – | – | V-tail configuration. |
| – | H-13G | 1061 | 52-7834 | 17.09.53 | 25.07.67 | |
| NASA29 N530NA | 204B | 2017 | – | 20.09.64 | current | |
| N532NA | OH-4A | 1 | 62-4207 | 01.04.65 | 23.01.73 | Acquired as N73917. Transferred to US Army. |
| N537NA | OH-13H | 2136 | 57-6207 | 16.06.68 | 05.04.72 | Acquired from JSC as NASA931. |
| N540NA | OH-58A | 41564 | 71-20703 | 01.08.72 | current | |
| N541NA | AH-1G | 20004 | 66-15248 | 18.12.72 | 01.03.78 | Transferred to ARC as N736NA. |
| N542NA | UH-1H | 4335 | 64-13628 | 04.04.73 | 01.03.78 | Transferred to ARC as N734NA. |

## NACA High Speed Flight Station (HSFS), NASA Flight Research Center (FRC), NASA Dryden Flight Research Center (DFRC), NASA Ames-Dryden Flight Research Facility (DFRF), Edwards, California

| *Reg'n* | *Type* | *C/n* | *S/n* | *From* | *Until* | *Remarks* |
|---|---|---|---|---|---|---|
| – | X-1 | – | 46-062 | 05.04.47 | 28.08.50 | In NASM, Washington, DC. |
| – | X-1/X-1E | – | 46-063 | 07.10.46 | 04.59 | On display at Ames-Dryden Flight Research Facility. |
| – | X-1 | – | 46-064 | – | 09.11.51 | Destroyed |
| – | X-5 | – | 50-1838 | 23.11.51 | 05.04.57 | In USAF Museum, Wright Patterson, AFB, Ohio. |
| – | X-5 | – | 50-1839 | 51 | 13.10.53 | Destroyed. Pilot: Major Popson. |
| – | X-1A | – | 48-1384 | 23.02.55 | 08.08.55 | Destroyed. |
| – | X-1B | – | 48-1385 | 01.08.56 | 26.01.59 | In USAF Museum, Wright Patterson, AFB, Ohio. |
| N822NA | 47G-3B1 | 6670 | – | 01.11.73 | – | Acquired from JSC as N948NA. |

# Appendix VII

# French Airacobras and Kingcobras

## French Bell P-39 Airacobras

List of 158 identified aircraft.

### P-39K:

42-4334.

### P-39N:

42-9085, -9087, -9193, -9202, -9341, -9371/9374, -9376, -9382/9384, -9387, -9389/9390, -9394, -9397, -9402/9405, -9407/9410, -9414, -9419, -9421, -9427, -9430, -9432, -9435, -9669, -9682, -9717.
42-18276, -18355, -18365, -18368, -18376, -18380, -18391, -18395, -18720/18721, -18727/18730, -18732/18734, -18736/18756, -18758, -18761/18767, -18769/18771, -18774/18779, -18781/18782, -18784/18785, -18816, -18819, -18977.

### P-39Q:

44-3023, -3055, -3117/3118, -3152, -3154, -3172, -3192, -3242, -3253, -3851, -3853, -3871/3872, -3881/3882, -3911, -3914, -3917, -3919/3920, -3922, -3925/3927, -3930, -3934/3935, -3937/3938, 44-32664.

The French used to identify American aircraft with the last three digits of the serial number; 26 other aircraft are known as such:
076, 083, 121, 188, 201, 317, 351, 366, 368, 375, 386, 433, 434, 436, 447/450, 455, 661, 873, 884, 891, 894, 921, 954.

## French Bell P-63C Kingcobras

List of 106 identified aircraft.

43-11543, -11566/11567, -11570, -11574/11575, -11582, -11590/11591, -11597/11599, -11606/11607, -11614, -11621/11622, -11625, -11629/11631, -11637, -11645, -11649, -11651, -11659, -11666/11667, -11674/11675, -11682/11683, -11691/11694, -11696/11697, -11706, -11714/11715, -11718, -11764.

44-4004, -4006, -4012/4014, -4020/4022, -4028/4030, -4036/4038, -4044, -4046, -4052/4054, -4060/4062, -4069/4070, -4076/4079, -4083/4086, -4092/4094, -4097, -4100/4102, -4110, -4117/4118, -4125, -4133/4134, -4141/4142, -4149/4150, -4158, -4165, -4173, -4182, -4189/4190, -4197, -4205/4206, -4214, -4311.

Three aircraft identified only by the last three digits of the serial number: 280, 793, 886.

## Appendix VIII

# Serial Numbers of Foreign Military and Civil UH-1s

**Foreign military UH-1s:** (identified aircraft; figures between brackets give local serial number)

**Argentine:** UH-1H s/n 69/15997, 73-22076 (AE-412), 73-22084 (AE-415), 77-22930 (AE-424)

**Australia:** RAAF, UH-1B s/n 62-4606/4613 (A2-384/391), 63-9784/9791 (A2-714/721), 63-13586/13593 (A2-1018/1025); UH-1D s/n 65-10041 (A2-041 then A2-085), 66-1166 (A2-166 then A2-649). UH-1H s/n 67-17178/17185 (A2-376/383), 67-17307/17312 (A2-505/510), 67-17568/17575 (A2-766/773), 68-15219 (A2-149), 68-16451 (A2-110), 69-15415 (A2-703), 69-15435 (A2-723), 69-15484/15490 (A2-484/490), 70-15845 (A2-455), 70-15915 (A2-915), 72-21579/21580 (A2-278/279), 72-21596/21597 (A2-295/296), 72-21611 (A2-310).
RAN, UH-1B s/n 63-8659/8661 (N9-881/883); UH-1C s/n 64-17621/17623 (N9-3101/3103), 65-12846 (N2-3104).

**Brazil:** SH-1D c/n 3202/3207 (FAB8530/8535).

**Chile:** UH-1H s/n 69-15110/15111 (181/182), 69-15177 (183)

**Honduras:** UH-1B s/n 61-0728, 63-8532, 64-13911 and 13943.

**New Zealand:** UH-1D s/n 65-9768/9769 (NZ3801/3802), 65-10114/10116 (NZ3803/3805), 69-15417/15420 (NZ3806/3809), 69-15650/15654 (NZ3810/3814), 74-22525 (NZ3815).

**Norway:** UH-1B s/n 60-3580 (580), 60-3584 (584), 60-3586 (586), 60-3591 (591), 60-3597 (597), 60-3613 (613), 61-688 (688), 61-699 (699), 62-1887 (887), 62-1937 (937), 62-1957 (957), 62-1992 (992), 62-1993 (993), 62-1994 (994), 62-1995 (995), 62-1996 (996), 62-2025 (025), 62-2086 (086), 63-8501 (501), 63-8588 (588), 63-13086 (086), 63-13087 (087), 63-13088 (088), 63-13089 (089), 64-14079 (079), 64-14082 (082), 64-13961 (961), 64-13962 (962), 64-13963 (963), 64-13965 (965), 64-13966 (966), 64-13967 (967), 66-14420 (420). UH-1C s/n 65-12853 (853), 65-12854 (854), 65-12855 (855), 65-12856 (856).

**Pakistan:** UH-1H s/n 70-16322.

**Panama:** UH-1B s/n 60-3604 (116), 62-1890 (102), 62-1895 (116), 62-1906 (111), 62-2076 (112), 63-8622 (117), 64-14050 (113), 64-14073 (114), 64-14076 (112) and 64-14100 (115).

**Peru:** UH-1D s/n 64-13802/13805 (FAP-623/626), 64-13842/13844 (FAP-627/629), 65-9764/9766 (FAP-630/632).

**Philippine:** UH-1H s/n 68-15290/15291, 69-15157, 15270, 15460, 15467, 16715, 72-21466, 21468, 21471/21472, 73-21731, 21733, 21759, 74-22319/22320, 22322/22323, 22373, 76-22657/22658, 22661, 22686/22690, 77-22955, 22959, 78-23175/23177.

**Singapore:** UH-1B s/n 60-3550, 3605, 61-0689, 0695, 0700, 0774, 0776, 0796, 62-1891, 1918, 1985, 2088, 2094, 4583, 4597, 12525, 63-8514, 8530, 8531, 8533, 8534, 8539, 8544, 8679, 8692, 8708, 12951, 63-13957, 13982 & 14077.

**South Korea:** UH-1B s/n 61-0725, 0735, 62-1977, 2007, 2103, 12542, 63-8524, 8540, 8560, 8582, 8613, 8614, 8673, 8698, 8734, 12921, 64-13926, 13939, 14003, 14010, 14040, 14054, 14081, 14087 and 14096.

**South Vietnam:** UH-1H s/n 66-16309, 16340, 16371, 16438, 16452, 16496, 16503, 16518, 16534, 16549, 16562, 16569, 16574, 16581, 16608, 16651, 16698, 16727, 16730, 16739, 16796, 16813, 16838, 16841, 16852, 17116, 67-17188, 17276, 17284, 17308, 17314, 17346, 17360, 17383, 17385, 17392, 17394, 17430, 17438, 17444, 17478, 17480, 17507/17509, 17730/17731, 17742, 17761, 17787, 17829/17830, 19504, 68-15218, 15242, 15247, 15257, 15298, 15315, 15353, 15358, 15384, 15398, 15428/15429, 15467, 15479, 15504, 15507, 15509, 15542, 15545/15546, 15575, 15603/15604, 15709, 15711, 15717, 15731/15732, 16078, 16090, 16146, 16161, 16188, 16207, 16219, 16231, 16255, 16260, 16280, 16287, 16317, 16377, 16379, 16390, 16393, 16422, 16424, 16442, 16444, 16464, 16493, 16506, 16533, 16539/16541, 16551, 16555, 16570, 16580, 69-15032, 15049, 15054, 15061, 15071, 15109, 15133, 15169, 15196, 15201, 15206, 15214, 15222, 15274, 15280, 15285, 15289, 15295, 15317, 15369, 15373, 15377, 15382, 15388, 15391, 15393, 15400, 15407, 15409/15410, 15426/15427, 15430,

15432/15433, 15437, 15444/15445, 15451, 15456, 15465, 15468, 15470/15471, 15504, 15511, 15513, 15516, 15520, 15522/15523, 15527, 15535/15536, 15538, 15543, 15546, 15549, 15554/15556, 15562, 15574, 15576, 15612, 15618, 15626, 15635, 15638, 15640, 15644, 15663, 15667, 15670, 15685, 15689, 15694, 15696, 15698, 15712, 15714, 15720, 15737, 15744, 15761, 15768/15769, 15774/15776, 15778, 15780, 15786, 15790, 15806, 15809, 15812, 15825, 15832, 15833, 15890, 15892, 15895, 15897, 15904, 15906/15907, 15955/15956, 15958, 16650, 16659/16662, 16664, 16666, 16670, 16693, 16704/16707, 16709, 16714, 16718, 16721, 16724/16726, 16732, 70-15705, 15713/15717, 15721/15722, 15725, 15729, 15737, 15740, 15748, 15751, 15786, 15793, 15800, 15803/15804, 15808, 15813/15814, 15816, 15831, 15840, 15842, 15868, 15874, 15921/15922 and 15924.

**Spain:** UH-1H s/n 70-15817/15828 (ET-303/312), 71-20125/20126 (ET-207/208), 72-21275/21277 (HE.10B-37/39), 73-21842/21849 (ET-217/224), 73-22068/22071 (HE.10B-51/54), 72-21525/21532 (ET-209/216), 72-21593/21595 (ET-313/315).

**Thailand:** UH-1H s/n 67-19480, 79-23402/23415.

**Tunisia:** UH-1N s/n 73-22054/22055.

**Turkey:** UH-1H s/n 69-15646, 69-15720, 69-15724, 71-20334, 20338, 72-21519, 21536/21537, 21543 and 21546.

**Uruguay:** UH-1B s/n 60-3565, 61-0703, 0713, 62-2105, 63-8711 and 8735.

**West Germany:** UH-1D s/n 64-13661/13662 (7 64-13806 (70-39), 64-13881 (70-40), c/n 8001/8002 (70-01/02), c/n 8101/8240 (70-41/80), c/n 8301/8504 (71-81/84).

## Aircraft transfered to US civil market: (read across three columns)

**UH-1A:**

58-2079/N93066, 58-3039/N707FW, 59-1644/N64286.

**UH-1B:**

60-3552/N8043Z, 60-3556/N3145F/N18SX, 60-3558/N90632.
60-3559/N37995, 60-3561/N92826, 60-3562/N22949,
60-3568/N9970F, 60-3573/N98163, 60-3583/N59367,
60-3587/N1901R, 60-3594/N96142/N508SC, 60-3595/N1902R,
60-3596/N1903R, 60-3598/N330WN, 60-3600/N1904R,
60-3604/N5022Q, 60-3606/N394HP, 60-3607/N3231F,
60-3612/N70512, 60-3614/N70264, 60-3615/N4237V,
60-3619/N2295J, 60-0687/N57HP, 60-0690/N2298E,
61-0694/N3361F, 61-0698/N70544, 61-0701/N46968,
61-0702/N404PD, 61-0705/N80479, 61-0712/N46928,
61-0718/N88992, 61-0720/N103MF, 61-0723/N9645A,
61-0724/N88987, 61-0733/N9050Q, 61-0738/N331WN,
61-0739/N96261, 61-0740/N88983, 61-0741/N91525,
61-0744/N98154, 61-0747/N3032F, 61-0748/N31341,
61-0750/N45731, 61-0753/N98102, 61-0756/N96142,
61-0758/N91307, 61-0761/N91348, 61-0762/N98126,
61-0763/N9050Q/N842M, 61-0765/N6991D, 61-0767/N87845,
61-0770/N88979, 61-0771/N98049, 61-0786/N9846F,
61-0787/N9993Q, 61-0791/N68077, 61-0797/N96206,
61-0798/N2252A, 62-1875/N85290, 62-1881/N58HP/EC-EHU,
62-1887/N91320, 62-1888/N5023U, 62-1890/N333WN,
62-1893/N96017/N204PJ, 62-1894/N64CC, 62-1900/N9066D,
62-1905/N665PS/N102FW, 62-1910/N105MF, 62-1912/N70547,
62-1915/N31213, 62-1922/N17765, 62-1923/N22961,
62-1924/N6NJ, 62-1926/N1564F, 62-1928/N59368,
62-1931/N91284, 62-1934/N6NJ/N206NJ, 62-1936/N1564F,
62-1944/N83985, 62-1949/N8503K, 62-1953/N50023,
62-1954/N910PD, 62-1956/N841M, 62-1960/N1565F,
62-1968/N98F, 62-1980/N63CD, 62-1984/N332WN,
62-1991/N2266T, 62-2026/N328WN, 62-2031/N91350,
62-2034/N87729, 62-2043/N31379, 62-2078/N50330,
62-2082/N5430G/N333WN, 62-2084/N832M, 62-2085/N83980,

62-2089/N1525T, 62-2096/N87765, 62-2097/N334WN,
62-4566/N61589, 62-4568/N87948, 62-4576/N61589,
62-4590/N70105, 62-4591/N335WN, 62-4598/N64789,
62-4601/N99675, 62-4603/N911CD, 62-4610/N234SJ,
62-4612/N345SJ, 62-4613/N444SJ, 62-12533/N394HP,
62-1253-6/N336WN, 62-12543/N96113, 62-12555/N80447,
63-8500/N337WN, 63-8503/N96119 63-8511/N96250,
63-8513/N99676, 63-8521/N46942, 63-8526/N104MF,
63-8528/N844M, 63-8529/N2295B, 63-8535/N91281,
63-8547/N96036, 63-8548/N46969, 63-8556/N98024,
63-8566/N8142W, 63-8606/N15SP, 63-8610/N5HF, 63-8615/N15SD,
63-8622/N5073X, 63-8636/N99478, 63-8646/N99634,
63-8864/N9434X, 63-8668/N9378A, 63-8676/N843M,
63-8699/N39SD, 63-8704/N64771, 63-8721/N64770,
63-8728/N88389/EC-EHV, 63-8731/N3295F, 63-9786/N123SJ,
63-9790/N456SJ, 63-12905/N5448, 63-12916/N5598G,
63-12950/N2956F, 63-13589/N888SJ, 63-13593/N999SJ,
63-14100/N50722, 64-13906/N406PD, 64-13907/N64496,
64-13914/N87944, 64-13930/N405PD, 64-13940/N91259,
64-13945/N5598E, 64-13948/N9044N, 64-13968/N87966,
64-13970/N87923, 64-13985/N22753, 64-14000/N65380/N50722,
64-14009/N88976, 64-14023/N266F, 64-14038/N87701,
64-14046/N92376, 64-14050/N3879M, 64-14057/N46884,
64-14070/N51929, 64-14073/N38880A, 64-14076/N845M,
64-14090/N90632, 64-14100/N50722.

**UH-1C:**
65-9521/N59RF/N68RF.

**UH-1D:**
62-12357/N81523, 63-8740/N8148C, 63-8775/N81526,
63-8785/N8149P, 63-12962/N81500, 64-13533/N81522,
64-13572/N8152Q, 64-13577/N81569, 64-13875/N8152J,
65-9596/N8151G, 65-9731/N8152G, 65-10023/N81518,
66-1192/N81568, 66-16078/N8146H, 66-16450/N81463,
66-16537/N81499, 66-16863/N8152K, 66-16942/N8149H.

**UH-1E:**
151271/N271GH, 151866/N5363G, 151874/N39M,
151875/N151LC, 151887/N118HS, 152428/N120FC,
153762/N911KK, 153765/N67RF, 154754/N159RR/N204AB,
154765/N98F, 154769/N9678Z, 154770/N821DH,
154944/N909KK, 154948/N204RW, 154949/N156RR/N116HS,
154953/N53SS, 155341/N118HS, 155342/N9173N,
155346/N7160J, 155348/N48SS.

**UH-1F:**
63-13144/N45770, 63-13154/N45773, 64-15479/N91471,
64-15481/N64709, 64-15487/N48158, 64-15488/N45774,
64-15497/N45776, 64-15524/N482DF, 65-7917/N480DF,
65-7933/N482DF, 65-7936/N981, 65-7938/N483DF,
65-7940/N484DF, 65-7947/N485DF, 65-7949/N486DF,
65-7952/N487DF, 65-7954/N488DF, 65-7955/N23021,
65-7961/N7403, 65-7963/N489DF, 65-1212/N490DF,
66-1213/N491DF, 66-1216/N9044N.

**TH-1F:**
66-1239/N38921, 66-1248/N67·163, 66-1250/N55781,

**UH-1H:**
63-8740/N8148C, 63-8775/N81526, 63-8785/N8149P,
63-8846/N338WN, 63-8848/N81785, 63-12962/N81500,
63-12979/N339WN, 64-13533/N81522, 64-13572/N8152Q,
64-13577/N81569, 64-13609/N8158Q, 64-13628/N734NA,
64-13685/N394M, 64-13723/N8160V, 64-13875/N8152J,
65-9596/N8151G, 65-9644/N8157G, 65-9705/N122FC,
65-9731/N8152G, 65-9956/N8158G, 65-10023/N81518,

66-1192/N81568, 66-16078/N8146H, 66-16450/N81463, 66-16537/N81499, 66-16863/N8152K, 66-16942/N8149H, 66-17192/N8159C, 67-17192/N8159C, 67-17850/N8159Z, 68-15254/N205SA, 69-15762/N46905, 69-15765/N8146M, 69-16663/N56RF, 70-16238/N8147Q, 70-16344/N37, 70-16398/N7042L, 71-20103/N81477, 70-20175/N8147G, 71-20304/N81464, 72-21478/N81473.

**UH-1L:**
157831/N474RR/N540AH/N540GH, 157854/N496N, 157855/N70410, 157858/N5107J,

**TH-1L:**
157815/N154RR, 157822/N155RR, 157831/N474RR, 157838/N838GH/N99G/N1JW, 157839/N8160G, 157844/N9770Y/N327FL, 5341/N118HS, 155342/N9173N, 155346/N7160J, 155348/N48SS.

**UH-1F:**
63-13144/N45770, 63-13154/N45773.

## Appendix IX

# Bell Helicopters Combat Losses – Vietnam War

| | | UH-1 | | AH-1 | | OH-13 | OH-58 |
|---|---|---|---|---|---|---|---|
| *Year* | *USAF* | *US Army* | *USMC* | *US Army* | *USMC* | *US Army* | *US Army* |
| 1963 | – | 2 | – | – | – | – | – |
| 1964 | – | 17 | – | – | – | – | – |
| 1965 | – | 39 | 16 | – | – | 3 | – |
| 1966 | – | 75 | 4 | – | – | 15 | – |
| 1967 | 2 | 174 | 15 | – | – | 20 | – |
| 1968 | 2 | 288 | 19 | 16 | – | 31 | – |
| 1969 | 6 | 222 | 9 | 41 | 2 | 1 | – |
| 1970 | 3 | 213 | 5 | 39 | 5 | – | 11 |
| 1971 | – | 148 | 1 | 43 | – | – | 16 |
| 1972 | – | 32 | – | 33 | – | – | 1 |
| 1973 | – | 1 | – | 1 | – | – | – |
| TOTAL | 13 | 1,211 | 69 | 173 | 7 | 70 | 28 |

## Appendix X

# Westland Sioux Production List

| *C/n* | *Line serial* | *Remarks* | |
|---|---|---|---|
| WA.310 | WA/N/1 | British Army (XT151) | |
| WA.311 | WA/N/2 | 〃 〃 (XT152) | scrapped 1976 |
| WA.312 | WA/N/3 | 〃 〃 (XT153) D-HOFD, | w/o 27.05.80 |
| WA.313 | WA/N/4 | 〃 〃 (XT154) ZS-HLX, | w/o 27.10.86 |
| WA.314 | WA/N/5 | 〃 〃 (XT155) D-HFFF, EC-EEJ | |
| WA.315 | WA/N/6 | 〃 〃 (XT156) G-BFEI | |
| WA.316 | WA/N/7 | 〃 〃 (XT157) | |
| WA.317 | WA/N/8 | 〃 〃 (XT158) | |
| WA.318 | WA/N/9 | 〃 〃 (XT159) | |
| WA.319 | WA/N/10 | 〃 〃 (XT160) G-BGAM, | w/o 26.05.79 |
| WA.320 | WA/N/11 | 〃 〃 (XT161) | crashed 14.02.66 |
| WA.321 | WA/N/12 | 〃 〃 (XT162) G-BFJN | |
| WA.322 | WA/N/13 | 〃 〃 (XT163) | w/o 23.10.74 |
| WA.323 | WA/N/14 | 〃 〃 (XT164) | w/o 19.06.75 |
| WA.324 | WA/N/15 | 〃 〃 (XT165) ZS-HFF, G-BHOI, F- . . . . | |
| WA.325 | WA/N/16 | 〃 〃 (XT166) | w/o 14.01.70 |
| WA.326 | WA/N/17 | 〃 〃 (XT167) G-BFYI | |
| WA.327 | WA/N/18 | 〃 〃 (XT168) D-HICE, | w/o 11.06.79 |
| WA.328 | WA/N/19 | 〃 〃 (XT169) | scrapped |
| WA.329 | WA/N/20 | 〃 〃 (XT170) G-BHBU, Soloy power, EC-DLK | |
| WA.330 | WA/N/21 | 〃 〃 (XT171) | w/o 25.11.65 |
| WA.331 | WA/N/22 | 〃 〃 (XT172) D-HAFK | |
| WA.332 | WA/N/23 | 〃 〃 (XT173) | shot down 23.06.67 |
| WA.333 | WA/N/24 | 〃 〃 (XT174) | w/o 18.04.73 |
| WA.334 | WA/N/25 | 〃 〃 (XT175) | accid 12.10.68 |
| WA.335 | WA/N/26 | 〃 〃 (XT176) | preserved Yeovilton |
| WA.336 | WA/N/27 | 〃 〃 (XT177) | w/o 06.02.67 |
| WA.337 | WA/N/28 | 〃 〃 (XT178) | w/o 07.04.66 |
| WA.338 | WA/N/29 | 〃 〃 (XT179) G-BFYF, PH-OFM, G-BFYF, VH-HMK | |
| WA.339 | WA/N/30 | 〃 〃 (XT180) G-BFEG, | crashed 09.07.79 |
| WA.340 | WA/N/31 | 〃 〃 (XT181) G-BGID | |
| WA.341 | WA/N/32 | 〃 〃 (XT182) D-HAFD | |
| WA.342 | WA/N/33 | 〃 〃 (XT183) ZS-HGZ | |
| WA.343 | WA/N/34 | 〃 〃 (XT184) | w/o 11.06.71 |
| WA.344 | WA/N/35 | 〃 〃 (XT185) | w/o 16.09.73 |
| WA.345 | WA/N/36 | 〃 〃 (XT186) G-BEBV, OE-AXP | |
| WA.346 | WA/N/37 | 〃 〃 (XT187) | w/o 02.06.66 |
| WA.347 | WA/N/38 | 〃 〃 (XT188) D-HOWD, EC-DVO | |
| WA.348 | WA/N/39 | 〃 〃 (XT189) | |
| WA.349 | WA/N/40 | 〃 〃 (XT190) | |
| WA.350 | WA/N/41 | 〃 〃 (XT191) G-BGXP | |
| WA.351 | WA/N/42 | 〃 〃 (XT192) 5Y-BDR, ZS-HLW | |
| WA.352 | WA/N/43 | 〃 〃 (XT193) D-HAFM | |
| WA.353 | WA/N/44 | 〃 〃 (XT194) G-BHAR | |
| WA.354 | WA/N/45 | 〃 〃 (XT195) G-BEHN, converted to Soloy power, accid 21.06.77, EI-BKG, G-BEHN, N8229C | |
| WA.355 | WA/N/46 | 〃 〃 (XT196) HP-789 | |

| *C/n* | *Line serial* | *Remarks* | |
|---|---|---|---|
| WA.356 | WA/N/48 | British Army (XT197),SE-HIF, OY-HCO, G-BPDY | |
| WA.357 | WA/N/49 | " " (XT198) ZS-HHX, | w/o 1980 |
| WA.358 | WA/N/50 | " " (XT199) HP-850? | |
| WA.359 | WA/N/51 | " " (XT200) | preserved Newark |
| WA.360 | WA/N/52 | " " (XT201) ZS-HLW | w/o |
| WA.361 | WA/N/53 | " " (XT202) D-HEEE, EC-DVM | |
| WA.362 | WA/N/55 | " " (XT203) ZS- . . . . | |
| WA.363 | WA/N/56 | " " (XT204) | w/o 03.04.69 |
| WA.364 | WA/N/57 | " " (XT205) D-HGGG | |
| WA.365 | WA/N/58 | " " (XT206) D-HAFQ, | w/o 13.06.60 |
| WA.366 | WA/N/61 | " " (XT207) D-HMHF, w/o 09.07.81, rebuilt, OE-AXS, D-HCXA | |
| WA.367 | WA/N/62 | " " (XT208) | w/o 17.03.72 |
| WA.368 | WA/N/63 | " " (XT209) D-HAUI | |
| WA.369 | WA/N/64 | " " (XT210) | w/o 25.11.69 |
| WA.370 | WA/N/65 | " " (XT211) G-BFOH, 5B-CGO, | w/o 05.09.88 |
| WA.371 | WA/N/68 | " " (XT212) D-HAFG, | w/o 15.07.81 |
| WA.372 | WA/N/69 | " " (XT213) G-BFLS, 5B-CFQ | |
| WA.373 | WA/N/70 | " " (XT214) G-BFJU, 5B-CEX, SU-BHB | |
| WA.374 | WA/N/71 | " " (XT215) | w/o 06.10.70 |
| WA.375 | WA/N/72 | " " (XT216) | w/o 30.07.66 |
| WA.376 | WA/N/73 | " " (XT217) 9M-AUO, Malaysian AF | |
| WA.377 | WA/N/76 | " " (XT218) | |
| WA.378 | WA/N/77 | " " (XT219) | w/o 26.02.67 |
| WA.379 | WA/N/78 | " " (XT220) D-HDDD | |
| WA.380 | WA/N/79 | " " (XT221) G-CHOP, | crashed 17.06.85 |
| WA.381 | WA/N/80 | " " (XT222) D-HIII | |
| WA.382 | WA/P/81 | " " (XT223) G-BGZK | |
| WA.383 | WA/P/84 | " " (XT224) G-BEBW, OE-AXU, D-HNFA | |
| WA.384 | WA/P/86 | " " (XT225) | w/o 17.03.75 |
| WA.385 | WA/P/85 | " " (XT226) | preserved Hong Kong |
| WA.386 | WA/P/87 | " " (XT227) G-BHKB, Soloy power | |
| WA.387 | WA/P/88 | " " (XT228) D-HAFR, OE-CXS, D-HHBB, OE-CXS | |
| WA.388 | WA/P/91 | " " (XT229) ZS-HLM, Soloy power | |
| WA.389 | WA/P/92 | " " (XT230) | |
| WA.390 | WA/P/93 | " " (XT231) | |
| WA.391 | WA/P/94 | " " (XT232) ZS-HIL, 3D-HZA, ZS-HIL | |
| WA.392 | WA/P/95 | " " (XT233) | |
| WA.393 | WA/P/96 | " " (XT234) G-BFVM | |
| WA.394 | WA/P/99 | " " (XT235) | scrapped 1976 |
| WA.395 | WA/P/100 | " " (XT236) | preserved Middle Wallop |
| WA.396 | WA/P/101 | " " (XT237) D-HAFL | |
| WA.397 | WA/P/102 | " " (XT238) | w/o 07.07.73 |
| WA.398 | WA/P/103 | " " (XT239) | |
| WA.399 | WA/P/105 | " " (XT240) | scrapped 1977 |
| WA.400 | WA/P/106 | " " (XT241) | accid 02.01.77 |
| WA.401 | WA/P/107 | " " (XT242) | accid 15.04.75 |
| WA.402 | WA/P/108 | " " (XT243) HP-850 | |
| WA.403 | WA/P/109 | " " (XT244) D-HATW, HB-XIF, OE-AXZ, D-HLBS | |
| WA.404 | WA/P/111 | " " (XT245) D-HHRK | |
| WA.405 | WA/P/113 | " " (XT246) | w/o 04.09.69 |
| WA.406 | WA/P/114 | " " (XT247) | |
| WA.407 | WA/P/117 | " " (XT248) G-BKNF, VH- . . . | |
| WA.408 | WA/P/118 | " " (XT249) G-BHBV, Soloy powered, G-SMRI | w/o 24.07.85 |
| WA.409 | WA/P/119 | " " (XT250) | |
| WA.410 | WA/P/120 | " " (XT498) | w/o 02.09.71 |

| *C/n* | *Line serial* | *Remarks* | |
|---|---|---|---|
| WA.411 | WA/P/121 | British Army (XT499) | |
| WA.412 | WA/P/122 | " " (XT500) G-BEWJ | |
| WA.413 | WA/P/125 | " " (XT501) G-BEHO, | w/o 23.06.79 |
| WA.414 | WA/P/126 | " " (XT502) | |
| WA.415 | WA/P/127 | " " (XT503) | w/o 05.05.73 |
| WA.416 | WA/P/128 | " " (XT504) | scrapped 1977 |
| WA.417 | WA/P/131 | " " (XT505) D-HHHH, ZS-HJT | |
| WA.418 | WA/P/132 | " " (XT506) | |
| WA.419 | WA/P/133 | " " (XT507) G-BEBX, OE-AXN | |
| WA.420 | WA/P/134 | " " (XT508) G-BGAI | w/o 04.06.73 |
| WA.421 | WA/P/135 | " " (XT509) | w/o 23.08.69 |
| WA.422 | WA/P/136 | " " (XT510) G-BHBE | |
| WA.423 | WA/P/137 | " " (XT511) ZS-HHB | |
| WA.424 | WA/P/139 | " " (XT512) G-BEPA, HB-XHB | |
| WA.425 | WA/P/138 | " " (XT513) | w/o |
| WA.426 | WA/P/140 | " " (XT514) D-HAFN, D-HAFW, D-HAFB | |
| WA.427 | WA/P/141 | " " (XT515) | scrapped 1977 |
| WA.428 | WA/P/142 | " " (XT516) 9M-AUP, ZS-HHA | |
| WA.429 | WA/P/143 | " " (XT540) | w/o 13.10.67 |
| WA.430 | WA/P/144 | " " (XT541) ZS-HLP, 3D-HLP | |
| WA.431 | WA/P/145 | " " (XT542) D-HAFH, EC-EAL | |
| WA.432 | WA/P/146 | " " (XT543) G-BFSJ | |
| WA.433 | WA/P/147 | " " (XT544) | w/o 27.11.70 |
| WA.434 | WA/P/148 | " " (XT545) G-BGOZ, | w/o 18.06.81 |
| WA.435 | WA/P/149 | " " (XT546) | |
| WA.436 | WA/P/150 | " " (XT547) | w/o 30.05.75 |
| WA.437 | WA/P/151 | " " (XT548) | |
| WA.438 | WA/P/152 | " " (XT549) | w/o 29.05.67 |
| WA.439 | WA/P/153 | " " (XT550) | |
| WA.440 | WA/P/154 | " " (XT551) ZS-HJT | |
| WA.441 | WA/P/155 | " " (XT552) D-HOBZ, D-HAUH | |
| WA.442 | WA/P/156 | " " (XT553) HB-XLX | |
| WA.443 | WA/P/157 | " " (XT554) D-HAKI | |
| WA.444 | WA/P/158 | " " (XT555) D-HAFS | w/o 30.10.80 |
| WA.445 | WA/P/159 | " " (XT556) D-HATA, HB-XIX, HB-XOA, EC-EBJ | |
| WA.446 | WA/P/160 | " " (XT557) ZS-HHB | |
| WA.447 | WA/P/161 | " " (XT558) | |
| WA.448 | WA/S/162 | " " (XT559) HB-XLE, D-HAFF | |
| WA.449 | WA/S/163 | " " (XT560) D-HAFF, HB-XKY? | |
| WA.450 | WA/S/164 | " " (XT561) D-HBLE | |
| WA.451 | WA/S/165 | " " (XT562) ZS-HHA, crashed 28.10.78, preserved SAAF Museum | |
| WA.452 | WA/S/166 | " " (XT563) | |
| WA.453 | WA/S/167 | " " (XT564) 3D-HLP, ZS-HLP | |
| WA.454 | WA/S/168 | " " (XT565) | w/o 31.03.68 |
| WA.455 | WA/S/169 | " " (XT566), D-HAFB | scrapped |
| WA.456 | WA/S/170 | " " (XT567) | |
| WA.457 | WA/S/171 | " " (XT568) G-BGTZ, 5B-CFJ, SU-BGT | |
| WA.458 | WA/S/172 | " " (XT569) 5B-CEW, 5Y-BDS | |
| WA.459 | WA/S/173 | " " (XT570) | scrapped 1976 |
| WA.505 | WA/N/47 | " " (XT798) | w/o 01.03.67 |
| WA.506 | WA/N/54 | " " (XT799) | w/o 29.03.68 |
| WA.507 | WA/N/59 | " " (XT800) | |
| WA.508 | WA/N/60 | " " (XT801) D-HHRW, OE-CXA | |
| WA.509 | WA/N/66 | " " (XT802) | w/o 14.05.69 |
| WA.510 | WA/N/67 | " " (XT803) | |

| *C/n* | *Line serial* | *Remarks* | |
|---|---|---|---|
| WA.511 | WA/N/74 | British Army (XT804) G-BHBY | |
| WA.512 | WA/N/75 | " " (XT805) | |
| WA.513 | WA/P/82 | " " (XT806) G-SOLY, 5W- . . . | |
| WA.514 | WA/P/83 | " " (XT807) G-BGMU | |
| WA.515 | WA/P/89 | " " (XT808) | w/o 19.11.67 |
| WA.516 | WA/P/90 | " " (XT809) | w/o 12.08.68 |
| WA.517 | WA/P/97 | " " (XT810) HB-XLH, EC-DSK | |
| WA.518 | WA/P/98 | " " (XT811) G-BFOI | w/o 31.07.86 |
| WA.519 | WA/P/104 | " " (XT812) D-HOAA, I-ELDE | |
| WA.520 | WA/P/112 | " " (XT813) | w/o 29.01.69 |
| WA.521 | WA/P/110 | " " (XT814) D-HASW | |
| WA.522 | WA/P/115 | " " (XT815) D-HAGO, OE-AXX | |
| WA.523 | WA/P/116 | " " (XT816) | w/o 24.03.70 |
| WA.524 | WA/P/123 | " " (XT817) | scrapped 1976 |
| WA.525 | WA/P/124 | " " (XT818) | w/o 18.12.75 |
| WA.526 | WA/P/129 | " " (XT819) | scrapped 1976 |
| WA.527 | WA/P/130 | " " (XT820) N . . . . | |
| WA.564 | WA/S/175 | " " (XV310) | w/o 22.04.70 |
| WA.565 | WA/S/181 | " " (XV311) G-BDIA, ZS-HGV | |
| WA.566 | WA/S/185 | " " (XV312) 8430M, A2631, G-BDVJ, 5B-CGI | |
| WA.567 | WA/S/187 | " " (XV313) G-BCZJ, N86731 | |
| WA.568 | WA/S/190 | " " (XV314) G-BDEE, ZS-HGB | |
| WA.569 | WA/S/191 | " " (XV315) G-BDHY, ZS-HFJ | |
| WA.570 | WA/S/197 | " " (XV316) | w/o 22.04.70 |
| WA.571 | WA/S/198 | " " (XV317) A2638, G-WHIT, OY-HDH | |
| WA.572 | WA/S/204 | " " (XV318) G-BCYY, | w/o 06.06.82 |
| WA.573 | WA/S/205 | " " (XV319) G-BCYZ, | w/o 11.08.88 |
| WA.574 | WA/S/211 | " " (XV320) G-BDHZ, ZS-HFI, | w/o 13.01.78 |
| WA.575 | WA/S/212 | " " (XV321) G-BCZK, | wfu 20.10.76 |
| WA.576 | WA/S/217 | " " (XV322) | w/o 06.05.71 |
| WA.577 | WA/S/219 | " " (XV323) G-BCZL, | w/o 25.07.77 |
| WA.578 | WA/S/220 | " " (XV324) ZS-HFF | |
| WA.579 | WA/S/174 | " " (XT824) | scrapped |
| WA.580 | WA/S/177 | South Yemen AF (401), G-BBVP | |
| WA.581 | WA/S/180 | South Yemen AF (402), G-BBZK, 3D-GAH | |
| WA.582 | WA/S/182 | South Yemen AF (403), | crashed |
| WA.583 | WA/S/184 | South Yemen AF (404), G-BBZL, SE-HME | |
| WA.584 | WA/S/186 | South Yemen AF (405), G-BBZM, HB-XFA | |
| WA.585 | WA/S/188 | South Yemen AF (406), | crashed |
| WA.586 | WA/S/176 | British Army (XT825) | w/o 14.08.69 |
| WA.587 | WA/S/178 | " " (XT826) G-BGAM, 5X-PAW | |
| WA.588 | WA/S/179 | " " (XT827) | |
| WA.589 | WA/S/183 | " " (XT828) | w/o 03.08.70 |
| WA.590 | WA/S/189 | " " (XT829) D-HECI | |
| WA.591 | WA/S/192 | " " (XT830) | w/o 19.09.73 |
| WA.592 | WA/S/193 | " " (XT831) G-BENG | |
| WA.593 | WA/S/194 | " " (XT832) | w/o 07.10.68 |
| WA.594 | WA/S/195 | " " (XT833) D-H . . . | |
| WA.595 | WA/S/196 | " " (XT834) G-BHBW, | w/o 24.07.70 |
| WA.596 | WA/S/199 | " " (XT835) ZS-HGX | w/o 02.12.82 |
| WA.597 | WA/S/200 | " " (XT836) | w/o 27.02.73 |
| WA.598 | WA/S/201 | " " (XT837) ZS-HGY | |
| WA.599 | WA/S/202 | " " (XT838) | |
| WA.601 | WA/S/203 | " " (XT839) G-BEBD, OE-AXO, D-HNFB | |
| WA.602 | WA/S/206 | " " (XT840) | w/o 27.03.75 |

| *C/n* | *Line serial* | *Remarks* | |
|---|---|---|---|
| WA.603 | WA/S/207 | British Army (XT841) G-BFJT, 5B-CEV | w/o 24.08.82 |
| WA.604 | WA/S/208 | " " (XT842) G-BHKC | |
| WA.605 | WA/S/209 | " " (XT843) | scrapped 1978 |
| WA.606 | WA/S/210 | " " (XT844) G-BERO, HB-XHM | |
| WA.607 | WA/S/213 | " " (XT845) | w/o 25.11.69 |
| WA.608 | WA/S/214 | " " (XT846) D-HLLL | w/o 26.08.86 |
| WA.609 | WA/S/215 | " " (XT847) | |
| WA.610 | WA/S/216 | " " (XT848) G-BHKD, D-HABY | |
| WA.611 | WA/S/218 | " " (XT849) | w/o 30.09.75 |
| WA.699 | WA/T/221 | " " (XW179) | preserved Stapehill |
| WA.700 | WA/T/222 | " " (XW180) G-BHNV | |
| WA.701 | WA/T/223 | " " (XW181) D-HAFJ | |
| WA.702 | WA/T/224 | " " (XW182) D-HAFZ | w/o 20.05.82, rebuilt |
| WA.703 | WA/T/225 | " " (XW183) D-HMNI | w/o 26.07.79 |
| WA.704 | WA/T/226 | " " (XW184) G-BEHP | w/o 28.06.80 |
| WA.705 | WA/T/227 | " " (XW185) G-BEGA | |
| WA.706 | WA/T/228 | " " (XW186) D-HAUS | w/o 01.06.78 |
| WA.707 | WA/T/229 | " " (XW187) G-BGKK, 5B-CEW?, SU-BGR | |
| WA.708 | WA/T/230 | " " (XW188) D-HKKK | |
| WA.709 | WA/T/231 | " " (XW189) HB-XMM, D-HATS | |
| WA.710 | WA/T/232 | " " (XW190) G-BFKM | |
| WA.711 | WA/T/233 | " " (XW191) | accid 23.08.69 |
| WA.712 | WA/T/234 | " " (XW192) G-BGFS | |
| WA.713 | WA/T/235 | " " (XW193) G-BHKW, 5X-HCC | |
| WA.714 | WA/T/236 | " " (XW194) | w/o 05.10.73 |
| WA.715 | WA/T/177 | " " (XW195) | w/o 21.05.75 |
| WA.716 | WA/U/238 | G-AXKK, G-17-1 | |
| WA.717 | WA/U/239 | G-AXKL, G-17-2 | accid 30.07.73 |
| WA.718 | WA/U/240 | G-AXKM, G-17-3 | |
| WA.719 | WA/U/241 | G-AXKN, G-17-4 | |
| WA.720 | WA/U/242 | G-AXKO, G-17-5 | |
| WA.721 | WA/U/243 | G-AXKP, G-17-6 | |
| WA.722 | WA/U/244 | G-AXKR, G-17-7 | |
| WA.723 | WA/U/245 | G-AXKS, G-17-8 | preserved |
| WA.724 | WA/U/246 | G-AXKT, G-17-9 | accid 06.10.81 |
| WA.725 | WA/U/247 | G-AXKU, G-17-10, G-MASH | |
| WA.726 | WA/U/248 | G-AXKV, G-17-11 | accid 31.01.74 |
| WA.727 | WA/U/249 | G-AXKW, G-17-12 | scrapped |
| WA.728 | WA/U/250 | G-AXKX, G-17-13 | |
| WA.729 | WA/U/251 | G-AXKY, G-17-14 | |
| WA.730 | WA/U/252 | G-AXKZ, G-17-15 | |
| WA.731 | WA/U/253 | G-AXLA, G-17-16 | scrapped |

# Abbreviations and Acronyms

AAFSS Advanced Aerial Fire Support System
AAH Advanced Attack Helicopter
ABW Air Base Wing
ACAP Advanced Composite Airframe Program
ACLG Air Cushion Landing Gear
ACLS Air Cushion Landing System
ACS Air Commando Squadron
AEFA Army Engineering Flight Activity
AFB Air Force Base
AFRES Air Force Reserve
AFSC Air Force Systems Command
AHB Attack Helicopter Battalion
AHC Assault Helicopter Company
AHIP Army Helicopter Improvement Program
APU Auxiliary Power Unit
ARRS Aerospace Rescue and Recovery Squadron
ARTI Advanced Rotorcraft Technology Integration
ARVN Army of the Republic of Vietnam
ASW Anti-Submarine Warfare
ATAS Air-To-Air Stinger
AvBat Aviation Battalion
AvCo Aviation Company
AvRgt Aviation Regiment
CAFT Combined Advanced Field Team
CavRgt Cavalry Regiment
CCTW Combat Crew Training Wing
C-FLEX Cobra-Fleet Life Extension
CLNAS Cobra Laser Night Attack System
CNO Chief of Naval Operations
CW Composite Wing
DNSARC Department of the Navy System Acquisition Review Council
DoD Department of Defense
ECM Electronic Counter Measures
EOTADS Electro-Optical Target Acquisition and Designation Subsystem
FAA Federal Aviation Administration
FAI Fédération Aéronautique Internationale
FBW Fly-By-Wire
FG Fighter Group
FLIR Forward-Looking Infra-Red
FS Fighter Squadron
FSD Full-Scale Development
FWW Fighter Weapons Wing
GTV Ground Test Vehicle
HC Helicopter Combat Support Squadron
HIDSS Helmet Integrated Display and Sight Subsystem
HMH Marine Heavy Helicopter Squadron
HMLA Marine Light Attack Helicopter Squadron
HMM Marine Medium Helicopter Squadron
HMT Marine Helicopter Training Squadron
HMX Marine Helicopter Development Squadron
HUD Head-Up Display
ICAP Improved Cobra Armament Program
IFF Identification Friend or Foe
IFR Instrument Flight Rules
IGE In Ground Effect
IR&D Independent Research and Development
JGSDF Japan Ground Self Defence Forces
JVX Joint Services advanced Vertical lift aircraft
LGM Laser Guided Munition
LHX Light Helicopter Experimental
LLRV Lunar Landing Research Vehicle
LLTV Lunar Landing Training Vehicle
LOC Localiser
LOH Light Observation Helicopter
LORAS Linear Omnidirectional Resolving Airspeed System
MAAG Military Assistance Advisory Group
MAC Military Airlift Command
MedCo Medical Company
MedDet Medical Detachment
Medevac Medical Evacuation
MMS Mast-Mounted Sight
MPLH Multi Purpose Light Helicopter
MPS Microprocessing Subsystem
MTO Mediterranean Theatre of Operations
NACA National Advisory Committee for Aeronautics
NASA National Aeronautics and Space Administration
NASC Naval Air Systems Command
NOE Nap Of the Earth
NTSH Near-Term Scout Helicopter
NVPS Night Vision Pilotage Subsystem
OEI One Engine Inoperative
OGE Out of Ground Effect
PACAF Pacific Air Forces
PRG Photo Reconnaissance Group
PTO Pacific Theatre of Operations
RPV Remotely Piloted Vehicle
SAR Search And Rescue
SOF Special Operations Forces
SOS Special Operations Squadron
TAC Tactical Air Command
TOW Tube-launched, Optically-tracked, Wire-guided missile
TRECOM Transportation Research Command
USAAF United States Army Air Force
USAF United States Air Force
USAFE United States Air Force Europe
USMC United States Marine Corps
USN United States Navy
UTTAS Utility Tactical Transport Aircraft System
UTTCO Utility Tactical Transport Helicopter Co
VDR Variable-diameter Rotor
VFR Visual Flight Rules
VMO Marine Observation Squadron
VOR VHF Omni-directional Range
VSCAS Variable Stability Control Augmentation System
VSS Variable Stability System
VTOL Vertical Take Off and Landing
VXE Antarctic Development Squadron

# Index of Aircraft Types

Page numbers in italics refer to illustrations only.

# Index of People